Consultants Business Development Guide

Carol Keyes, CSP, CRC, CCM
J. A. Rodriguez, Jr., CSP
Pamela Walaski, CSP, CHMM

Editors

American Society of Safety Engineers
PARK RIDGE, ILLINOIS, USA

Copyright © 2015 by the American Society of Safety Engineers
All rights reserved.

Copyright, Waiver of First Sale Doctrine
All rights reserved. No part of this work may be reproduced or transmitted in any form or by any means, electronic or mechanical, without the permission in writing from the Publisher. All requests for permission to reproduce material from this work should be directed to: Manager, Technical Publications, American Society of Safety Engineers, 520 N. Northwest Highway, Park Ridge, IL 60068.

Limits of Liability/Disclaimer of Warranty
While the publisher and authors have used their best efforts in preparing this book, they make no representations or warranties with respect to the accuracy or completeness of the contents of this book, and specifically disclaim any implied warranties of merchantability or fitness for a particular purpose. The information is provided with the understanding that the authors are not hereby engaged in rendering legal or other professional services. If legal advice or other professional assistance is required, the services of a competent professional should be sought.

Library of Congress Cataloging-in-Publication Data

Consultants business development guide / editors, Carol Keyes, CSP, CRC, CCM, J. A. Rodriguez, Jr., CSP Pamela Walaski, CSP, CHMM. – First Edition.
   pages cm
 Includes bibliographical references and index.
 ISBN 978-0-939874-07-1 (alk. paper)
   1. Business consultants. 2. Consultants–Handbooks, manuals, etc. I. Keyes, Carol A. (Business consultant) editor. II. Rodriguez, J. A., editor. III. Walaski, Pamela, 1959- editor.

HD69.C6C6476 2015
001–dc23
                    2011053318

Text Design and Composition: Cathy Lombardi, Liberty NY
Cover: Reed Design Studio
Project Editor: Jeri Ann Stucka, ASSE
Managing Editor: Michael F. Burditt, ASSE

Printed in the United States of America

21 20 19 18 17 16 15   7 6 5 4 3 2 1

TABLE OF CONTENTS

Preface   v

Acknowledgements   vii

Foreword   ix

About the Editors   xv

Chapter 1: Assessing Your Abilities (Eldeen E. Pozniak)   2

Chapter 2: Creating a Business Plan (Sam Gualardo)   38

Chapter 3: What about the Money (Financial) (Deborah Roy)   78

Chapter 4: Insurance Needs (Diana Stegall)   118

Chapter 5: Legal and Regulatory Issues (Adele L. Abrams)   144

Chapter 6: Marketing and Sales (Linda Tapp)   190

Chapter 7: Networking (Katharine Hart)   244

Chapter 8: Client Retention: How to Develop Successful Client-Consultant Relationships (Katharine Hart)   280

Chapter 9: Ethics and Other Professional Issues (Daniel J. Snyder)   318

Chapter 10: After the First Year (Donna Pearson)   344

Chapter 11: Making It Work on Your Own (Robert N. Andres, Jeffery C. Camplin, Paul Gantt, J. Terrence Grisim, Steven High, John P. Lesenganich, Chris Ross, Debby Shewitz, and Dave K. Smith)   386

Suggested Readings   423

Index   425

PREFACE

Becoming a professional safety consultant may seem, at first glance, to be an ideal job: You would be your own boss, take only the work you wanted to do, set your own hours and all the money you make would be your own.

The reality of becoming a successful professional safety consultant, however, can be quite different, and a lot more work than you originally imagined. The *Consultants Business Development Guide* will help you plan out and set up your consulting business, from what type of business you want to be (sole proprietor, partnership, or head of your own company) to how to evaluate you consulting business after the first year (and thereafter). Each chapter sets out a topic that consultants need to deal with, including:

- Business plans
- Finances
- Legal and regulatory requirements
- Insurance
- Marketing and sales
- Employees and subcontractors
- Networking
- Ethics
- Workers' compensation
- Getting and retaining clients

At the beginning of each chapter, There is a list of "Questions to ask" yourself about the topic covered. By the end of the chapter, you should have a much clearer idea of what you need to do and how to do it.

Some of the special features included in this book are:

- Consulting Skills Self Appraisal Form
- Sample Fee Schedules for services
- Estimated cost samples and profit and loss statements
- Sample Certificate of Liability Insurance
- Sample Worksheet—Determining How Much Insurance You Need
- Common Contract Terms
- Federal Employment Laws: Coverage and Scope
- State Employment Laws

- Sample Six-Month Marketing Action Plan
- Sample Proposal: Needs Assessment and Development of OSHA Compliance Plan
- Creating a Client Consultant Contract
- Client Resistance Type, Definition and Example chart
- Consultant Values Exercise
- ASSE Code of Professional Conduct
- BCSP Code of Ethics
- ABIH Code of Professional Conduct

Each chapter in the *Consultants Business Development Guide* is written by a professional safety consultant, and the last chapter contains essays by a number of safety consultants regarding the lessons they have learned as a consultant, providing the reader with real-life examples of the opportunities and challenges involved in being a professional consultant. The editors have decades of experience as independent safety consultants and provide commentary to further educate the reader in the intricacies of becoming a successful safety professional consultant.

Whether you are considering becoming a professional safety consultant or are one already, the *Consultants Business Development Guide* is a vital resource that can be read and referred to again and again for practical advice and guidance.

ACKNOWLEDGEMENTS

As with many books such as this one, there are many additional contributors that deserve to be mentioned. Below are those to whom we owe a debt of gratitude for their contributions to this book.

First, to the authors for their hard work, the results of which you will see as you read this guidebook.

Second, each chapter had at least one peer reviewer who was chosen by the authors for their content knowledge and expertise. Their task was to assure that the content was technically accurate as well as to suggest additional information to enhance the quality of the chapter.

Our thanks to those peer reviewers: Mary Beth (MB) Deans; Ed Dyna, CD, CRSP, CSP; Terrence Grisim, CSP, CDS, CPSM, ARM; Joe Keenan, MBA, CSP; James "Skipper" Kendrick, CSP; Jack Luckhardt, CSP, ARM; Karen Mastroianni, EdD, MPH, COHN-S, FAAOHN; John H. Mitchel; Heather Murphy; Jeff Richardson; and Péllo Walker.

Third, to Janet L. Keyes, CIH. She was, for all intents and purposes, the fourth editor and spent countless hours reviewing every chapter with the goal of making sure that they flowed smoothly from one to the other and were consistent in the use of terms and the overall voice. She also made sure to note cross-references between chapters. Janet is a Certified Industrial Hygienist and founding partner of Complete Health, Environmental & Safety Services, Inc. (CHESS), a safety consulting firm in Minnesota.

FOREWORD

"Whatever you do, you need courage. Whatever course you decide upon, there is always someone to tell you you are wrong. There are always difficulties arising which tempt you to believe that your critics are right. To map out a course of action and follow it to the end, requires some of the same courage which a soldier needs."

Young People's Weekly
From Mary Allette Ayer's book, 1908

You've picked up this guide book because you are considering, or are already working in, a consulting business. It can be exciting and terrifying to start your own consulting practice. For some, this might be the next logical step in your career. For others, it may be a big leap. It may come about because you have been downsized, rightsized, or simply laid off. For others, it may grow from a dislike for working with others. It may be a transitional option between jobs, or it might be a definite career choice.

Venturing out as a consultant means venturing into a business, whether doing part-time work on the side, as a sole practitioner, or in a multi-office firm with many consultant-employees. Whatever direction you take, this guide is designed to provide assistance with the ground work and decision making.

Consulting is a business. While you have technical expertise and knowledge, it will become apparent as you work through this guidebook that running a business, even doing consulting part-time, requires additional skill sets. Some people have or develop those skills (marketing, sales, bookkeeping, management, and so forth), and some find running a business is not what they want to do.

As the quote above pointed out, people may tell you that you've made the wrong decision, regardless of what that decision is (to start a consulting business or not). To be successful, you need to be passionate about what you do. But, aside from providing training or program development or audits (the technical side), you need to be able to sell your services. You need to have a vision of what you want to do. You need to be able to network and market, and ask people to pay for your services. You need to know what to charge to make a living, or at least cover your basic business expenses. You need to pay taxes and payroll, even if it is paying yourself. In addition, you need to invoice for your services, so you can pay those taxes and the payroll. You need insurance: health, general liability, professional liability, and maybe workers' compensation. That's the business side.

All of that may seem overwhelming, but it is manageable. And it is the reason why we put this book together. All of us who worked on this guidebook kept one thought in mind: What did we wish we knew then that we know now? Every single occupational safety and health (OS&H) professional who participated in the development of this book did so because we believe in the importance of having such a critical resource for our colleagues. It is a resource that we, who have all run successful OS&H consulting practices of varying configurations, wish we had when we started. Although we would have still made some mistakes along the way, we know we could have benefited from the wisdom of those who were successfully doing what we were just diving headlong into.

As we went through the process of concept to outline to first, second and final drafts, we all had one goal in mind: to create a comprehensive and usable reference tool that would have answered the questions we all had at the beginning and in the early days. Many of us who have been in business for numerous years have also wished for a resource that would help us evaluate our business. We wanted something that could help us refresh and revise our current business to help it grow and flourish.

We also realize that consulting takes many forms. Along with helping the OS&H professional starting his or her own business, this guidebook may be useful to those who have been in business for one or two or ten years. It may also help those who work in a consulting capacity, but not for a consulting firm, such as loss control representatives or OS&H professionals who oversee and guide multiple sites.

As we can all attest, the process of becoming successful OS&H consultants isn't easy, in part because while we may all be technically proficient, we may not be business savvy or, at the very least, are limited in our ability to actually run a business, even though we may understand parts of the process. It's the lack of understanding of basic business concepts and the inability to develop those skills and abilities that are more likely to derail the best dreams and plans for a successful consulting practice. Even if you have had a significant role in your organization's management team, running a business on your own requires a different skill set that has to be learned, practiced, and mastered.

How This Book Came to Be

This guide book is a project of the American Society of Safety Engineers' Consultants Practice Specialty (ASSE CPS). As a group of safety consultants, we often mentored others who were considering or starting consulting businesses. Over the years, we would provide advice to others, offer suggestions and provide mentoring opportunities. We talked about putting in writing the guidance we were dispensing, and wished there was a good resource for safety consultants.

We'd hear remarks about safety consultants, some derogatory ("It's easy to be a consultant," "You make lots of money for little work," "Your time is all your own; you don't have to account for it") and so on. While there may be some nugget of truth in these statements, there is a lot more to it.

Consulting will likely require that you step out of your comfort zone, whether that means asking people to pay for your expertise, having to actually invoice for your services (you don't get paid unless you invoice), having to understand contract language, or learning about social media, you will find challenges along the way. This guidebook will help you identify those challenges, provide ideas on overcoming them, and help you decide if you want to take them on.

As you will read in chapter after chapter, this is not always an easy path. It requires balancing work and the rest of your life. Your time only partially belongs to you; it also very much belongs to your clients. If you don't work, you don't get paid. You also become your own boss, with more control over decisions than working for someone else.

What to Expect from the Guidebook

Each chapter starts with questions to ask yourself about a specific topic. Then there is a short biography of the chapter's author. The authors have very different backgrounds that influence their chapter. This provides you with a wide scope of expertise and views on consulting.

This should not be your only resource. We've listed additional resources within the chapters, as well as at the end of the book. Just as clients may consult with you on OS&H issues, you should consult with appropriate professionals. At the very least, such professionals should include an accountant, an attorney, and an insurance agent.

There are plenty of other great resources for developing a business plan, for marketing, for small business accounting, and so forth. This guide is geared for the OS&H professional, providing sometimes general and sometimes specific information about the business aspects of safety, such as insurance issues you may not have considered, ethical dilemmas you may face, how to secure clients, and how to keep them.

How to Best Use This Guidebook

This guidebook is intended to help you frame some of the most critical questions you will need to ask yourself as you begin the process of opening a consulting practice and making it work. We address everything we think you might need, and probably things you may not have thought of.

We encourage you to take notes as you read through the chapters. (Even with years of running a consulting practice, we took notes for our business.) There are exercises throughout the chapters, designed to help you master the information from the chapter, and to make the information your own.

The chapters are arranged in what we considered a logical order, from considering this career choice to developing a business plan, setting up your business (insurance, legal considerations) to bringing in the work (marketing, developing clients), to keeping the work coming (retaining clients, ethics) to planning beyond the first year. Even so, each chapter is actually free-standing. You could read this in order, read only the chapter that currently applies to your situation, or work through the chapters in any order.

Some topics are covered in several chapters, from difference angles. For example, contracts and contract language are mentioned in the chapter on business plans, in the legal and regulatory chapter, as well as in the marketing chapter.

The chapters include the following information:

Chapter 1: Assessing Your Abilities
- Identifying your strengths and weaknesses before you start
- Helping you to determine whether your personality and skills are a good fit or whether you should perhaps consider some type of partnership where you can find one or more people who can balance out the necessary skills

Chapter 2: Creating a Business Plan
- Identifying the need and purpose of a business plan
- Setting forth the essential components of a business plan, including how you will finance the initial start-up, identifying competition, creating a niche market based upon your skills, and

bringing in outside professional to assist, such as an accountant, lawyer, and IT specialist
- Elucidating the funding and financial considerations when starting a business
- Examining the use of contracts to manage and transfer risk

Chapter 3: What about the Money (Financial)
- Setting rates
- Understanding financial statements to help determine whether your business is making money or not
- Discussing taxes and accounting considerations
- Providing information on invoicing and collecting fees

Chapter 4: Insurance Needs
- Determining what type of insurance and how much you need, and how to go about finding a carrier and necessary coverage
- Providing a detailed discussion on property and general liability, professional liability/errors and omissions, medical/health insurance, life insurance, and workers' compensation/disability insurance

Chapter 5: Legal and Regulatory Issues
- Identifying the proper business structure for your endeavor (sole proprietor, LLC, or corporation)
- Considering when to enter into contracts with clients, for office space and equipment, and with other consultants (subcontracting)
- Covering employment law, including taxes and considerations when hiring, along with other legal issues

Chapter 6: Marketing and Sales
- Examining the types of marketing/advertising resources from traditional to more contemporary (i.e., social networks)
- Utilizing different avenues for marketing
- Developing a specific marketing plan and a marketing action plan
- Developing proposals

Chapter 7: Networking
- Focusing on building relationships as a key element of building your business
- Using networking as an extension of marketing
- Discussing strategic alliances and networking for all business resources from clients to vendors and employees as well as other OS&H professionalsncovering the advantages of using this method for client development

- Focusing on the need to create your own professional development plan, which is typically handled by an employer

Chapter 8: Client Retention: How to Develop Successful Client-Consultant Relationships
- Converting prospects and initial clients to long-term or future clients
- Developing your brand and reputation, taking into consideration your values
- Developing client relationships and recognizing possible pitfalls

Chapter 9: Ethics and Other Professional Issues
- Defining ethics and helping to identify potential conflicts of interest
- Addressing such areas as what to do when a client asks for something outside of your expertise, or how to handle situations when a client does not follow through on recommendations that may present an imminent danger to their workforce

Chapter 10: After the First Year
- Identifying what you've learned and evaluating how your business has developed
- Identifying your strengths for future business growth
- Identifying potential problems and addressing them before they pose a real danger to you and ongoing operations
- Defining issues around expanding your business and managing growth

Chapter 11: Making it Work on Your Own Terms
- Providing a series of essays from fellow consultants that address how they have managed to balance life and work and enjoy both. These essays represent the varied ways in which some of your fellow OS&H professionals have managed to succeed with a consulting practice, whether they are a solo shop, part of a larger firm with multiple offices, working part-time, and dealing with young children, grown children and no children.

We encourage you to spend some time exploring each chapter and the accompanying resources not only as you begin to develop your consulting practice, but as you grow and succeed.

All the work on this guidebook, from conception to submitting it for publication, was done on a volunteer basis. Proceeds from this book go to the American Society of Safety Engineers (ASSE), and a scholarship fund sponsored by the Consultants Practice Specialty.

ABOUT THE EDITORS

CAROL A. KEYES, CSP, CRC, CCM is the president and co-owner of Complete Health, Environmental & Safety Services, Inc. (CHESS, Inc.). CHESS provides safety, environmental and occupational health consulting, primarily for smaller businesses. The company's clients range from municipalities to automotive repair to manufacturing facilities. CHESS, a women-owned business, was started in 1993 by Carol Keyes and Janet Keyes, CIH.

Carol is a Certified Safety Professional, Certified Rehabilitation Counselor, and Certified Case Manager. She is an OSHA authorized instructor, and has completed advanced training in ergonomics design and assessment. Prior to founding CHESS, Carol worked in the area of workers' compensation as a Rehabilitation Counselor. She is a Professional Member of ASSE, and active with the Consultants Practice Specialty, having served as editor for *The Advisor*. She was awarded Safety Professional of the Year by the Consultants' Practice Specialty. Carol is also very active with Northwest Chapter of ASSE, serving twice as secretary.

In addition to overseeing all of the business operations of CHESS, Carol provides guidance on OH&S issues to approximately 100 active clients. She works extensively with other business owners, both as their consultant and as a fellow small business owner. Carol has over 25 years of small business management experience (CHESS is the third business she has owned). Carol presents frequently to local associations, chambers of commerce, and business groups on topics such as general safety, program development, workplace violence, emergency planning, and workers' compensation.

J. A. RODRIGUEZ, JR. is CEO of Make My Day Strategies LLC. He is an elected Voluntary Protection Program (VPP) Participants' Association Board member, an *EHS Today* Magazine Safety Leadership Institute Board member, a patented inventor, and a U.S. OSHA VPP Special Government Employee. He is an accomplished global Fortune 100 EHS professional, and an ASSE Professional Member.

J.A. is a credentialed safety instructor for the University of Alabama at Birmingham. He was named by *EHS Today* Magazine as one of the 50 people who most influenced Environmental, Health & Safety in 2013. He is also a writer for several industry publications and social media outlets, including *EHS Today* Magazine, and *JenningsWire — The World of Success*. He has written for several ASSE practice specialty publications, and is author of the book, *Not Intuitively Obvious — Transition to the Professional Work Environment*.

J. A. is an inspiring keynote speaker, a frequent presenter at national safety conferences for various organizations, and an expert analyst for media programming, including top 100 national radio and television stations. Tens of thousands follow him on Twitter, and his LinkedIn profile is one of the most viewed in the world. He is also an avid philanthropist, devoting his resources toward assuring the availability of a college education for underprivileged youth.

PAMELA WALASKI is the Regional Manager, EHS Services, for Compliance Management International (CMI). In her current position, she is responsible for managing and growing CMI's western PA office. Prior to this position, she owned and operated her own consulting business (JC Safety & Environmental, Inc.) for 10 years. She holds both the CSP and CHMM designations.

Pam is a Professional Member of ASSE. At the time of publication, she was Administrator for the Consultants Practice Specialty and Vice Chair of the Council on Practices and Standards (CoPS). She was also a member of both the Society's Nominations and Elections Committee and By-Laws Committee, the Student Section Liaison for the Western Pennsylvania Chapter, and a member of the Indiana University of Pennsylvania Safety Science Advisory Board.

Pam received the Safety Professional of the Year Award for the Council on Practices and Standards in 2014, the ASSE President's Award, and the ASSE WISE 100 Women of Safety in 2011.

Pam presents regularly at national level conferences, company safety meetings and insurance seminars on the topics of risk management, risk and crisis communications and safety management systems. She has been a presenter at the ASSE Professional Development Conference for 10 consecutive years.

Pam is a regular contributor to *The Advisor, Professional Safety, The Synergist, EH&S Today, Safety + Health* and was Section Coordinator for the 2nd edition of *The Safety Professionals Handbook*, published by ASSE in June 2012. Her book, *Risk and Crisis Communications; Methods and Messages*, was published by John Wiley & Sons in September 2011. She also received second place from the editors of *Professional Safety* for her article on risk and crisis communications, published by *PS* in June 2010.

Questions to ask:

Do people regularly ask for and use my advice?

What is my vision of being a consultant?

Do I have what it takes to run a business?

Do I have the characteristics and skills that will help me succeed?

Chapter 1

Assessing Your Abilities

BY ELDEEN E. POZNIAK BA, BSC, CEES, CHSC, CHSMSA, MIIRSM, CMIOSH, CRSP

Eldeen is the owner of Pozniak Safety Associates Inc., and has been operating as an independent consultant, business owner, and entrepreneur for almost 20 years. Consulting on an international basis, she has owned consulting firms abroad. Her recent focus is on the two consulting firms she owns now, one in Canada and one in the United States. She has learned about the skills and traits that are necessary to survive and thrive within this role through trial, error, and support. Eldeen is committed to enhancing and moving the safety profession forward in a progressive fashion, and providing some food for thought; this chapter is just one way to help fulfill that goal.

EVERYONE KNOWS the famous phrase from William Shakespeare's play *Hamlet*—"To Be or Not To Be." Is that the question you're grappling with? Not, we hope, in Shakespeare's context of whether it is better to live or die, but rather whether it is better to continue as you have been or to brave the world of OS&H consulting. This book will explore why you might be looking at consulting, and what it takes to be a consultant. This chapter is fairly narrow in scope; it will help you ask some questions to assess your readiness, and explore the characteristics and skills that will help you be successful.

As you begin the process of understanding what it takes to be a successful consultant, the first area to explore is your personality; whether it meshes with what are commonly considered to be the required attributes for someone to succeed in OS&H consulting. Don't assume that you will fail if you are wanting in some areas; it just means that you might have some difficulties or need to find a way to work with what you have. As we will discuss, there are plenty of ways to be able to strengthen your deficits. But an honest appraisal of your strengths and weaknesses is a critical first step. By the time you finish reading this chapter, you should be able to answer the broad questions at the beginning of the chapter, which will help you assess your overall ability to be successful as a consultant.

THE VISION AND REALITY OF BEING A CONSULTANT

I have found many differences between what I thought being a consultant was and what I now know to be true. Do you have the vision of being a high-powered wealthy consultant, breezing from one project to another, with an exciting life filled with numerous gourmet lunches and exciting international travel, while the money just pours in? In reality, this may be part of it, but it usually takes time and hard work to grow your consulting business to that level. I have been to places that have been exciting and wonderful, places I never dreamed I would get to see. I have also been in locations where the hotel door does not lock, the weather is bad, and McDonald's is considered fine dining. Furthermore, income levels don't tend to be the same year after year, especially as market situations change. We consultants often talk about "feast or famine," or reminisce about times gone by when, as employees, we could regularly expect a three-percent annual raise.

You've probably heard people who run consulting businesses talk about the joy of being their own bosses: setting their own hours, being in charge of scheduling their own time, and only doing work that interests them. The reality is that while we often talk about flexibility and control of our time, there generally seems to be a special project that demands extraordinary hours from us, or working for clients who seem to want to control our time instead of the other way around. As is true with most safety consultants, I have pulled long days, worked on weekends, and from hotel rooms and airports. I have done training on the graveyard shift, and then frantically rushed to the next client meeting. I have been up until 3:00 a.m. preparing for a presentation or finishing up a report, and I have taken that job that I really don't like to do, because it will pay this month's bills.

The fundamental reality is that being a consultant is not a surefire way to get rich, it is not considered by one and all as a prestigious role in society, and it is not an easy way to make a living. For most consultants, the job consists of a range of demands, as they juggle multiple clients and projects, as well as juggling the requirements of running a business. I have had moments of self-discovery when I questioned my choice to be a consultant that occurred when eating alone at a diner in some random town or when trying to balance work and life. I have juggled scheduling my work projects with time for the

...major causes of small business failure are incompetence of the owner (46%), and unbalanced experience or lack of business knowledge and entrepreneurial experience (30%).

mundane parts of running a business, such as invoicing and developing marketing strategies, all the while trying to squeeze in time with family and friends, doctor and haircut appointments, and any other semblance of a personal life.

Being a OS&H consultant out on your own is hard work, and the success rate is not that high: 70% of consulting businesses will fail within 10 years (Shane 2008) and the U.S. Department of Labor estimates that 50% of all small businesses fail (BLS 2013). The statistic analytical group Statistic Brain, using information culled from Entrepreneur Weekly, U.S. Small Business Development Centers, Bradley University, and the University of Tennessee, found that the major causes of small business failure are incompetence of the owner (46%), and unbalanced experience or lack of business knowledge and entrepreneurial experience (30%). Some of the most common management mistakes that contribute to small business failure include going into business for the wrong reasons, burn out, family pressures, lack of market awareness, and limited understanding of basic business financials.

But don't put the book down yet: I don't want to scare you. I just want you to realize that it is not all glamor, or as easy as some of us make it look. For me, it has been hard work, and has come with benefits as well as difficulties. I am trying to get you to consider what your idea of what it takes to be a consultant is, and whether it is close to reality. Going into the safety consulting business is not guaranteed to provide financial success. But for me, it has provided numerous opportunities to satisfy my appetite for adventure, as well as a desire for personal and professional growth and satisfaction.

WHY COMPANIES HIRE CONSULTANTS

When I started to consider the independent consulting lifestyle as a career choice, I was advised to take a look at why organizations or companies hire an OS&H consultant. I asked myself, "Why might I get that phone call?" for a consulting opportunity in the first place. I needed to consider what the client might see as my function, as this would determine my role, competencies, and qualifications. It would also help me visualize how my consulting business could be positioned to take advantage of these opportunities.

In my opinion and from my experience, people hire OS&H consultants for the following key reasons:

1. To solve a problem by gathering and evaluating information and using that to provide guidance in various forms. The hiring organization might:

- Be looking for someone to provide a shortcut to knowledge and information that does not already exist in the organization.
- Be in need of a consultant to provide solutions to specific challenges and situations. This would-be client often asks the question, "What are other organizations doing to solve this?"
- Want an experienced, objective, and unbiased outsider point of view to provide a perspective on the dynamics of situations that may be hard to see or understand from the inside.
- Want to validate ideas that have already been discussed and are being considered.
- Want a facilitator to bring out the voices of people within the organization who have valuable opinions but who are often not easily heard by those with decision-making authority.

If this is the need coming from a prospective client, the questions I ask myself are:

– Do I have the wisdom, experience and knowledge needed to provide what is being asked of me?
– What safety-specific and industry- or business-related tools and knowledge do I have that allow me to assess, evaluate and create solutions?
– Do I have a network of people that I can fall back on to get the right answers in areas where I may not be so strong?
– Can I facilitate and/or provide answers to safety and organizational questions?
– Do I have the ability to make my client feel comfortable with me and trust me?

2. To supplement staff or conduct a specific project. The organization might:

- Need a specific professional service that does not exist in the organization or simply need extra manpower to get a particular job done, usually within a specific or shortened time frame.
- Want to be able to access the network of contacts or knowledge of a consultant to expand upon the expertise that is available.
- Have discovered that it can save money by hiring a consultant rather than hiring a full-time employee(s), generating savings from not paying benefits or administrative overhead.

If this is the need coming from a prospective client, the questions I ask myself are:

- What is my specialty/expertise, and what gap can I fill for the organization?
- Do I have a unique skill(s) that is currently in demand by organizations?
- What makes my skills distinctive, and sets me above other consultants that are out there? In other words, why would they choose me?

3. To facilitate, motivate or act as a catalyst. Organizations might:

   - Need someone who can get things going to facilitate, create or implement a system. Often, a consultant can come in and get a project moving faster than internal departments can due to bureaucracy, company culture, employee morale, internal politics, or other issues that can get in the way when an organization is trying to institute change.

   If this is the need coming from a perspective client, the questions I ask myself are:

   - Can I get things done at the pace expected by the organization?
   - Am I a change agent who can understand, communicate, and utilize a management of change philosophy?
   - What are my strategies for implementing change, and achieving objectives?

4. To make unpopular decisions. Organizations might hire a consultant because they:

   - Need to make a decision they know will be unpopular or that has been difficult to sell thus far. In these cases, an organization may have the consultant provide information or an opinion to validate or legitimize support of an unpopular direction or perhaps to stir the pot to get members of the organization to look at things in a different way.
   - Are looking for someone who has the ability to articulate a position or opinion in a neutral way or in a way that appears to maintain objectivity, while keeping the members of the organization focused on the topics at hand.

If this is the need coming from a prospective client, the questions I ask myself are:

- If I am brought in to make or support an unpopular decision, and if I am not appreciated for my position or called back to do any ongoing work, can I live with that?
- If I make a difficult decision or communicate bad news, will that affect my belief about my professional expertise or ethics?
- Do I have the soft skills to handle difficult situations or difficult people within an organization?

5. To present, teach or implement new business ideas and procedures. The organization might:

- Require new, specialized skill development, and call in a consultant to jumpstart that process.
- Need to ensure that internal changes are implemented with consistent information, and so use a consultant to oversee or completely implement that process.

If this is the need coming from a prospective client, the questions I ask myself are:

- Am I an effective trainer or instructor? Can I communicate information that may be new or complicated in a way that is easily understood by employees at different levels in the organization?
- Am I a strategic thinker? Can I help an organization look internally at how it functions and facilitate a change in a process or a procedure?

THE TYPES OF PEOPLE WHO SEEK TO BECOME CONSULTANTS

In our careers, most of us have seen or worked with an external OS&H consultant who has provided one of the above-mentioned services, and afterwards we have said to ourselves or even to others, "I could do that!" As noted in the introduction, many people believe that they have the specific skillset or expertise needed to be successful at consulting. They are confident in their abilities, and believe they could perform effective outsourced training, conduct thorough risk assessments, or provide advice and consultation to solve difficult safety-related problems. They may also feel confident that they possess sufficient entrepreneurial or business attributes to enable them to start and run successful consulting businesses. The types of people who try their hand at consulting are varied, but in general they seem to fall into four major categories.

Challenge Seekers

Challenge seekers are the types of people who are in jobs that do not challenge them or utilize their talents to the fullest potential (or so they believe). They may have reached their peak level of job responsibilities within an organization, or they may have job-hopped for the past few years because the challenges of each position were not sufficient to keep them motivated and satisfied with their work life.

For those seeking to increase professional satisfaction by challenging themselves with a career that requires the ability to constantly adapt and be flexible in aptitude, time and work style, as well as to be able to juggle multiple clients and a variety of projects combined with the demands of running and marketing a business, consulting may fit the bill.

Seasoned Experts

These are experienced OS&H professionals who have spent many years in the occupational health and safety field developing their skill set, and now are thinking of going out on their own. This group can take advantage of their business contacts and years of experience to create a high demand for their services because their specialized knowledge is needed. This type of potential consultant has typically established respect and credibility in a specific area or areas of the field and, therefore, often has a higher opportunity for success. Often, these types of consultants realize fairly lucrative payment for their services once they have established themselves and their business.

"Life Changers" or "Transitioners"

These are people who have recently experienced a life-changing event, such as being laid off or downsized, who want to supplement an existing job by moonlighting, who are nearing retirement and want to continue to work but not full-time, or who are already retired and are finding themselves bored.

For me, entering consulting was not because I needed to survive being laid off or downsized, it was because ... I wanted more control over my own life.

The first, the recently laid-off, is one where life changes have created an urgency to solve problems related to having enough income to survive or, if married/in a partnership, continue to contribute to the income of a household. This type of potential consultant is not necessarily desperate, but may simply see the life-altering event as an opportunity to branch out into consulting, possibly because he or she always wanted to do so, or possibly because the current job prospects are not good. Sometimes, these situations are meant to serve as a bridge to a more permanent job; sometimes, what was originally intended to be a temporary solution turns into a permanent one because of necessity or, more happily, success. Unfortunately, the opposite is also true, where a solution that you hoped would be permanent ends due to lack of success.

For me, entering consulting was not because I needed to survive being laid off or downsized, it was because of my desire to work from home while I cared for a parent and a child. I wanted more control over my own life. Because of that, combined with what I saw as a need in the market, I pushed myself into trying part-time consulting as a test before jumping in with both feet. As with many potential consultants in this category, I was seeking increased flexibility and control of both my professional and personal life.

If you find yourself disenchanted with your current supervisor, work responsibilities or organization in general, realize that, even though as a business owner you won't have a typical boss, you are accountable to your clients in much the same way. Even though you do have some say in what, how and when you undertake a project, at the end of the day it's still your job to make sure it gets finished, while still earning enough to pay the bills so that you are not living in a van down by the river.

New Graduates

Recent graduates might consider starting a consulting firm because it seems like a natural outgrowth of their academic experience. They are used to being successful at short-term projects, doing research to increase their knowledge level, and enjoy having bursts of intense work followed by calm periods. They may feel they have a great idea, and want that freedom of being on their own. I have known of a few consultants who started consulting with little or no professional experience. Each says that going out on their own with so little experience and with few, if any, clients lined up was a very risky move.

Working for well-established consultants can help you gain the type and level of experience that you would not have otherwise been able to find on your own

While I would not personally recommend starting a consulting business right out of the gate, if you are determined that this is the path you want to take, then consider following one of two early career tracks that I have observed will increase your chances of long-term success:

1. Target smaller organizations for your client base, and
2. Working as a subcontractor.

Often, targeting small to mid-sized companies can provide better opportunities, as these organizations understand that the services delivered are at a reduced price because of your inexperience. However, because the organization is small and may not have extensive funds to outsource its OS&H needs, or because its size means that the hazards are not that unusual and the services that are needed don't command high fees, the fit between an inexperienced consultant and the organization's needs is perfectly acceptable.

Being able to recognize opportunity is necessary if consulting is being considered at any stage in your career. Being able to provide potential clients with the confidence that using you will allow them to successfully complete the project will be beneficial selling points. Effective use of this strategy allows you to have the opportunity to work on a variety of projects without having to waste time understanding the bureaucracy of a large organization in order to secure their work.

Working as a subcontractor is also a good option for those with limited professional experience. Working for well-established consultants can help you gain the type and level of experience that you would not have otherwise been able to find on your own. It can also provide valuable mentoring relationships to aid in both professional development and in understanding the complicated aspects of running a business. Both allow you to gain experience, build mentoring relationships that are valuable and establish a track record for service delivery, all of which may lead to the ability to branch out on your own in the future. (Many chapters in this book address subcontracting. Chapter 2, "Creating a Business Plan," and Chapter 5, "Legal and Regulatory Issues," can provide some additional guidance on working as a subcontractor.)

While the reasons individuals seek to become consultants are varied, no one reason will ensure success over the other. Regardless of your reason or your level of experience and education, there are challenges and issues that all would-be safety consultants must understand and address to ensure success. What does contribute to success is knowing what it takes to succeed, and having the professional skills and personality characteristics that can contribute to success.

KNOWING WHAT IT TAKES TO BE A CONSULTANT

No matter which of the above categories you might find yourself in, the draw to enter consulting can be strong because of the perceived opportunity to learn and grow, achieve personal and professional satisfaction, make a difference in the implementation of OS&H programs for your clients, meet new people, and obtain financial rewards. However, it is important to understand that, while owning a business represents independence and freedom on some level, this reward is accompanied by the risk and uncertainty that the business owner assumes. By entering consulting, you are saying goodbye to the predictability, routine, normality, and safety of a regular job. You're venturing out on your own into unknown territory, where you will need to survive (in part) by your OS&H and business wits, not by a paycheck that appears every two weeks without questions.

> *My willingness to uncover my weak areas has gone a long way to help me get to where my business is today.*

The following questions are intended to give you some insight into whether you have really considered what being a consultant means. They will help you assess whether you have the personality traits needed to become a successful consultant or whether you are just trying to escape a job situation that is unsatisfying.

Over the years, I have read many articles that posed questions, and those listed here are many of these that I asked myself before I started and found helpful. In some respects, I think my honest appraisal of myself helped me to succeed. My willingness to uncover my weak areas has gone a long way to help me get to where my business is today. I still made some mistakes along the way, failing to see potential problem areas that I should have dealt with before I started. We all are human in that respect. But I present them to you as my own personal and professional "lessons learned" in the hope that they will help you. I strongly encourage you to honestly assess yourself before getting started. I also suggest you consider asking a trusted friend, family member or colleague to look at these questions and to do his or her own assessment of you, so you can benefit from another outside opinion.

- Do people frequently ask me for my advice and follow it?
- Do I have the skills, knowledge and experience that companies will pay for? Is there a need for the services that I want to sell? Can I offer something my competitors don't?
- Do I enjoy finding solutions to problems and experimenting with new ways to do things?
- Can I get up and start work without being told to do so? Can I keep on task without someone mentoring me? Can I meet deadlines?
- Am I in good health? Can I manage without health insurance and other benefits at first or can I afford to pay for those?
- Can I recover from emotional setbacks?
- Am I a leader? Am I effective when I am in control of a situation? Do I like being in control?

- Am I self-confident? Am I competitive and a risk taker?
- Am I a good listener and good communicator, both one on one and in groups?
- Do I keep my goal clearly in mind when there is something that I want? Am I persistent?
- Do I have the interpersonal skills to make sales and manage clients?
- Do I have a lot of energy? Can I work long hours and unconventional schedules for an unknown length of time?
- Can I sleep at night without knowing when I'll see revenue? Do I have a financial safety net? Do I have a decent credit rating? Can I afford to take this risk? Can I recover if I don't succeed?
- Am I organized? Am I comfortable with answering the phone, answering emails, and managing the books, while still trying to deliver services I can be compensated for?
- Will my family support my decision?

As you explore embarking on a consulting path, doing an honest self-assessment will increase the possibility of your success. As stated earlier, research and trial and error helped me but together the following chart below, and the accompanying discussion identifies skills and characteristics that I believe can help you succeed in consulting. While it is not an inclusive list, it is a good place to start for conducting your own self- assessment.

Figure 1 (adapted by Pozniak) provides a comprehensive illustration of the characteristics that are essential for success in OS&H consulting. Each quadrant addresses a different characteristic area. The details about each of these quadrants and their associated characteristics are addressed in the section below.

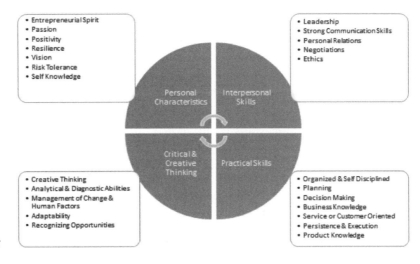

Figure 1
Successful Characteristics of OS&H Consultant

Personal Characteristics

In this area, you need to look at what you bring to the table regarding your intrinsic personality type, including values and beliefs, such as those I have listed below. In my experience, they are typical of successful consultants.

Vision

Most successful consultants have a vision, a "big picture," and the ability to explain and inspire others to see it as well. It is important to have a vision of what you want, and dissatisfaction with the present to either take the step to become a consultant or to take your business to the next level. In John Kotter's book, *Leading Change* (1996), he postulates that leading change depends on a defined dissatisfaction with the present, which creates a vision for how things should be, and a clear idea of the first steps to be taken to get there.

Your passion needs to align with an unmet need, and the values of the potential organization or client.

What is your focus? What is your vision for growth and change in your professional vision? What are the first steps for you? Do you have the ability to look at an organization or a problem, including your own, and see where things can be improved?

Entrepreneurial Spirit

Numerous articles, in publications including *The Harvard Gazette*, *Forbes* and *Entrepreneur*, along with web sites focusing on entrepreneurship, refer to the necessity of not just believing that you have a good business idea, but the additional ability to organize, operate, and assume the risk for the business venture to ensure success. Such publications emphasize the critical need to have an "entrepreneurial spirit;" the enthusiasm, excitement, initiative, and commitment to an idea, as well as the dedication and will to succeed, that is needed to overcome the initial and ongoing difficulties and demands. Establishing a name for yourself, setting up your business, and trying to win a critical project can be an intimidating experience.

Do I have a strong desire to be in control of my own destiny and succeed? Am I willing to commit time and effort to my goals? Can I keep moving forward when setbacks keep getting in my way?

Passion

In my experience, successful consultants have a passion for what they do and how they do it. No one personifies this characteristic for me as much as Richard

Branson, the founder of Virgin Airlines. His passion for what he does and for life is contagious and inspirational. One of Richard Branson's personal principles that really resonates with me is, "There is no greater thing you can do with your life and your work than follow your passions—in a way that serves the world and you" (Anderson 2013). I have always had a desire to be a change agent, stemming from my deep internal belief that things can be better, can be safer and can be changed through a tailored, persistent, and consistent application. I am passionate about our profession because I truly believe in the meaning and purpose of it.

... leading change depends on a defined dissatisfaction with the present, which creates a vision for how things should be, and a clear idea of the first steps to be taken to get there.

As a consultant, you will need something to carry you through the days when you don't make any money, you have no clients, and nothing seems to be going your way. It is your passion for what you do that will help keep you going, that will push you though the hard times. Be careful not to fall into the fallacy that says, "As long as I am doing what I love, the money will eventually come." Simply doing what you love is not enough. Your passion needs to align with an unmet need, and the values of the potential organization or client. If your passion is selling blue fire extinguishers but the regulation states only red ones are to be used, you will be out of business quickly. Passion alone won't guarantee success, but life is tough enough without being dissatisfied with or even hating what you do for a living.

What do you have passion for? Does that enthusiasm align with what potential organizations and clients need?

Positivity or Optimism

Being a positive or optimistic thinker will be an advantage in getting you through the tough times that all consultants experience occasionally, regardless of how long you have been in business, your specific business model or the types of clients you serve (Carver & Scheier 2001). There have been times when working with specific clients has been particularly trying for me. In some cases, their problems created great difficulties within the organization; by the time I was brought in to assist, emotions were high, and people were entrenched in their opinions and processes. The overall mood can be contagious; in more than one situation, I have found myself feeling very stressed as well. If I did not have a positive outlook in general and a belief in my ability to assist, I could have easily been drawn into the drama, and into the poisoned environment that I was there to help fix.

Over the years that I have been in consulting, I have had some tough times and have had to make many unpleasant business decisions. Sometimes, those decisions involved not working with specific clients or other consultants anymore because of our different approaches or ethics. My personal philosophy is to see every challenge as an opportunity, because that positive outlook and confidence helps to carry me through.

Do you see challenge and change as an opportunity? Is your personal outlook one of a glass half-full, or half-empty?

Resilience

This is that quality that allows one to be knocked down by life, a negative business turn, or a project that does not turn out well, and to come back stronger than ever. It is the ability to adapt and manage adversity, stress, and even trauma, while being open to feedback. Psychologists report that what makes someone resilient is a positive attitude, optimism, flexibility, the ability to regulate emotions, and the ability to see bumps in the road as feedback from which to learn (U.S. Department of Education 2013). There is no sitting back, and letting someone else pick up the slack when it comes to consulting; you are the only one with the ability to make yourself and your work a success. For me, this meant having to change my business structure, focus, and OS&H services to survive some turbulent times.

Top consultants and business owners never stop learning.

Can you pick yourself up when things don't go as planned? Does adversity make you stronger or more determined to succeed?

Risk Tolerance

Being in business for yourself is a form of legalized gambling. You need to have a high tolerance for the ambiguity and uncertainty that characterizes the first years of your consulting practice. Banking on winning that proposal that you are sure you have in the bag, only to learn that you did not win it because of a pricing or approach difference, is not for the faint of heart. Before you begin your consulting venture, it is important that you understand all the risks as well as the rewards, and then learn how to best manage them. For me, one of the main rewards for getting involved in consulting was being able to spend more time with my family, and when the balance did not work out, I ended up risking family relationships. Only after reprioritizing and rethinking my business model was I able to salvage some of those relationships.

Are you able to take risks and make decisions when situations are uncertain?

Self-knowledge and Investment

You need to know your strengths, weaknesses, motivations, and even biases, since you operate from them every day. Blaise Pascale, the French mathematician and philosopher (1623–1662) said, "We must learn our limits. We are all something, but none of us are everything" (Quotes.net 2014). Being able to take a genuine look at yourself and your business potential and to be able to realistically outline your business goals, plans, activities, and your ability to deliver on them is essential for success. You have to be willing to admit when you don't know something, when you have made a mistake, or when you need someone's help. Consultants cannot know everything and should not be expected to know everything.

Having a weakness does not mean you have to strengthen it to succeed. It means that you can surround yourself with others who have that strength and use them as a resource. I am not suggesting that you should not take time to increase and improve your skills and expertise. Top consultants and business owners never stop learning. They read business and marketing materials because these resources will improve their understanding of the skills needed to run a business successfully. They join associations and clubs to network and to learn secrets of success. They attend seminars, workshops and training courses, even if they think they have already mastered the subject matter to ensure that they are current. Never stop investing in the most powerful, effective and best business tool you have—you.

Do you have a basic understanding of your own strengths and weaknesses? Do you know how to figure them out? Are you willing to invest time in continually improving yourself?

Interpersonal Skills

There is no doubt that relating well to people, so you can form stable and trusting business relationships, is essential to your success. This is true whether it be with your clients, your team members, or your suppliers. Since consulting typically involves more than one person (even if it is just you and the client), you need to be able to work well with a variety of people. You need to have effective people skills to help you obtain the work or project, then use those skills to build a trusting relationship to ensure the success of your project, and create a possible repeat business situation.

Individual success in consulting has been shown to be related to the number, quality and depth of relationships. . . .

Leadership

Your ability to communicate, negotiate, influence, persuade, and inspire others to do what you want or need them to do is indispensable to almost everything you do in successfully running your consulting business. These skills are effective in everything, from getting the contract to helping clients foster and implement the changes you are recommending. As I have come to understand through my experience and my readings, commonly accepted characteristics of leaders are charisma, enthusiasm, shared ethical grounding, and a desire to build integrity within an organization (SBA n.d.) Successful leaders can competently assist an organization to ensure goals and objectives are accomplished.

Good leadership starts with self-development; understanding the perceptions, motivations, strengths and weaknesses that make up your own leadership style. Further, your leadership style needs to be effectively demonstrated in your client interactions. While the focus of this chapter does not permit a lengthy discussion of leadership styles and development, a number of theories on the topic of leadership and leadership styles can easily be found in any book store or via an Internet search. You can also join local organizations in your community that focus on leadership development. I have found both reading and participating in such organizations to be helpful.

I believe that different situations demand different leadership approaches. I have found success by developing a style of flexibility and awareness, using different skills as needed for different situations and different clients. At times, I have worked hard to develop reasonable, logical recommendations that are correct according to regulations that my clients have promptly ignored, usually because of resistance to change within the organization and/or individuals. I believe I have several choices at that point: I can walk away if I believe that I have done all I can within the scope of providing assistance and advice, or come back with a different strategy or communicate in a different way to turn that type of situation around.

What type of leader are you? Are you effective in fostering and implementing change in organizations or programs?

Strong Communication Skills

Communicating effectively is key to consulting success. You can possess stellar knowledge in occupational health and safety, but if you cannot share it in a way that is both meaningful and understandable, your knowledge is less effective. As a consultant, you must be able to effectively present information to a diverse audience, from the CEO to a floor employee, which includes the ability to present your ideas and vision both verbally and in writing.

Strong active listening and empathetic listening skills are also critical. Ed Hrycenko, my father, had many sayings about communication, and how it motivated people. He used to say, "You were given two ears and one mouth — use them accordingly." Applying this axoim has helped me learn to effectively draw out important information in my consulting relationships, allowing me to know more about the company and its issues, thus increasing my overall effectiveness. Good communication skills help you gain an understanding of your customers' needs and the business environment in which they operate, so you can then work to fulfill those needs. The ability to discuss and negotiate projects, clarify roles and responsibilities, and outline contract inclusions need to be a part of your overall communication attributes.

Communicating effectively is key to consulting success.

Your ability to "schmooze" is important. Those extroverts who have it or the introverts who can turn it on have a distinct advantage in the world of consulting. Having the ability to easily strike up conversations helps you establish comfortable relationships with many types of people. Having these skills and utilizing them will vastly improve your chances of success.

Do you have strong presentation skills, exceptional writing ability, and sensitive listening skills? Can you enter a room full of strangers and engage in conversations easily? Do you like to network?

Personal Relations

Individual success in consulting has been shown to be related to the number, quality and depth of relationships, according to research done by Keith Ferrazzi (2005). The ability to relate to others and to fit in, the capacity to understand and manage relationships with others, and the ability to understand and accurately express oneself verbally and nonverbally and interpret the words of others is extremely important for a number of reasons in the consulting world, including modifying the consultant approach in order to more comprehensively address client needs. If you want to do work in some countries and cultures (e.g., Asia Pacific, Middle East), developing relationships first is a critical predecessor to even being considered or given the opportunity to consult.

Since effective consulting requires working well with others, you have to be able to get along with people in general. Often, you are seen as an outsider in the beginning of projects and client relationships. You need to be able to win the confidence of strangers, who may be initially suspicious or even threatened by your presence. You must be able to listen to, speak to, understand and interact with other people in order to assist and provide advice.

It is also helpful to have the skills and focus to form personal relationships with people in the same industry, whether peers, allied consultants, or possible competitors. You will benefit from what they offer, and they may benefit from knowing you. How close you are to them is up to you; you will need to decide, based on what fits in with your business plan. They may be just be connections on LinkedIn, but their perspectives on an issue posted in a discussion could turn out to be an important piece of information for you. Then there are others with whom you might want a stronger connection, getting to know them well enough to e-mail them for a small favor or to ask them if they would be interested in getting involved in your new project. With yet others, you may form a more transactional relationship, where there is a significant level of trust and respect. Relationships at this level include those people who serve as your mentors and trusted advisors.

Relationships with your clients can also become more than just a business relationship. I have several of these. They are people who, from the earliest days of my consulting business, fit with my values. Over time, we have worked at building a relationship, both individually and organizationally. These relationships are worth the effort to develop and sustain because they frequently create huge opportunities. They have had long-term impacts on my consulting business.

Do you have connections and relationships to mentors, peers, and clients? How well do you relate and interact with others? Do you understand the cultural aspects of the country, business, or individual? Can you connect with people and form relationships?

Ethics

As consultants, we face ethical dilemmas every day of the week. Having high ethical standards, including integrity, honesty, respect, fairness, empathy and trustworthiness and the ability to maintain confidences, are values and principles that must govern our actions. Conflicts of interest, conflicting personal relationships, lack of ability to do the job, being aware of insider information, and client requests for unethical work are a few of the possible negative ethical dilemmas that have crossed my path along my consulting journey. Often while providing consulting services I am privy to a lot of insider information, including interesting and confidential things about my client's operations, business plans, and strategies. Some organizations require signing a confidentiality agreement, along with turning in all documents and papers; others are more casual about the confidential information they allow you to see. Regardless of the organization's practices, a consultant cannot misuse the information obtained in the working relationship.

Are you prepared to turn away clients if they ask you to do something that you feel is unethical?

Some specific examples of ethical situations I have encountered have been when clients asked me to not include specific things in reports or to retest specific measurable data so that it is more beneficial than the original results. In one situation, my solution was to retest as requested, but to supply both sets of data and recommend that another organization conduct follow-up testing to verify the accuracy of my data. As for written reports, I have been willing to soften or reword, but have not excluded items that I felt needed to be included.

One ethical dilemma that I often run into is when a client approaches me for direct work when I have subcontracted another professional to do the work, or if I am the subcontractor. Being approached to bypass, or having consultants who are subcontractors on a job pass out their cards and encourage direct contact can and does happen. Having clear agreements and good understanding of those you work with or for is important, as some may not have the same business common sense or ethics as you do.

Choosing the ethical way will not only allow you to sleep better at night (because you are not going against something that you believe in), but your reputation will be kept intact, and your liability will be decreased. I refer to and follow the ethical codes of both the Canadian Society of Safety Engineering (CSSE) and the American Society of Safety Engineers (ASSE), as I am a professional member of both organizations. These provide me with a framework and guidance as I make my ethical choices. You should also reference Chapter 9, "Ethics and Other Professional Issues," for a more in-depth discussion.

Do you know what your line is? Have you reviewed your profession's codes of ethics to decide your direction? Are you prepared to turn away clients if they ask you to do something that you feel is unethical? Are you really qualified to do the work that your client is hiring you to do? Do you already have far too many jobs lined up to be able to adequately handle a new one? What are you willing to do if your employees or subcontractors do not follow the same ethics?

Critical and Creative Thinking Skills

As a consultant, you must be able to analyze and evaluate a situation, clarify concepts and ideas, seek possibilities, consider alternatives and solve problems. Critical and creative thinking skills are needed to enable you, as the consultant, to generate new ideas and alternative possibilities, and even to discover or imagine an entirely new way of approach for your clients.

Analytical and Diagnostic Abilities

As a consultant you must be able to size up the situation and people, analyze an organization's processes, and diagnose problems in a quick and accurate way. These activities are a part of every consulting project; they need to be accurate from the beginning, or it can result in problems down the line. Objectivity, curiosity, conceptual outlooks, and inductive reasoning are some key qualities in being able to assess the real needs of the client, as those needs are often not stated at the beginning of the project or even known to the client.

Can you identify, explore and organize information and ideas to interpret, sequence, compare and appraise information? Can you pose questions to identify and clarify information and ideas? Are you open and fair-minded?

Creative Thinker

Your perspective as an outside expert is what is most often valued by your potential clients, as you are often asked to see things that others closer to the situation failed to see, or could see but were unable to resolve. You will need to explore the problem and be able to provide alternative solutions, to guide your client's actions. Knowing more than one way to resolve a tough problem; imagining the different possibilities; connecting ideas and weighing the alternatives; putting these ideas into action: these are essential skills in the consulting business.

I have been successful in enhancing my own creative thinking skills and in engaging the creativity of the client representatives I work with through the use of tools such as process mapping, predictive reasoning, alternative story endings, and blue sky exercises. These tools, easily researched, learned, and utilized, are not much different than some of the processes we use within our safety profession, such as risk assessments and job task analyses, where we define the steps in the task, identify potential hazards and alternative procedures, and then identify all possible controls to address the hazard and risk. If you are looking to improve your creative thinking skills, I highly recommend that you investigate some of these.

In addition to using creative thinking with clients, you will need to apply this skill within your own business. One of the most frustrating situations that I and many others faced when starting up our consulting practices was scarce resources, both financial and otherwise. This is where my creative thinking skills really came in handy. In one situation, I found myself with limited computer resources necessary to market myself and my consulting business effectively. I approached a local advertising and media class instructor and convinced that instructor to use my consulting practice as a project, providing me with some advertising design and advice for free. Another example was attending local safety association meetings, such as the monthly meetings of the local chapter of CSSE, and networking my little heart out, making myself known by putting a unique twist on questions posed to the group. Word of mouth, my different way of looking at the situation, and relationship building soon helped me get projects.

Are you good at generating ideas, possibilities, and actions? Can you see existing situations in a new way, identifying alternative explanations, and seeing or making new links that generate positive outcomes?

Management of Change and Human Factors

At times, you have to be an armchair psychologist to understand yourself, let alone to understand the underlying motivations of your clients and their organizational culture to such a degree that you can facilitate change in the way they function. Knowledge of organizational behavior and internal motivation is becoming recognized by consultants and other OS&H professionals as key to helping guide clients. For me, learning, understanding, and implementing some of key concepts in this area helped me in setting up and growing my consulting business, helped me assist my clients, and helped me create a niche in the consulting world. Some of my best resources, which I recommend to you, include John Kotter's change management principles (Kotter 1996), Dan Petersen's system structure and underlying failure concepts, such as organizational traps and decision to err information (Petersen 2003), and Menzel's change agent skill information (Menzel 1975).

Understanding human personality, attitude formation, and motivation is useful to help us guide our clients to implement changes in their safety management systems and program initiatives. Having knowledge in these areas can not only assist you in your analysis and development of recommendations, but also in successful implementation. Before I understood organizational psychology and management of change philosophies, I would provide my recommendations to the client, and leave it up to them to determine how to implement them, or I would provide a few suggestions built upon what I had seen work in other organizations, and hope that those would work for that particular client. Now that I have changed my process, using my knowledge of ways to understand, implement, and manage organizational change, my success rate has increased. The amount and types of consulting I do reflect the success I have achieved by implementing what I learned.

Do you have a basis of knowledge or experience, a template, tool or philosophy to follow that facilitates individual and organizational change or habit formation? Do you understand how individual and group beliefs and behavior affect safety culture?

Adaptability

In my opinion, having the ability to adapt or be flexible is one of the greatest strengths a consultant can have. I believe every successful business owner and consultant must be willing to improve, learn, refine, and customize his or her service to continue to give the clients what they want (Reeves & Deimler 2011). Sometimes, things do not go as planned; in an era of heightened business risk due to globalization, new technologies, greater transparency, and the volatility of business operating margins, consultants often come and go. To survive and thrive, we need the ability to perceive and respond to the current and future business environment and help our clients restructure and re-institutionalize behaviors and processes that allow them to adapt. We need to welcome new ideas, be willing to try new approaches, and see creating change in our own consulting business and in our clients' organizations as an important part of the way we both do business.

When I started in consulting, I targeted a specific industry, the forest and manufacturing industry, but as that market changed, I had to adapt to other industries, such as mining and construction. I initially provided specific safety programs and initiatives (ergonomics consulting, hazard and risk analysis). Although those services are still a part of my consulting practice, to sustain my organization, I expanded my services to satisfy client demands such as contractor management, safety culture assessment, and soft skill training for safety supervisors. For me, adaptability was the characteristic that took my business from having a narrow specialty to being more diverse, as I needed to adapt to market demands to stay profitable. It allowed me to be flexible and to respond to changes without being paralyzed with fear and uncertainty.

Adaptability has allowed me to be more creative with my client recommendations, and to bring more value in the proposed options. It is crucial to maximize your impact with each client as you apply the right tools and provide the right deliverables. Often, our consulting projects have some of the same constraints that we have in our own consulting businesses, including time management, limited budgets and people, data availability, different levels of cooperation, and varying levels of interest or worth. But if you are able to respond to the environment you find yourself in, build the best process based upon your knowledge and experience, and employ the best techniques you can in the best way you can within the constraints you have been given for your client and for your consulting business, your success will be enhanced.

How do you keep an eye on your market? Do you have a plan for change, growth and adaptability? When your consulting environment can be unpredictable, how can you apply forecasting and analysis to ensure your business continuity? Do you take enough time to analyze and explore options?

Recognizing Opportunities

Understanding your clients' wants and needs can provide your consulting business with a greater opportunity to provide support to those clients. It can also earn you a loyal client base and ongoing referrals. You can identify opportunities by observing trends, solving existing problems for organizations, and seeing how they apply elsewhere, and by finding gaps in the market place. Even if you think you have found a new opportunity, you need skill, ability, risk, and timing to take advantage of it. Analyze the feasibility of the opportunity so that you can readily provide the product or service people want at a price they are willing to pay.

Is there an improvement in the goods or services that you offer that can put you ahead of your competitors? Can you "horizon gaze" and spot a trend or a new hot topic? Can you recognize an opportunity as it presents itself?

Practical Skills

As a consultant you must have sound theoretical and technical knowledge, be able to plan, organize, and think on your feet, and have the ability to apply or "get your hands dirty."

Organized and Self-disciplined

As noted previously, being a consultant gives you the freedom to organize your work in your own way, and to set your own hours. It is great to be your own boss, with no one looking over your shoulder telling you what to do and when to do it. But not having this structure can make it easy to procrastinate or forget things that need to be done.

Because time management is an important part of being organized, create a system for yourself that addresses such items as inclusion of regular work hours, and the means to keep track of those things that you need to do. If you cannot control your tendency to procrastinate, you will not get things done, and if you don't get things done you won't keep your clients. I have used computer-based programs, such as Microsoft Outlook, and concepts, such as the Bring Forward System, to remind me of what I need to do that month, week, or day. Without a direct supervisor, you need to keep your own schedule, be your own manager, balance your own books, and even be your own secretary, or make sure it gets done by someone else.

Do you like to plan your day, week, and month? Do you do what's easiest or do you do what's right? Do you complete a task when you say you will?

Planning

Planning is the process of determining your future, deciding what actions to take, and why, how, when, and in what order. Planning helps you adapt to the demands of your projects, the day-to-day details of managing a business, and the overall mission that guides the future of your consulting business in a systematic fashion: keeping them all in perfect harmony. You need to anticipate what you have to do, as well as influence and control how it is done. You have to have the ability to handle both the day-to-day operation of the business, as well as to make the decisions that determine your future, and all of that needs to be balanced with providing your clients with the services that keep you in business.

Prioritizing is an important part of planning and time management within your own business activities, as well as with client projects. Some days you can be inundated with client meetings and work, when everything seems due at once. To handle those, you have to learn to prioritize and balance the workload, focusing on the most important tasks. In my experience, planning is most effective when you have clearly established short-term and long-term goals. I have had success using the SMART concept—Specific, Measurable, Achievable, Realistic and Time Limited (Doran 1988)—to set the goals, objectives, and plans for both my consulting company and for my clients. I have even expanded it to SMARTER, adding Evaluate and Reevaluate to ensure that my intended targets are not forgotten.

Decision Making

Problem solving and decision making are important skills for business, as well as for life. Many consultants and organizations are familiar with conducting a SWOT Analysis, which is a simple framework used to evaluate your consulting business, client organization, or programs for Strengths, Weaknesses, Opportunities and Threats. You can then use the analysis to develop strategic plans and initiatives. I have also used other frameworks and tools, such as de Bono's Six Thinking Hats (de Bono 1985) not only to understand how I make decisions, but to assist my clients and their organizations with their decisions. De Bono's methodology assigns six hats, each with a different color, to six distinct ways the human brain can be challenged: objective, intuitive, negative, positive, creative, and process. By metaphorically wearing the different hats, decision makers can organize their thoughts into decisions. If I know which "hats" or attributes my clients and I naturally default to, then make the conscious choice to put on the other hats, we are able to make more complete and inclusive decisions.

When facilitating a client's decision-making processes, I have found it key to first create a constructive environment: establishing objectives, agreeing on processes, involving the right people, and having open honest creative communication. I can then introduce my decision-making model, in which our plan is to come up with good alternatives, explore those alternatives, choose the one we think is right, check the decision, communicate it to those affected, and then move into action, implementing it.

Do you have tools or a well-defined process to structure your decisions? Can you determine the real issues before making a decision? Do you consider a variety of potential solutions and perspectives before making a decision? Do you include the key stakeholders?

BUSINESS KNOWLEDGE

The rest of the chapters of this book will guide you through much of the basic business knowledge you need to develop your business concept and to structure the main functional areas of business (marketing, finance, and operations). Here, suffice it to say that you will need to have basic bookkeeping skills and knowledge regarding account payables, receivables, budgeting, and payroll. You will also need to know something about systems to track time and expenses. Whether you keep full control over this area, or if you outsource it, you have to manage your money wisely; it is the lifeblood of any business enterprise. Business planning, asset management, operations management, and marketing must become a part of who you are and what you do.

I have found business knowledge is not only the key to successfully running my own consulting business, but it also provides me with a better understanding of my clients' needs and the business environment in which they operate, increasing my credibility with them. As a profession, we continuously point out it is key that we, or at least the good business case for safety, need to be around the leadership table. I demonstrate that by using a technical skill, such as calculating a return on investment. Other times, I demonstrate that credibility in understanding and being able to communicate the applicability of concepts of organizational group behavior, such as that of Hersey and Blanchard's Situational Leadership Model (Hersey and Blanchard 1988), which involves telling, selling, participating, and delegating to facilitate growth. Remember this is not just about "name or concept" dropping, but actually being able to discuss, apply, and utilize the concepts. If we know, understand, and have the ability to communicate and apply business concepts, language, and systems, it goes a long way in moving safety toward more a business risk-based system versus just a compliance focus.

> *Business planning, asset management, operations management, and marketing must become a part of who you are and what you do.*

Can you aim integration of the safety solutions you are selling into everyday business processes, improving those by addressing the real-world needs? What do you do to ensure that you understand the business needs of both your own business and that of your clients? How do you tie in your service or product to the clients' overall business strategy, structure, and culture?

Service or Customer Oriented

To build your business, you need to be motivated by understanding and meeting your clients' needs. Your success is not solely because you have the best prices or the best product or services; it is because you understand your clients' needs and the business environment in which they operate. Everything you do must be client-focused. That includes your polices, payment options, operating hours, presentations, and advertising. You must know who your customers are, know what they need, and know what they want. You need to find ways to work in collaboration with them, to be their partner in business, so they become the clients we all want, the valued repeat clients.

What does "customer-oriented" really mean to you? How are you aligning your consulting capabilities with your clients' needs?

Product Knowledge or Technical Skills

Your client is buying your knowledge or technical skill. You must have a thorough grounding in theoretical and practical aspects of the health and safety disciplines; of the laws, regulations, guidelines, standards and codes; and the elements of occupational health and safety management systems and programs. Technical skills that apply to the specific job and project requirements are necessary; most of us have acquired those through our education and training and through field experience. But it is important to keep in mind that you cannot know and do everything. Saying "I don't know" is an honest answer to a question, but even better is to say, "I don't know but I know someone who does or I will find someone who can help us." Rather than turning a potential client away, you may have now created a new business opportunity.

There are different paths that can be taken in OS&H consulting. The most obvious are becoming either a generalist or a specialist. A generalist usually focuses on universal OS&H system improvement of an organization. These consultants often combine many skills to provide service to their clients. A specialist focuses on one particular area of OS&H expertise, such as fall protection, industrial hygiene, or return-to-work programs. The specialist may also service a specific industry sector, such as healthcare or construction. These consultants narrow their service delivery areas. Many consulting businesses successfully provide both general and specialized services, by hiring specialists or by creating business arrangements with others to broaden the types and levels of services they provide. You can read more about whether to specialize, generalize or partner with others in Chapter 2, "Creating a Business Plan," and about understanding your market niche in Chapter 6, "Marketing and Sales."

Do you have a skill or knowledge that people need and are willing to pay for? Are you a generalist or a specialist?

> ... "quality is commitment; it is self-motivation that distinguishes successful entrepreneurs from those that fail."

Persistence and Execution

All successful business owners, including OS&H consultants, have a long-term vision, but they are also relentlessly focused on the activities in the here and now that allow them to achieve their vision. Lenko wrote that, "quality is commitment; it is self-motivation that distinguishes successful entrepreneurs from those that fail. It is the common thread in the life and biographies of those that have succeeded new enterprises. It is the one quality which entrepreneurs themselves admit is critical to the success of their initiatives" (Lenko 1995).

Everything you do must be client-focused. That includes your polices, payment options, operating hours, presentations, and advertising.

Are you persistent? Do you have the ability to keep working on your vision day after day?

Tools to Assist You

The overview I have provided above is a compilation of skills and characteristics that I believe, and the literature suggests, you will need to be a successful OS&H consultant. Think carefully about the material I have presented. Answer the questions at the end of each section. But don't stop there. I recommend that you further evaluate your ability to become a successful consultant.

Many free assessment tools are available. I've found these three to be useful:

1. The GoForth Institute specializes in providing individuals with the skills they need to start and grow a small business. One of their tools is a Self-Assessment Guide for Entrepreneurs developed by Leslie Roberts (2010).
2. The U.S. Small Business Administration offers another online version called The Small Business Readiness Assessment.
3. The Canadian Society of Safety Engineering (CSSE) *Consulting Skills Course* uses a comprehensive tool for assessing your skills as a consultant. The scoring indicates your skill sets and success rates. The higher your ranking, the more likely you are to succeed. This tool is provided in Figure 2 below.

The Canadian Society of Safety Engineering (CSSE) and the American Society of Safety Engineers (ASSE) both offer seminars for people who want to start a consulting business. I have taken the former course, and I highly recommend it. It provides an in-depth opportunity to assess your skills and characteristics, and provides you with additional information about the aspects of consulting that are discussed in this book.

Consulting Skills Course - Certified Health and Safety Consultant (CHSC)

Consulting Skills Self Appraisal Form No. 1

Rate yourself along each of the following dimensions:

	Low					High
Diagnostic Abilities						
Objectivity	1	2	3	4	5	6
Curiosity	1	2	3	4	5	6
Organization and analysis of data and information	1	2	3	4	5	6
Recognition of patterns, trends, underlying issues	1	2	3	4	5	6
Reasoning	1	2	3	4	5	6
Solution and Implementation Skills						
Imagination	1	2	3	4	5	6
Planning	1	2	3	4	5	6
Design and facilitation of change	1	2	3	4	5	6
Understanding human behaviour, motivations, attitudes	1	2	3	4	5	6
Courage	1	2	3	4	5	6
Teaching	1	2	3	4	5	6
General and Specialized Knowledge						
Current theory and research findings on OH&S	1	2	3	4	5	6
Contemporary thinking on best practices	1	2	3	4	5	6
Detailed expertise in one or more OH&S content areas:						
Safety Engineering	1	2	3	4	5	6
Safety Management	1	2	3	4	5	6
Training	1	2	3	4	5	6
Emergency Response	1	2	3	4	5	6
Fire Prevention / Protection	1	2	3	4	5	6
Security	1	2	3	4	5	6
Environmental Protection	1	2	3	4	5	6
Ergonomics	1	2	3	4	5	6
Risk Management	1	2	3	4	5	6
Occupational Hygiene	1	2	3	4	5	6
Occupational Medicine/Nursing/Health	1	2	3	4	5	6
Mechanical Engineering	1	2	3	4	5	6
Organizational Development	1	2	3	4	5	6
Toxicology	1	2	3	4	5	6

(continued....page 2)

CSSE
Canada's safety, health and environmental practitioners
www.csse.org

Figure 2 Consulting Skills Course—Certified Health and Safety Consultant (CHSC)
Source: Canadian Society of Safety Engineers (CSSE).

Consulting Skills Course - Certified Health and Safety Consultant (CHSC)

Consulting Skills Self Appraisal Form No. 1   (continued from page 1)

	Low					High
Knowledge of management disciplines:						
Finance / Accounting	1	2	3	4	5	6
Human Resources	1	2	3	4	5	6
Administration	1	2	3	4	5	6
Purchasing	1	2	3	4	5	6
Operations Management	1	2	3	4	5	6
Production	1	2	3	4	5	6
Marketing	1	2	3	4	5	6
Knowledge of applicable laws, statutes, regulations, and standards	1	2	3	4	5	6

Communications Skills

	Low					High
Listening ability	1	2	3	4	5	6
Writing ability	1	2	3	4	5	6
Oral presentation	1	2	3	4	5	6
Conversational	1	2	3	4	5	6
Verbal intervention	1	2	3	4	5	6

Marketing and Selling Ability

	Low					High
Identification of prospective clients	1	2	3	4	5	6
Cold Calling	1	2	3	4	5	6
Preparation of advertising concepts and materials	1	2	3	4	5	6
Development of marketing plans and strategies	1	2	3	4	5	6
Preparation of proposals	1	2	3	4	5	6
Prospective client interview skill	1	2	3	4	5	6
Perseverance	1	2	3	4	5	6
Being friendly and cheery	1	2	3	4	5	6

Managerial Skills

	Low					High
Leading project teams	1	2	3	4	5	6
Cost control	1	2	3	4	5	6
Constructively disciplining	1	2	3	4	5	6
Giving feedback	1	2	3	4	5	6
Coordinating production of reports and presentations	1	2	3	4	5	6
Praising	1	2	3	4	5	6
Developing and maintaining systems for tracking of time and expenses	1	2	3	4	5	6
Motivating	1	2	3	4	5	6
Personal organization	1	2	3	4	5	6

(continued....page 3)

CSSE
Canada's safety, health and environmental practitioners
www.csse.org

Figure 2 Consulting Skills Course—Certified Health and Safety Consultant (CHSC)
Source: Canadian Society of Safety Engineers (CSSE).

Consulting Skills Course - Certified Health and Safety Consultant (CHSC)

Consulting Skills Self Appraisal Form No. 1   (continued from page 2)

	Low				High	
Personal Attributes						
Ethical standards	1	2	3	4	5	6
Empathy	1	2	3	4	5	6
Trustworthiness	1	2	3	4	5	6
Positive thinking	1	2	3	4	5	6
Self-motivation	1	2	3	4	5	6
Ability to find reward in one's own work	1	2	3	4	5	6
Team player	1	2	3	4	5	6
Willingness to travel	1	2	3	4	5	6
Energy	1	2	3	4	5	6
Self-awareness	1	2	3	4	5	6

Figure 2 Consulting Skills Course—Certified Health and Safety Consultant (CHSC) *Source:* Canadian Society of Safety Engineers (CSSE).

At the time of this publication, these CSSE and ASSE courses offered are great resources. You can visit the CSSE website (http://www.csse.org) to see when the next offering will be by clicking on the "Professional Development" tab. My fellow chapter author and colleague Deb Roy also conducts a seminar for ASSE entitled "Becoming an Effective OS&H Consultant". You can visit the ASSE website (http://www.asse.org) to see when the next offering will be by clicking on the "Professional Development" tab.

Your Family and Friends

To this point I have only lightly touched upon the importance of your family and friends with regard to the success of your consulting business. This is a start-up as well as a continued business, and the family balance issue that is seldom mentioned in text books. But it is one that I believe contributes greatly to success or difficulty in your consulting business. It isn't easy to give up the comforts of a corporate world to start a consulting business. Without the support of your family and friends, the already difficult journey into the consulting world can be even more challenging. A Bloomberg *Business Week* magazine article on the importance of support systems stated that one-third of people who set out on their own don't have

Because of my experiences, I recommend that you create several business plans....

sufficient support systems among spouses and friends, and that the amount and strength of those supports contributes to the success and failure rates, as well length in business (*Bloomberg BusinessWeek* 2011). Sometimes instead of encouraging you, unsupportive people are saying, literally or figuratively, "Go back to work, you're never going to make it on your own," or "I don't like this lifestyle."

When you start your consulting journey, your family is affected, and not always in a positive way. I found in my early days that I was emotionally and financially drained. My time was focused on getting things going, which took away from my family. When my expectations of the consulting business and myself were not the same as those of my family and friends, resentment and conflict grew, and contributed greatly to the breakup of my marriage. When I look back, I see some things that I should have done differently. I needed to secure my family's support, and I needed to give more consideration to my family's participation and expectations about the new consulting business. I needed to be more strategic with my finances, to ensure that my family understood we would have reduced revenue in the household for a period of time. I should have created a firm separation of "house and state," so if I needed to buy equipment for the business, my spouse would understand that it was a necessity, not me wasting our money.

... the family balance issue ... is one that I believe contributes greatly to success or difficulty in your consulting business.

We all needed to understand more clearly the family sacrifices that would need to be made, and agree on the family benefits that would result. I should have talked more openly with family members about my work. In the beginning, I operated my consulting business from my home. My family had no idea what was going on or how hard I worked; they just knew I was home all day, and that became a large source of misunderstanding and conflict.

Because of my experiences, I recommend that you create several business plans, two more than what is described in the following chapter. Create a family business plan, in which family members determine the overall goals of the family, and the resources needed to achieve those objectives. Create an individual plan, to help each family member determine his or her own personal goals, and how to balance those needs with the family and business needs. And, of course, create a typical business plan. But make sure that one addresses such issues as ownership and management control, family involvement in the business, and overall strategic direction of the business.

Don't forget to include a plan and supporting communication to balance family life with consulting life. Many consultants and family members fail to realize how many hours you have to put in to make the business successful. Plan to have family time, where you remember you are not the "boss" at home, and where you focus on making your family your most important client.

CONCLUSION

If you have most of the characteristics and skills I have described above, I believe you have a very good chance of succeeding as a consultant. But if there are activities or skills listed at which you are not very proficient or which you simply don't like to do, this won't necessarily bar you from success. Most thriving consultants, including everyone who participated in writing this book, will tell you that from the time they started out, they had an idea about their strengths and weaknesses. As they opened their business and began to see some success, they made a conscious decision to improve on certain skills and tasks and delegated the rest to others, either by hiring staff or by partnering with others in some fashion. In all likelihood, some of the consultants who struggled or did not succeed had much less self-awareness.

Like many, when I started, I did not excel at everything I have written about in this chapter, nor do I to this day. Initially, I mistakenly thought that I had to know and perform every aspect of the business; be the product, know the market, and have the business financial focus. I found that I was spending much of my time trying to do the things I did not do well. And I was unhappy. A wise person told me to find my weaknesses and strengthen them. That was good advice to a point. But, after a time of being frustrated by struggling to perform some aspects of the business that I really did not like or had limited knowledge about, I realized that I could, instead, surround myself with others who are strong where I am weak, with others who like to do the things I do not.

> When I sought quality assistance in the areas I was not good at and did not enjoy (finances), I could then focus on what I loved: consulting and marketing.

If your strength is the product—your knowledge and expertise within the occupational health and safety field—and you have a natural ability to market, but your weak area is business structure and financial attention, then work with others to bring those to the table. When I sought quality assistance in the areas I was not good at and did not enjoy (finances), I could then focus on what I loved: consulting and marketing. As a result, my business became more successful, and I became much less frustrated. Focus on spending your time on doing what you're good at, and surround yourself with others to support the other areas to guarantee success.

Before I close, I have a few final pieces of advice, from an existing consultant to a potential consultant. The first is to do what you enjoy. What you get out of your business is the sum of what you put into it, whether it is personal satisfaction, financial gain, stability, or enjoyment. So, if you don't enjoy and have fun with what you're doing, in all likelihood it will be reflected in your business—and its likely lack of success. If you enjoy what you're doing and have a passion for it, the chance for success is much higher. Life is too short to invest the time in starting and growing a business that does not give you satisfaction and joy.

The second piece of advice is to take what you do seriously. To be successful, you have to have passion behind what you do, and truly believe in what you do. Not taking business seriously, getting sidetracked, losing motivation or focus on task has resulted in some of my consulting peers seeking employment back in organizations.

Let me leave you with one last quote from Henry Ford, "Whether you think you can, or think you can't—you're right."

In this opening chapter, I have attempted to set the stage for the rest of this book on effective OS&H consulting by helping you assess your own skills, abilities, and personality characteristics. I believe it is important that you enter consulting with a clear idea of your strengths and weaknesses, particularly with regards to the practice of consulting. I have created a framework to evaluate yourself those against essential characteristics in four major areas and by answering them, provides you with a roadmap as you begin your journey. In the next chapter, "Creating a Business Plan," you will be given a different roadmap that will help you understand the essential components of effective business plans. You will learn the importance of spending time researching and writing your business plan before you start. This plan will become the foundation of your consulting practice and, as you grow, it will continue to provide a framework for keeping it running.

BIBLIOGRAPHY

Anderson, Erika. 2013. "11 Quotes from Sir Richard Branson on Business, Leadership, and Passion" (retrieved November 3, 2014) www.forbes.com

Bloomberg. BusinessWeek Small Business May 2011 (retrieved from www.businessweek.com).

Canadian Society of Safety Engineering (CSSE). 2014. *Consulting Skills Course* (retrieved November 3, 2014) https://portal.csse.org/professional_development/consulting_skills_for_the_o%26s_professional.htm

Carver, C.S. & Scheier, M.E. 2001. "Optimism, pessimism, and self-regulation" *Optimism and Pessimism: Implications for Theory, Research, and Practice*, pp. 31–51. Washington, D.C.: American Psychological Association.

Collins, James C., and William C. Lazier. 1995. *Beyond Entrepreneurship: Turning Your Business into an Enduring Great Company*. Englewood Cliffs, NJ: Prentice Hall.

Coolahan, Craig, Goulet, Tag, and Archibald, Marg. *Become a Business Consultant* (retrieved July 20, 2013) www.fabjob.com/tocs/business consultant-toc.pdf.

Dalley, Jeff, and Bob Hamilton. "Knowledge, Context, and Learning in the Small Business." *International Small Business Journal*. April-June 2000.

de Bono, Edward. 1985. *Six Thinking Hats*. Little Brown and Company.

Doran, George. "There's a S.M.A.R.T. way to write management's goals and objectives." *Management Review Journal*, November 1988.

Drucker, Peter F. 1986. *Innovation and Entrepreneurship: Practice and Principles*. New York: Harper & Row.

Ferrazzi, Keith. 2009. *Who's got your Back: The Breakthrough Program to Build Deep, Trusting Relationships that Create Success—And Won't Let You Fail*. NY: Broadway Books.

Ferrazzi, Keith with Tahi Raz. 2005. *Never Eat Alone and Other Secrets to Success, One Relationship at a Time*. NY: Currency Doubleday.

Gray, Douglas. 1990. *Start and Run a Profitable Consulting Business*. 3rd Ed. North Vancouver, British Columbia; Bellingham, WA: Self-Counsel Press.

Hamilton, Barton H. "Does Entrepreneurship Pay?" *Journal of Political Economy*, June 2000.

Hersey, Paul and Blanchard, Kenneth. 1988. *Management of Organizational Behavior: Utilizing Human Resources*. Englewood Cliffs, NJ: Prentice-Hall.

Kotter, John. 1996. *Leading Change*. Boston, MA: Harvard Business School Press.

Lenko, Mitch. "Entrepreneurship: The New Tradition." *CMA—The Management Accounting Magazine*. July–August 1995.

McGrath, Rita Gunther, and Ian MacMillan. 2000. *The Entrepreneurial Mindset*. Boston, MA: Harvard Business School Press.

McLaughlin, Erin. 2012. *An Emotional Business: The Role of Emotional Intelligence in Entrepreneurial Success*. Denton, TX: University of North Texas.

Menzel. R. 1975. "A Taxonomy of Change Agent Skills." *The Journal of European Training*, 4(5), 289–291.

Petersen, Dan. 2003. *Techniques of Safety Management: A Systems Approach*. 4th ed. Des Plaines, IL: ASSE.

Powell, Alvin. 2013. "Fueling the entrepreneurial spirit" (retrieved November 23, 2014) www.news.harvard.edu/gazette/story/2013/08/fueling-the-entrepreneurial-spirit/

Reeves, Martin and Deimler, Mike. "Adaptability: The New Competitive Advantage." *Harvard Business Review*, July 2011.

Ries, Eric. 2011. *The Lean Startup; How Todays Entrepreneurs Use Continuous Innovation to Create Radically Successful Businesses*. NY: Crown Publishers.

Roberts, Leslie. 2010. "Self-Assessment for Entrepreneurs" (retrieved November 23, 2014) http://www.goforthinstitute.com/resources-templates.php.

Ronstadt, Robert. 1985. *Entrepreneurship: Texts, Cases & Notes*. Dover, MA: Lord Publishing.

Shane, Scott. 2008. *Illusions of Entrepreneurship: The Costly Myths that Entrepreneurs, investors and Policy Makes Live By*. New Haven, CT: Yale University.

Statistic Brain. Retrieved from www.statisticbrain.com.

Timmons, Jeffry A. 1989. *The Entrepreneurial Mind*. Andover, MA: Brick House Pub. Co.

Tuckman, Bruce Wayne. 1992. *Educational Psychology: From Theory to Application*. Fort Worth, TX: Harcourt Brace Jovanovich College Publisher.

Tuckman, Bruce W. with D. Moneth. 2001. *Theories and Applications of Educational Psychology*. 3rd Ed. New York: McGraw Hill.

Tuckman, Bruce and Jensen, Mary Ann. 1977. "Stages of small group development revisited." *Group and Organizational Studies Journal*, 2, pp 419–427.

U.S. Department of Education, Office of Educational Technology. 2013. *Promoting Grit, Tenacity and Perseverance: Critical Factors for Success in the 21st Century* (retrieved November 24, 2014) www.pgbovine.net/OET-Draft-Grit-Report-2-17-13.pdf

U.S. Department of Labor, Bureau of Labor Statistics. 2013. "Business Employment Dynamics" (retrieved November 20, 2013) www.bls.gov/bdm

U.S. Small Business Administration. n.d. *Is Entrepreneurship for You?* (retrieved November 24, 2014) www.sba.gov/content/entrepreneurship-you.

_____. n.d. *Small Business Readiness Assessment*. https://eweb1.sba.gov/cams/training/business_primer/assessment.htm

Questions to ask:

Have I ever run a business before? If not, do I know what it takes to do so?

Have I taken the necessary time and the required thought to plan for my success?

Do I know what my business goals are, and how I expect to accomplish them?

Do I have a roadmap that will guide all of my business's operations, from financial to sales and marketing to operations?

Have I considered what services I will be providing, and where I might find clients who will purchase these services?

Do I understand what external services I might need to get help with (accounting, marketing, etc.)? Will I get those services from internal partners or external contractors?

Have I thought about how I will finance my business? How much start-up money will I need (if any)? Will I need to seek outside funding?

Since there are various business structure legal and tax options, do I have a good understanding of the pros and cons for the structure I will be using to start my consulting business?

CHAPTER 2

Creating a Business Plan

BY SAM GUALARDO, MA, CSP

Samuel. J. Gualardo is President of National Safety Consultants, Inc., with offices in Salix, PA and Ormond Beach, FL. He holds a B.S. in Safety Management and a M.A. in Labor/Industrial Relations and is a CSP. His firm has been providing expertise in safety management systems, safety culture change, regulatory compliance, and expert testimony since 1984. His Management-Based Safety System is used by numerous organizations globally.

Sam served as President of the American Society of Safety Engineers (ASSE) in 2000–01 and President of the Board of Certified Safety Professionals (BCSP) in 2010. In 2011, Sam was awarded the honor of Fellow, the highest achievement in the EHS profession, by ASSE.

A<small>LMOST</small> 30 <small>YEARS AGO</small>, I ventured into the world of OS&H consulting. I was asked by a business association executive director if I would be interested in doing some training on job safety analyses. I showed up, did a few hours of training for some supervisors for a company and received a nice check, which immediately was spent to purchase a lawn tractor. I had a few acres of grass to cut and many leaves to rake. A shiny new lawn tractor made the job much more enjoyable. I was immediately hooked. One job led to another, and as I sit here after many years, I am wondering where the time has gone. I am also reflecting on how consulting in OS&H not only benefited my life but the lives of many others along the way.

Maybe you too have made the decision to hang your shingle out. But have you thought about all of the significant issues that may cause your success or failure? The decision to start a business is an easy one. The work required to make it succeed is a little more difficult.

I have met tens of thousands of OS&H professionals throughout my career. Many have believed that consulting work can be done by anyone. I thought the same before diving in. However, after running a successful consulting firm since 1984, I will be the first to tell anyone that it takes more than having expertise in the many disciplines of our profession—much more!

BUSINESS PLANNING FOR THE CONSULTANT

The consulting business is not for the faint of heart. Many more OS&H professionals fail at consulting than succeed. In most cases, the successes and failures hinge on proper preparation or the lack thereof. Consequently, your preparation for entering this world must be taken seriously. This chapter will provide some groundwork for the development of a business plan, which you may be tempted to sidestep in your rush to get your consulting business going. But I caution you not to do so. A business plan will help you organize your thoughts around your business. This chapter is intended to highlight many of the issues you need to consider as you prepare for this new adventure.

The technical work you perform as an OS&H consultant is very different from running a formal business.

The most important consideration before moving forward is to clearly understand that consulting is a serious business. The *technical work* you perform as an OS&H consultant is very different from running a formal business. Remember, the easy part is doing the actual consulting work; the more difficult part is running the business. You may be great technically, but are you suited to running a business? (To better assess your entrepreneurial abilities, see Chapter 1.) If your answer is yes, you *must* start it the correct way, with building a business plan. You may be asking, why bother? You think you already possess the skills and fortitude to make a go of consulting. You may want to get off the ground quickly, and think that the steps required to develop a business plan will get in your way.

Think of it this way: A pilot does not begin a flight without putting together a proper flight plan. Not doing so could produce a catastrophic outcome. The same holds true for you. Without a good business plan, prepare to crash and burn! You may get off the ground, and may fly for a while. But eventually, you just may run out of gas as a result of the overwhelming pressures consulting work can place on you and those who depend on your success. Spending the necessary time now to develop your plan will prevent much pain down the road.

A business plan is an essential tool that forces you to think before you act. The old adage, measure twice and cut once, is the perfect analogy. The business plan forces your mind into thinking through whether you are equipped to start, build, manage and grow your business. Keeping a business going by attracting, satisfying, retaining, and expanding your client base is what proper business planning will help you do.

The Need for a Business Plan

I have learned several very important things after consulting now for nearly 30 years. First, it is not okay to try to be all things to all clients. Selecting and specializing in a few areas of service will help you hone your expertise, and it will make your business planning more manageable. In the beginning, I did not do that very well. I spent much time trying to come up to speed on the issues my clients wanted to focus on next. I learned quickly that I was spending a lot of uncompensated time having to master many issues. Trying to be a jack of all trades and a master of none was very time-consuming and financially unproductive.

> *. . . the most important lesson I learned, is that the consulting business is just a little about OS&H consulting. . . .*

Second, producing revenue takes constant work. It simply does not drop into your lap. Even with your best clients, you need to continually prove your worth and add value to their business, or they will not be your best clients for long. Proper business planning will help you to stay focused on meeting your existing and future clients' needs.

Third, you have to be willing to accept that maybe what you have to offer is not suited for everyone, and that is OK. Trying to spend time selling someone what they will never buy can be frustrating and time-consuming. Identifying target markets and target clients will be critical to your success and your sanity. Proper business planning will help you do just that.

Finally, probably the most important lesson I learned, is that the consulting business is just a little about OS&H consulting and a lot about business. Realizing that you will need to master an entirely new set of skills may help you make the decision that OS&H consulting is really not what you thought. Going through the rigors of creating a high-quality business plan will get you to that decision point quickly.

As you begin to think about entering OS&H consulting, there are several issues you must consider that a business plan will force you to flesh out. Failing to spend ample time thinking through and properly addressing these issues could make or break your business, your reputation, and could be financially devastating to you personally. As an OS&H professional you would invest ample time in researching the best solution to solve a technical problem. Similarly, you need to think of a new business venture as a problem that you need to address. Your problem statement for this situation is just a little different. It essentially boils down to whether you have what it takes to become a successful entrepreneur versus possibly performing less work and assuming less risk working for someone willing to pay for your expertise as a full-time employee.

The Purpose of a Business Plan

A business plan is a comprehensive document that defines your business goals, how they are expected to be accomplished, and who will be accomplishing them. They can be written to target those working within the business to guide their activities, or they can be focused externally to address the stakeholders who may be investing in the business and the customers the business is trying to reach. Internal participants are those involved in operating the business. External participants are those who have a stake (financial or otherwise) in ensuring the business is launched and operates successfully. A great resource for the development of a business plan is the United States Small Business Administration (SBA). These resources provide clear and concise direction to anyone deciding to start a new business venture. They even provide assistance for those businesses that are already in operation and wish to grow (SBA n.d. d.).

Business plans are comprehensive planning documents that address all of the aspects required to initiate, sustain, and grow a business. Business plans typically do not follow a cookie-cutter approach. Rather, they are defined by the business goals and by those who have a vested interest in developing or reviewing them. The size of the consulting firm may also be a determining factor in the breadth and depth necessary for the business plan. However, regardless of size, several key areas are required to be fleshed out within the business plan: finance, operations, marketing, human resources, accounting, and legal/contract issues. An OS&H professional desiring to begin or expand a consulting business has the same ultimate goal as individuals planning to build or expand a Fortune 500 company—financial success. A solid business plan is at the heart of that success.

The complexity of your plan will depend on your short- and long-term goals. For example, if your goal is to become a sole proprietor, your plan may only need to contain several elements to ensure you have considered some key issues. However, if your goal is to become a full-service, one-stop-shop consulting firm with a stable of workhorses having talents in many diverse areas, your plan will obviously be much more complex. Additionally, the more eyes beyond yours that will critically review your plan, the deeper, more diverse and complex your plan will need to be. And all of this work will need to be done well before you land your first client. Spending ample time to develop your plan may be necessary to just get off the ground. Consider it as your first project. Understand that doing it well may be a true predictor of your future success.

A stark reality is that most new businesses fail. (See "Ten Common Causes of Business Failure" and "Top Ten Reasons Why Businesses Fail.") Ultimately, the primary goal of any good business plan is to help the writer, the business partners, staff members or external stakeholders make sound decisions so the business won't fail. A poorly devised plan could potentially lead to bad decisions. A well thought-out business plan will not guarantee success of the business, but it will certainly increase its odds for success.

A safety consulting start-up business plan will need to sufficiently address the following questions.

1. What problem will the firm's product and/or service solve?
2. What niche, if any, will it fill?
3. What is the solution to the problem, and is this solution different from potential competitors?
4. Who are the customers?
5. How will products and/or services be marketed and eventually sold?
6. What is the size of the potential market?
7. How will the firm conduct business to generate revenue?
8. Who are the known competitors?
9. How will a competitive advantage be established?
10. How will the business grow?
11. Who will direct the business operations and decision-making, who will individually contribute, and what external resources will be necessary? Do they have the required qualifications?
12. What are the current strengths, weaknesses, opportunities and threats associated with the business (SWOT analysis)?
13. How will the business be resourced and capitalized?
14. What are the legitimate financial projections?
15. Most important, when if ever, will it make financial sense to leave the stability of a full-time, salaried position and be able to support yourself with the revenues of the business?

Substantial amounts of research and heart-wrenching thought will be required to develop the answers before making the decision to put pen to paper to begin drafting your plan. If you have taken the time to consider these questions successfully, it is time to get to the task of developing your plan, which is step one on the road to developing your new venture.

One last suggestion before you begin is to read examples of completed business plans. Many of us are visual learners, and seeing a few good examples will aid in understanding the concepts discussed throughout this chapter. Several good business plan examples for service-providing firms, such as a consulting business, can be found under the "Other Resources" section at the end of this chapter.

BUSINESS PLAN ELEMENTS

A business plan should follow a defined outline of major elements. Each of the following elements may not need to be fully addressed within every business plan and some may not need to be discussed at all. For example, you may not have an internal management team if you are a sole proprietor. Perhaps there is nothing unique about your services, so you may not need to have anything defined with respect to intellectual property. However, your outline should start with attempting to define all potential areas that need to be addressed versus ignoring them. Take the time to think through the potential implications of every element to your business before deciding it does not apply.

. . . the executive summary is probably the most important section of a business plan.

Performing an Internet-based search will provide you a plethora of business plan templates that can be utilized. Additionally, many software firms have created templates to make it easy to develop a business plan. Software that I used years ago was named Business Plan Pro. (See "Other Resources" at the end of this chapter.) Since then, many other promising templates have hit the Internet. (See Live Plan in the "Other Resources" section at the end of this chapter for one example of the type of business plan development template sites available). If you choose to purchase a template, I would recommend you review a number of types of templates before you buy (see entry on "Top 10 Reviews" under "Other Resources" at the end of this chapter). Regardless of which outline you choose, take some time to compare and contrast several before deciding which works best for you. Or create your own version, taking the best from several templates.

Regardless of which way you go, most plans will have the following elements:

1. Executive Summary
2. Mission Statement
3. Company Description
4. Market Analysis
5. Organization & Management
6. Management Team
7. Business Organizational Structure
8. Business Ownership
9. Organization Oversight

10. Service or Product Line
11. Lifecycle Implications
12. Intellectual Property
13. Research and Development (R&D) Activities
14. Marketing & Sales
15. Funding
16. Control of Information
17. Regulatory Issues
18. Plan Revisions
19. Appendix

Executive Summary

I have learned over the years that the executive summary can either get your proposal or great idea to see the light of day or to hit the circular file. As a result, the executive summary is probably the most important section of a business plan. Although it is the first section of your business plan, it should be the last section that is developed.

The executive summary is where you will sell your firm and its capabilities to the reader. In this section, you will explain what your company is, what it will do, and why it will be successful; in other words, it is a thumbnail sketch of your entire business plan. Working hard on a great executive summary will be very important if you need financial assistance, since outside investors will want to be confident that you have a good plan before investing. And even if you are not in need of financial assistance, this section ensures that you can succinctly define your business and its goals, setting the stage for the rest of the plan that becomes your roadmap towards your success.

The executive summary will vary depending on your business, its proposed structure, and whether it is a new business or an existing one. However, except for those items below, which address historical issues, the following at a minimum should be included:

- ***The Mission Statement:*** Defines the overall end goal of your business.
- ***Company Description:*** Discusses when your business was organized, the key business leaders, their specific roles, the number or employees, and your physical business location(s).
- ***Products and Services:*** Covers the major products and services your business provides, along with a very brief description of them.
- ***Market Analysis:*** Describes your target market, key competitors, and what differentiates your business from similar ones.

- *Financial Information:* Includes your current financial and investor information, such as profit and loss statements, accounting balance sheets, cash flow analysis, and investor contributions.
- *Historical Performance:* Demonstrates company growth and financial performance. Graphs and charts can be useful as long as they are simple and easily discernible. (Obviously, this section is not applicable for new businesses.)
- *Future Objectives:* Discusses your desires for future growth, expansion, new business lines, new products, and so on.

It is extremely important that the executive summary be just that, a summary. Do not make the mistake in believing that the reader will want complicated or detailed information. It must be well thought out, simple, concise, and powerful, and should be no more than a few pages; it is even better if you can get it all on one page. Additional details will be found in the full plan if the reader desires to go there. Your job is to get them there.

For start-up consulting entities, there are other considerations. A start up may have limited information that can be included. For example, a start-up company will have no financial history. As a result, there should more in the executive summary discussing how the business is envisioned, who will be running it, and their experiences and backgrounds.

Mission Statement

The mission statement is a concise sentence (or two) that clearly states why your company is in business or plans to be in business. According to Entrepreneur.com, it should convey "the essence of your business's goals and the philosophies underlying them. Equally important, the mission statement signals what your business is all about to your customers, employees, suppliers and the community (Entrepreneur.com, n.d.).

An example of a clear and concise business statement from a consulting firm following these principles is provided below. Included with this mission statement are the values that support their overall mission.

Company Description

The company description is a more detailed review of the nature of your business, the customers you plan to serve, and why your firm has an advantage over the competition. Consider including the following elements in the company description section:

> **JSM Consulting Mission Statement and Values**
>
> JSM Consulting is a national consulting firm that specializes in developing and implementing programs that enhance your company's efficiency and effectiveness. Our mission is to exceed our customer's expectations by providing real value and delivering results.
>
> *Our Values*
>
> We believe that partnering with our customers is critical to our success.
>
> We believe in measuring the success of our projects to our customer's satisfaction.
>
> We believe that building the basics of good organization leads to reduced costs with overall improved results.
>
> We believe that honesty and ethical conduct should permeate our business and personal life (JSM Consulting 2004).

- What your business does or plans to do;
- The customers you plan to serve;
- What your business is trying to help clients do;
- Why and how your products and services will satisfy the clients;
- Actual or potential clients that your business serves or plans to attract;
- What competitive advantage your firm offers that separates your business from the competition and ensures your success. This may include your market niche, your personnel and their experience, the business location, pricing, and value-added services.

Market Analysis

The market analysis section is a very important component of the business plan. This section must essentially prove you have a market to serve and that your business can match the needs of the market with what you provide. Defining your target market is at the heart of your success. This section addresses your in-depth knowledge of who your business intends to attract as buyers of your products and services.

To properly develop this section, you must have detailed qualitative and quantitative research data to substantiate your analysis. A report specific to your business plan's target audience can be developed and incorporated into your plan. There are many fee-based firms that provide market data, market intelligence, and market trends, etc. A quick Internet search will yield numerous entities selling that expertise, or you may also obtain free assistance from the SBA through their network of Small Business Development Centers (SBDCs), which provide a vast array of technical assistance to small businesses and aspiring entrepreneurs. SBDCs are typically affiliated with colleges and universities but may also be housed within a state government entity, depending on your locality (SBA n.d. d). The Service Corps of Retired Executives (SCORE) is "a nonprofit association dedicated to helping small businesses get off the ground, grow and achieve their goals through education and mentorship" (SCORE.org n.d.)

A comprehensive market analysis should include the following:

1. ***Industry Description and Future Outlook.*** This section should discuss your specific industry segment. It quantifies its current size and historic growth rate, market trends and direction (e.g., life cycle stage, projected growth rate), and the major customer groups within your industry.
2. ***Target Market.*** This section further defines and reduces your market potential to a size that will match with your firm's capabilities and resources. Spending ample time trying to narrow your target market may be crucial to your success. At some meals, my eyes are bigger than my stomach. After the meal, I feel bloated and my performance suffers. The same holds true for many businesses. Trying to be all things to all people will increase the likelihood of failure. Finding a few good customers and serving them well with the capacity you have will be a good formula for success. As you become successful, you will have the opportunity to grow, opening more potential markets.

   A good example of defining a target market is how Colonel Sanders started his empire, Kentucky Fried Chicken. He started by selling fried chicken from the trunk of his car. He had one product, no fixings, and a tank of gas. He may have thought big, but started small satisfying a very narrow focused market, consisting of a handful of hungry folks willing to pay a reasonable price for a good product. Now there are more Kentucky Fried Chicken franchises in China alone than all the other franchises combined.
3. ***Client needs.*** This section identifies the specific needs of your customers. It also covers why those needs are not being met by the existing purveyors of services and what differentiates your consulting

practice. Beyond that, the specific demographics of the target clients (their location, their business purchasing cycles) are discussed. Depending on when you pull the trigger to start your business, its initial success can be influenced by these factors. Selling snow cones to people who live in Alaska in the middle of winter would not be a good business plan. Careful consideration of similar issues may be strong factors in your success or failure as well.

4. *Market size.* This section defines the size of your target market segment. Specifically, you want to try to find hard data regarding how much money your target market spends on your proposed services. As stated previously, these data can be purchased from a fee-based, market analysis firm. However, with some legwork, you may find free information from a library, your local SBDC or SCORE.

5. *Market gain potential.* This section is a determination of how many clients you can reasonably plan to service within your target market as a percentage of the overall available. Being reasonable in this estimate is important from a financing and revenue expectation perspective. It should never be overstated or a guess. Your estimate should begin with the end in mind. For example, if you have two employees who are willing to work a typical eight-hour work day, 240 days per year, you can't expect to provide adequate OS&H consulting services to Walmart on a global scale. Although this may be a great long-term goal, understanding your capabilities and limitations is important to your success.

6. *Pricing and margins.* Your pricing structure can also be highly instrumental in your success or failure. (For a detailed discussion on pricing, see Chapter 3.) Pricing involves more than setting the bar slightly above or below the market average for your products and services. Pricing involves establishing a defined structure, setting desired gross margin levels, defining discounts, and determining what qualifies a client for a discount. Your pricing structure must be clearly documented, firm, and applicable to all clients. Your firm should never be ashamed to charge a fair price for your products and services. Pricing your services on the fly can and will cause your credibility as a consultant and a business professional to be challenged.

7. *Cash flow.* Cash flow is the blood that pumps through the heart of the business. Without cash flow, the heart stops pumping. Many budding consulting firms forget this most important concept. They are technically competent and can attract clients. But they forget

> *Good cash flow... can be improved by associating with sound businesses and through the use of good contracts with favorable payment terms that favor your firm verses your client.*

that collecting the money and paying the bills is just as important as providing the service or selling the product. Before the business begins, you need to define how the billing process will occur, if late charges will be applied, how collections will occur when clients do not pay their bills, and whether a retainer arrangement will be necessary. Your firm may have great technical OS&H expertise but you will quickly learn that having business savvy with respect to cash flow can be more important for your short- and long-term survival.

One of the most important considerations regarding cash flow is that you need to set money aside for three major reasons. First, consulting does not produce a steady stream of revenue. There will always be highs and lows in your business regardless of the current economy. Eating, feeding your family, and paying the mortgage do not wait for the revenue to flow in. Second, unless you are operating from the Cayman Islands, substantial revenue will need to be set aside to pay taxes. Third, you will need money for business bills that will not wait for that late-paying customer to pay your invoice. Good cash flow is never guaranteed. But it can be improved by associating with sound businesses and through the use of good contracts with favorable payment terms that favor your firm verses your client.

It can also be helped immensely by requesting some payment in advance in the form of a retainer, which I typically do with law firms in the form of a case retainer. (For more information regarding the importance of cash flow, please see Chapter 6.)

8. *Competitive analysis.* Understanding your market size and how much revenue is being generated by your competitors within that market is quite different than understanding your competitors. The importance of this issue is often underestimated. Your business plan needs to include the extensive research you have conducted to thoroughly understand your competition. Determining what your competitors are offering takes personal research. Interviewing the competition, its principals and employees, accessing their informational brochures, talking with their clients, and reviewing print ads in trade periodicals are all good ways to gain insight into what your competitors are offering.

Once your research is completed, you need to define your competitor's products and services in detail. As part of this analysis, you need to define:

- your primary and secondary competitors and their market share;
- your firm's strengths and weaknesses, as well as those of the competition;

- how your business may impact their market share, and how they could impact yours;
- what your entry into the market may do to competitors' future marketing strategies; and
- barriers that may threaten your ability to be a recognized and viable competitor within the market segment, including marketing costs, client recognition, investment cost, personnel, decision-maker access, industry recognition, credibility, technology, location, etc.

Organization and Management

As part of your business plan, describe how your business will be organized and managed both directly (day to day) and indirectly (oversight). This section should include your company's organizational structure; specifics regarding who owns your company; who will be managing your company and their specific skills, education and experience; and, depending on how your business is structured, a description of your Board of Directors and their qualifications.

Describe in detail who will specifically be performing the various major day-to-day and oversight functions of your business operation. Their experience, qualifications, education, and so on, should be included, along with the specific acumen they bring to the table that will be instrumental to their success and that of the business. This section should include responsibilities by individual functions such as marketing, sales, accounting, and legal to give the reader assurances that all of the major functions typical of a successful business are being managed effectively. In larger consulting practices, these functions may be handled by dedicated personnel, such as human resources, marketing, and accounting.

Identifying who is responsible for the above functions becomes especially important in small consulting firms, which lack internal professionals managing just these functions. If you are a small or solo firm or you are planning to create one, juggling these activities will be difficult and time-consuming. You will need to dedicate the necessary time to each of these issues (or ensure that they are done by someone else) or your firm simply will not flourish. For example, if you are spending your time performing consulting work for clients and not marketing your services to others, you may find yourself in a situation where the old client business has dried up and new client work is not in the pipeline. Similarly, if you do not spend ample time minding your cash flow and accounting, it will quickly catch up with you and impact your firm's solvency. Regardless of size, if those functions are not clearly assigned at the outset and appropriate time is not allotted for them, they probably will not be done or not done well.

A detailed description of your planned compensation, benefits, retention, and career advancement processes should also be included in this section.

The Board of Directors (BOD) should be addressed here as well. Whether or not you have one is often determined by your size and corporate type (see below and Chapter 5 for more details). This section should include who is being named to the BOD, how long their services are being requested, and how you plan to compensate them for their services. If no BOD is named, I would strongly suggest that you consider at least an external advisory group Using an Advisory Board, which is typically not compensated, is a great way to get free advice and guidance on issues you or your internal management team does not fully understand. Creating an advisory board with individuals who have amassed great business and technical credentials will help provide instant credibility and reader perception of managerial horsepower. Most consultants have come across a myriad of professionals in their careers and in personal lives to whom they have looked up for their insight into various issues. Your Advisory Board should consist of these types of people, trusted colleagues or professionals. For your Advisory Board, look for people who are going to challenge you and your decision-making. You want them to keep you and your organization out of harm's way and to guide you toward success.

Whichever direction you take, the credentials of this group should be included in your business plan. Specifically include:

> *Creating an advisory board with individuals who have amassed great business and technical credentials will help provide instant credibility....*

- Names;
- Positions on the board or advisory group;
- Extent of involvement with company;
- Background; and
- Historical and future contribution to the company's success.

If you are contemplating starting a consulting business with numerous employees, an organizational chart is a good way to define personnel and differentiate functions. This chart will need to include a narrative description of functions and assigned personnel, ensuring that nothing will be missed or unnecessarily replicated as the business becomes operational. Taking the time needed to do this step and do it well will demonstrates to potential employees or investors that the business was well thought out, not developed in a hurried fashion. It will also help prevent situations where the left hand did not know what the right hand was doing.

Management

The success or failure of a consulting business may be, in large part, a result of the quality of those who are managing various business functions or the ability of the primary consultants to act as business function managers and not just technical consultants. Although OS&H consulting may be your primary service deliverable, managing the company successfully will be one of the most critical factors in assuring your services are marketed, advertised, delivered and, compensated for properly and in a timely manner. You can have the best product in the world, but if the business is not managed properly to sell that product, the business is likely to fail and potential customers will never realize its benefits.

You will need to assure the reader of your business plan that the people managing your business have the requisite experience needed to produce success well beyond their knowledge of OS&H disciplines. Provide ample information and backgrounds on key players in your business. If you are a solo practice, you may need to reference external advisors whom you have hired to assist you with those functional areas where you are weak. Resumes should be provided and should include the following information:

- Name;
- Position (include brief position description along with primary duties);
- Primary responsibilities and authority;
- Education;
- Unique experience and skills;
- Prior employment;
- Special skills;
- Past track record;
- Industry recognition;
- Community involvement;
- Number of years with company;
- Compensation basis and levels (make sure these are reasonable—not too high or too low); and
- Quantification of specific past achievements aligned with their defined function.

Business Ownership

In this segment of your business plan, you will outline the formal legal structure you plan to utilize in establishing your business entity, along with the requisite ownership information. It will define whether your business is organized as a C corporation, a Subchapter S corporation, a limited liability company (LLC), a partnership or limited partnership, a sole proprietor, or another legal entity defined by your business domicile. Various types of business structures are identified below and are discussed in more detail in Chapter 5, including how to decide which structure fits best for you (Nolo.com 2013).

Sole Proprietorship

A sole proprietorship is a simple structure and is used by many to begin their business. A sole proprietorship is an unincorporated business owned and operated by a single person. In this type of business, there is no differentiation between you and the business. You make the money and have full access to your profits, but are also responsible for the debts, losses, and liabilities of the business. Some lawyers maintain that a sole proprietorship may not be the best structure for a firm that provides OS&H consulting services; however, many accountants disagree. As will be recommended in Chapter 5, it is wise to seek counsel of both before making your decision.

Limited Liability Company

Many consulting practices organize a limited liability company (LLC). This legal structure provides the limited liability features of a corporation and the tax efficiencies and operational flexibility of a partnership. It can be well suited for consulting businesses.

C Corporation

A corporation (sometimes referred to as a C corporation) is a separate legal entity owned by shareholders. This means that the corporation itself, not the shareholders, is held legally liable for the actions and debts the business incurs. C corporations are more complex from a tax and accounting perspective, but many believe they offer better liability protection for a consulting business.

Partnership

A partnership is a corporation where two or more people share ownership. This type of business structure can be good as long as the partners understand and accept that they are responsible for an equal portion of the financial and business gains as well as an equal portion of the losses. Many partnerships fail because unequal balance places strain on the partners. Additionally, you must have total faith in your partners. Partnerships are very much like a marriage. Many work well, while many struggle and fail. Before considering a partnership arrangement, some thoughtful soul searching needs to occur. Before deciding, meeting with a lawyer will help you and your prospective partner(s) decipher the potential pitfalls and benefits this arrangement can produce.

S Corporation

An S corporation (sometimes referred to as an S corp) is a corporation created through an IRS tax election. You effectively declare that this is the way you want to be perceived by the taxing authorities. This type of corporation can avoid double taxation (once to the corporation and again to the shareholders). In this scenario, profits and losses pass directly to the owners.

Once you have established your corporate structure, the following ownership information should be incorporated into your business plan:

- Business corporate structure type;
- Names of owners;
- Percentages of ownership;
- Extent of involvement with the company;
- Forms of ownership (i.e., common stock, preferred stock, general partner, limited partner);
- Outstanding equity equivalents (i.e., options, warrants, convertible debt);
- Common stock (i.e., authorized or issued); and
- Management profile of each owner.

PRODUCTS AND SERVICES

The next section of your business plan is where your products and services are described. In this section, you want to pay special attention to describing how your products and services will benefit potential clients. In particular, you need to show how your products and services are different from other similar firms and why customers will choose your firm as compared to potential competitors. This section may be extremely important to potential investors whose interest is dependent upon your products and services being substantially different from others. You should also include ample discussion on any future product or services that are being planned for along expansion projections.

Life-cycle Implications

If your product or service has a life cycle or is seasonal in nature, factors that may influence future sales need to be addressed. For example, if you are providing OS&H consulting services to Federal Emergency Management Agency (FEMA) only during hurricane recovery efforts, this should be clearly specified. Although it seems that this would make it difficult to earn a living and have continual cash flow, some firms narrow their scope to these types of activities and are content to do so. Some make their firms work by combining life-cycle services that complement each other and are able to generate enough business. Others may just work part time and are not totally dependent on consulting income.

Any readers of your plan need to know if life-cycle or seasonal implications can have an impact.

Intellectual Property

Depending on the product or services you offer, your business may have intellectual property that is in need of protection from unapproved use. Much of what you develop for use with your clients may contain intellectual property. Information with respect to existing or anticipated copyrighted written materials and products that are or could be patented should be discussed in this section. Trade secrets should also be discussed.

For example, over the years, I have invested countless hours into developing and perfecting the Management-Based Safety Process© (MBS). The MBS Process is licensed to our clients through contract language for them to use after they have been trained. This is my bread and butter, which I must guard to effectively protect my livelihood. Some consultants will formally and legally register the copyright of their work products (PowerPoint slides, etc.) to advise others that they are prohibited from using them without their permission. Others will simply mark their work product using copyright references.

Finally, legal agreements, such as non-disclosure and non-compete agreements, should be detailed in this section. These agreements are important first to ensure that your products and services will not be disclosed to anyone without your consent by your clients or employees. They also serve to protect your firm from employees or partners leaving your firm and effectively "stealing" your client base and/or your work product. Detailing what is owned by your firm versus what employees and/or partners develop or have developed previously needs to be documented with explicit contract language. For example, if a new partner brings a new product to the firm, it must be determined in advance who owns the product once the partnership is consummated, and who owns the product if the partnership is terminated.

RESEARCH AND DEVELOPMENT (R&D) ACTIVITIES

With consulting businesses, it is important to continue reinventing your service and product offerings to meet current and future market needs. Consequently, continually being involved with research and development (R&D) is crucial to growth and sustainability. The OS&H business has changed radically over the past 20 years. From a broad perspective, safety, health and environmental functions have converged in most work environments. Those consulting practices that have changed with it are surviving. Those who failed to keep pace with the constant change have struggled and, in some cases, disappeared. Button manufacturers were totally caught off guard when zippers emerged in the manufacture of clothing. My guess is that many button manufacturers hastened their demise by not keeping abreast of technological changes in the marketplace and by not striving to be the leader of that change. In the world of OS&H consulting, it is much more difficult to offer only industrial hygiene services in the marketplace. Most clients want a broader spectrum of services from their retained firms.

Listing planned and current R&D activities will show the reader of your business plan that you are already thinking ahead. If your plan will only be developed for your eyes, you will benefit from having thought about the implications of research and development. One good article on the reasons why businesses fail is "Ten Common Causes of Business Failure" (OnStrategy.com 2008). In this article, you will quickly learn that staying abreast of products and services, as well as where your competitors are heading, is important.

It is my opinion that, over the last 20 years, many OS&H consultants missed the boat regarding the impact of ergonomic-related injuries and illnesses on the profession and consulting opportunities. Had they been ahead of the curve, a ton of new business opportunities could have been generated. Combustible dust may be over the next horizon. Keeping in tune with cutting-edge issues by staying abreast of NIOSH research and OSHA's regulatory agendas can be instrumental in this endeavor (CDC 2014).

MARKETING AND SALES

Marketing is both a science and an art. Its goal is to create customers who are willing to spend their money on what you are selling. Without customers, you have no business. Without a good marketing strategy, you have no business being in business!

Marketing Strategy

Developing a product and service line is the easy part. Getting someone to purchase it initially and make repeat purchases is a little more difficult. Overcoming this difficult task can be accomplished with a good marketing strategy. Your marketing strategy will outline specifically how your consulting practice plans to attract and retain customers. Effective marketing requires much research, along with trial and error. Learning about potential clients and their needs through purchased mailing lists and analytics is available for any industry sector. However, marketing is not an exact science, so buyer beware!

There are issues common to every good marketing strategy to ensure you are thinking and doing what will be necessary to drive sales and repeat business (sometimes referred to as customer loyalty). As I am writing this section, I am on my way to London passing through Dulles Airport. I just departed my earlier flight on my preferred airline and will shortly be boarding my preferred airline to London. Why did I choose this airline? Why do they have me coming back time and time again? The short answer is they treat me well and have gained my loyalty over the years. But the real answer is that it all started with effective marketing strategies on their part.

There is no single way to approach a marketing strategy; your strategy should be part of an ongoing business evaluation process and unique to your company.

There is no single way to approach a marketing strategy; your strategy should be part of an ongoing business evaluation process and unique to your company. However, there are common steps you can follow that will help you think through the direction and tactics you would like to use to drive sales and sustain customer loyalty. An overall marketing strategy should include these four different components:

- *Market penetration.* This discusses the specifics of how you plan to get clients to consider your products and services over those with which they are currently comfortable. You will also discuss untapped client potential or areas that no similar consulting firm has penetrated yet.
- *Growth.* This area will discuss how you plan to grow your business. It could take the form of increasing market penetration, acquiring like businesses, or branching out your business into new products, services or distribution territories.
- *Distribution.* This section will discuss how your products and services will ultimately get into the hands of users. Whether you will use the Internet, direct sales, or offer your products and services under some other arrangement, such as a strategic alliance, will need to be vetted.
- *Communication.* How will your customers hear about your products and services? Will you use the Internet to promote your business? Will special sales and marketing promotions be undertaken? Will advertising be done and in what form will it take? Will you engage a public relations firm to get you noticed? Will direct sales be used to attract clients or will they be solicited printed advertising and marketing materials, such as brochures, catalogs, flyers, and so forth. These are all important areas that will need explored.

A more in-depth discussion on marketing is found in Chapter 6 (with additional information in Chapters 7 and 8). After you have developed a comprehensive marketing strategy, you can then define your sales strategy. This covers how you plan to actually sell your product.

Sales Strategy

With respect to sales of your products and services, two areas will need special consideration:

- **Sales approach.** This is vital to your business. Again, you can have the best products and services in the OS&H business but if they are not sold properly, they will die on the vine. You will need to assess whether you will use inside or outside sales personnel and how they will be affiliated with your firm. Additionally, how these personnel will be compensated will be a large factor in your success and, potentially, theirs. Perhaps you will just rely on the Internet and word of mouth as your sales strategy. Regardless of which approach you use, this area needs to be thought out in advance.
- **Primary sales activities.** Sales activities are essentially what you are planning to do to attract customers. Listing prospective clients and then prioritizing high-potential clients who are worth initially pursuing will be important, so you do not waste precious time, as well as limited labor and monetary resources.

> *Defining how much time you will allocate to sales activities is important to ensure that proper time is expended in attracting and retaining clients.*

Defining how much time you will allocate to sales activities is important to ensure that proper time is expended in attracting and retaining clients. Being a great consultant is not enough! Being a great business person will determine your success in the OS&H consulting field. Sales analytics will need to be developed and reviewed to ensure you are spending your time and resources wisely. For a more detailed discussion on sales, please refer to Chapter 6.

Marketing Campaigns

Over the last several years, analytics has become an integral part of most successful marketing campaigns. For example, through the use of the Google Ads process, my firm's website collects all types of analytical data on clients who visit my site looking for information or services matching their Internet search criteria. If they do not contact us first, we can use these data to target certain client types and industry sectors. But keep in mind that what works to attract one client may not work for the next. So, reinventing this strategy is also necessary at times.

FUNDING

Some funding is necessary for start-up consulting practices, regardless of size. The larger the firm, the higher the start-up cost, but even a small solo practice needs business cards and a computer. Beyond those basics, the development of a website, stationary, start-up advertising, marketing materials, insurance, legal and accounting services, office supplies, equipment, infrastructure, banking services, and so forth, are examples of costs that must be allocated. In many cases, you may not have any clients to generate start-up income. Therefore, funding for these basic services must be identified. You also need to consider ongoing costs such as website hosting, advertising, replenishment of marketing materials and office supplies, rent, utilities, and vehicle maintenance, to name a few.

As noted above, even small solo practices need some upfront funds to get started. My business actually started that way in 1984 by just dabbling in a little training work here and there. However, when I got serious about developing my specialized lines of business, my need for capital increased so that I could purchase equipment and provide for marketing along with legal, accounting and investment expertise. What started as a way to have a few extra toys in the garage grew quickly into a legitimate source of income for my family.

Don't forget to consider that with growth, there will be additional cost burdens. You have heard the phrase that it costs money to make money. The larger your firm gets, the more that becomes a reality. Some OS&H consultants just dabble in business part time. Others however, begin with the end in mind, considering the business as more than just an additional source of income. They are serious from the outset and realize that a serious business venture will require serious capital.

If you are contemplating building a strong, diverse and viable consulting business, external funding may be necessary in the start-up stages and/or down the road for growth. As a result, a funding request may be necessary. You may want to try to put other people's money to work for you but before doing so, those "other people" are going to want to see how their investment will be used. Your bank, in the way of credit or a line of credit, is a typical source of capital. SBDCs and other similar organizations may be able to suggest funding sources in your local area that are interested in investing in small businesses. Your local banker may also have some suggestions for you.

If you decide to pursue external funding, each source will have specific requirements for the type of information required to proceed. Typically, you need to be prepared to identify at least the following:

- Initial funding needs in terms of both capital investment and operating funds.
- Growth-oriented operating and capital expansion needs.
- Planned use for the funds. For example, will they be used for capital expenditures, operating working capital, debt retirement, acquisitions, selling your business, etc.?

Ample details are required to make creditors comfortable with approving your requests. Proving to them that these funds will be used wisely will be critical to your success in obtaining them.

When defining your funding requirements, be sure to break out the funding that your business operation will need initially, and then, in later years. Whether the funds will be debt-based (what you pay back) or equity-based (what you plan to give up as part of your business, such as ownership position or stock shares) needs to be clearly specified.

FINANCIAL OUTLOOK PROJECTIONS

If you plan to just moonlight as an OS&H consultant, some of the financial information discussed below may not be necessary. However, if you are serious about this undertaking, financial data will be at the foundation of your business and an important building block of your plan. The purpose of financial projections is to prove that your business can successfully launch, develop, sustain or possibly even expand. Without going through the pains of developing this, your enthusiasm may lull you into a position of making uninformed decisions that are not based on fact.

Financial outlook projections are one of the most difficult parts of developing the business plan.

Financial outlook projections are one of the most difficult parts of developing the business plan. However, your estimates need to be credible in order to assure potential employees and/or investors that you will be capable of surviving and, for investors, providing a return on their investment (ROI) in your business. Similarly, if you have already quit, or are deciding to quit, your 9-to-5 job and commit to a consulting business, a cash reserve will be necessary. You simply will not be able to start a consulting business and have instant cash flow. Generating work will take time, and producing revenue from the work performed will take even longer. Depending on your clients, it may take 30, 60 or even as much as 90 days for them to pay your invoices. Typically, invoices follow work performed, and they also take time to create and send. Consequently, being able to project the finances of your business is critical to understanding how to survive, especially in the first year or two when it may be tough to break even, let alone make a profit.

Similarly, properly projecting where you will be in the short term may prevent you from having to live on your savings or the income of your spouse until your cash flow improves. This section should be developed only after you have thoroughly analyzed and researched the market and talked to those in a similar capacity. You must obtain a real world understanding and perspective of your potential and realistic capabilities. This is an area where you definitely want to be very conservative.

Historical Financial Data

If your business is already operational, you should include historical financial data in your business plan. (If you are not yet operational or are not relying on outside funding, this section can be omitted.)

Typically, creditors will want to see financial performance data from the past three to five years before they will be willing to loan you capital. They will be looking to determine specifically how you handled your financial affairs, how you attracted clients and translated them into steady income, how your income was used to pay down debt and expenses, and whether your business is growing or stagnating. Financial data necessary for this section includes income, balance, and cash flow statements. (For more information on these types of documents, see Chapter 3.) Additionally, the collateral you have to offer to ensure debt payment must be included in this section to give creditors confidence in your ability to pay possible loans or lines of credit extended.

Future Financial Projections

All businesses, regardless if they are start-up or operational and whether or not they are looking for outside investment, will need to develop financial data illustrating future financial projections. This budget-related data is typically limited to a short time frame, such as five years, and should include income projections, balance sheets, cash flow statements, and major or capital expense budgets.

Admittedly, this may be difficult to create as a solo start-up practice. You may need to begin with a simple budget, demonstrating what income will be necessary monthly to offset known expenses and then build it out over time. Typically for new businesses, the data should be projected in a monthly to quarterly format initially. Operating businesses can show the data on a quarterly to annual basis. But in either case, three to five years should be projected.

It is important that financial projections match your funding requests. Inconsistencies in your projections will send creditors a red flag and you will be back to the drawing board. Any assumptions in your data should be fully explained. A short analysis of your data, using charts and graphs, may be helpful in telling the story.

CONTROL OF INFORMATION

Keep in mind that your business plan is just that—*your* business plan. Although you will be potentially reviewing its content with others, plans for your business should remain confidential, and access to your plan should be controlled. To accomplish that, you may consider keeping a distribution record. Doing so will also permit ease of updating and maintaining the business plan when changes to the content are needed. Finally, you should also strongly consider putting a confidentiality clause in your plan to deter it from being misused if it gets into the wrong hands.

REGULATORY ISSUES

There are myriad regulatory requirements affecting your business. These are not the regulations affecting your clients and the services you are performing for them (e.g., the Occupational Safety and Health Administration (OSHA) and the Environmental Protection Agency (EPA)). Instead, these regulations affect your business with respect to how it is intended to be performed. For typical consulting firms, these regulations involve business tax and business proprietor regulations, safety and environmental regulations, and employment law regulations. Numerous others may be applicable as well if you do government contract type of work.

This section will not only list all the regulators and significant regulations that your business must comply with, but it will cover how you or your management team plan to ensure compliance along with the potential regulatory compliance costs. A word of caution: If your goal is to just offer your services domestically, tax and licensing implications may not be so significant. But if you decide to sell your products and services internationally, the costs to comply with the laws of the many countries within which you plan to operate may be so restrictive that your business cannot become or remain viable.

PLAN REVISIONS

Business plans are not a once-and-done project. They need to be reviewed and revised continually, as it is easy for any business to get off track without proper attention to the overall plan for its operations and as the environment in which it operates changes. At the very least, reviewing your plan should become an annual exercise for you. Beyond that, the plan should be revised when major changes occur or business expansions are projected. For example, if you decide to go from a part-time OS&H consultant to full-time, a rigorous review and revision will be necessary to ensure you have properly analyzed all of the necessary implications of this change. Expanding a product or service is another example of when a plan should be reviewed and revised, although this change may not require such a comprehensive analysis. Lastly, any hire or a senior level consultant is another example of something that should require plan review.

Business plans are not a once-and-done project. They need to be reviewed and revised continually....

APPENDICES

The final sections of your business plan are the appendices. These sections should be structured to provide supplemental information to support and augment your business plan. It should not be information previously included within the body of your plan.

Typically the appendices include, as applicable:

- Credit history (personal and business);
- Resumes of key individuals;
- Product and service brochures (if already developed);
- Letters of reference;
- Market research;
- Licenses, permits or patents;
- Legal documents;
- Office leases;
- Physical facility descriptions and building permits;
- Contracts (blank and executed); and
- Business advisory consultants being used or proposed to be used. (e.g., attorney, accountant, public relations firm, financial advisor).

OTHER BUSINESS START-UP AND BUSINESS PLANNING CONSIDERATIONS

The following items are not necessarily part of a formal business plan, although sometimes details about them should be included. These additional areas are those that you should give some time and consideration to determine if they apply. If warranted, incorporate them into your plan.

Subcontracting

Subcontracting is a business model that is often considered by start-up OS&H consulting firms with limited financial and/or talent resources. In some cases, you or your firm can act as a subcontractor to other firms. This will definitely aid in cash flow while you build your own clientele. You or your firm can do this for certain projects where there is the attraction of quick revenue or there is an opportunity to grow professionally by accepting challenging assignments.

In other cases, if your firm is very successful in the short term, limited staffing or other resources may force you to subcontract work to others to just satisfy contractual requirements. The biggest advantage of hiring a subcontractor is that it eliminates obligations owed to regular employees on your payroll. They can be utilized or not at any time with limited strings attached. Consequently, this promotes flexibility in addressing business upturns and downturns. Subcontracting can also assist with managing large or seasonal projects where the internal resources are non-existent or to create a scalable organization with a limited overhead resource investment.

In a typical subcontractor arrangement, the OS&H consultant meets with the client to propose a solution to meet the client's needs. The consultant then develops a plan and cost proposal. If the client decides to execute the contract, the consultant is responsible to get the work done, with the assistance of the subcontractor(s) or in a combination of consultant and subcontractor(s). The consultant is ultimately responsible for reviewing the work after completion and/or supervising its progress to ensure quality. The consultant is also responsible for collecting the contractual fee upon project completion and paying the subcontractor.

Another advantage of hiring subcontractors is that less recordkeeping is necessary on the part of the business owner. For example, regular employees require tax and benefit withholding and expense documentation. With subcontractors, those responsibilities will rest on their shoulders and not on those of your business. In the United States, the business owner employing a subcontractor is only obligated to keep track of subcontractor work hours and earnings and, if over $600.00, file IRS Form 1099s annually.

Using subcontractors also allows a business to manage itself more prudently. In consulting, it can be feast or famine. You may not be able to afford regular employees and the expenses associated with them; their burden can present significant challenges at payroll time if the cash flow from work generated is not there. Ancillary expenses can also be minimized or eliminated as subcontractors are not typically afforded fringe benefits, insurance coverage, office space, and equipment.

It is very important to spell out contractually that your subcontractors are not employees and must pay their own taxes and benefits.

Work specialization can also be a strong determining factor in the decision to use subcontractors, as a business may need certain expertise not held by current regular employees. This expertise may be needed on either a short-term or long-term basis. It can be in the form of technical assistance (e.g., engineering) or of an administrative nature (e.g., payroll services). The use of subcontractors can assist a business in focusing its efforts on its core competencies without being distracted and eventually overwhelmed with trying to perform work that requires extensive training and experience to master.

Additionally, you may need to hire subcontractors if your firm's resources become spread too thin, and deadlines are looming. This can sometimes be the only alternative in satisfying a contractual obligation. Using subcontractors can also permit the billing out of additional hours and providing key players sufficient time to concentrate on the business' operational functions.

There are some things to consider before hiring subcontractors. First, it may be helpful to create a stable of well-qualified, reliable subcontractors that you can call upon when needed or before you need them. Your goal is to find the best available talent within your resource constraints. Surrounding yourself with excellence will be beneficial to your long-term success. When this is done, you may want them to sign a contract with your business to ensure their availability when needed. The last thing that you want to occur is to enter into a contract and find that you do not have the resources to fulfill it. However, be aware that retaining such availability may come at a price, especially for those subcontractors who work for numerous consulting companies and may not want to be tied down to one business, especially if there is no guarantee of work.

Second, you need to take the time to validate the references of all subcontractors. They may be your good friend or relative, but their work ethic or lack thereof can have a major impact on your business. You need to treat subcontractors the same as you would for a person you are considering hiring for a salaried position, as they are often the face of your business. Thus, it is critical that they portray the image you want when exposed to your clients.

Third, always establish and execute a formal contract. Subcontractor contract templates can be quickly accessed free online or from legal resource firms, where you may need to pay an upfront fee. Regardless of the sources, it is always prudent to have any contract you use reviewed by an attorney. (For an example of one that can be quickly developed online, see the "Other Resources" section at the end of the chapter.) Your contract must have confidentiality, work product protection, non-compete and termination clauses embedded. Payment terms, including actual subcontractor remuneration and time frames for payment, must also be well defined. This will ensure that your products, services, and clients will not be pilfered and under what conditions you can terminate the agreement.

It is very important to spell out contractually that your subcontractors are not employees and must pay their own taxes and benefits. It would be prudent to understand the differences between employees and independent contractors in the eyes of taxing authorities and to ensure proper language is contained in your contract. The Internal Revenue Service website is a good resource to learn about the difference between employees and subcontractors (IRS 2010). You also want to discuss the ramifications of classifying someone as subcontractor or employee with your accountant and your attorney.

Defining the exact scope of work, deliverables and deadlines is a necessary part of your subcontractor agreement. This will provide clear direction from the beginning of the assigned project and not leave any question unanswered. Include the subcontractor in defining this scope, so if there are any challenging issues, those can be addressed up front.

Fourth, your clients must know up front that you will be using subcontractors. Even though that language may be contained deep within your contract with them, advising them that qualified subcontractors will be used is the right thing to do to avoid any surprises or embarrassment.

Fifth, treat subcontractors fairly and honestly. Remember they may be the face of your business. You can't afford to have a disgruntled subcontractor just like you can't afford to have a disgruntled employee. After you develop a trustworthy subcontractor pool, your job as the business owner is to treat them well. Compensating them well and providing an occasional perk will go far in developing a very good long-term, fruitful relationship.

Depending on how well your business grows, you may need to evolve from subcontractor relationships to partnerships or salaried employees. Although subcontracting can have many benefits in the short term, at some time, reliance on known internal support may be more prudent and comfortable. At that point, you may need to trade off the expense in overhead, payroll, taxes, and so on, for stability, growth and enhanced work product or service control. Although this should be a well thought-out and calculated decision, in many cases it is difficult and is dependent upon the potential ability to expand if more human resources were available.

Tax Consultation

As a business owner, you have a responsibility to make sure your business is operating within the confines of the taxing authorities in your jurisdiction. In the United States, businesses are taxed at the federal, state and local levels. Depending on your business structure, tax laws and requirements can become extremely complicated. Finding a good certified public accountant (CPA) who specializes in small business will be worth the effort to avoid making mistakes in this all-important area. Get referrals from others before signing on.

Taxes on business profits are essentially handled the same way for sole proprietorships, partnerships, and LLCs. Businesses such as these are often referred to as pass-through businesses. This essentially means that all profits generated and losses incurred pass directly through to the business owner. They are then accounted for on personal tax income tax returns. All unincorporated businesses are required to pay income taxes on all net profits of the business. In these entities, even if all of the profits are kept in the business checking account, are not spent, and are awaiting upcoming expenditures, owners are obligated to report their share of these profits as income on their tax returns.

On the other hand, owners of a C corporation do not account for their portions of the corporate profits on their personal tax returns. Corporations are separate legal entities from the owner. Owners are, however, required to pay taxes on profits they actually receive in the form of salaries, bonuses, and dividends. The C corporation also pays taxes at corporate income tax rates on any profits left in the company. These are referred to as retained earnings. Corporations are also responsible for tax payments on any dividends paid out to shareholders. Owners of a C corporation are not required to pay personal income taxes on profits they don't receive. Corporations enjoy a lower tax rate than most individuals for a substantial portion of profits. Thus, depending on the revenue generated and the tax rates, a C corporation and its owners may realize a lower combined tax bill than the owners of an unincorporated business that earns the same amount of profit.

Corporate income tax rules create additional paperwork, time, effort, recordkeeping, and tax filing obligations. It can be very complex for large businesses with accounting staffs. It can be overwhelming for small businesses that don't have the time, energy, and in-house expertise to keep abreast with complicated rules and tax filing requirements. Thus, a good CPA and possibly the use of a bookkeeper on a part-time basis may be beneficial.

Financial Planning and Advisement

As has been noted previously, you will need to identify external advisors to assist with operational management issues, as well as issues ancillary to running and sustaining a successful business. Financial planning expertise is one of those areas. After all, you are probably not deciding to go into business to simply make ends meet. Your goal should be to maximize your business' profitability as payment for your hard work.

. . . you will also need to invest the time, energy, and resources needed to control your risks: risks to yourself, your workers, and your business.

There are two significant areas of consideration with respect to financial planning and advisement. The first area deals with managing your business and the implications of cash flow, tax planning, risk management, and business continuity. Everyone venturing into a consulting business needs to address these issues. The second area deals with protecting yourself and dealing with the issues related to retirement, business sale, or dissolution. It may not need to be addressed immediately but will need to be at some point.

Taking a realistic perspective from the beginning of your business planning process is important. This mindset should carry through as you consider issues that may be on the distant horizon. Accordingly, financial planning will help with setting and meeting goals, managing risks associated with your business, reducing taxes, investing your profits and retirement, and succession planning.

Planning for Your Retirement

You need to consider planning for your retirement at the beginning of your consulting career. Whether you are moonlighting as a solo consultant just to have some extra money or whether your business is your sole livelihood and everything in between, at some point you will probably want or need retire. Since this is a reality for most, retirement planning should be considered during the early stages of your business. You need to consider the various retirement savings options available within your business structure, their tax advantages, and whether additional planning and investment options need to be explored. Chances are you will not be able to live off of the proceeds from the sale of your business, even if it is marketable. Additionally, you will need to think about whether you will outlive your savings based on projected longevity estimations. Thus, retirement planning cannot wait until later, as too often, later never comes.

Managing Risk

Your OS&H consulting practice is aimed at helping others to recognize, evaluate, and control risks effectively. But you may have never considered that you will also need to invest the time, energy, and resources needed to control your risks: risks to yourself, your workers, and your business. Structuring your business properly, managing your assets, and purchasing liability insurance can go a long way in this endeavor. You need to ensure that you and those who depend on you are protected as well. What if your income stream is disrupted or stopped suddenly? If some form of disability affects you or key personnel? What if key partners, workers or clients decide to leave? What if your business suffers some catastrophic loss? Planning for these eventualities up front through insurance and other risk management strategies cannot be overlooked. Pretending that they will never occur is not prudent for any successful business. Consider if your client base did this. You would have no business! (Please refer to Chapter 4 for more information on risk transfer options.)

Personal Tax Planning Strategies

As the old saying goes, the only things certain in life are death and taxes. Depending on your perspective, fortunately or unfortunately, we must give to Caesar what belongs to Caesar! But giving more to Caesar than he deserves is foolish. As I work with my tax advisors, I continually advise them that I want to do everything morally and ethically correct. But I also want to ensure I am not overpaying. Making sure your books are kept in a timely and proper manner is an important first step in this process. Understanding and planning for legitimate tax deductions is the next step. Preparing and filing your taxes on time is the last step. The assistance of someone qualified to assist you, such as a CPA or a bookkeeper, will be worth every penny you invest, especially if you make some mistakes along the way.

PLANNING FOR THE NEXT FRONTIER

As stated earlier, only death and taxes are certain in life. As a result, you should invest some time thinking about how your business will be dealt with when you are no longer around. I currently have two children in the OS&H profession. Maybe someday they may take an interest in my consulting practice. That would be wonderful and the easiest option. Right now, they are not ready, as both need experience to fully understand and practice in my niche area. But what if that does not happen? What will I need to consider for protecting my wife if I die first? Will the business be dissolved and how will this occur?

How will the business assets, including physical property, investments and intellectual property, be dispersed? Even if my children take over my business, who will lead it? Will they be equal partners, equal shareholders, officers, and so on? Those are all estate planning questions that need to be addressed early on. Spending the money to consult with estate planning attorneys will be an investment that pays huge returns in the end.

Wealth Building

The primary goal of any business is to make it successful. If you are fortunate enough to become successful, you will need to consider how your wealth will be invested and protected. Making your wealth is only half the battle in business. Keeping it is the other half. Seeking the assistance from a financial advisor is a very important step. Picking the right one is just as important.

I have learned over the years that there are two types of financial advisors. First are those who want to make money off of your wealth through investing it for you and selling you investment products. Second are those who are willing to give you purely fee-based advice without anything "clouding" their view. The second type is the best from my perspective. I was fortunate to benefit from the partnership of such an advisor for many years. Then the economy downturn occurred, and he began pushing commission-based products. Within a few months, we parted company.

Great wealth managers will help you clearly and sometimes painfully understand the implications and strategies for the accumulation of wealth and distribution at various times in your business and personal life cycle. They will also help you understand how you should be preserving your wealth, legal tax avoidance, and protection from creditors, if the need arises. Finding a great financial advisor or team who will be willing to look at your entire picture, fully considering all the previous areas discussed, is hard to find. But it is well worth the search. Great wealth managers will be worth their weight in gold! As was impressed upon me by my wonderful grandmother when I was very young, in life you pay for what you get and you get what you pay for. This was great advice for a young impressionable kid. It is also great advice for any successful business owner.

> *... there are two types of financial advisors ... those who are willing to give you purely fee-based advice ... [are] the best from my perspective.*

Using Government Certifications (Such as DBEs)

As you go through the process of writing your original business plan or revising it, you might want to consider investigating the various government-based certifications for which your business might qualify. For certain consulting businesses, obtaining government certifications is a way to assist with both business planning and marketing. Government certifications are typically available if you are a minority-owned business, a women-owned business, a veteran-owned business, a business owned by a person with a qualifying disability, or a small business (or combinations of the above).

Government certifications offer a consulting business several advantages in the marketplace. The first is that the proposal review process for some public sector contracts award additional points to businesses possessing certain types of government certifications. In a tight competition, these additional points can help the certified business rise above others and obtain a bid. The second is that some proposal processes offer a set-aside for businesses with qualifying certifications so that a certain proportion of the bid or total project award must be given to a certified business. Finally, in larger projects that involve prime contractors, the prime contractor's overall bid for a project can be enhanced through the use of a certified business as a subcontractor. In some cases, the bid requires that a certain portion of the total price be assigned to a subcontractor who meets specific qualifying certifications. All of these advantages can provide substantial work for your consulting business; in fact, some consulting businesses subsist almost entirely on these types of projects. As you go through the process of business planning, you should evaluate how certifications might assist you.

Certifications are generally awarded by governments or government entities. They can be federal, state or local. Each one has its own set of requirements that must be met for certification. Therefore, this process will require some research on your part to see what might be available to you. The most widely available one is the federal government's 8(a) program, administered by the Small Business Administration (SBA n.d. d). Another one is the HUB Zone certification, which is designed to help small businesses in specific rural and urban areas and is based upon the physical location of the primary office (SBA n.d. c.).

Applying for a certification requires that you provide very specific information about your business, its ownership, and its finances. It will not require that you seek outside assistance to complete the application process; however, you may want to look for some help the first time you try. Many free or low-cost services are available to assist you in the process. SBDCs typically offer this type of help (SBA n.d. e.) There are also many other state or local entities that can help you; an Internet search will turn up many possibilities.

Once you become certified, it is up to you to market your certification and find opportunities. To help, SBDCs and other organizations provide resources, workshops and meetings where you are able to promote your business and develop leads. Many of these services are either free or very low-cost.

One last point: you must be able to maintain the minimum qualifications throughout the life of the certification. Some are awarded annually and others have longer terms. Any material changes in your business' operations must be reported when they occur. Each certifying organization will also determine the process for recertifying your business and will provide directions on how to do so. Failure to comply with the requirements for certification or the recertification process will jeopardize your certification and may also subject your business to fines and the loss of business.

CONCLUSION

I have learned from experience that starting a business is hard work. Running it is even harder. And sustaining it can be downright painful at times. Anyone who begins a business needs to understand this reality. But most rarely do, so they start with wild enthusiasm. They convince themselves that nobody can live without their product or service. They learn very quickly that life existed before their business, and it will exist long after it has failed. Start with the understanding that your product or service is one of many for clients to choose from and that it may not be the best deal for the price; that is the reality. Believing that you can fail quickly, consuming your life savings or a bank loan is also a reality-based starting point. Reality is also understanding at the outset that an OS&H consulting business is very time consuming to get off the ground. It will take away from your "fun" time.

Finally, unfortunately, most business start ups do not succeed. This is a stark reality (statisticbrain.com 2014). In many cases, this occurs because proper business planning did not occur in the beginning. When push came to shove, shove was a little stronger and the party was over, so to speak! Although your business will be hard work, proper business planning will make it enjoyable and fun. And, if your business is not enjoyable and not fun, it is probably time to go to work for someone else.

I have learned from experience that starting a business is hard work. Running it is even harder.

Over the years, my business has been blessed in many ways. I have never had a shortage of work or a bad client relationship. This just didn't happen. Proper planning and execution was a large part of this. But, giving back was also instrumental in my success. I firmly believe that God gave me some wonderful talents and gifts. Sharing what I have learned, and the wealth I have reaped with others along the way was at the core of my success. This was well above having and executing a solid business plan and is worth your consideration. Great historical leaders are not remembered for what they had. They are remembered for what they did with what they had along the way, to positively impact the lives of others. Good luck and fortune in your new endeavor.

If the information in this chapter has not deterred your enthusiasm for beginning an OS&H consulting business, it is time to get off the couch and start developing your business plan. If you don't, someone else will, and that person will be reaping the many rewards that consulting has to offer, not to mention enjoying a few new toys in the garage maybe.

I have tried to give you, the prospective consultant, an essential framework for establishing your consulting practice by developing a comprehensive business plan. You can see that each one of the items of a business plan is critical to the initial set up. I have also given you the beginnings of needing start-up funding, as well as the identifying some ongoing costs of running a consulting practice. I have also a discussed how important it is to evaluate financial projections in order to see whether or not your consulting practice is viable. Now it is time for us to look at finance from a different and somewhat deeper perspective, including setting rates, collecting fees, and learning to read and understand some vitally important business financial statements.

BIBLIOGRAPHY

Benton, Patty. 2005. *Using Subcontractors* (retrieved December 2013). ezinearticles.com/?Using-Subcontractors&id=112703

Business Wealth. 2004. *Ten Common Causes of Business Failure* (retrieved January 2014). http://businesswealth.com.au/business/starting/advice/failure.asp

Centers for Disease Control (CDC), National Institute for Occupational Safety and Health (NIOSH). n.d. *The National Occupational Research Agenda (NORA)* (retrieved January, 2014). http://www.cdc.gov/niosh/NORA/

Entrepreneur.com. n.d. *How to Write Your Mission Statement* (retrieved October 27, 2014). www.entrepreneur.com/article/65230

Goltz, Jay. January 5, 2011. *Top Ten Reasons Small Businesses Fail* (retrieved March 8, 2014). boss.blogs.nytimes.com/?s=/Top-10-Reasons-Why-Businesses-Fail

Internal Revenue Service (IRS). 2010. *Employee vs. Independent Contractor—Seven Tips for Business Owners* (retrieved November, 2013). http://www.irs.gov/uac/Employee-vs.-Independent-Contractor—Seven-Tips-for-Business-Owners

JSM Consulting. 2004. *Mission Statement and Values* (retrieved October 27, 2014). www.jsm-consulting.com/?page=Mission

Larson, Aaron. 2013. *Contract Law: An Introduction* (retrieved December 2010). www.expertlaw.com/library/business/contract_law.html

Laurence, Beth. n.d. *Choosing the Best Ownership Structure for Your Business* (retrieved September 2013). www.nolo.com/legal-encyclopedia/business-ownership-structure-choose-best-29618.html.

Mahoney, Jessica. n.d. *The Advantages of Using Subcontractors* (retrieved November 2013). www.ehow.com/info_8750661_advantages-using-subcontractors.html#ixzz2ffTJ3Cd2

Nolo.com. n.d. *Choose Your Business Structure* (retrieved September 2013). www.nolo.com/legal-encyclopedia/business-structures.

Occupational Safety and Health Administration (OSHA). 2013. *Fall 2013 Unified Agenda* (retrieved January 2014). www.osha.gov/pls/oshaweb/owadisp.show_document?p_table=UNIFIED AGENDA&p_ID=7071)

OnStrategy. 2008. *Ten Common Causes of Business Failure* (retrieved October 27, 2014). www.onstrategyhq.com/resources/ten-common-causes-of-business-failure

Priebe, Jim. n.d. *Financial Planning for the Business Owner* (retrieved December, 2013). http://www.ehow.com/info_7748235_financial-planning-business-owner.html

Service Corps of Retired Executives (SCORE). n.d. *About SCORE: We Help Small Businesses Like Yours* (retrieved October 27, 2014) www.score.org.about-score

Small Business Administration (SBA). n.d. a. "8(a) Business Development Program," (retrieved December 2013). www.sba.gov/category/navigation-structure/contracting/contracting-support-small-businesses/8a-business-development-program.

_____. n.d. b. "Creating Your Business Plan" (retrieved July 2013). www.sba.gov/category/navigation-structure/starting-managing-business/starting-business/how-write-business-plan

_____. n.d. c. "HUBZone Program." (retrieved December 2013). www.sba.gov/category/navigation-structure/contracting/contracting-support-small-businesses/small-business-cert-0

_____. n.d. d. "Starting and Running a Business" (retrieved March 9, 2014). www.sba.gov/category/navigation-structure/starting-managing-business/

_____. n.d. e. "Small Business Development Centers (SBDCs)," (retrieved October 27, 2014). www. sba.gov/tools/local-assistance/sbdc

_____. n.d. f. "Thinking About Starting a Business" (retrieved July 2013). www.sba.gov/thinking-about-starting.

Statisticbrain.com. 2014. "Startup Business Failure Rate by Industry (retrieved October 27, 2014). www.statisticbrain.com/startup-failure-by-industry/

Wikipedia.com. n.d. a. "Contract" (retrieved November 2013). en.wikipedia.org/wiki/Contract.

_____. n.d. b."Business Plan" (retrieved July 2013). http://en.wikipedia.org/wiki/Business_plan

OTHER RESOURCES

"10 Top Ten Reviews" n.d. *Business Plan Software Product Comparisons* (retrieved January 2014). business-plan-software-review.toptenreviews.com/

BPlan. "Business Plan Pro." n.d. (retrieved December 2013). www.bplans.com/ppc/template-offer-lt/

Google. "Adwords." www.google.com/adwords

"Live Plan by Palo Alto Software," n.d. (retrieved January 2014). www.live-plan.com/ppc/ipad-homepage

RocketLawyer.com. n.d. *Free Subcontractor Agreement* (retrieved November, 2013). www.rocketlawyer.com/document/subcontractor-agreement.rl

Questions to ask:

Are you prepared to do what it takes to make money in OS&H consulting?

Have you thought through the type of services you will offer? Are they high, middle or low level services?

What rate will you charge for your services? Did you prepare a rate schedule?

What pricing method do you anticipate using?

Are your salary expectations realistic, based on your proposed rates and your willingness to work?

Have you practiced how to price your services?

Do you know how long it will take to complete each type of work?

Will you use employees or subcontractors? If so, how will they fit into your business model?

What ongoing expenses do you anticipate?

What equipment or services will you need to start your business?

What financial software will you use?

Do you have an accountant to help you set up your books? Are you comfortable reading financial statements?

How will you invoice for your services? Did you write up a collection strategy?

Chapter 3

What about the Money (Financial)

BY DEBORAH ROY, MPH, RN, COHN-S, CET, CSP

Deborah is currently Corporate Director of Health, Safety and Wellness at L.L. Bean, Inc. in Freeport, Maine, where she leads staff and consults with senior management globally. In 1990 she started SafeTech Consultants, Inc., providing chemically related training and consulting. Deborah served as President/Owner of SafeTech, managing employees until 2007, and then selling the training portion of the business to a former employee. From that time on, she has accomplished her corporate role and maintained SafeTech on a part-time basis. She continues to provide consulting in global safety and health management systems, sustainability, and control of chemical risks. Deborah received her BSN from Northeastern University in Boston and her MPH in Occupational Health and Safety from the University of North Carolina. She has written numerous professional articles and presents at national and international conferences. Deborah has also taught consulting courses at ASSE conferences since 1999.

AT THIS POINT in the book, you may be wondering how you are going to pay for what it takes to run a business, as well as asking, "Isn't the reason for being a consultant to make lots of money and work fewer hours?" Here is where you might start thinking, "How do I price my services, and how much money can I make?" However, if you haven't done the planning for your business, as outlined in Chapter 2, "Creating a Business Plan," those questions might be premature. First consider:

- How much are you planning to work?
- What type and complexity of services will you will offer?
- Where will your office will be?
- Will you have employees?
- What kind of upfront expenses do you expect?

Answering these questions will help you determine how many hours you would need to work and what price you will need to charge in order to achieve your salary expectations.

PRICING FOR SERVICES: AN INTRODUCTION

The most common OS&H consulting questions are: What rate do I charge? How do I figure out a dollar value for the work or project? How do I get paid quickly? I'll try to give you some ideas so that you can be not only a qualified consultant but a financially successful one, too. And I hate to burst your bubble, but most consultants who are financially successful today have worked hard to get there.

You may already be familiar with pricing services or have a good idea of what the going rate is for the services you provide. When I started my business, I was pretty comfortable with how to determine my rates. I had worked in a corporate role for an international environmental consulting firm, so I was familiar with rate schedules and pricing proposals. Also, much of my work in the first year of business was HAZWOPER (Hazardous Waste Operations and Emergency Response) training and related consulting. Since the OSHA regulation, 29 CFR 1910.120, was new at the time, business was plentiful, and the range of pricing for these required courses was known. After being in business for a few years, though, I found that I was working hard and had plenty of work, but I wasn't making as much as I thought I should, given the many hours I was putting in. With the help of a local Small Business Development Center (SBDC) funded by the U.S. Small Business Administration (SBA), I did some analysis of my rates and realized that for consulting and custom training courses, I was not charging enough! The analysis of the custom training courses consisted of comparing all the expenses incurred (including a portion of overhead) to the fees I charged to the client. What I found was that my profit margin was quite small and would not support the business for some training projects. In the case of consulting, I did a competitive analysis of rates based on the type of services and my experience. I found I was providing high-quality, high-level services but charging less than my competitors. Lesson learned: Evaluate rates on an ongoing basis.

Setting a rate is an important part of the consulting business. Different types of clients are looking for different types of services. The price they will pay varies tremendously.

DETERMINING RATES

Setting a rate is an important part of the consulting business. It makes sense to spend some time thinking about what your rates should be and why. You can always adjust your rates along the way, but if you start off too low, quickly transitioning to a higher rate might be difficult for existing clients. On the other hand, starting with rates that are too high might keep you from acquiring some clients, although depending on the client, the industry or the type of work, high rates may be appropriate. Different types of clients are looking for different types of services. The price they will pay varies tremendously. Being successful as a consultant means finding clients that are the right fit for you and what you offer. Sometimes the company is too small to afford your consulting services and would be better served by obtaining free services through its trade association or the Occupational Safety and Health Administration (OSHA) consultation program. You may still be able to help the company by referring the contact to an appropriate resource. I've actually had businesses come back to me years later as clients, because in the past, I connected them to the right service at the time when they were small. And you never know who they might tell about the few minutes you spent on the phone with them, making sure they received the help they needed.

Just because potential consulting work exists doesn't always mean you should accept it! I know that sounds counterintuitive, but trust me, it's true.

Other potential clients may be unrealistic about the cost of safety and health services, budgeting too little to complete the work. In that case, if you agree to work at the price they want to pay, you could end up giving away hours of work or risk not completing the requested tasks. These same clients who are unrealistic about costs often require much more of your time and energy than other long-term clients with whom you develop a business relationship over the years. Just because potential consulting work exists doesn't always mean you should accept it! I know that sounds counterintuitive, but trust me, it's true. I once had a client ask me to quote on a major update of their construction safety policy and procedure manual, based on a paper copy shown to me at a meeting. The electronic copy was sent to my company by e-mail two weeks before the document was due. Unfortunately, my employee (an experienced consultant) didn't look at the document until a week later. It turns out the client sent us a document that was twice as long as the paper copy that I had reviewed and needed significantly more work. They claimed this was the correct document. Because I felt that my reputation was at risk, we completed the work correctly, on time, and for the quoted price, despite the fact that it took twice as much time as was proposed. And this experience is not uncommon in consulting!

As a sidebar to this story, this same client did admit to me up front that he was using my firm because it was a Department of Transportation (DOT) approved Woman-Owned Business under the Disadvantaged Business Enterprise (DBE) program. (You can find more about government certifications in Chapter 2, "Creating a Business Plan.") It turns out this client had been warned by the DOT that he needed to use more DBE contractors on his government projects. After this first assignment, we were asked to do numerous other projects. I declined to participate in any future work for this company. Ironically, my firm had DBE status for about 15 years. This was the only client that hired my firm for that purpose. The other clients hired us because of our qualifications and the quality of the work, and they received the DBE credit as a bonus. That was a great lesson for me: no matter what the revenue for the project, it might not be worth the time and effort. It also taught me to trust my intuition. I knew that the client came to us for the wrong reason, and I should have said no from the beginning. Another lesson learned.

Let's get to the discussion of rates. There are a variety of approaches in the management and engineering consulting literature. What I will offer here is what I have used or seen in OS&H consulting. Keep in mind that even if you use a logical approach to setting your rates, the market will ultimately impact how high your rates can be for a given type of project, which assumes the services you wish to offer match up to what your potential clients want to buy. It takes both the right type of services and the right rate to be successful in consulting.

> *I tend to think of pricing as two steps. The first is to determine the hourly and/or daily rate, and the second is to determine the pricing method.*

I tend to think of pricing as two steps. The first is to determine the hourly and/or daily rate, and the second is to determine the pricing method. Why start with rate detail before process? I think of rate first, since it will be used in the calculations once you determine the process to use, or pricing method. Since most of us started by selling time, the hourly rate is where I will start. Note that there are other ways to make money in consulting beyond selling time, but I'll address that later.

Rate Options

Multiplier

The multiplier is commonly used by engineering firms to determine the basic rates (Association of Consulting Engineering Companies, p. 1). Engineering is the closest field to OH&S, so it is often a good starting place. For an idea of multipliers used in other professional disciplines, see the article by Higgins, called "The Successful Consultants Guide to Fee Setting" (2010, 23). To use this approach, start by determining your proposed salary. For example, let's say you are an experienced OH&S professional with significant expertise and an advanced degree or designations, such as a CSP or CIH. Your goal is to have a salary of $100,000 per year. Divide that salary by 2,080 hours (40 hours a week,

52 weeks a year) and you will get to $48.10/hour. This is the base. Multiply the base by your set multiplier. Environmental engineering firms often use some rate between 3 and 4. If we use 3.5, then the hourly rate will be $168.35 and the daily rate will be $1,346.80. It is easiest to then round to the next $5 or $10. Your hourly rate might be $170, and your daily rate might be $1,350. In this example, if you billed 2,080 hours a year, the gross revenue for your firm would be $353,600. Sounds great, doesn't it? Consulting is looking really good!

However, if you start a firm as a solo consultant, you will still need to perform administrative and marketing functions; take vacations, holidays and sick time; pay for insurance, such as health, liability, unemployment, and workers' compensation; attend conferences for professional development; and cover other business expenses and taxes. What may initially look like profit or additional compensation is really the cost of doing business. The other challenge is that when you are starting out working solo, only about 50% of your time will realistically be billed (Coutu 2013, 1). With experience, and depending on the amount of administrative and marketing support you have (and that costs money), 65% is realistic, I've found. Now let's look at the example again.

Salary of $100,000 divided by 1,040 potential billable hours
(2,080 hours at 50% time)
    = $96 base hourly rate
    X multiplier of 3.5
    = $336 billing rate per hour

A rate of $336 per hour might be appropriate, depending on the industry you are working in and your degree of knowledge, but it might be too high if you are competing with lots of other similar OH&S consultants. Let's look at the example again for an experienced consultant who is able to bill 65% of his or her time. In this case, the hours worked would be 1,352 and the base hourly rate would be $74. This would produce an hourly rate of $259, or $260 after rounding. This rate may be more competitive and still allow for a good income, depending on the type of work and the geographic area.

Sometimes, firms use a different multiplier for different client industries.

Sometimes, firms use a different multiplier for different client industries. For example, one large environmental consulting firm that I worked for many years ago used a lower multiplier for petroleum clients, since there was significant competition in that area of business. For all other industrial clients, the multiplier was higher. In the case of OH&S, you might use a multiplier of two or slightly less for commodity work that can be done by many consultants in the field. Examples of commodity work in OH&S could include the writing of safety policies and procedures for standard OSHA topics, such as respiratory protection or hazard communication, or could be basic level safety training in that type of topic. This is the kind of work that an associate level staff OH&S professional is qualified to perform. Using the example above with 65% billability, multiplying the rate of $74 per hour by a multiplier of two would bring the hourly rate down to $148. Depending on the market, this rate could still be too high, pricing you out of the market. Think about the type of consulting work you will be offering when considering your salary goal. Unless you are willing to work considerable hours beyond forty, it's not likely that you'll be able to draw a $100,000 salary by just selling time based on commodity OH&S work. Either your salary will be lower or the complexity and rarity of the consulting work being offered will need to be greater. So consider your salary goal based on the market, not just what you consider to be your worth or what you need for income. This moves us to addressing competitive rates.

> ...there is nothing wrong with commodity services!...at lower rates, you will need an efficient system to produce the consulting volume needed to make the financials work long term.

Competitive Rates

In some cases, it's simple to just match your rates to the competitor's rates. When I started to provide HAZWOPER training in 1990, the eight-hour refresher course was typically about $150 per person for an open enrollment course. Initial 40-hour courses varied from around $700 to $800 per person. Price was not as much a differentiator as quality of materials and equipment, instructor-to-student ratio, creativity of instruction and specificity to the student group. For example, most of my firm's clients were engineering and geotechnical firms because of the network that I had established while in my former corporate role. This population of educated professionals wanted value during their non-billable training time, not just a certificate. So each year, we redesigned the course from scratch, addressing the OSHA-required material, but focusing on content that was relevant to the audience, and including new safety and health concerns each year. Over time, this allowed my firm to gain significant market share and keep clients long term. As a result, pricing was able to move beyond the competition. That doesn't mean no competitors offered $99 courses; they did. But even if an occasional client chose that option, they always came back to us, due to the quality of the courses my firm provided.

When using a competitive rate, think about where you want to be in the market. Do you want to be at the high, median or low end of the market? The continuum of OH&S services is broad; your education, designations, experience, the type of industry, and the amount of competition can affect the value of the services offered. Are your services high end, meaning they add more value, require a higher level of expertise, utilize a proprietary methodology, or provide something different? Are your services mid-level and have some barrier to entry, such as a CSP or CIH designation? Or, are your services commodity services that could be provided by a safety professional with a couple of years of experience? Keep in mind, there is nothing wrong with commodity services! Just understand that at lower rates, you will need an efficient system to produce the consulting volume needed to make the financials work long term. One way to do so is to hire junior-level staff to provide commodity services, while you engage in more challenging and lucrative projects. For example, OSHA ten-hour courses for general industry or construction are quite popular. If your potential client network is strong, this may be a great option, depending on your geographic area and industry experience. Many OH&S consultants are approved trainers for these courses and, consequently, the price is often lower than other safety and health training or consulting. But if you have a good product and take the time to develop great course modules upfront, you or your junior staff may be able to teach these courses over and over for a reasonable profit. Just remember that the revenue produced has to cover not only your salary and benefits (and any employee salaries), but also taxes and all the other expenses of a business.

Once you know the level and type of services, how do you actually find out what your competitors are charging, and what the going rate should be? This will depend on the type of service. For training that may be offered on an open enrollment basis, all it takes is an Internet search. For example, I did a search for live OSHA ten-hour courses and found courses in different parts of the U.S. with prices ranging from $100 to $200 per person for the course. Depending on what the client needs are, the number of students in the course, or the geographic area, your course could be within that range or outside of it. I also found online courses that were offered for $59 per person. So think about how to differentiate your offering if it looks like the same service is offered online. It is possible to market the value of live courses compared to online ones. What would make your services more attractive to a client?

Another way to determine the going rate is to utilize your network of colleagues to find someone who might be offering or buying similar services, but who is not in your geographic area. For example, you might be planning to offer a small company your services as a part-time safety manager, for a few hours a month. You could use the multiplier method to determine a rate, but how do you know if it is in the ball park? Ask two or three colleagues you know in the OH&S field, but who are working outside of your market area. They may be willing to give you an idea of what they have seen or what they are personally charging. Understand that not everyone will be willing to share. Price fixing is illegal (see the definition below), so don't expect to have a consultants' professional meeting and all agree upon a price. The idea is to validate your calculations in the market, not to have all competitors agree to set the same price. You will still need to test the market, based on your skills and experience and the services you offer. Your price may be the same as a competitor, but should be derived based on your own method.

Dealings with Competitors: Price Fixing

Price fixing is an agreement (writtten, verbal, or inferred from conduct) among competitors that raises, lowers, or stabilizes prices or competitive terms. Generally, the antitrust laws require that each company establish prices and other terms on its own, without agreeing with a competitor. When consumers make choices about what products and services to buy, they expect that the price has been determined freely on the basis of supply and demand not by an agreement among competitors. When competitors agree to restrict competition, the result is often higher prices. Accordingly, price fixing is a major concern of government antitrust enforcement (FTC 2013, p. 1).

Rate Schedules

Traditionally, fee schedules are provided to clients as part of the proposal or quote. If the consultant is solo, then rates listed will be the daily or hourly rate (as calculated previously) plus the payment terms and conditions. The rate schedule could also have rates for different types of services. For example, I have often seen expert testimony quoted at one and a half times the usual hourly rate. See Figure 1 for a sample solo consultant rate schedule. If the firm has employees or has subcontractors billed as part of the firm, then the rate schedule will list the rate by title for each level of employee. The type of work or the industry may also warrant more than one rate schedule. See Figure 2 for a sample rate schedule for a firm with employees. Note that rate schedules are dated and should be updated as appropriate. As I mentioned earlier, it is to your benefit to regularly review your rates. I would recommend updating your rate schedule at least annually.

Figure 1
Sample Rate Schedule I

> **Solo Firm**
> **RATE SCHEDULE I**
> Effective January 1, 2014
>
> | SERVICE | RATE PER HOUR |
> |---|---|
> | Professional consultation | $275.00 |
> | Delivery of depositions, responses to subpoenas, case review or expert testimony | $425.00 |
> | Professional instruction (includes preparation time) | $4,400 per day |
>
> (Based on a minimum of ten students)
>
> TERMS: NET 14 days. A finance charge of 1.5% per month will be assessed for amounts 30 days past due. Mileage is charged at the current IRS rate. Travel time will be billed at $135.00/hour. Out-of-town travel (meals, lodging, car rental, air fare, etc.) and other direct expenses will be billed at cost.

Figure 2
Sample Rate Schedule II

> **Firm with Employees**
> **RATE SCHEDULE II**
> Effective January 1, 2014
>
> | SERVICE | RATE PER HOUR |
> |---|---|
> | Professional consultation | |
> | Principal | $250.00 |
> | Senior Consultant | $200.00 |
> | Consultant | $175.00 |
> | Technician | $150.00 |
>
> TERMS: NET 30 days. A finance charge of 1.5% per month will be assessed for amounts 30 days past due. Mileage is charged at the current IRS rate. Travel time will be billed at half of the hourly rate. Out-of-town travel (meals, lodging, car rental, air fare, etc.) and other direct expenses will be billed with a 5% service charge.

Developing a Pricing Process (or Method)

Now that you have worked out your rate, the next step is to determine your process or pricing method. That method will vary depending on the type of consulting work that you provide and, to some extent, the type of client. Is the work ongoing, based on an hourly or daily rate, and a certain number of hours per month? Is the work based on a number of employees trained and that number is not known until the class? Is the work a discrete project with a known beginning or end with little dependence on the client? Is the work dependent on other client work or information that may impact the timeline or consulting hours? The key is to consider the complexity of the work and what the fair price is for the level of work: low, median or high end of the market, given the known variables. This does take some practice, and I'll explore how to shorten the learning curve later in the chapter.

Method 1: Time and Materials

Based on my 20+ years of experience in OH&S consulting, this appears to be, by far, the most common method of determining a price. The consultant considers the amount of time it would take to complete the project and estimates the hours, then multiplies that by the previously determined rate. Depending on the size of the project, this may be based on an hourly or daily rate. The work may consist of a single project or multiple projects or phases. Expenses are then estimated separately, if applicable and a total estimated cost is shown. Since this is an estimate for a given scope of work, it is critical that you spell out how any changes to the scope of work will be handled in the proposal. For example, you could add:

> The costs of providing these services are based on an estimate of time, materials, and expenses for the given scope of work and reflect a not-to-exceed figure. Our invoice will include only the actual costs of the

---

SAMPLE METHOD #1
Time and Materials

WORKSHOP—COSTS

Preparation and Instruction
30 to 45 minute Workshop Presentation:
$450 per one hour (minimum)	450.00
Panel Discussion: up to 3 hours @ $200 per hour	600.00
Workshop Cost	**$1,050.00**

Expenses
Travel Time to/from Anytown, USA (8-9 hours) @ $100/hour	$900.00
Meals (1 day × $50/day)	50.00
Airfare	400.00
Hotel	200.00
Airport parking	35.00
Expense Cost	$1,585.00

TOTAL (Estimated) COST	**$2,635.00**

Note: This example has a minimum of $450 for the Workshop Presentation. If you are doing small projects or presentations, it is a good idea to offer the work with a minimum. This will make it worth your while to leave the office!

Figure 3
Estimating Costs I

Figure 4
Estimating Costs II

> **SAMPLE METHOD #1**
> Time and Materials
>
> *Itemized Costs*
>
> Cost for the noise survey, dosimetry and report are as follows:
> Initial noise survey with Sound Level Meter:
>
> | | |
> |---|---:|
> | 4 hrs @ $225/hr | $ 900.00 |
> | Sound Level Meter rental: 1 day @ $50/hr | $ 50.00 |
> | *Written report: 2-4 hours @ $225 per hour | $900.00 |
> | Travel to/from Anytown, USA: 1 hour @ $100/hr | $ 100.00 |
>
> **Subtotal for noise survey $ 1,950.00**
>
> **Dosimetry for up to 6 individuals in a single day:
>
> | | |
> |---|---:|
> | 4 hours @ $225/hr | $ 900.00 |
> | Dosimeter rental: 6 units @ $35 per day | $ 210.00 |
> | Download dosimetry data and add to written report: | |
> | 2 hours @ $225 per hour | $450.00 |
> | Travel to/from Anytown, USA x 2: 2 hours @ $100/hr | $ 200.00 |
>
> **Subtotal for dosimeter testing $ 1,760.00**
>
> **TOTAL ESTIMATED COST $ 3,710.00**
>
> *Time range is shown to allow for flexibility. Only actual hours used will be invoiced.
>
> **Additional dosimetry may be added as needed.

completed work. Additions to the scope of work must be approved in writing by XYZ client and will be billed at cost.

See Figure 3 and 4 for two different examples of the cost section of a proposal using the time and materials method.

The type of services provided by an OH&S consultant may vary widely. Larger projects can be broken down into phases or over time, such as calendar quarters. The key is to either estimate the range of time for each element or the maximum time expected. No client wants to find out when they receive the invoice that you needed double the estimated time to complete the work. If the scope changes during the project, it's in your best interest to let the client know right away and negotiate a solution. Scope creep is a common problem that can be avoided by clearly stating what you will and will not do in the proposal and sticking to it. If the client wants to expand the scope, add an addendum to the contract or letter of agreement and make sure the additional cost and/or timeframe is clear. See Chapter 6, "Marketing and Sales" for more information on proposals.

> *If the client wants to expand the scope, add an addendum to the contract or letter of agreement and make sure the additional cost and/or timeframe is clear.*

Training services are commonly provided by OH&S consultants. Such training is often required by OSHA, EPA, or DOT regulations. Depending on the nature of the course, there may be significant preparation time involved to customize a training course for a client or to develop a course with new content. Consider whether not you will be able to reuse content in the future. For example, an OSHA 30-hour course could be developed in a module format, which would include not only the required modules but some elective modules that are likely to be requested. This preparation time upfront would make it easy to put together and provide the courses with little extra work later on. As discussed in a previous section, this is how commodity courses can be offered in the volume needed to produce sufficient revenue and still be of high quality.

Custom courses may need all new content, development of learning activities, or at least tailoring to the client industry or situation. In this case, preparation time may be up to twice the hours of instruction. Be sure to propose custom courses with either a line item for preparation or build it into your rate for instruction, as shown in the Figure 1 rate schedule.

What about student materials? Would you charge for those? Some OH&S consultants include printed materials in the cost of the course, some charge a per-person fee for manuals on top of the instruction/preparation fees, and some charge only for additional books, such as emergency response guidebooks or OSHA regulation books. A lesson that I learned early was not to list a cost for preparation of the manuals. I had a large client for whom my firm provided anhydrous ammonia emergency response training at about twenty of their plants. In my first year working with this client company, its Corporate Safety Director asked if I would just provide the master for the materials so that the plant could produce the materials and not incur the additional cost for manuals and shipping. I reluctantly agreed to do so. When I flew in and arrived at the plant at about 5 p.m. the day before the three-day class was to begin, I found the plant safety coordinator at the copier trying to copy 25 packets. Needless to say, the packets were thrown together, and didn't look very professional. That was the last time I agreed to have a client produce the materials! From then on, I added the cost to the training fee for this type of course, and it was never an issue again. We continued to provide training for this client for over ten years, and they paid the additional cost without a problem.

Method 2: Overhead Rate

The overhead method is commonly used on government projects. Since these agencies typically reserve the right to audit your financials for the sake of transparency, I would suggest working with an accountant to determine your actual

SAMPLE OVERHEAD RATE
Pricing for Government Contracts

Direct Labor: 10 days @ $300/day	$3,000.00
Overhead: 0.50 X 3,000	1,500.00
Other Direct Costs:	
Printing	350.00
Travel	700.00
Express Charges	100.00
Total ODC	1,150.00
Total Costs	5,650.00
Profit: 15%	847.50
Total Price	**$6,497.50**

(*Source:* Holtz & Zahn 2004, 227.)

Figure 5
Estimating Overhead

overhead before submitting a government proposal that requires this method. An example of how to calculate your overhead rate can be found in Higgins (2010, 7-10). Note that, according to Holtz and Zahn (2004, 227-228), a new consultant may need to start with a provisional overhead rate until financials for a full year are available. Using a conservative rate of 50% means that your fee for the project would be 50% above and beyond your salary. Profit is then added to that dollar amount. A more typical overhead rate may be 75%. Keep in mind that this type of government work is often a commodity project, so if your overhead is too high, you might not be in the best position to compete. See an example of proposed costs using the overhead method in Figure 5.

Method 3: Fixed Price

This is a common method for OH&S training or consulting when there are multiple OH&S consultants who can provide a type of service or when an organization has a policy that requires bids for work above certain dollar values. The key for fixed price work is to have a clear idea of the tasks and the time involved. The client organization may be focused on containing costs, or they may just be looking for a creative approach within a reasonable cost range or budget. Either way, be sure you know what you are pricing, the extent, the time frame and the locations. An example would be an audit. Consider each of the following potential scenarios when developing a fixed price bid for audits. The physical audit may be in one building or an entire campus. The documentation may exist at another location. The client contacts or individuals who must be interviewed could be at a third location, or multiple audits may be in several different geographic areas, requiring significant travel time. The final audit report could be simple or complex. Without careful attention to detail, it is very easy to price a project too low and lose money in the process. Don't forget the scope creep that I mentioned earlier. Be sure that your quote addresses how additional work will be approved before it is completed. Otherwise, you may not be able to recoup the cost of work later added by the client.

> *The key for fixed price work is to have a clear idea of the tasks and the time involved.*

A word about responding to a request for proposal (RFP): Before responding to an RFP, be sure to consider your chance of success, and determine if the benefit outweighs the cost (i.e., time). Many OH&S consultants routinely bid on consulting work. It may be a great way to get exposure to a potential client company and develop long-term work, but it does require effort, and may take considerable non-billable time for a new consultant who has limited experience pricing work. Organizations have different reasons for offering RFPs. Sometimes the preferred bidder is already chosen, and the additional bids are used to validate the choice. Sometimes organizations are not sure of the cost of the work and want to determine the budget needed for future work.

In my business, I only occasionally respond to RFPs. One day, I had a call from a corporate environmental manager in New England with whom I worked when she worked for another client firm. She asked if my firm was going to bid. I told her that my rates were typically too high to win a bid on price, and that our focus was on creative approaches and high-quality work: 50% on overall approach, 25% on creativity, and 25% on price. She asked me to consider responding, and I decided to do so. This bid required onsite presentations from each consulting firm, and interviews with the group of decision makers. We were up against several well-known national firms. And yes, we won the bid! This resulted in six months of project work for one of my staff, and three years of additional work after that first project. In this case, the benefit definitely outweighed the cost.

Method 4: Retainer

If a client would like to reserve your time on an ongoing basis, a retainer may be the best method to use. This means that the client pays for a specific number of consulting hours per year (Kaye 1997, 196). Some experienced OH&S consultants have retainers that also detail the tasks to be completed within a time frame, such as a year, but this approach is more complex and requires the consultant to have a clear understanding of the time needed for each task.

Retainers are often paid on a monthly basis and are usually to the advantage of the consultant. This work provides regular income and allows scheduling of other projects in between. For example, I had several retainers for many years. This allowed my clients to have quick response time and priority if they had an urgent matter that needed risk communication, a serious safety issue that needed investigation, or evaluation of an employee indoor air quality or chemical exposure concern. My clients saw the value and, most of the time, they didn't use all the hours committed to the retainer.

Payment for a retainer can be set up a variety of ways. It can be paid monthly, quarterly, or annually in advance. Some clients may need a routine invoice for a retainer to satisfy internal accounting requirements. It is a good idea to spell out what kind of work is considered to be outside of the retainer; that way, if the client requests work that is excluded from the retainer, you would need to submit a separate proposal, and the client would need to pay a separate fee for that work.

> *Although most consultants reduce the regular hourly rate for a retainer. . . . I usually start at a ten-percent reduction.*

What rate do you use for a retainer? This will depend on the hours per month or year allotted to the client. Although most consultants reduce the regular hourly rate for a retainer, there are no set guidelines for how much to discount the retainer rate. I usually start at a ten-percent reduction. Other consultants reduce their rates by up to 20 or 25%. If you have a regular rate of $220 per hour, for a year-long retainer of four hours a month, the retainer rate per hour may be $200 an hour, or $800 per month. For additional hours, you might reduce the rate to $175 or to $150 per hour, depending on your starting rate and the type of work the client wants. Retainers can also be used for clients who want to hire safety, loss control, environmental, or industrial hygiene services on a monthly basis. The client would have your availably locked in for a maximum number of hours per month. In that case, be sure the type of services offered and the arrangement is clear, so that you can book other consulting work around it.

Method 5: Value-based

Alan Weiss has been writing and speaking about value-based fees for a number of years. (You can read more about Alan Weiss and his ideas around consulting and creating value for the client in Chapter 6, "Marketing and Sales," Chapter 7, "Networking," and Chapter 8, "Client Retention."). He defines value as "the degree of improvement to the client represented by the achievement of the objectives. These may be quantitative (2 percent increase in sales) or qualitative (there will be much less stress for me)" (Weiss 2009a, 294). Other consultants use different terms, such as "solution-based fees" (Coutu 2013, 1). The concept involves selling the client on the results of your work, as opposed to the inputs such as time and methodology. The client therefore is making an upfront investment in the outcome, not paying after the fact for specific tasks or number of hours of work. In this case, you would still need to build a relationship with the client to determine their needs and objectives, but in the value-based approach, the measures might not be completion of a training program, but what the participants will do with the information after the session. This adds value for the client instead of just providing a piece of paper that states that the individual has been trained. The approach allows for a single fee, or a fee plus expenses. My personal caveat for new OH&S solo consultants is that it is still necessary to learn how much time tasks will take you and get an idea of the market rates. This is the only way I know of to understand the difference between the cost of the services and the highest price the market will bear.

Value-based consulting is typically used for more complex consulting assignments....

To further illustrate value, I'll relate a conversation that I had with a client and professional colleague, whom I will call Jack. Jack has a doctorate and is an experienced hydrogeologist and environmental consultant. He uses a different value-based approach. If a task would take a mid-level consultant 16 hours to complete but, due to his expertise, the task would take Jack two hours to complete, then his fee is the equivalent of 16 hours. Keep in mind, Jack is not billing for 16 hours, but for the value provided to the client. That means that, although his regular hourly rate is $500 per hour, he is not billing his time. In this example, the fee based on his time (even with a high rate) would only result in $1000. By using a value-based fee, Jack's value would result in a fee of $3200. As a highly sought-after consultant, Jack knows that the client wants his expertise and is willing to pay for it. This means that the focus of the initial conversation with the client is based on the client's needs, and how Jack can meet those needs, not on price. That doesn't mean that the fee is not addressed. It is addressed either at the end of the conversation or provided in the proposal. The client agrees to the fee, rather than the number of hours involved in completing the project. As I mentioned earlier in the training example, line items often just allow the client to focus on reducing the price. If the price needs to be reduced, then the work (or in this case, the value) should be reduced. Your goal should not be to work for free unless you are doing so deliberately to market new services or to consciously volunteer for a non-profit organization.

Value-based consulting is typically used for more complex consulting assignments, not for volume-driven commodity training or inspections where the client's objective is to document regulatory compliance, as opposed to behavior change or problem solving. The client in value-based consulting is buying a solution from a consultant with a proven track record and a high level of expertise. The client, in this case, is not focused on the path or tasks, but on the outcome. New consultants will need experience to determine the number of hours needed to develop the solution and would likely either aim too low for the given amount of work, or aim above what the client will pay (i.e., market price). In the OH&S field, this value-based consulting may be appropriate for some types of audits, major risk reduction, implementation of safety or environmental management systems, safety culture change, OH&S organization designs, recruiting OH&S professionals, or sustainability projects. If you are interested in the value-based method, other books by Alan Weiss that include the topic are *Value-Based Fees: How to Charge—and Get—What You're Worth* (2008) or *Million Dollar Consulting* (2009b). As noted previously, Chapters 6, 7, and 8 also include concepts by Alan Weiss.

Method 6: Contingency

The idea behind a contingency fee in consulting is that you could reap large rewards if you take a risk and assist the client in meeting a set goal. An all-contingency fee in OH&S consulting is probably not the best pricing method. I remember some years ago, a consulting firm was offering to reduce workers' compensation premiums for a fee equal to 10% of the client's savings. All of us in the OH&S field likely know this only works in the consultant's favor when the client organization starts with virtually no systems in place to control workers' compensation costs. If a best-practice client wants to reduce workers' compensation premiums, it will take a long time, and other factors may interfere with reaching the goal in the allotted time frame. In addition, the client may not fully implement the recommendations of the consultant. In addition, other factors, such as changes to the method to calculate the Experience Modification Rates or state workers' compensation laws, may reduce savings or even increase costs. The consulting firm in this example dropped this offering later on because it turned out not to be profitable. There are situations where a base fee plus contingency might be appropriate for OH&S consultants. In this case, extra effort or expertise might be suitably rewarded by taking such risk.

Determining Project Length and Time

One of the most difficult consulting tasks to conquer is determining how long it will take to complete a project. This was the case for my employees even when I provided the structure. For a new consultant, understand that you will have a learning curve to overcome. First, the work will take longer than you think

> *In general, plan on twice the preparation time for each hour of training, assuming you know the topic and are not learning the basics as you go.*

until you have a repeatable process in place; and second, you will need some time to develop templates or modules that will speed up the work and create efficiencies later on. Even spelling out the work to be done or the value to the client in the proposal will take more non-billable time in the beginning. It does get better, but taking the time to develop repeatable processes when you have time, early in the business life, will pay dividends later.

So what do I mean? Let's take training, for example. If you have expertise in a particular area such as fall protection, you might spend significant time for the first client in developing a manual, scenarios, and training exercises. These could be modified for other clients in the future. Since you might have more available time when you are just starting out, the research and development time can be longer. All your time may not be billable for the first client. But now you have the tools to provide high-quality services, with much less preparation time, for the next client. In general, plan on twice the preparation time for each hour of training, assuming you know the topic and are not learning the basics as you go. Even for commodity training, training that you will perform over and over, if your fee is based only on instruction time, you will lose money. Some portion of preparation time should always be included in the price. It is up to you whether you want to price preparation and delivery separately. I found that a single fee that included both worked best for me.

For other types of OS&H consulting, consider all the variables that might occur. If you are writing policy and procedure manuals or web content, include time for someone else to proof the documents or format them. For audits, include enough time to not only tour the facilities but to review all the appropriate documents and interview employees and management. For both of the above, if there are any topics or unusual types of work or equipment, be sure to include time to research the issues and/or provide reference material. You can spend a lot of unbillable time on research if you don't include research time in the project costs. For reports, assume that the writing will take 1.5 times as long as you think it will and build in time to produce a draft for the client to review before a final version. This doesn't mean the client writes your conclusions. It just means that most clients will review a document to be sure the terminology used is appropriate to the culture of the organization and that they understand the recommendations. Reserve the right to invoice the client at the draft stage if they want more than a week to review the draft. Build in time to finalize the report as well. Above all, as each project is completed, keep track of the time each task takes and document it. I know that this is not what most of us like to do. But, trust me, you will get better at projecting time once you have done several similar projects, and can determine whether or not the last one was profitable. This is one of those areas where practice makes perfect.

Subcontracting Fees

You can either have other consultants subcontract to you or you can subcontract to someone else. (A broader discussion on using consultants as part of your business plan is addressed in Chapter 2.) I'll start with the latter. If you are asked to subcontract or collaborate with another firm that has acquired the work, you will need to consider the circumstances and the long-term consequences. Subcontracting may be a short-term strategy for a new consultant, or it may be a long-term strategy for a consultant who isn't interested in acquiring the work or marketing his or her firm. From a financial perspective, this type of arrangement is a partnership that requires fairness for all involved. Look at the transaction as having three components: the first is the acquisition of the work, the second is the methodology, and the third is the execution (Weiss 2009b, 180 et al.). The firm that acquired the work would usually be paid a portion for getting the work, and may also have developed the methodology. If that is the case, then your role is to execute the work. If, for example, the hourly rate to the client is $300 per hour, the other firm would receive $200 per hour, and you would receive $100 per hour.

This example assumes that the other firm is hiring you for "boots on the ground" and not for the purpose of developing the work methodology. If you perform the second and third portions of the transaction, then you might receive $200 per hour, and the other firm may receive $100 per hour. If the other firm has most of the expertise but it needs you for a special component that it doesn't have, then it may be appropriate for you to offer to participate at a higher rate. After all, they will still be able to mark up your fee, and they will make their profit primarily on the bigger portion of the project. All of this is negotiable.

There are some OS&H firms where the expertise is to acquire work for a variety of consultants, and then charge those consultants a fee. This could be a percentage of the total cost of the work or a flat fee. Regardless of the fee structure, be sure to have clear expectations of your role. The firm acquiring the work (unless otherwise specified in writing) owns the relationship with the client company. If you are asked to provide consulting to the client directly, the ethical approach would be to refer the client back to the other consulting firm contact that owns the relationship. If the client company is one for whom you wish to provide direct consulting work in the future, then subcontracting may not be appropriate, unless the limits of the relationship are clarified up front. See Chapter 9 for more information on consulting ethics and on subcontracting.

If you or your consulting firm is going to hire subcontractors, then determine if this will be your business model or an occasional strategy to win larger projects that require more "boots on the ground." For example, audit projects at multiple sites or safety culture interviews may require more staff than you have. If that is the case, you may be able to develop a network of qualified consultants with the skills you need to perform these tasks. This consulting work would then be acquired by your firm, and the methodology set by you as well. The subcontractor rate can be negotiated, as mentioned above. The arrangement has to be equitable for all if it's going to work in the long term. If both sides have done their homework, are clear on their overhead costs, and base consulting rate needed, the client will receive good quality work at a fair price.

If you are going to provide a rider on your professional liability insurance for subcontractors or provide space, equipment, or travel costs to them, these costs will need to be factored into the fees you are charged by the subcontractor. These represent costs to you, and a benefit to the subcontractor. Your alternative is to have the subcontractors maintain their own professional liability insurance (with verification to you), as well as to provide the other resources they need. And yes, the subcontractor will need to submit invoices to you. In addition to the Internal Revenue Service (IRS) rules for determining whether a person is an employee or contractor, some states have laws or workers' compensation requirements for potential contractors. See the Chapter 4, "Insurance Needs" and Chapter 5, "Legal and Regulatory Issues," for more information on this topic.

Travel Expenses and Other Fees

Your approach to travel expenses and other fees should be outlined in the terms and conditions as shown in the rate schedule examples in Figure 1 and 2 on page 87. Some consultants pass through expenses to clients with no additional charge. Others add on a handling fee of five, ten or fifteen percent. In OS&H consulting, mostly I have seen no additional charge for these expenses. Keep in mind, if you need to use a credit card to charge airfare or other large expenses well ahead of when you will be paid, you will have carrying costs that you may need to recoup with a handling fee. As an alternative, some consultants invoice expenses when occurred, such as at the time a flight is booked. Examples of travel expenses would be coach airfare, hotel, meals, tips, ground transportation (or mileage at the current IRS rate), and parking fees. Sometimes, additional fees are spelled out such as expedited shipping charges (e.g., FedEx). Other times, office expenses, such as copying, printing, or telephone services, are specifically noted as overhead, and not charged separately. Whatever approach you decide to use, it should be clear to the client what is included, and what is not.

Depending on the project, travel costs may be estimated or a range provided. If the actual geographic sites have not yet been determined, an estimated travel cost may be offered, based on an average for a certain number of plant sites. For example, $1000 per location × 10 locations = an estimate of $10,000 for travel. This will work if you are flying short distances from a major metropolitan area or driving, but for many of us airfare costs are quite variable. Hotel and other fixed costs may be easier to estimate. Be sure to organize all travel expenses before invoicing the client. These should be itemized on the invoice in categories but, in most cases, the actual receipts should be retained by you and properly stored. They may be needed should an IRS audit occur at a later date.

> *The typical approach in both engineering and OS&H consulting is to invoice travel time . . . at half the billable rate or half the time at the full rate.*

Travel time is an important component in consulting. Depending on the extent of the client locations and type of work, a significant amount of time may be spent traveling by plane, train, or automobile. The typical approach in both engineering and OS&H consulting is to invoice travel time dedicated to a single client at half the billable rate or half the time at the full rate. For example, if your billing rate is $200 per hour, the travel time will be $100 per hour. So what hours do you bill? I would include the time driving to the airport, the time in the air and between flights, and the time to the plant or hotel. I often have a full day of eight or ten hours of just travel time on each end of a project. For car travel, some consultants charge travel time outside of their metropolitan area; others charge only mileage. I charge both travel time and mileage outside of my metropolitan area.

What if some plane or train time allows you to perform work for another client? Ethically, the time is split accordingly, not double-billed. Another version of this scenario is if you have two clients in a single geographic area. Trips to them may be combined; this way, each client only pays for half the travel time and expenses. Typically, no documentation is provided to the client other than the total number of travel hours, and costs itemized on the invoice. Being honest with a client can foster a long-term business relationship that, in my experience, can translate into a loyal, long-term client.

Billable Time and Revenue Mix

As discussed previously when determining billing rate, billable time is the number of hours billed vs. the number worked. To calculate billable hours, just divide

> **REVENUE EXERCISE**
>
> **Part I**
>
> | Sources of Revenue: | | Dollars | Hours |
> |---|---|---|---|
> | Consultation: 500 hours × $100 .... | = | _____ | 500 |
> | Training: 10 sessions @ $5,000 (20 people @ $250 each)....................... | = | _____ | 265 |
> | Reports: 10 @ $150 .... | = | _____ | 10 |
> | Retainer Agreements: 2 @ $12,000 .... | = | _____ | 300 |
> | Educational Seminars: 6 @ $1,000 .... | = | _____ | 80 |
> | | Totals | _____ | 1,155 |
>
> **Part II**
>
> **Billable Time**
>
> a) 2000 hours × 60% = _____ available hours.
>
> b) _____ available hours × $100.00 per hour = _____ total billable revenue.
>
> **Part III**
>
> Which method produces more revenue; having a revenue mix or billing time?

Figure 6
Boosting Revenue

the number of hours billed by the number of hours worked. This number will vary, depending on the total workload of the individual. For example: If you work forty hours, and twenty of those hours are billable, then you are 50% billable. Some portion of your work week will be devoted to administrative work, such as bookkeeping, marketing, and other tasks related to running the business. Efficiencies in these areas can improve the bottom line. A solo consultant will usually be between 50 and 65% billable, depending on efficiencies and experience.

Since consulting time billed is limited by the number of staff and hours worked, then one way for OS&H consultants to increase their income is to broaden the revenue stream. This can be accomplished by providing different combinations of services to increase the total revenue produced. Figure 6 is a simple example of a revenue mix that goes beyond selling time. Complete the exercise to see the difference.

Initial Business Funding

How much money does it take to start an OS&H consulting business? Many variables determine this, such as the type of business. As discussed in Chapter 2,

"Creating a Business Plan," and Chapter 5, "Legal and Regulatory Issues," some consultants remain solo and work out of their homes. Others have outside offices with employees. Some might need to purchase equipment or lease classroom space, and others just need a phone and a computer. In addition to the cost of office equipment and travel expenses, one expert suggests $10,000 to $20,000 for each of the first two years and $10,000 in the third year (Tuller 1999, 17). (In today's dollars, the necessary amounts may be higher, depending on the type of consulting and your marketing plan.) These funds are intended to pay for marketing and operating expenses during the time that income is limited. This assumes that you have business and are bringing in revenue sufficient to cover your basic income during this time, or that you have alternate sources of income to support yourself. Another option is to secure a line of credit that can be used to cover business expenses until cash flow stabilizes. More information on a business line of credit can be found later in this chapter on page 115. Figure 7 shows an example of the income potentially produced in six-month increments for the first three years.

In this example, I used a rate of $200 per hour for the calculations. Note that, as billable time increased, less marketing was accomplished. The subsequent six-month period has less total income. This is part of the learning curve in the first three years of business, often considered the make or break time frame of any business. As an OS&H consultant, you need to learn how to efficiently add clients for the future while performing billable work. The point of this example is to show you that the revenue stream is not typically linear,

SOLO CONSULTANT
Projecting Income in the First Three Years

TIME PERIOD	AVAILABLE HOURS	MARKETING HOURS	ADMIN HOURS	BILLABLE HOURS	TOTAL INCOME
1st six months	968	726	242	0	0
1st year	968	726	146	96	$19,200
3rd six months	968	484	242	242	$48,400
2nd year	968	630	193	145	$29,000
5th six months	968	388	96	484	$96,800
3rd year	968	340	96	532	$106,4000

(*Source:* Adapted from Tuller 1999, 15–16.)

Figure 7
Projected Income

especially in the first few years. Putting in the time needed for marketing and maintaining cash flow are critical knowledge for any consultant.

ACCOUNTING

According to the American Institute of CPAs:

> Accounting is often called the "language of business" because it deals with interpreting and communicating information about a company's operations and finances. Accounting is extremely important to any company because the financial information, as interpreted by CPAs [certified public accountants], allows executives to make informed business decisions-decisions that help those companies become more successful.... Everyone works with and uses accounting ideas, whether they're managing a business, investing money, or just deciding how to spend their paycheck. In business, accounting links the past with the future. It provides decision-makers information about recent financial activity, as well as information and recommendations useful for forecasting future events (AICPA 2013, 1).

If you are going to run an OS&H consulting business, there are some basic accounting functions that have to be accomplished, whether you have the skills and experience or not. Understanding financials and hiring the right assistance are key, even if you have no intention of doing the bookkeeping yourself. Hiring a qualified accountant to set up your books is a good idea. Just like we have designations such as CSP and CIH, and not all safety professionals or industrial hygienists are certified, the accounting field has the designation of CPA, and not all accountants are CPAs. Ask your trusted friends or small business colleagues whom they use for an accountant. Many CPAs cater to small businesses and can help you set up accounting software, assist in setting up financial recordkeeping, or determine the tax consequences of legal entity options. A CPA may also prepare financial statements, estimate taxes due, prepare and file tax returns, and provide general business financial advice.

Even if you hire a CPA to set up your financial system and a bookkeeper to do your routine bookkeeping, I would strongly recommend that you take the time to learn the basic concepts of accounting and how to read profit and loss statements and balance sheets. For those of you who just want to read a book on the topic, there are plenty available if you do a Google search. I recommend a book by Rhonda Abrams, *Six-Week Start-Up: A Step-by-Step Program for Start-*

ing your Business, Making Money, and Achieving Your Goals (2013, 202–221). Abrams is easy to read, and has a number of other books that I have found helpful. Why should you bother to learn more about financials when you can hire the expertise? Let me tell you a story.

An OS&H colleague of mine, whom I will call Tom, asked me for help with his ten-year-old business. This was a very successful firm with employees and an office that they owned, in a large metropolitan area. Tom had a business partner who ran the business side, and he, as the credentialed OS&H professional, was the president of the firm and did business development. When the economy started to falter, so did the business. Tom realized that with the drop in revenue he had to do something, but he had no idea what to do! It turns out that he didn't know how to read financial statements and had not been paying attention to which lines of business were profitable and which were not. For ten years the business grew, and the cash was always there.

So what did he do? We sat down, and I taught him how to read his own profit and loss statement, balance sheet, and cash flow analysis. By asking him questions about the day-to-day operations, it became clear that he didn't have enough work for all of the employees, and that expenses were out of control. Tom committed to cutting expenses (including his own salary) for the next three months and doubling his personal marketing efforts. After that, he would reevaluate the number of employees, and determine if any layoffs were needed. Like any of us, he didn't want to start with layoffs. And in this case, there were other options. But keep in mind, if you start a business and decide to hire employees, this will always be a risk.

How do you read financial statements? Your accountant can help with this if you don't have experience, or you can read a basic financial statements book, but here are the basics. The income statement represents a flow of funds through the company during the reporting period. That period would be indicated as January 1–December 31, 2013, or "fiscal year 2013." This report, also referred to as an earnings statement or statement of profit and loss (P&L), answers the question of how much the company made for that period. Figure 8 shows a sample P & L for an OS&H firm. Note that the income of $76,180.00 at the top of the P & L (fourth line under income) can be compared to expenses grouped for open enrollment training of $25,567.51 (on the next page under expenses). Whatever the work is that you provide, be sure that you set up your software to capture the specific income and expenses so you know what work is profitable and what is not. Note that this P & L statement example is on an accrual basis, meaning the income is recorded when billed, and expenses are recorded when they are incurred, not when the cash goes in or out. A business

SAMPLE PROFIT & LOSS STATEMENT

Jan–Dec 2013

Ordinary Income/Expense
  Income

Consulting Income	$114,911.90
Honorariums	826.36
Training Income-Custom	114,650.78
Training Income-Open Enrollment	76,180.00
Total Income	306,569.04
Expense	
Advertising	9,114.23
Automobile Expense	1,535.72
Bank Service Charges	37.03
Cleaning & Maintenance	723.50
Client Gifts	216.70
Computer Services & Supplies	2,643.93
Conference & Education	1,719.55
Contributions	725.00
Copier	
Maintenance	2,700.00
Total Copier	2,700.00
Depreciation Expense	4,584.00
Dues and Subscriptions	1,595.00
Equipment Delivery	0.00
Equipment Installation	75.00
Equipment Rental	358.00
Insurance	
Health	4,989.60
Life	287.50
Business owners	331.00
Disability Insurance	733.80
Liability Insurance	6,985.00
Work Comp	512.00
Total Insurance	13,838.90
Interest Expense	1,724.73
Miscellaneous	
Recruitment Exp.	196.31
Total Miscellaneous	196.31
Office Expense	819.22
Office Supplies	5,596.55
Outside Services	12,439.11

Figure 8
Profits and Losses

SAMPLE PROFIT & LOSS STATEMENT (cont.)

	Jan–Dec 2013
Payroll Expenses	
Taxes SUTA	1,334.03
Taxes-FICA	10,461.37
Taxes-FUTA	169.40
Wages	136,749.96
Total Payroll Expenses	148,714.76
Pension Contribution	4,097.25
Postage and Delivery	3,076.51
Printing and Reproduction	269.94
Professional Fees	830.00
Publication & Books	1,026.62
Refund	360.00
Rent	
Storage	−424.33
Rent - Other	14,054.62
Total Rent	13,630.29
Repairs	
Equipment Repairs	
Multi-gas meter	291.40
Total Equipment Repairs	291.40
Total Repairs	291.40
Storage Equipment	0.00
Taxes	
Property	175.83
State	206.55
Total Taxes	382.38
Telephone	6,689.42
Open Enrollment Training	
Meals	619.58
Refund	1,650.00
Books & Manuals	9,000.76
Caterer	10,433.19
Change	20.00
Facility	2,130.00
Instructors	755.00
Supplies	958.98
Total Open Enrollment Training	25,567.51

Figure 8
Profits and Losses

SAMPLE PROFIT & LOSS STATEMENT (cont.)	
	Jan–Dec 2013
Custom Training	
Meals	405.94
Travel	12,008.73
Total Custom Training	12,414.67
Travel Expenses	
Meals	385.93
Travel Expenses - Other	403.36
Total Travel Expenses	789.29
Utilities	
Gas and Electric	380.13
Utilities - Other	242.70
Total Utilities	622.83
Total Expense	279,405.35
Net Ordinary Income	27,163.69
Other Income/Expense	
Other Income	
Interest Income	407.42
Other Income	360.30
Total Other Income	767.72
Net Other Income	767.72
Net Income	**$27,931.41**

Figure 8
Profits and Losses

has a choice of using either the cash or accrual method for recording income and expenses.

So why do you need a profit and loss statement? It's a way to monitor how your consulting business is doing financially, usually on a monthly or quarterly basis. It also tells you, as I mentioned previously, whether or not a specific project or line of consulting work is profitable. This information allows you to adjust your pricing, business services or reduce expenses to keep the business profitable. Another reason to prepare a P&L is that it is required by the IRS, in order to determine your profit that is taxable.

The balance sheet is a snapshot of the company on any given day, usually the last day of the reporting period. For this reason, the balance sheet will show the date it was compiled, such as December 31, 2013. The left side (or top) of the balance sheet lists the assets, or what the company owns. On the right side (or bottom) are the liabilities, or what the company owes, and the shareholders' equity, or the funds contributed by the stockholders. The two sides must balance, so the balance sheet can be summarized as assets equal liabilities plus shareholders' equity (A = L + E). See Figure 9 for a sample balance sheet.

So why do you need to prepare a balance sheet? Like the profit and loss statement, the balance sheet is another tool to evaluate your business. It really tells you how healthy the business is at a given point in time; in other words, it shows what the business owns verses what it owes.

SAMPLE BALANCE SHEET

Dec 31, 2013

Current Assets	
Checking/Savings	
Checking-My Bank	$4,576.29
Checking-My Bank	
SBA Loan	3,079.65
Checking-My Bank - Other	−3,079.65
Total Checking-My Bank	0.00
Savings-My Bank & Trust	21,261.82
Total Checking/Savings	25,838.11
Accounts Receivable	
Accounts Receivable	32,001.05
Total Accounts Receivable	32,001.05
Total Current Assets	57,839.16
Fixed Assets	
Furniture and Equipment	95,888.52
Software	
Accum. Amort-Software	−583.00
Software - Other	583.00
Total Software	0.00
Accum. Depreciation	−82,497.00
Vehicles	
Accum. Dep'n-vehicle	−14,460.00
Vehicles - Other	26,844.90
Total Vehicles	12,384.90
Total Fixed Assets	25,776.42

Figure 9
The Balance Sheet

SAMPLE BALANCE SHEET (cont.)

Dec 31, 2013

Other Assets	
Organization Costs	
Accum. Amort.	−900.87
Organization Costs - Other	900.87
Total Organization Costs	0.00
Total Other Assets	0.00
TOTAL ASSETS	**$83,615.58**
LIABILITIES & EQUITY	
Liabilities	
Current Liabilities	
Accounts Payable	
Accounts Payable	6,378.20
Total Accounts Payable	6,378.20
Other Current Liabilities	
Accrued FICA/Medicare	1,653.02
Accrued FUTA	4.97
Accrued SUTA	11.03
Federal Withholding Payable	2,892.75
FICA withholding payable	1,339.70
Medicare W/H	313.32
Prepayments	10,990.91
State withholding payable	2,814.00
Total Other Current Liabilities	20,019.70
Total Current Liabilities	26,397.90
Long Term Liabilities	
Loan Payable #3	6,017.73
SBA Loan	6,384.78
Total Long Term Liabilities	12,402.51
Total Liabilities	38,800.41
Equity	
Capital Stock	11,570.44
Retained Earnings	5,313.32
Net Income	27,931.41
Total Equity	44,815.17
TOTAL LIABILITIES & EQUITY	**$83,615.58**

Figure 9
The Balance Sheet

A Word About Taxes

Note that the P & L sample in Figure 8 is for an OS&H consulting firm that is a Subchapter S corporation under U.S. IRS rules. As mentioned in Chapter 5, "Legal and Regulatory Issues," this means that the tax liability flows through to the owner. In the Figure 8 example, the P & L shows only a small amount of tax paid, property tax and state tax on purchases. The remaining net income (otherwise known as profit) of $27,931.41 will flow through to the owner's personal tax return, in addition to whatever salary is earned. That total amount will then be taxed accordingly at the end of the year. That doesn't mean that income tax is just paid the next year on April 15. Depending on your income level, income taxes may need to be paid monthly or quarterly to the IRS. Your accountant can determine the frequency of payments needed, help you to set up electronic payments, and prepare your tax returns.

Many new small business owners are unaware that their former employers paid a number of taxes on their behalf, such as unemployment, Medicare or Social Security tax. Unemployment is governed by each state, and the tax rates vary widely. Your state's department of labor will usually be able to provide information on unemployment insurance taxes and rates. The Social Security and Medicare taxes are federal, and actually have two parts. The employee pays half, up to a certain income limit, and the employer pays the other half. When you are self-employed, you will end up paying both halves of the tax, often called the self-employment tax. The rates vary, based on the whims of Congress. For 2014, employees pay 6.2 percent on income under $117,000 for the Social Security tax, and 1.45 percent of all income for Medicare. Employers pay a Social Security tax rate of 6.2 percent. The Medicare tax rate is 1.45 percent. If you are self-employed, the Social Security tax rate is 12.4 percent on income under $117,000 through the end of 2014. The Medicare tax rate is 2.9 percent on all income (SSA 2014, 1). These payroll taxes are in addition to the tax on your salary (income tax) and tax on the business profits.

Invoicing

For you to receive payment for services rendered, you will probably have to send an invoice to your clients. If you provided the client with a proposal, and you are using an accounting software program, this is relatively easy. It does, however, take time and it is one of those administrative tasks that will impact your billable time. This is an area that you may want to turn over to a bookkeeper when you can afford to do so, but most of us do the work ourselves at the beginning. Your

Timing of invoices should be addressed with the client before the work begins.

accountant can help to set up your invoice format, and advise you on various invoice methods.

The invoice method will depend on the pricing method for the work. For example, if the work is based on time and materials, the invoice might show the total number of hours for the project with the price per hour. If you have different rates for the different personnel working on a project, then group the hours worked for each professional. Expenses would then be listed separately in groups. A total project cost would be shown at the bottom. Depending on the terms you established with your clients, the invoice might note that payment is due in 10, 14 or 30 days. Some consultants provide a discount of 2% to 5% if fees are paid by a certain date or upon receipt of the work product. This may be to your advantage for large projects where you have subcontractors, lab fees or rental equipment to pay for promptly. In that case, receiving payment quickly, even at a discount, might be less expensive than paying interest on a business line of credit.

Retainers might be billed at the beginning of the year and the terms may be monthly or quarterly payments. Regardless of the pricing method, all invoices should be straightforward and clear to avoid a client withholding payment until further detail is provided. If the client uses purchase order (PO) numbers, be sure the invoice includes the number. Even if the client doesn't require their use, POs are often advisable since you are ensured that the dollars are allocated. Otherwise, payment can be delayed until the funds are allocated. Even though the work and fees are initially agreed upon, when the invoice reaches the client's accounts payable department it's an entirely different story! Invoices can be provided to the client by hand, electronically by e-mail or sent by paper mail.

Timing of invoices should be addressed with the client before the work begins. If the project is in phases, then invoices may be sent at the end of each phase or at the completion of a deliverable. Again, be sure this is clear. Any confusion tends to hold up payments. Open enrollment courses are usually paid prior to the course in order to secure a space for the participant, similar to registration for a national professional development conference. This has the advantage of providing cash flow to cover the class expenses and to pay trainers who might be subcontractors or employees. Be sure to establish and post on your website and materials a clear cancellation and substitution policy. I always allowed substitutions but cancellations required at least 48 hours' notice or the fee was forfeited.

. . . a better way to think of collections is as a process that continues throughout the project. . . .

When should the client pay your fees? As above, this may depend on the type of work. Although my clients typically paid for the work after it was completed, it is common now to request an upfront payment from the client prior to the commencement of work. This may be one third or one half of the total fee. In that case, the client may request a statement that shows the partial payment at the beginning or the payment might be shown, and deducted, on the final invoice.

How should the client pay your fees? Again, this will likely vary by client. Some clients will pay by paper check. This is still by far the most common payment method. Other clients may want to use ACH (Automated Clearing House) transfers. This is an electronic payment system used by both government and private businesses because it is considered cheaper and faster than processing paper checks. Your accountant or your bank can provide more information on this payment method. Finally, your client may want to pay by credit card. This may speed up acceptance of a proposal since a client can pay your upfront partial fee this way. Since most companies issue purchase cards to personnel with purchasing authority, this is also becoming common. Keep in mind, although it is fairly easy to set up the ability to receive credit card payments on a Smart Phone or tablet computer with a card reader or app these days, there are still fees associated with these services. Consider who your clients are now or will be in the future, and whether or not it makes sense to provide alternative payment options.

Collection Strategy

As a consultant, you might first think of invoicing the client when you have completed the project. But a better way to think of collections is as a process that continues throughout the project, to be sure the client is satisfied and informed, so nothing holds up the payment of your fees. This means that you are organized, know if you are meeting the project milestones on schedule and have been communicating with the client about the status of the project all along the way. If the client asks for changes to the scope of work, you are obtaining signed change orders. If the timeline needs to change due to client information not being available, then the client is informed in writing and has agreed to a new completion date. All of these components during the project will simplify the collection process and, quite honestly, help your reputation as a consultant.

In my corporate role, we had hired a qualified solo consultant to produce a training program that my staff of CSPs didn't have the time to develop. A week after the due date of the work product, my staff contact called the consultant and asked about the status. It turned out the consultant had an emergency project for another client and didn't get our work done. There was no e-mail or call from the consultant regarding the problem prior to the due date.

If you were the consultant, how would you handle the project? In this case, the consultant apologized and said he would work over the weekend to get it done. He missed the second deadline as well and said it was more work that he thought it would be! Not only did he not meet the deadline, he left money on the table since the project should have been quoted for more time. When the work was finally delivered, it was good work. But what kind of impression did this leave? How comfortable would my staff be in the future counting on this consultant if we have a tight deadline? How did I feel signing for the invoice when it arrived a month after the project was finally completed?

The fact is that everything you do in conducting the project affects not only your reputation but your ability to secure new work and your ability to receive payment. So the business side of consulting, such as properly estimating time, preparing clear proposals, sticking to the timeline, communicating changes, and invoicing accurately and promptly, will go a long way to adding to your expert OS&H skills.

Once the project is complete, it's time to invoice. The process will be based on the terms that you have previously outlined on your rate schedule and/or in your proposal. Part of your collection strategy should be to consider how quickly you will invoice clients. Keep in mind that the sooner you send the invoice, the quicker you will receive payment. And no, it doesn't make you look desperate to invoice promptly. It's just good business.

If you wait until the end of the month and do all your invoicing for work completed that month, you will not only likely forget details (if they are not written down) but you also risk waiting at least another month to get paid. If you are requesting a paper check, most companies have a certain day of the week that they process those checks. If you have a client for whom you do regular work, it is in your best interest to know what day that is. How do you find that out? Ask your contact or call the accounts payable department for the client company.

How soon after the project completion do you invoice? I suggest that you invoice once you know the client is happy with the work. For straightforward projects, check back a couple of days after work product delivery and ask if there are any questions. That is a nice opportunity to thank the client and even ask for a testimonial comment for your marketing materials or website if they are thrilled with the work. At this point you can verify to whom the invoice is going and to what e-mail or physical address. If the project has phases, just verify with the client that the phase is complete and then invoice. I found that I prepared invoices more or less weekly. This meant there was cash flow coming in on a pretty regular basis.

How do you deliver invoices? These days, it's easy to use accounting software to build a customized invoice for your business and then send invoices by e-mail. Some clients may still require a paper copy. Either way, be sure the format is clear and that the document has your business address and phone number. You can even load an electronic copy of your business logo onto the invoice so that all your materials have a cohesive brand.

Now that the client has your invoice, how long do you wait for payment? Here is where having a routine collection procedure comes in. If the client has agreed to your terms of payment, you have the right to receive payment on that schedule, within reason. So, for a solo consultant, it is not unusual to have ten or fourteen-day payment terms. You could have a policy where you wait two days after the due date and then contact the client. Your policy should specify how you contact the client, either by e-mail or phone call. My policy was to call the client contact, and ask for the status of the payment.

If you use a routine collection process, 99% of the time you should be paid within a reasonable timeframe without significant effort.

Having been on both the client side and the consultant side, I would strongly recommend that follow-up. The reason is that in larger organizations, there are lots of places in the process that an invoice can become lost or delayed. The client is often embarrassed by the red tape within their organization and will have your invoice tracked down and paid promptly. This is particularly true if you have a special skill set that the client wants to continue to tap into. They will do everything they can to make sure you are paid promptly!

That one follow up call usually results in payment within a week. But there will be some clients that will require further follow-up. The second step then should be to make another contact within a set period such as another week or two. The second contact might be an e-mail follow up with your same client contact or, if this is a regular client, you might by now have made contact with the accounts payable department. Even in a large client organization, there is usually someone assigned to a certain type of bills or a range of billers. Just call the department and ask who could provide the status of your invoice. Be prepared to offer the date of the invoice and the invoice number. At this point, the invoice may need to be resent or it may be in process. A word about offshore back office services – some larger companies are using offices that are offshore to process accounts payable and receivable. In this case, the client may require that you send electronic invoices or to be paid by ACH or credit card. It is also possible that you will only be able to communicate with the processors by e-mail, if that. In that case, your client contact may be the only option for follow-up of past due invoices.

If the first two steps don't result in payment, then consider your third step for the rare situation where you have not been paid yet. Do you give up at this point? Only you can determine if the effort is worth the fees that are due to you. At this stage, some consultants will send a new invoice with late fees added. If you choose to do this, the late fees should have been clearly stated on your terms. Another option would be to turn the work over to a collection agency. The agency will then do the follow-up and take a percentage of your fees as payment.

In my business, I always talked to the client up front about the terms and considered the size of the client organization and the complexity. For example, a Fortune 500 client, utility company or government agency may want payment terms of 45 or 60 days, but for a small consulting business, they will usually modify their policy if you ask. I had many annual sole source projects with long-term clients. Even when other consultants told me they didn't receive payment for 60 to 90 days, my firm was paid within 30 to 45 days by the same organization. The key is to create the expectation and do the follow-up.

Non-routine Collection and Write-offs

If you use a routine collection process, 99% of the time you should be paid within a reasonable timeframe without significant effort. The process may not be what you enjoy doing but it will be worthwhile in the end. There are some circumstances that may be out of your control. Examples would be if the client went through a sudden bankruptcy, financial collapse or if a catastrophic event (unrelated to your project or even geographic area) caused the company to close. In these cases, it is always possible that you will have outstanding invoices and become an unsecured creditor.

In the case of bankruptcy, you should receive an official notice of the client bankruptcy. The notice will have instructions on how to proceed to be considered for some portion of payment. Although it is possible to receive some payment, it may be a long shot and take a year or more. This may be when you decide to write off the debt for non-payment. Your accountant can help with this type of adjustment to your financial records.

In the more than twenty years that I have been in business, most of my clients have paid within a reasonable period of time, and required zero, or occasionally one follow-up. Some did require two, and a handful required more. One client was a well-known technology company. I did work for one of their local plants. I used my collection process and started sending invoices with interest, 30 days after the invoice was due. I then called the client contact and later the accounts payable department on a monthly basis. After five months I received a check for the original amount due. No interest was included. I decided to call that good.

About six months later, I received a bankruptcy notice for the company. That explained the protracted payment. I have received bankruptcy notices for eight or ten client companies over the years, all of which were well-known national firms. In each case, we had completed work for the company shortly before the bankruptcy was declared, but had already been paid. I've been very fortunate not to write off any bad debt in all this time. I strongly believe that having a collection system and sticking to it really does make a difference. At the beginning, you may have to do the collections yourself. As the business grows, you could have an administrative person or contract bookkeeper handle these tasks. In my case, because I established the collection process and did it myself, it was much easier to train someone else to do it later on and to make sure my customer service expectations were met. If you hire someone to establish the process for you, it is in your best interests to know how and what will be done.

Considering Credit

Even if you have a good collection process, it is always possible that the amount or timing of payments will not be sufficient to pay all the bills at some point. Assuming you are not lavishly spending money the business doesn't have in the receivables pipeline, this is where obtaining credit might come in handy. Credit may be obtained from your suppliers. For example, you can request payment terms of 30 days by completing a credit application for vendors that you use. Or, you can use a business credit card which will allow you move the payment due timeframe out by at least three weeks. As long as you can pay off the full payment due each month, this may be all you need. Otherwise, just like with personal credit cards, the interest and fees will quickly dwarf the principal and make it harder to pay off.

Another business option if you have good personal credit is to establish a business line of credit. This can be done through a bank with which you have a relationship early in the life of your business. It is a good way to prove you are a good credit risk in the future when you might need funds to expand your business. The business line of credit allows you to borrow money when you need it to pay bills and then only pay interest on what you used, not the total amount available. For example, if you have a $10,000 line of credit and need to pay $2,000 of bills from the account, you would only pay interest on the $2,000 used that month. This assumes you have accounts receivable sufficient to cover this amount or more. Most banks will require you to clear the line (i.e., pay it off completely) at least once, for 30 days a year. Over time, as you show appropriate use of a line, it is possible to negotiate higher amounts or lower interest rates and to either have no clearance requirement or to only clear once every three years.

CONCLUSION

If you have positive answers to these questions at the beginning of the chapter, and those posed by in other chapters up to this point, then welcome to the business side of consulting. You now should have the tools to start a business and an idea of some of the financial pitfalls that you can avoid along the way. Consulting involves not only providing your OS&H expertise to clients but doing so in an organized way that results in a satisfying career and the requisite financial rewards.

Now you have a basic understanding of how to set up your consulting practice to be profitable by making sure that you are charging enough for your services. You also have several rate-setting models that will help you to read and understand some basics financial statements. You also have to know how to protect the assets you are working so hard to build. One of the many ways consultants do so is by transferring the risk through insurance. In the next chapter, you will discover the various types of business insurance that are essential to obtain to manage your risk. You can look at your practice to identify what can go wrong and protect yourself by having effective insurance policies.

BIBLIOGRAPHY

Abrams, Rhonda. 2013. *Six-Week Start-Up: A Step-By-Step Program for Starting Your Business, Making Money, and Achieving Your Goals*. 3rd ed. Palo Alto, CA: The Planning Shop.

American Institute of Certified Public Accountants. 2013. *What is a CPA?* http://www.aicpa.org/becomeacpa/gettingstarted/frequentlyasked questions/pages/default.aspx#What_is_a_CPA

Association of Consulting Engineering Companies (ACEC). 2013. *Fee guidelines*. http://www.acec-nb.ca/en/resources/guideline/

Coutu, Andrea. 2013. *Consulting Fees/rates*. http://consultantjournal.com/blog/setting-consulting-fee-rates

Federal Trade Commission. 2013. *Price Fixing*. http://www.ftc.gov/bc/antitrust/price_fixing.shtm

Higgins, William. 2010. *The Successful Consultants Guide to Fee Setting*. http://mindwareincorporated.com/blog/wp-content/uploads/The-Successful-Consultants-Guide-to-Fee-Setting.pdf

Holtz, Herman. & Zahn, David. 2004. *How to Succeed as an Independent Consultant*. 4th Ed. New York: John Wiley & Sons.

Kaye, Harvey. 1997. *Inside the Technical Consulting Business*. 3rd Ed. New York: John Wiley & Sons.

Social Security Administration (SSA). 2014. *Social Security and Medicare tax rates; maximum taxable earnings*. http://ssa-custhelp.ssa.gov/app/answers/detail/a_id/240

Tuller, Lawrence. 1999. *The Independent Consultant's Q & A Book*. Holbrook, MA: Adams Media Corporation.

Weiss, Alan. 2009a. *Getting Started in Consulting*. 3rd Ed. Hoboken, NJ. John Wiley & Sons.

Weiss, Alan. 2009b. *Million Dollar Consulting*. 4th Ed. New York: McGraw-Hill.

Weiss, Alan. 2008. *Value-Based Fees: How to Charge—and Get—What You're Worth*. 2nd Ed. San Francisco, CA: Pfeiffer.

Questions to ask:

What kinds of insurance will I need as a consultant, and how do I determine what type(s) I will need?

Are there new risks from owning my own business that I need to consider?

How does the way my business is set up (sole practitioner, partnership, company/corporation with employees) affect the types of insurance I need, and the cost?

What is property and general liability insurance? Will I need that as a consultant?

How will becoming a consultant affect my homeowner's insurance, my auto insurance, and my life insurance?

What is umbrella insurance and when do I need it?

Under what circumstances will I need to have workers' compensation?

What is professional liability or E&O (errors and omissions) insurance, what does it cover, and when do I need it?

What types of retirement plans are available for consultants, and what are the advantages of each?

What types of medical insurance are available, and what are the advantages/disadvantages of each?

Do I need disability insurance and if so, under what circumstances?

What are the types of life insurance, and what are their advantages and disadvantages for consultants?

What types of insurance will I need if I have subcontractors, or if I am a subcontractor for another consultant or company?

What kind of coverage do I need if something goes wrong due to work performed by a subcontractor?

What are the best sources for finding insurance for my consulting business?

Chapter 4

Insurance Needs

BY DIANA STEGALL, CSP, CFPS, CPCU, ARM

Diana Stegall, CSP, CFPS, CPCU, ARM, is a loss control consultant for United Heartland in Minneapolis, Minnesota, consulting with businesses of all sizes, ranging in industries from healthcare to non-profits to manufacturing. She has been involved in safety for 25 years, assisting clients with their risk management efforts, and helping them identify potential risks to their business as a whole. She enjoys digging into contracts, including insurance contracts, and identifying sections that are one sided to ensure a balanced agreement. Diana has been very active in the American Society of Safety Engineers (ASSE), receiving the Society Safety Professional of the Year in 2005, and Culbertson awards for volunteer service in 2004 and 2011.

You have assessed your ability to be an OS&H consultant. You've developed a business plan, identifying the products and services you'll provide and how much you'll need to charge (see Chapters 2 and 3). Have you included all of your expected expenses? What about insurance costs? Will your current homeowners' and auto policies cover your business equipment? Are there new risks from owning your own business that you need to considered? What if you contract out work: Do you have coverage if something goes wrong due to work performed by a subcontractor?

Insurance is often seen as a necessary evil. Evaluating your insurance needs requires you to look at what can go wrong, just as you are optimistically planning on how to make your foray into consulting a success. Unappealing though it may be, having the right insurance (and the right amount of insurance) can make the difference in your business's survival after an unintended event. Insurance is there to "make you whole." It may be used to provide you with the financial resources to replace damaged or stolen equipment. It could pay legal expenses for property or other damage caused by your actions (or inaction), or medical expenses if a third party is injured on your property. Insurance can cover medical expenses and lost wages if your employee is injured at work. Also, it can pay for damages (property or personal) that may occur from the work performed by a subcontractor. Insurance can also help with your financial goals and protect your family if you are injured in your new venture.

As a business owner, your insurance needs include protecting yourself, protecting your employees, and protecting your business. As an individual or part of a family, you needed certain types of insurance with which you are probably familiar, such as auto, life, and health insurance. But now you will also need to consider some other types of insurance that are likely to be new to you, such as property insurance, general liability insurance, disability insurance, workers' compensation, and professional liability (or errors and omissions) insurance. A big part of determining what insurance you need involves finding the right advisor, and knowing what questions to ask.

This chapter will introduce you to what types of insurance are available, what types of coverage you need to consider as you start and as your business grows, and what questions to consider as you explore your insurance options.

DETERMINING HOW MUCH AND WHAT INSURANCE YOU NEED

If you have that entrepreneurial spirit, thinking about the negative things that can occur does not come easily. You want to be sure, however, that you have the right amount of insurance coverage to protect you, your family, and your assets in this new venture. Appendix B, "Determining How Much Insurance You Need," will help to guide you through this process.

... having the right insurance (and the right amount of insurance) can make the difference in your business's survival. . . .

Several factors determine your insurance needs. What services will you be providing? What equipment do you need to provide that service? Will you be working from your home, or will you rent an office? How can someone be injured or something be damaged while you are providing services, or as a result of the service you provided? If you are consulting in an environment with constant change (such as a construction project), the chance of something going wrong is greater than in a fixed environment. What is your business structure? (Sole proprietorships and partnerships allow a claimant to go after your personal assets, so you may need more protection if that's your business structure.) Do you have employees? How much of a loss can you afford out of pocket to replace damaged or stolen property, to repair your vehicle, or to live on if you're temporarily disabled? All of these items impact what insurance policies and what policy limits you need.

Take a look at your business plan. How can the resources you need for your business (different types of property, reputation, employees) be damaged or hurt? What are the potential financial consequences of that occurring? What assets, such as your investments and savings, do you currently have that you could use to pay for that loss? As previously mentioned, your corporate structure will determine if the assets to consider are those of the business or your personal assets (see Chapter 5). If you have a sole proprietorship or a partnership, both your personal and business assets will need to be included.

Let's look at a property exposure and insurance decision from a personal insurance perspective. You drive an older model car. You may decide to drop the physical damage coverage on the vehicle, if the premium for the coverage is more than the value of the vehicle. It is a fairly straightforward, cost/benefit decision. You feel comfortable that you can repair or replace the vehicle for less than the cost of the insurance. Liability exposures are different. The potential amount of the claim is unknown. If you run into the back of someone's vehicle and injure the vehicle occupants, your insurance policy will cover the actual injuries to a certain amount (and your state typically sets a minimum required amount). Your insurance, up to your policy limits, will cover damage to the other vehicle and costs if the vehicle occupants decide to sue you. If your limits are less than the awarded financial damages, any amounts still owed would come out of your assets. These would not be limited to your savings or investments (excluding your 401k or IRAs, as those are exempt from creditors). *Any* assets, including your home, your vehicle, and your personal possessions, can become part of a settlement.

So, when you are looking at how much insurance coverage you need, consider the financial assets you want to protect. If the business is being sued, the business's assets are considered during any settlement. But remember, if your business setup is a sole proprietorship or partnership, your personal assets would also be included. Bottom line, when deciding how much coverage you need, make sure you're covered for an amount equal to the total value of the assets you need to protect.

As you're just starting out, your business assets may include a computer, electronic tablet, smart phone, or camera. You may have specialized equipment for industrial hygiene work. If you are working out of your home, your office space is an asset. Your transportation to and from your clients is also an asset. Appendix A, at the end of this chapter, provides some initial guidance on identifying your assets and coverage needs.

Keep in mind that insurance is a risk-financing mechanism. It is a way to pay for losses (or claims), instead of having to pay for them yourself. Before you can determine how much coverage you need, evaluate what other personal and business resources you have available to pay for any potential losses. For example, your current automobile policy probably has a deductible. The deductible amount was (ideally) determined based on how much you felt you would be able to afford out of pocket if something happened to your vehicle. For the other types of insurance, you will need to make a similar determination. When you consider purchasing any type of insurance, you'll want to look at the cost of various deductible levels and make risk-based decisions to purchase a certain amount of coverage at a reasonable cost. This usually means accepting a higher deductible, which you will need to cover from your personal and business financial resources. For example, if your business property were lost or damaged, what equipment could you afford to replace from your other resources?

For disability insurance, what other sources of income could you rely on? Do you have savings you could use? What about other family member income? How long could you get by without your income? What amount of income do you need to prevent a financial hardship? Don't plan on relying on Social Security alone; if approved, Social Security does not kick in until the fifth full month of disability, and then only if the disability is expected to last 12 months or longer.

Your life insurance needs should not change significantly just because you are a consultant. Term insurance tends to be popular since, it is for a specific time frame; for example, until the children are out of college, at which point the amount of coverage could be lessened. Whole life features level premiums to age 100, and has a cash-value provision. In universal life, a portion of the funding goes to the insurance coverage, while the other premium is invested.

Business Owner's Policy (Property and General Liability)

Does your homeowner's policy cover your business personal property? It may or may not; it depends on the type of homeowner's policy you have, and how much personal property you use primarily for business purposes. Each insurance company offers different levels of homeowner's policies, based on the coverage you want or need. They have different exclusions, cover different perils (things that must happen, such as a fire or a windstorm, to have the loss covered), and provide different limits. As you might suspect, the broader the coverage is, the higher the cost. Most of these policies, however, follow the general policy language and rules of the Insurance Services Office (ISO).

Keep in mind that reading the policy documents . . . you have to read all the way through. . . .

If you haven't read your insurance policy since you first purchased the insurance (you did read it then, right?), now is a good time to do so. Take note of the coverage limits, and the different coverage sections. Many insurance companies will allow you to access your specific policy documents through their Web site, if you cannot find your actual policy. Keep in mind that reading the policy documents is like reading any regulation; you have to read all the way through, and ensure that you have read the exclusions and exceptions sections, as well as the definitions.

The HO-3 is an ISO homeowner's "special" form that provides more coverage than the broad form. The HO-3 form is for stand-alone housing units. Other forms are used if you rent or are in a condominium. Condominium refers to a type of ownership; these are usually townhomes, but may also consist of single-home units where you are only responsible for "studs in," and the association is responsible for the exterior of the building. The coverage and limits for personal property apply, regardless of type of dwelling, and whether it is owned or not. Where the "broad" form only covers those perils (things that can cause loss) if they are mentioned, the "special" form covers perils unless they are specifically excluded.

Before we get into what is and is not available for coverage under a standard homeowner's policy, I want to mention the importance of looking at the type of valuation included on your policy. The two major ones are actual cash value (ACV) and replacement cost. Assume you have a three-year old laptop that is damaged due to a fire. Under an ACV policy, the adjuster will look at what a similar model would cost new, and then subtract depreciation for the age of the laptop. For that state-of-the-art model you purchased three years ago, you may receive one-half or less of what it would cost you to replace it. With replacement cost coverage, whatever it costs to replace the laptop with a similar new model is what the insurance company will pay, minus any deductible, of course. The replacement cost coverage is more expensive, but how much can you afford to pay out of pocket if there is a loss? This question of how much can you afford to pay out of pocket applies to all of your insurance policies.

As you review your homeowner's insurance policy, pay particular attention to the section on personal property. This is separate from the limit of coverage on your actual dwelling (the building), and is usually specified as a percentage of the dwelling coverage limit. For renters or those in a condominium, the amount is specified by you. Your personal property is covered for the perils that apply to the dwelling. For example, under the broad or named peril form, damage to personal property from windstorm and hail is not covered if a window was left open and rain gets on your computer. It would only be covered if the window had been broken by the storm, or a tree falling on the roof had caused the opening. Under the special form, the damage would be covered, even if a window had been left open by your teenager.

> *The standard homeowner's policy also excludes personal liability coverage or property damage arising out of business activities.*

Specific amounts of coverage are provided for certain types of personal property. Your personal property is covered, even when it is away from your home. For example, only $2500 of coverage may be provided for items normally used for business purposes when at your house, but only $500 of coverage may be provided for business items away from your house; for instance, in a car or at a client's facility. In addition, business data stored on paper or electronically is not covered (another reason to be sure you have regular back-ups that are kept offsite).

The special homeowner's form also provides coverage for damage to property of others, up to a predetermined amount. Damage arising out of business operations, however, is excluded. The standard homeowner's policy also excludes personal liability coverage or property damage arising out of business activities. There are two exceptions, though: If either your revenue was less than a predetermined amount during the prior year, or the claim occurred when you were involved in volunteer activities, coverage for personal liability would apply. Most homeowner's policies specifically exclude coverage for professional services (more on coverage for professional services later).

You can add endorsements, attached to your homeowner's policy, to provide coverage for your business operations. The ISO version is called HOMEBiz, and is available in most cases if:

- the business is owned by you or you and relatives,
- it is operated out of your home (the premises listed on the declarations page),
- the premises are used primarily for residential purposes,
- you have no more than a predetermined number of employees, and
- gross annual receipts are less than a predetermined value.

Once you have more than the predetermined number of employees or your gross annual receipts are more than the predetermined amount, you will need to purchase commercial insurance or a business owner's policy. The specific requirements on receipts and/or number of employees through your homeowner's insurance company may vary from the standard policy language.

The commercial or business owner's policy typically includes:

- the full personal property limits for your business property,
- business personal property away from the premises for up to a predetermined amount,
- theft limits, higher than those for homeowner's insurance, for credits and money up to a predetermined level, and
- accounts receivable, loss of business income and extra expense to help you recover after there has been a covered cause of loss at the actual cost, for up to a predetermined length of time.

This extra expense coverage in the commercial or business owner's policy may include recovering any lost electronic business data. If you are leasing an office, your lease may require that you have a specified amount of property and general liability coverage.

The commercial policy also covers:

- products/completed operations coverage up to the personal liability limit on your policy;
- personal and advertising liability (claims that occur when another company is referenced without permission in your advertising, or from making false claims in your marketing materials) up to twice the limit for combined personal liability and medical coverage to others;
- medical payments to others, up to the policy limit; and
- damage to property of others, higher than that for homeowner's insurance, up to a predetermined level.

It does *not* include professional liability (also known as errors and omissions, or E&O) coverage. In addition, you may still need a personal articles policy or rider, if the amount of personal property you will have away from the premises is greater than the predetermined level.

General liability insurance is designed to protect you from claims made by a third party; i.e., someone who is not part of the insurance contract. It covers the claims/damage for someone who is injured on your premises. An example would be if someone slips and falls at your office, and goes to the doctor. It also covers property damage or injuries that you or your employees cause. For example, while waiting at a construction site, your employee leans up against a piece of equipment. The equipment starts to roll, and runs over some pallets of finished product. In both of these cases, the claim would be covered under your general liability insurance, along with legal costs to defend you, if needed. Since the employee was not performing professional services at the time of the injury, in most jurisdictions, this would be different from the types of claims that would be covered under the professional liability policy.

General liability policies can either cover claims on a claims made or an occurrence basis. For claims-made policies, the policy only covers claims that are reported during the policy period, regardless of when the actual injury/damage occurred. Policies that provide coverage on an "occurrence" basis cover injuries/damage that occurred during that policy period, regardless of when the claim is actually made.

This might not seem like a major distinction, but it can be. The person who was injured may not realize the extent of injury for several months or years. If you just have an occurrence-basis policy, and a claim is made for something that happened years ago, the insurance policy you had those many years ago will not pay, since the injury did not occur while that policy was in effect.

> *General liability insurance is designed to protect you from claims made by a third party....*

If you have been in business for several years without a general liability policy, a claims-made policy may be more expensive. You can purchase "tail" insurance to fill in the gaps between the different insurance policies. It is always important to let your insurance carrier know as soon as you suspect that there may be a claim. Otherwise, the carrier may take the position that you were misrepresenting your claims history.

The other item to review in the commercial or business owner's policy is what legal expenses are covered. Are they included in the loss limit, or is there a separate duty-to-defend clause? This may seem like a minor distinction, but legal expenses can quickly use up your limits of insurance in case of a lawsuit, leaving you unprotected.

Auto Insurance

Auto insurance is much simpler. As long as you are driving a personal passenger vehicle (pickup, van, SUV, car), you may not need a commercial vehicle policy. This depends on your state and on the percentage of time you drive your vehicle for business. I highly recommended that you check with your insurance carrier for use, coverage, and policy type requirements. At least annually, you should evaluate your insurance limits and verify that they are adequate for your current exposures. Most state minimum requirements are not sufficient in case of a serious crash. Given the number of drivers who have only the minimum coverage limits and, if you are injured in a crash, even if you are not at fault, your insurance may end up paying under the uninsured/underinsured motorist provisions. As mentioned under how much coverage is needed, consider additional limits to better protect your personal assets.

Umbrella Insurance

> *Umbrella policies stipulate what the underlying policy limits must be.*

Umbrella policies are designed to provide additional liability coverage in case of a catastrophic claim, lawsuit, or judgment. The limits are over or on top of the coverage limits (like an umbrella) provided in existing auto or business owner policies, and allow you to purchase additional liability protection for a minimal additional premium. This is based on the assumption that most of your claims will be within the underlying policy limits, and that the umbrella carrier will not have to pay out claims, at least not frequently. If you are looking for a cost-effective way to protect your financial assets from a catastrophic claim, consider an umbrella policy. The coverage for these policies tends to be broader than what is covered on the underlying policy, often including causes of loss not covered by the underlying policies. If there is a claim that is not covered under your general liability policy, for example, if it is covered by your umbrella policy, that policy "drops down" to provide coverage for that claim. When this drop-down coverage comes into play, there is generally a deductible that you would then need to pay.

For example, let's say your business owner's policy has a general liability limit of $500,000. You purchased an additional $1,000,000 umbrella policy. If you have a covered $750,000 claim, your general liability policy will take care of the first $500,000, and your umbrella policy will take care of the remaining $250,000. Without the umbrella policy, you would have to come up with the $250,000 balance.

Umbrella policies stipulate what the underlying policy limits must be. Like the deductible on your auto insurance, the higher the underlying policy limits, the more affordable the coverage.

Keep in mind that you can purchase a personal or a commercial umbrella policy. Many personal umbrella policies will provide some coverage for libel or slander. They will not, however, cover liability arising from business activities, other than the use of a private passenger automobile. Although a commercial umbrella policy may be a little more expensive and require higher underlying limits, many will provide coverage on top of your professional liability policy. The exclusions for umbrella policies vary dramatically from insurance company to insurance company, so be sure you are familiar with the exclusions on any policies you are considering.

The underlying policy limits are also critical. If these are not maintained (i.e., if you change your underlying policies and policy limits), your umbrella policy may be determined to be null and void. It is also important to ensure that the underlying liability policy and the umbrella policy both use the same claims basis, either occurrence or claims made.

Workers' Compensation

Workers' compensation is a program that is state regulated and requires companies to provide insurance to pay for work-related injuries to their employees. The first time you put someone on your payroll, you will likely need to provide workers' compensation coverage for any injury or illness that arises out of, and in the course of, employment. Family members are often exempt from this requirement.

In the excitement of starting their businesses, many consultants have neglected to purchase workers' compensation insurance. Then they had to scramble to find a way to pay for an employee's injury. Even in an office environment, there are hazards: slips and falls, repetitive motion injuries, or cuts and burns. If you do not have workers' compensation coverage but have your state's minimum number of employees where it is required, you can be penalized, and no one likes to pay unnecessary fines.

Workers' compensation covers medical care related to the injury, disability benefits, . . . and occupational therapy.

Since this is a state-regulated program, the requirements vary from state to state. Some states will allow sole proprietors to purchase workers' compensation to cover themselves. In most states, you purchase workers' compensation insurance from the private marketplace, similar to other insurance coverages. In monopolistic states, such as North Dakota, Ohio, and Washington, insurance is purchased directly from the state.

Workers' compensation covers medical care related to the injury, disability benefits (typically after a waiting period, which varies from state to state), and occupational therapy. The cost of this insurance is based on your payroll, your operations, and what your claims are in relation to companies of a similar size that provide a similar service.

To characterize companies providing similar services, classification codes have been developed over the years. Most classification codes are very broad, covering all anticipated types of job duties for a particular company (the prevailing class code). Most states, other than California, New York, Delaware, Pennsylvania, and New Jersey, utilize the class codes published by the National Council on Compensation Insurance (NCCI).

The classification codes determine, in part, how much you will be charged for workers' compensation insurance. Some class codes can be broken out of the prevailing class code for your business. These are clerical/administrative, outside sales, and (sometimes) drivers. If your employees are simply providing administrative support, the rate of insurance is less than if they are climbing around on construction sites. Your insurance agent can help you determine the correct classification code for your operations.

Indemnity claims (injuries where there are lost wages) impact your future premiums more than injuries where the person is brought back to work within the waiting period, which is typically three days.

Professional Liability/Errors and Omissions (E&O) Insurance

As a safety professional with a corporation, professional liability or errors and omissions (E&O) insurance is something most of us don't really think about.

We assume that if something happens due to our professional services, we are covered under our company's general liability policy. That may not have been the case when you worked for someone else, and it certainly is not the case now that you're on your own.

A consultant had been asked to look at the art room in a school, because there were concerns about the different materials used (clays, glazes, and so on). Since there was time after that evaluation, the client took the consultant through the hockey rink, which was in the midst of a renovation. Scaffolding covered most of the bleachers, where they were putting some of the final touches on the project. Later that winter, a spectator was hit in the head by a hockey puck. During the renovation, they had changed the bleachers, but had not adequately changed the Plexiglas protection. The consultant was personally sued. Fortunately, his personal professional liability coverage protected him from the lawsuit.

> . . . a general liability policy . . . specifically excludes those items when they arise out of your professional services.

How many times have you focused on a specific area during an audit or while providing client service, and potentially overlooked a different hazard? As a consultant, professional liability or E&O insurance is often overlooked, but it is critical to protecting your assets.

While a general liability policy covers bodily injury, personal injury, and property damage that occur on your premises, it specifically excludes those items when they arise out of your professional services. That is where professional liability, or E&O, insurance is needed. It covers situations when someone claims we have been negligent or made an error, or omitted information that ended up causing financial loss, bodily injury, or property damage. Even when we are exercising best practices and not going beyond our scope of knowledge, there can still be a professional liability claim. For instance, you sign a contract indicating that you will perform a specific service. You perform that service, yet the client does not feel that the service measured up to the desired standards, so the client files a professional liability claim.

This can also be a concern when we are asked to determine if a client is in "compliance with OSHA" or other regulatory authority. Before you agree to a project that includes that condition, you need to recognize that if OSHA (or EPA, or DOT, and so on) comes in shortly after your project is over, and finds something wrong, even if that condition was not present while you were there, you are potentially open to a professional liability claim. Avoid this trap. Let the uninformed consultant make those promises, not you. As a safety professional, advise your client that what you report is a snapshot in time and place and that, as conditions change, so do the risks and levels of compliance with the regulations. Ultimately, you do not have control over the work environment.

The professional liability policy provides defense costs. As with general liability insurance, it is important to determine if the policy includes a separate "duty to defend" or if any legal expense depletes your limits of insurance. Some policies also include coverage for libel and slander; that is, damage caused by what you have written or said. Some may cover you if, by chance, you have infringed on material covered by copyright (Can you say "clip art in presentations?"). There may be a provision where you have ultimate veto rights on any settlements. This provision exists since, as a consultant, you want to protect your reputation. Settlements can make it appear that you have done something wrong, even when it was just a matter of the insurance company trying to avoid additional legal expenses.

Several professional associations, including ASSE, have designated providers who offer professional liability policies to their members, which are crafted specifically for safety consultants. If you go through someone other than those designated providers, you want to be certain that the professional liability policy includes provisions to cover contingent bodily injury and property damage caused by your professional services.

E&O coverage is typically only offered on a claims made or reported basis. If you switch insurance companies, you may want to purchase "tail" coverage, if possible, to cover any gaps in coverage. When you get ready to retire or sell your business, you will want to ensure you have tail coverage for any unreported claims that may be outstanding. As with your general liability policy, it is important to let your carrier know if something has occurred that may result in a claim; that improves the chances of coverage, especially if you are changing insurance companies.

This is another policy where a thorough review of the exclusions is critical. Many professional liability policies automatically exclude coverage for environmental damages. If you are providing environmental consulting services, this policy is of little benefit.

Regardless of your corporate structure, you need professional liability insurance. The cost of the coverage will vary, according to your number of employees, the services you provide, if you use subcontractors, and the extent of coverage. For example, if you provide mold services or work on construction projects, your exposure is higher, so the costs will be higher. The difference may be not enough to pursue that type of service.

Policies are designed for specific types of services. If the services that you provide change, you will need to let your insurance company know. Otherwise, the carrier can deny a claim or cancel a policy, based on misrepresentation. Policies are also state-specific, so if you expand into a different territory, you need to keep your agent informed.

Personal Loss Exposures and Risk Financing

As with professional liability coverage, once you are out on your own, you are responsible for your personal loss exposures. These include areas such as retirement income, life insurance, medical coverage, and disability insurance. A certified financial planner (CFP) or insurance agent can be very helpful here, so let's provide some information to get you started.

Your retirement planning options as a consultant will depend on how you set up your company. Regardless of your corporate set-up, you can open an individual retirement account (IRA) or a Roth IRA and contribute to it throughout the year. With the traditional IRA, deductions are exempt from state and federal taxes (based on income limits that change annually). Withdrawals are taxed as ordinary income. Roth IRA contributions are not tax deductible, but there is no tax on the distributions.

Two other options are a SEP (simplified employee pension plan) and a qualified plan. The SEP allows your business to make contributions into a traditional IRA plan on your behalf and for any employees you may have (up to 100 eligible employees). Annual contributions are optional. If you are self-employed (a sole proprietor) you are allowed to make contributions for yourself. The business can contribute up to a maximum percentage of your compensation or up to a certain monetary limit. The contribution for all employees, however, has to be equal. Under this option, the company may not have another retirement plan.

A qualified plan is another option for making tax deductible contributions to a retirement plan if you are a sole proprietorship or partnership. You determine if you want it to be a defined benefit (contributions are based on what is needed to provide definitely determinable benefits for the participants) or a defined contribution plan. The defined contribution plan can be either, a profit-sharing plan, where the amount contributed to the plan each year is not fixed, or a money purchase pension plan, where contributions are fixed. For more information on retirement plans for small businesses, see IRS Publication 560 (IRS 2013).

Life Insurance

The need for insurance coverage changes throughout the years. As you start your consulting company, now is a good time to review those needs. Considerations include: how much money is needed for funeral expenses, debt elimination (if that is a goal), family living expenses, special needs (college fund for children, for example), or a retirement income for your surviving spouse. Keep in mind that not everyone needs life insurance. If no one is dependent on your income, you do not need life insurance.

There are two main types of life insurance: term and cash value (which includes whole, variable, and universal). Term life tends to be the most cost-effective. You purchase the term insurance, typically for a set number of years. The premium is based on your age, your health (some policies require a physical to get the best rates), and the amount of coverage at the time you purchase the insurance.

Cash value life policies include an investment component. Either a set amount of money is paid up front or a level premium amount is paid through the end of the policy (typically the death of the policy holder). The premiums above the actual insurance cost are invested; that is what provides the cash value. With whole life policies, the insurer pays an annual dividend of a specified amount, and the account value increases tax deferred. With variable universal life policies, the policy holder can direct the investments. For universal policies, the investments are usually more fixed. Most allow you to take out a loan, based on the cash value of the policy. The initial expenses for these types of policies tend to be higher but they decrease the longer you have the policy. If you miss a payment, you may forfeit both the policy and its cash value.

Let's go back to the statement that if no one is dependent on your income, you do not need life insurance. Your business itself may be dependent on your income. There are situations where a life insurance policy enables the orderly succession of your business. For instance, if you have a business partner, each of you could have a life insurance policy on the other. If your business partner passes away, the death benefit would enable you to purchase the other half of the business. A financial advisor or insurance agent can help you determine if this type of buy/sell agreement makes sense for your situation.

One provision included in many life insurance policies is the accidental death benefit. This benefit provides double the face amount of the insurance policy if you die as the result of an accident. Since, at least initially, your death may not be covered by workers' compensation insurance, this benefit provides your beneficiaries with some financial assistance in case the unthinkable should happen.

How much life insurance do you need? The amount of insurance should be sufficient to make up the income deficit when you die without your beneficiaries having to take from the principal part of your investment (versus the investment earnings). To determine the necessary life insurance death benefit, take the amount your beneficiaries will need on an annual basis to not deplete the principal of your investments, and multiple it by 20 (depending on the financial advisor, the number to use for the calculation can range from 10 to 25). Your advisor or agent can help you with the calculations.

Medical Insurance

This is another potentially new expense that you need to consider. If you are married or in a long-term relationship, can you be covered under your partner's coverage through work? Under the Affordable Care Act, health care exchanges have been set up in each state to help you find coverage, and fines will be assessed for not having coverage. If you are currently healthy, medical insurance may seem like an unnecessary expense, but staying healthy is going to be even more important as a consultant. There are no paid sick days. If you are not able to work on a regular basis due to illness, your earnings and your ability to build your business will be impacted.

Can you afford to provide medical insurance for your employees? As your company expands, you may want to consider this option. Under the Affordable Care Act, small employers can use a federal site to help them design and select health insurance for their employees. Providing comprehensive health insurance can help your business attract and retain employees.

If you are a sole proprietor and either decide to not buy a workers' compensation policy that provides you coverage, or you are in a state where you are not allowed to cover yourself on a workers' compensation policy, the type of health insurance you buy becomes even more important. Think about what your day-to-day work environment will be: Will you be primarily in the office or classroom, or will you be in mines, on jobsites, and working around potentially hazardous materials? The Affordable Care Act covers preventive office visits, but what if you have a serious injury due to work? How much can you afford to pay out of pocket? What health care policy is right for you?

Whether you are looking for coverage for yourself or your employees, the variety of health insurance plans continue to change. There are high-deductible plans, which have high upfront, out-of-pocket expenses, but lower premiums; catastrophic plans, which are really designed for a catastrophic event, and do not provide preventive services; and health maintenance organizations (HMOs), which provide coverage within a specific network of doctors. HMO coverage tends to be pretty extensive, with low premiums, copays, and low deductibles. Preferred provider organizations (PPOs) and point-of-service policies (POSs) have an in-network and out-of-network option, with greater coverage and lower or no deductibles as long as you stay within the network. Because of the flexibility, the premiums tend to be somewhat higher than an HMO. Indemnity plans are what many consider traditional health insurance. You can choose your doctor, pay a deductible for the policy year, and then pay 20 percent of the bill once the deductible is met. These tend to have a higher premium than the other types of plans.

Disability Insurance

Most consultants will not have a sustainable income if they are not able to work. If something happens, either due to an accident or a health issue, disability insurance can help replace your income until you are back on your feet. Many of the insurance companies that provide homeowners' insurance also have disability policies. In addition to the income replacement policies, policies are available that will make your mortgage or loan payments for you. Although you may not think you need to worry about disability, just over 1 in 4 of today's 20 year-olds will become disabled before they reach the age of 67 (SSA 2011).

Subcontractors and Insurance Coverage

When you're just starting out as a consultant, you may have other consultants who ask you to do work on their behalf. Maybe the work falls within your specialty. Maybe they have several projects going on that prevent them from taking on this particular project for their account. What are the special insurance considerations for working as a subcontractor?

If there is an actual contract involved, it is important that you read it through to understand what is required of you. Even if you have known the person for whom you are doing the work for many years and have a great relationship, the best way to keep that great relationship is to understand what is expected of you. If you do not understand parts of the contract, ask for clarification. There may be some provisions that the end client wants included. Sometimes these requests make sense; other times, they are part of the standard contract language that the company uses.

One of the requirements you may see is to add the contractor (or the client) as an additional insured.

One of the requirements you may see is to add the contractor (or the client) as an additional insured. Additional insured status means that your insurance policy will cover the person/company that you name as an additional insured as if they were you, the insured, for the work you are performing for them. The specific insurance limits and type of policy may be specified. If something you do on the project causes bodily injury, physical damage, personal injury, or other harm (depending on the policy), and the injured party files a claim against the contractor, your policy will provide the same legal defense and coverage to that person that it would provide to you. This means that your policy limits will be divided. If your limits are $100,000, that limit now has to cover the contractor and you. If you have $50,000 of defense coverage per occurrence, that $50,000 is now split between defending you and the contractor. Cooperation in defending the claim is critical; otherwise, you may have expenses that are not covered.

Do you have to add your contractor as an additional insured? It depends on the contract. This may be driven by the end client or the contractor. It is important to understand the concerns that the contractor has, and how your part of the operation can cause harm. Sometimes, you will be able to make the case that this provision is not necessary, and that providing them with a certificate of insurance, which shows that you have coverage, will satisfy their legal department.

There is an additional fee for additional insured status, which varies by insurer and by your operations.

What if the shoe is on the other foot, so to speak? Your business has really taken off, and you need to use a subcontractor, either because you are very busy, or because a client has a request that you do not feel is in your area of expertise. What do you need to require for insurance?

For the best protection, you should have the subcontractors add you as an additional insured on their professional liability policy. You should also require them to have policy limits that are the same as yours. If their limits are less than yours, are you comfortable with that limit, based on the scope of work that they will be performing? Keep in mind that once their limits are exceeded, you may not have coverage.

Most professional liability/errors and omissions (O&E) policies automatically cover employees (a W-2 relationship). Subcontractors would need to specifically be added. What you don't want to have happen is: A claim is filed against you for work the subcontractors performed; the subcontractors didn't have insurance (or did have insurance, but the limits were not sufficient); you didn't add them as an additional insured; and you are now liable for their work, but do not have insurance coverage. In that case, your company assets (plus your personal assets, in the case of sole proprietorships and partnerships) are used to pay any claims or settlements.

Subcontractors can be included in your workers' compensation calculations....

General liability insurance tends to work the same way in terms of subcontractors. Each policy can have different provisions, however, and you should pay close attention to who is considered an insured. The home business policy would provide very minimal coverage if the subcontractor was injured while performing the job (unless workers' compensation was required), and would not pay at all for any injuries due to professional services. For maximum protection, you should be added to the subcontractor's general liability policy, in addition to the errors and omissions policy, as an additional insured.

The other common provision, when it comes to subcontractors, is obtaining certificates of insurance (COI). COI do not provide the certificate holder (that is, you or your client) with any insurance coverage. They simply let the certificate holder know that the insurance coverage exists, who the insurance carrier is, what the limits are, and when the limits expire. If the insurance coverage lapses, if the insurer is cancelling the policy, or there has been a decrease in policy limits or other significant changes to the policy, the insurance carrier has to notify the certificate holder.

If you need to provide a COI to a client, the contract will indicate the coverages that are required, the limits for each type of coverage, how long they have to be in place, and any exceptions or additional conditions. The request may require, for example:

Business/General Liability Insurance:
- $1,000,000 per occurrence
- $1,500,000 aggregate
- $1,500,000 products/completed operations total limit
- $1,000,000 personal injury/advertising

There may also be other requirements for automobile insurance, if there are commercial vehicles, workers' compensation insurance with certain employer's liability limits, or professional liability insurance. The time limit will typically be "as long as the contract is in place." If your current limits are less than requested, or the request for insurance and/or limits does not make sense, based on the services you will be providing, you can try to negotiate with your client. Otherwise, you will need to increase your policy limits, add coverages to accommodate the request, or decide that the project is not worth the increased insurance costs.

The good news is that almost all insurance agencies that deal with commercial accounts are familiar with obtaining certificates of insurance for their clients, and can do so within a few days of the request. You can have them forward the certificates directly to your client, or have them sent to you for delivery to your client.

Just as it is best practice to have any of your subcontractors add you as an additional insured, you should also request certificates of insurance, based on the types of services they will be providing on your behalf, and the types of coverage that are required. Appendix A contains a typical Certificate of Liability Insurance form.

Subcontractors can be included in your workers' compensation calculations, since coverage may (unknowingly) be provided for them. One consultant made certain to include her employee payroll information, used in determining workers' compensation premium, but did not include the subcontractor's payroll; they were subcontractors, after all. The company was audited, a common practice in workers' compensation, to ensure that the payroll was appropriately classified. Since records had not been kept of the subcontractor's professional liability policies, the amounts paid to them were added to the employee payroll, increasing the workers' compensation premium.

Finding Coverage

Starting out, it may be simplest to talk to the agent for your existing homeowner's policy, since there is an existing relationship, and many agents can handle small business questions and policies. If you want to forge new relationships, you have the choice of two main types of agencies: independent agencies and company agencies. Company agencies include some of the better known insurance companies. These agencies are typically contractors with that insurance company, selling only their company's products and services.

Independent agencies represent many different insurance companies. Every independent agency tends to have a different niche: the size of clients, contracts with certain insurance carriers but not others, or expertise in a special field. With an independent agency, you may have more options for addressing your business insurance needs as you grow. The key is to find an agent with whom you can relate, who listens to your concerns, and who is able to explain why that particular policy, coverage, or limit is important for you.

Since professional liability insurance for consulting services is a very specialized product, you want to be sure that the agency you work with understands the scope of your work, and can help you find the right type of policy.

Before deciding on which agency you are going to go with, get several offers in writing from different agencies, looking at different combinations of coverage and different coverage limits. You will want to compare the coverage, the limits, the perils covered, who is considered an insured, the exclusions, and the exceptions. But that is just the beginning. Even though we like to think of insurance companies as being stable, that is not always the case. Many no longer exist. There are a few quick ways to review an insurer's financial stability. The first is the A.M. Best rating. A.M. Best Company provides a financial stability and credit risk rating to insurance companies (A.M. Best 2014). Unfortunately, they do not make it easy to look up the information on their Web site, but you can enter, "What is the Xyz Company's AM Best rating?" in a search engine, and it will take you to the most recent press release. Anything rated "A" or higher means that, at the last review, its financial strength was considered excellent or superior. Although something with a "B" rating might be sufficient for your purposes, there are some companies that want their contractors to have insurance policies with an "A" rated carrier. Some property management companies will require that your property coverage is with an "A" rated carrier.

Standard and Poor's (2014) and Moody's (2014) also rate the financial stability of insurance companies. They also make it difficult to find the ratings on their Web sites, although Moody's does allow you to register for free to find access to the information. The ratings agencies all use different criteria, so the ratings may vary from organization to organization. You can also check the insurance company's Web site, or simply ask your agent to provide you with the data. You want to be sure that the company providing your insurance is financially stable in case you do have a claim.

In addition to the financial ratings, you can check consumer experience with that particular company. Better Business Bureau online and Consumer Reports are two of the many consumer rating agencies available. There are also general reviews through some search engines. Keep in mind that people are more likely to post a review when they have had a bad experience than when things have gone the way that they wanted.

There are a few quick ways to review an insurer's financial stability.

Appendix B is an "Insurance Comparison" worksheet to help you with this process.

CONCLUSION

Much of the insurance protection that you had as an employee is now your responsibility. Based on the products and services you have planned to provide, do you have enough insurance, and is it the right type? Without the right coverages and coverage limits, you put yourself, your family, and your company at a financial risk. Simply overlooking a hazard at a client's site that ultimately causes an injury can pull you into a lawsuit: Do you have coverage for that? Can you easily recreate your business data, such as client information, accounting information, client reports, industrial hygiene results, if you lose your laptop (either physically or if the computer crashes)?

Knowing the types of coverage and the limits of that coverage can provide peace of mind when something happens. As you go down this path, here are a few things to keep in mind:

- Insurance tends to be regulated state by state. If you expand your operations into another state, you need to know what that state's requirements are.
- Find insurance advisors who listen to you and whom you can trust. Do they have their own E&O policy in case they misadvise you? Do they fully understand your operations? Are they able to provide policies that are relevant to your operations, and the specific services you'll provide, or do they suggest a standard type, or one geared towards accountants or other unrelated professions? Do the policies allow you room to grow and expand your business, or will you be looking for new policies in a few years?
- Don't make the mistake of thinking you can't afford professional liability/E&O insurance.

Take a look at your business plan and your current insurance policies. Talk to your current agent about your business plans, and determine what coverage and limits make sense for you at this point in time to protect you and your family, now and as your business grows.

I have discussed some of the OS&H consultant's liabilities here as they relate to insurance. Chapter 5 discusses the liabilities and ways to mitigate them as they relate to legal and regulatory compliance issues.

BIBLIOGRAPHY

A.M. Best. 2014 "About A.M. Best"(retrieved December 16, 2014). www.ambest.com/about/

BizFilings. 2012. "How Much Property and Liability Insurance is Enough for Your Business?" (retrieved December 16, 2014). www.bizfilings.com/toolkit/sbg/office-hr/security-and-insurance/property-and-liability-insurance-needs.aspx.

Clancy, Carolyn M. 2011. "How to Get a Good Value When Choosing a Health Plan," *Navigating the Healthcare System* (retrieved December 20, 2013). www.ahrq.gov/news/columns/navigating-the-health-care-system/110111.html.

Consumer Reports. n.d. "About us" (retrieved December 16, 2014). www.consumerreports.org/cro/about-us/index.htm

Council of Better Business Bureaus. 2014. "About." (retrieved December 16, 2014). www.bbb.org/council/about/council-of-better-business-bureaus/

Internal Revenue Service (IRS). 2012. "Retirement Plans for Small Business" (Publication 560) (retrieved December 16, 2014). www/irs.gov/publications/p560/index.html

Javens, Melanie. "Complete Equity Markets." Phone Interview, October 10, 2013.

Moody's Investor Relations. 2014 "About Moody's" (retrieved December 16, 2014). www.moodys.com/Pages/atc.aspx

Nyce, Charles, ed. 2008. *Personal Insurance*. 2nd ed. Malvern, PA: American Institute for Chartered Property Casualty Underwriters/Insurance Institute of America.

Scism, Leslie. 2012. "Life Policies: The Whole Truth," *Wall Street Journal* (retrieved December 20, 2013). http://online.wsj.com/news/articles/SB10001424052702303296604577450313299530278

Social Security Administration (SSA). 2014 "Fact Sheet: Social Security" (retrieved December 16, 2014). www.ssa.gov/pressoffice/basicfact.htm.

_____. 2011. "What You Need To Know When You Get Social Security Disability Benefits" (retrieved December 20, 2013). www.socialsecurity.gov/pubs/EN-05-10153.pdf.

Standard and Poors. 2014. "About us" (retrieved December 16, 2014). www.standardandpoors.com/about-sp/main/en/us.

Wall Street Journal. n.d. "How to Insure Your Home" *Wall Street Journal*, accessed December 1, 2013. http://guides.wsj.com/personal-finance/insurance/how-to-insure-your-home/.

_____. n.d. "How Much Car Insurance Do You Need?" *Wall Street Journal* (retrieved December 1, 2013). http://guides.wsj.com/personal-finance/insurance/how-much-car-insurance-do-you-need/.

APPENDIX A

CERTIFICATE OF LIABILITY INSURANCE

DATE (MM/DD/YYYY)

THIS CERTIFICATE IS ISSUED AS A MATTER OF INFORMATION ONLY AND CONFERS NO RIGHTS UPON THE CERTIFICATE HOLDER. THIS CERTIFICATE DOES NOT AFFIRMATIVELY OR NEGATIVELY AMEND, EXTEND OR ALTER THE COVERAGE AFFORDED BY THE POLICIES BELOW. THIS CERTIFICATE OF INSURANCE DOES NOT CONSTITUTE A CONTRACT BETWEEN THE ISSUING INSURER(S), AUTHORIZED REPRESENTATIVE OR PRODUCER, AND THE CERTIFICATE HOLDER.

IMPORTANT: If the certificate holder is an ADDITIONAL INSURED, the policy(ies) must be endorsed. If SUBROGATION IS WAIVED, subject to the terms and conditions of the policy, certain policies may require an endorsement. A statement on this certificate does not confer rights to the certificate holder in lieu of such endorsement(s).

PRODUCER	CONTACT NAME:
	PHONE (A/C, No, Ext):	FAX (A/C, No):
	E-MAIL ADDRESS:
	INSURER(S) AFFORDING COVERAGE	NAIC #
	INSURER A :
INSURED	INSURER B :
	INSURER C :
	INSURER D :
	INSURER E :
	INSURER F :

COVERAGES   CERTIFICATE NUMBER: REVISION NUMBER:

THIS IS TO CERTIFY THAT THE POLICIES OF INSURANCE LISTED BELOW HAVE BEEN ISSUED TO THE INSURED NAMED ABOVE FOR THE POLICY PERIOD INDICATED. NOTWITHSTANDING ANY REQUIREMENT, TERM OR CONDITION OF ANY CONTRACT OR OTHER DOCUMENT WITH RESPECT TO WHICH THIS CERTIFICATE MAY BE ISSUED OR MAY PERTAIN, THE INSURANCE AFFORDED BY THE POLICIES DESCRIBED HEREIN IS SUBJECT TO ALL THE TERMS, EXCLUSIONS AND CONDITIONS OF SUCH POLICIES. LIMITS SHOWN MAY HAVE BEEN REDUCED BY PAID CLAIMS.

INSR LTR	TYPE OF INSURANCE	ADDL INSD	SUBR WVD	POLICY NUMBER	POLICY EFF (MM/DD/YYYY)	POLICY EXP (MM/DD/YYYY)	LIMITS	
	COMMERCIAL GENERAL LIABILITY						EACH OCCURRENCE	$
	☐ CLAIMS-MADE ☐ OCCUR						DAMAGE TO RENTED PREMISES (Ea occurrence)	$
							MED EXP (Any one person)	$
							PERSONAL & ADV INJURY	$
	GEN'L AGGREGATE LIMIT APPLIES PER:						GENERAL AGGREGATE	$
	☐ POLICY ☐ PRO-JECT ☐ LOC						PRODUCTS - COMP/OP AGG	$
	☐ OTHER:							$
	AUTOMOBILE LIABILITY						COMBINED SINGLE LIMIT (Ea accident)	$
	☐ ANY AUTO						BODILY INJURY (Per person)	$
	☐ ALL OWNED AUTOS ☐ SCHEDULED AUTOS						BODILY INJURY (Per accident)	$
	☐ HIRED AUTOS ☐ NON-OWNED AUTOS						PROPERTY DAMAGE (Per accident)	$
								$
	UMBRELLA LIAB ☐ OCCUR						EACH OCCURRENCE	$
	EXCESS LIAB ☐ CLAIMS-MADE						AGGREGATE	$
	☐ DED ☐ RETENTION $							$
	WORKERS COMPENSATION AND EMPLOYERS' LIABILITY Y / N						☐ PER STATUTE ☐ OTHER	
	ANY PROPRIETOR/PARTNER/EXECUTIVE OFFICER/MEMBER EXCLUDED? (Mandatory in NH)	N / A					E.L. EACH ACCIDENT	$
							E.L. DISEASE - EA EMPLOYEE	$
	If yes, describe under DESCRIPTION OF OPERATIONS below						E.L. DISEASE - POLICY LIMIT	$

DESCRIPTION OF OPERATIONS / LOCATIONS / VEHICLES (ACORD 101, Additional Remarks Schedule, may be attached if more space is required)

CERTIFICATE HOLDER	CANCELLATION
	SHOULD ANY OF THE ABOVE DESCRIBED POLICIES BE CANCELLED BEFORE THE EXPIRATION DATE THEREOF, NOTICE WILL BE DELIVERED IN ACCORDANCE WITH THE POLICY PROVISIONS.
	AUTHORIZED REPRESENTATIVE

© 1988-2014 ACORD CORPORATION. All rights reserved.

ACORD 25 (2014/01)   The ACORD name and logo are registered marks of ACORD
(Reprinted by ASSE with permission and courtesy of ACORD Corporation)

APPENDIX B

Work Sheet—Determining How Much Insurance You Need

Financial Assets

Item	Value
Savings	_____
Investments	_____
Other Income	_____
Home Value	_____
Other	_____
Total	_____

(This will provide a guide on your personal assets that may be at risk in case of a liability claim as well as assets you can pull on in case of your disability or injury)

Business Personal Property

Item (computer, camera, etc)	Replacement Cost
_____	_____
_____	_____
_____	_____
_____	_____
Total	_____

Employees? ___ Yes ___ No   If yes, workers' compensation

(Anticipated) Monthly Income   _____

(Anticipated) Monthly Expenses   _____

How many months of savings are available?   _____

Does your lease for office space require a certain amount of coverage? If, so, what amount?

Work Sheet—Insurance Comparisons

Property

What is the deductible? _____

Are there coverage limits for specific types of property? Yes / No

If so, what are they? _____

What are the covered causes of loss? _____
_____

Is coverage based on actual cost value or replacement cost? Actual / Replacement

What are the limits if the business personal property is off-site?
_____

Do I have coverage if I rent equipment? Yes / No

If so, are there any exclusions related to causes of loss? Yes / No

If so, what are they? _____

Liability (Professional/E&O and General)

Is coverage based on a claims made or occurrence basis? Claims / Occurance

What are the policy limits? _____

Does the E&O policy cover contingent bodily injury and property damage? Yes / No

If I subcontract work, are my subcontractors covered? Yes / No

If so, at what cost? _____   _____

General

What is the name of the insurance company? _____

What is their financial rating? _____

What is their consumer rating? _____

Questions to ask:

What corporate form will work best for me; will I be solo, or have partners?

Who will create and review the contracts that will be needed for client and business purposes?

Will I need to hire legal, insurance, or accounting professionals to help guide me through the formation of my business, to help me with payroll, tax withholding, employee benefits, employer tax and FICA contributions, payment of corporate property and income taxes, and obtaining appropriate insurance coverage to protect my business and myself against lawsuits?

Will I hire full- or part-time employees, or subcontract with other firms or individuals to provide services to clients on a contractual basis?

Will I be doing work with the federal government as a contractor? That could raise debarment for the company, and security clearance issues for its personnel.

Do I know the federal, state, and local employment laws with which I need to comply?

Will I have OSHA, MSHA, or state safety and health compliance issues, outside my normal areas of practice, that I will need to address?

Will I operate from my home or use leased or purchased office space? If leasing, will I have personal liability for payments under the lease if my business goes under, and for how long?

Do I understand legal liability and privilege considerations so that malpractice claims can be avoided?

Chapter 5

Legal and Regulatory Issues

BY ADELE L. ABRAMS, ESQ., CMSP

Adele L. Abrams is an attorney, safety professional, and trained mediator who is president of the Law Office of Adele L. Abrams P.C. in Beltsville, MD, and Denver, CO, a ten-attorney firm focusing on safety, health, and employment law nationwide. Adele is a certified mine safety professional. She provides consultation, safety audits and training services to MSHA- and OSHA-regulated companies. Adele is a regular columnist for numerous magazines on legal, employment, mine, and occupational safety/health issues, and is co-author of several books related to mining, construction, and occupational safety and health. She is on the adjunct faculty of the Catholic University of America, where she instructs on Employment and Labor Law. A graduate of the George Washington University's National Law Center, she is a member of the Maryland, DC and Pennsylvania Bars, the U.S. District Courts of Maryland, DC, and Tennessee, the U.S. Court of Appeals, DC, 3rd and 4th Circuits, and the United States Supreme Court.

So you are ready to hang out a shingle . . . how exciting! You are an expert in your field, and now you are prepared to share that expertise with your clients. Building an independent consulting practice can be rewarding. But to minimize the risk of turning a good experience into a nightmare, you have a number of legal issues you need to deal with, and many others of which you should be aware. As a new business owner, you are about to plunge into a legal and regulatory world where you do not have expertise, and where missteps can cost you your business, your reputation, and even your freedom. Legal and regulatory issues simply cannot be ignored: they won't go away!

INITIAL CONSIDERATIONS FOR CONSULTANTS

When I left a large law firm over a dozen years ago to go solo, both to practice safety and health law and to provide occupational safety training and consulting services, I had a lot of experience under my belt in my subject matter areas. What I did not anticipate were the legal and regulatory hurdles I would face initially, from incorporating my business, to obtaining lines of credit and a business loan (as a "woman-owned small business"), to entering into a contract for office space, to learning what fees and taxes would apply to my business, and when such filings were due.

> *When applying for small business loans and corporate credit cards, I found that my personal credit score could be affected by the credit usage of my firm. . . .*

Getting professional malpractice insurance was a given. But, as my business grew, and I took on an administrative assistant, I was introduced to the wonderful world of payroll tax deductions, IRS and state filings, workers' compensation and unemployment insurance forms, fees and filing requirements. I recognized the need for general liability insurance as well, to cover my business property and the potential exposure, if a client or third party were to be injured at my worksite. I also learned how prudent it was to obtain professional liability insurance (in my case, legal malpractice insurance, but other insurance needs for consultants are discussed in Chapter 4, "Insurance").

When applying for small business loans and corporate credit cards, I found that my personal credit score could be affected by the credit usage of my firm, and that this information, in turn, could influence public information such as Dun & Bradstreet ratings. This can be important if you want to consult for federal, state or local governments and must pass their contractor screening. After consultation with a tax professional, I decided that the "S" corporate structure was the best for my circumstances, and I was assisted in forming a "professional corporation" under Maryland law.

When I entered into agreements with consultants, using them as subcontractors, I had to consider whether they were truly subcontractors or were employees who only appeared to be subcontractors, because misclassification of workers is a high-priority prosecution area for both the federal IRS and the U.S. Department of Labor (particularly in light of employee size limitation triggers for insurance benefits under the Affordable Care Act, which has sparked misclassification actions). Misclassifying can carry significant consequences.

Because my practice eventually required employees, I also had to consider what benefits I would offer to them. That is a continually evolving area in the wake of new laws, such as the Affordable Care Act, for which, at the time this is being written, the implementation requirements by small businesses are still being determined. I learned as well that, in my state, I was required to offer COBRA benefits (extension of medical insurance coverage) to departing employees, even though my company fell well below the federal 25-employee minimum threshold.

Failure to know what laws apply to your business, now and as it grows, can end in litigation and enforcement actions, the consequences of which can bring a business and its owner to their knees financially!

CORPORATE FORM CONSIDERATIONS

Before opening your doors or website to new clients, consider what corporate form and business structure your enterprise will take. There is no right or wrong structure—the analysis is situation-specific—but several factors will influence what structure you choose. Key concerns include considerations of personal financial liability, personal criminal liability, commitment and shielding of personal assets, and whether you will have one or more partners or investors/shareholders. Tax liability, or more bluntly, selecting a form that will allow you to pay minimal taxes and take maximum deductions, is another consideration. All of these will influence the corporate or partnership form you select.

Prior to forming a business entity, you need to:

- Determine what financial resources you have available;
- Consider the area of commerce in which your business will practice (e.g., will you seek state or government contract work, will you offer training for clients); in my case, since I am also an attorney, I will offer legal advice); and
- Determine whether the business would be best suited to a general partnership, a sole proprietorship, or a limited liability company (forms that, in some states, have fewer formal corporate recording formalities or complex tax filings) or a formal corporation with shareholders, which would have the maximum paperwork requirements in terms of bylaws, mandated meetings with minutes, and tax filings.

The following discusses some of the corporate form options available to consultants, with a caveat. Corporate tax and licensing requirements vary state by state. It is outside the scope of this chapter to be able to cover these often-changing regulations and tax codes.

In addition, federal taxing requirements are constantly updated, and as this is written, more tax changes are under consideration by Congress. This book is not a replacement for legal or accounting advice, and should not be construed as such. Consult your professionals for personalized recommendations.

The typical corporate forms include:

- General corporations (C corporations)
- Close or S corporations
- Limited liability corporations (LLC)
- Partnerships
- Sole proprietorships

Most states require registration and payment of corporate formation fees; some even impose property tax on office equipment, which must be considered as start-up and ongoing expenses. This influence where you choose to locate, or at least incorporate, your business. Generally, a business will need to have a registered agent in each state in which it will do business, but check your state-specific laws on this issue. A registered agent is simply a person, available during normal business hours, who can accept service of legal documents on your behalf.

General Corporations

. . . the C corporation is the corporate form that offers the greatest shielding of personal assets and other liability.

The principal form of business organization is the corporation, sometimes referred to as a C corporation. It has the chief advantage of limiting the liability of its investors. For a newly minted solo consultant, this may be more bureaucracy than you will want to deal with. But if multiple consultants decide to band together to form an enterprise, this becomes a more viable option. Other possible organizational methods for individuals or small numbers of participants are discussed below.

The business and affairs of a corporation are managed under by a board of directors, who may be actively involved in the work of the corporation, investors or designated third parties. The number of directors is typically set forth in the corporate charter.

The corporate charter and bylaws of a corporation will designate the number of directors, qualifications (if any) for the position, and the election process. It will include issues involving votes, such as what constitutes a quorum, and whether actions are approved by a simple majority or a supermajority. Often, state laws will provide direction or mandates on corporate structures.

Corporations can issue securities, such as stocks, the terms and conditions of which are decided by the board of directors. In such situations, corporations will have shareholders, who have a vote on whether to amend the corporation's articles of incorporation, merge with other corporations, sell corporate assets or dissolve the corporation (Abrams et al., 2011). It is critical to address the liquidation process when forming the corporation, specifying how corporate assets will be converted to cash and distributed to shareholders after payment of all debts, when the corporation eventually ceases to exist.

Publicly traded corporations are subject to many other legal requirements, outside the scope of this book, such as the Sarbanes-Oxley Act and regulations of the Securities and Exchange Commission (SEC). However, occupational health and safety (OH&S) consultant practices are highly unlikely to be publicly traded unless they are working as part of a larger national or international company.

While the most complex to initiate and maintain, the C corporation is the corporate form that offers the greatest shielding of personal assets and other liability. Although most consultants will rarely deal with mine safety issues, you should be aware that the Mine Safety & Health Administration (MSHA) is permitted to personally fine "agents of management" of corporations and LLCs (but not partnerships or sole proprietorships; there is conflicting case law as to S corporations) if they are found to have been involved in a high negligence violation. If your business will involve a significant amount of training or consulting work at mines, this would be an additional consideration.

Close Corporations and S Corporations

Close corporations and S corporations are considered informal, or less structured, business entities. The IRS defines an S corporation as one that elects to pass corporate income, losses, deductions, and credits through to shareholders for federal tax purposes.

Shareholders of S corporations report the flow-through of income and losses on their *personal* tax returns, and are assessed tax at their *individual* income tax rates. This allows S corporations to avoid double taxation on the corporate income. S corporations are responsible for tax on certain built-in gains and passive income, such as rental income or income from a trade or business activity in which the shareholders do not materially participate (IRS 2014b). Conversely, shareholders of a close corporation do not enjoy the ability to avoid corporate taxation, and may be subject to double taxation of earnings on corporate and personal tax returns.

Shareholders of S corporations report the flow-through of income and losses on their personal tax returns, and are assessed tax at their individual income tax rates.

For these informal corporate entities, there will be no open market for shareholders to dispose of shares and there may be limits on transfer of shares (e.g., limited to family members). It is permissible to have only one shareholder:

the owner/operator. Under normal circumstances, a close corporation will be released from annual meeting requirements, unless requested by a shareholder.

Formations of S corporations are made on the federal level. In order to qualify as an S corporation, you must complete Internal Revenue Service Form 2553, and submit it to the IRS. Conversely, the IRS does not recognize the close corporation formation. This type of business formation is regulated on the state level, and so requirements for close corporation formation vary by state. Because not all states recognize close corporations, this type of business formation may not be available in your state.

Limited Liability Companies (LLCs)

Some states offer an alternate form, the limited liability company (LLC). This business form gives owners limited personal liability for the debts and actions of the organization. The LLC offers the flexibility of a partnership, with the legal shields of a corporation. It can involve a single member (the owner) or multiple members (individuals, corporations, other LLCs, and even foreign entities).

Because this is similar to a corporation, expect to have to file articles of organization with the state for the record, and have a registered agent. Additional members can be added over time, which allows for investment and expansion of the business enterprise. If the business was initially formed as a partnership, it can often be converted to an LLC, if that corporate form is seen as more desirable for tax purposes or to shield personal assets more effectively, as long as all partners approve.

When choosing an LLC, you and any additional members will want to set up an operating agreement to establish the manner in which the business will be managed, controlled and operated, and whether any members will have limited authority for such activities. The agreement will also need to specify how earnings and other assets will be distributed, how new members can be admitted, and how the company will be dissolved or terminated.

Partnerships

A general partnership is created any time two or more individuals form an organization to conduct business as co-owners, to share profits, control, and liability. Unlike corporations, in some states, a partnership does not require any legal documentation or filing of business records with the government. Each partner serves as an agent of the other, for legal purposes, and can bind the partnership when transacting business, such as signing leases or contracts for purchases or services. Normally, partners cannot transfer their interest unless all remaining partners agree (absent a contractual agreement to the contrary). Therefore, if actions will require consent of both/all partners, this should be spelled out in writing in order to have legal effect.

Because there is no corporation created, under most state laws each partner's personal assets have exposure in the event that the partnership is sued and loses, and partners are typically "jointly and severally liable" for damages in both contract and tort cases (e.g., personal injury, negligent training, or supervision). It may be possible to obtain an umbrella insurance policy associated with other personal insurance to protect at higher levels (umbrella insurance was discussed in Chapter 4). Consult an insurance professional as to options, because umbrella policies linked to home property insurance may have exclusions for business-related claims that arise offsite.

Some states recognize what are known as limited liability partnerships (LLP), where none of the partners have personal liability for the debts or obligations of the partnership. Under an LLP, partners can have limited voting authority over specified matters. Partners' interests in the organization are freely assignable and, therefore, easily transferred (Abrams et al., 2011). However, partners exiting the arrangement may retain liability for actions taken while they were still a partner. As hybrids of a partnership and a corporation, LLPs will need to register in many states, and there may be additional fees involved.

Of course, some budding consultants may be tempted, after reading this, to go solo and avoid the partnership or corporate route for simplicity's sake. As a sole proprietor, you may be able to work out of your basement, print your own business cards, and get initial assignments via your network of contacts. But once your business starts thriving and becomes profitable, there can be tax consequences, so if you're considering going solo, consult a tax professional.

Moreover, as a sole proprietor, your personal assets will be on the line if you're sued. You may find it more costly as an individual to get professional liability insurance in the amounts you would want, and your state or local government may have restrictions on what types of work can be performed from a home office under zoning restrictions. These are all factors to consider when determining how to organize your consultancy.

Sole Proprietorship

You may decide to keep things simple initially and operate as a sole proprietorship. Generally, this makes the most sense if you are operating from home or have only a short-term rental on office space (long-term leases for office space usually involve committing for a two- to five-year period initially), and if you will have no employees. State laws will vary on this business form, so check with your local authorities.

In general, a sole proprietorship is a form of business in which one person owns all assets of the business. The downside is that the sole proprietor is solely and personally responsible for all debts of the business, including any uninsured claims made by clients or third parties. Because this is an unincorporated business form, the owner will also be personally responsible for tax obligations. The Internal Revenue Service (IRS) has a link for information on federal requirements applicable to sole proprietorships (IRS 2014c). Your state may have its own filing requirements.

TAXES AND LICENSING FEES

As you contemplate business formation, I cannot stress enough the importance of discussing tax consequences with an appropriately certified tax professional, and doing your homework about business licenses that may apply to your activities.

Even selecting the state in which to incorporate (which may or may not be the same state where you are located) can have significant financial and tax consequences. For example, Delaware has long been viewed as a very corporate-friendly jurisdiction, with a regulatory environment marked by clarity and flexibility and a court system known for acting quickly and effectively in resolving corporate litigation. More than half of Fortune 500 companies are incorporated in America's smallest state (Abrams et al., 2011, Chapter DE). However, incorporating there would be of little benefit for a sole proprietor or a partnership.

Talk often to your tax adviser. Tax codes change constantly....

Depending on the corporate form selected, the corporation may have to file a separate tax return, with its income and expenses completely separated from those of its owners/investors. Depending upon current tax laws, which change frequently, you may be subject to paying taxes based on the alternative minimum tax; you will want to consult a tax advisor for further details. Other corporate or partnership formats may instead have income and tax liability "flow through" an individual shareholder's tax return.

You have many tax issues to consider and to discuss with a tax advisor, starting with the most basic: What can be claimed as business expense deductions? For example, if you are working out of your home, what percentage of home expenses would be tax deductible? These questions can be more complex than you may have anticipated, so check with a professional before buying that large screen TV for your home, thinking it is deductible because you can occasionally use it to review safety audit photos.

Another consideration is business incentives that some states offer in economically distressed areas, to encourage capital investments and location of corporations in such areas that employ local residents; for example, the New Jersey Urban Enterprise Zones Act (NJSA 52:27H-60 et seq.). Such laws offer tax credits and exemptions for certain types of businesses. If you are located in such a jurisdiction, this may be a consideration in whether or not you decide to incorporate.

Talk often to your tax adviser. Tax codes change constantly, and there are 50 differing state and local tax requirements as well (for example, as a "professional corporation" registered in Maryland, I have to pay a state corporate property tax annually, separate and apart from my corporate and personal income tax returns). It is very easy to make errors, if you are not diligent in learning your obligations at the outset. It can be very expensive to correct omitted mandatory tax payments and penalties!

Finally, you will need to find out whether your jurisdiction, or the jurisdictions where you have clients, charge sales taxes on your services. State tax laws can be complicated, to say the least; I once had to file a separate tax return in another state simply because I had provided $3,000 worth of services there. Some states impose a sales tax on all sales of tangible personal property, such as safety manuals or training videos, but would exempt personal services. Where sales tax is imposed, it usually must be collected and remitted by the seller (you, the consultant). Failure to do so would subject you to prosecution.

CONTRACTS

Contracts are a fact of life in any type of business. As a professional consultant, you'll need to pay special attention to some contract areas. Contracts are generally written by lawyers, for lawyers, and may contain unfamiliar terms. I've included a glossary of common terms in Appendix A to this chapter, but consider obtaining professional review and advice before binding yourself legally.

Many form contracts contain boilerplate language, under which you waive your right to litigate any breaches and must agree to binding arbitration, perhaps under the law of a distant state. Often such "adhesion contracts" are used by large companies when they hire consultants. Sometimes, an in-demand consultant can set his or her own desired terms. As in most things, the party with superior bargaining strength can usually dictate the final terms, but don't be afraid to ask for changes you might feel are necessary (e.g, length of a lease, amount of deposits).

There are many types of contracts that one could potentially enter into, but among the most common are:

- Contracts for offices and facilities
- Contracts with clients
- Contracts with other consultants (subcontractors).

Contracts for Office Space and Facilities

If you have made an initial decision to have an office space outside of your home, which is particularly necessary if you will have clients meet with you and need a conference space or if you plan to have employees (assistants) or partner consultants, your first order of business will be to acquire real estate.

Most new businesses will lease, rather than make a commitment to buy, an office space. Office suite operations that will allow you to add space as needed, and that share a conference space, administrative support for phones and/or minor secretarial work, may be a good starter option. If you opt for an office space of your own, you may soon find that you need to bring on a full- or part-time support person to answer phones and to assist with mailings, copying, and perhaps accounting.

While there is no one-size-fits-all solution to the right initial setup, the one thing you can count on is contracts. Contracts for real estate leases, and purchase or rental of items and services such as a photocopier, telephone, and Internet service, and so on, will generally be boilerplate contracts created by the vendor. These tips should help you understand what you are agreeing to:

- Read the entire contract carefully to understand what commitment you are making. Are you pledging personal assets to back up your fledgling corporation or partnership?
- Understand, based on your business entity choice, whether you will have a personal obligation to pay the rent on a leased space even if your business goes belly-up.
- Determine what recourse you have as the renter for breaches by the landlord (such as problems with electrical services, a leaking roof, or broken plumbing), and whether the contract allows you to go to court or whether you are limited to binding arbitration. Binding arbitration, which is often included in contracts, prevents you from going to court and having a judge or jury rule on your case with appeal rights to a higher court. Instead, a trained arbitrator substitutes as a judge and his/her decision is final, with no right of appeal.
- Figure out if you are agreeing to litigate in a different state from where you are located.

These are all issues that may be negotiable, depending on the state of the real estate market.

Contracts with Clients

You will also need to create contracts to use for your services with clients. It is impossible to provide examples of all relevant types of contracts here, as consulting practices can differ so widely, but see Chapter 6, "Marketing and Sales" for a sample proposal.

At a minimum, a contract should clearly describe:

- the identity of the parties;
- an execution date and the date(s) of the services;
- a detailed description of the scope of work to be performed (consider whether this will be a single event for the client, or an ongoing relationship);
- the rate(s) being charged (which may vary depending on services provided, such as whether field work or trial testimony is involved), and when those rates are subject to change over time;
- whether you can contract or subcontract out all or part of the work;
- payment schedules and consequences for breach (such as whether reasonable interest will be charged);
- "hold harmless" clauses and disclaimers, if appropriate (for example, a clause under which one or both parties agree not to hold the other responsible for losses or legal liabilities); and
- how breaches will be litigated (trial versus arbitration), and where (your home state, the state where you are incorporated, or the state where the client is located or where your work is performed, are common choices).

Other issues that either you or the client may want to address are insurance coverage, indemnification in the event that one party gets sued as a result of the other party's negligence, and clarification that you are a contractor and not an employee of the client. If you have questions about the contract you've drafted or been asked to sign, you would be wise to consult an attorney who focuses on transactional and business matters.

Contracts with Other Consultants

Subcontractor Liability and Risk Management

If you retain someone to be an independent contractor to your business, that person may have his or her own contract for you to review and sign, or you may be able to dictate the terms and conditions. Contracts can be on an assignment-by-assignment basis or can be longer term, depending on your needs. Typically, in addition to the general contract terms discussed above, you will want to include:

- a cancellation provision,
- whether a notice period is required on either side, and
- whether there will be liquidated damages and attorney fees paid in the event of a breach (e.g., your contractor walks off a job in the middle of time-sensitive environmental sampling or fails to provide you with verified, timely records of training he/she has conducted for your client).

Legal liability arising from activities of your subcontractors ... at a client jobsite is one of the most difficult risk exposures to address and properly manage.

Legal liability arising from activities of your subcontractors undertaking activities on your behalf at a client jobsite is one of the most difficult risk exposures to address and properly manage. Unless you adequately prequalify and train your subcontractors, or require them to come to you pre-trained and with appropriate certifications, and ensure proper coordination of activities with all parties involved in a project, your company can face civil penalties or even criminal prosecution from government safety agencies. When feasible, it is also a good idea to obtain copies of subcontractors' certificates of insurance and, if they are not insured, consider whether they can be included under your own insurance. More information on insurance issues can be found in Chapter 4.

Another concern is exposure to tort liability arising from personal injury or wrongful death claims under the *"respondeat superior"* doctrine (in which a "master" is liable in certain circumstances for the wrongful acts of his "servant" and a "principal" is liable under the same theory for the acts of his "agent"). Of course, using your own employee instead of a contractor can still result in imputed liability, so you must exercise appropriate oversight either way!

In one case I was involved with, an injury to one contractor at a jobsite was deemed to be the partial responsibility of another. The resulting jury awards were in excess of $15 million, a figure often outside the liability insurance policy limits of small consultants. Therefore, selecting your subcontractors without exercising due diligence can be devastating to a corporation, and even more so to a partnership or sole proprietorship where personal assets are at risk.

Professional Liability Exposure and Insurance

It is advisable that consultants obtain professional liability insurance coverage, personally and/or for your partnership or corporation. In addition to facing possible legal claims arising from contractual disputes, OS&H professionals can also be sued for tort actions including: negligent training, negligent supervision, and even negligent inspection (e.g., if conditions adversely affecting safety, health or the environment are not discovered or disclosed during audits, and damage results as a consequence of uncorrected conditions). In addition to providing guidance on appropriate coverages for the nature and scope of your business, the professional liability insurer may also be willing to review contracts you have drafted, as it is in that company's interest to protect you from suits.

Regulatory Compliance and Contractor Prequalification

As discussed elsewhere in this chapter, regulatory compliance is expected of consultants just as it is of the companies they serve. In addition to citation and penalty exposure for their own actions while on a client's jobsite, under OSHA and MSHA enforcement practices, a consultant who engages a subcontractor may be held liable for the subcontractor's violations under the agencies' multi-employer worksite doctrines as the "controlling employer." But getting a duplicative OSHA or MSHA citation based on another company's misdeeds has ramifications that go well beyond your compliance history with the Department of Labor. Such violations can normally be introduced as proof of negligence *per se* in tort actions brought by a subcontractor (or his/her estate) or by third parties for injuries or fatalities suffered at the worksite. It often does not matter if the defendant was the "creating employer" (the employer whose company created the hazardous condition or permitted the violative action) under these circumstances.

You will also want to know if the subcontractor has the liability and workers' compensation insurance coverage you require, perhaps adding you as an additional insured.

It is prudent practice to decide on a corporate policy for contractor and subcontractor utilization in advance of retaining one. Because the "low bid" often represents skimping on key safety practices, you will want to:

- Verify the company's written safety programs and training documentation (the "trust but verify" approach);
- Check references;
- Review the bidding subcontractor's compliance and injury/illness history with OSHA and MSHA (available free on the agencies' websites);
- Check your subcontractors' workers' compensation experience modification rate where applicable;
- Ensure that they have the necessary certifications and licenses to perform the work you are assigning to them; and
- See if they have professional or trade association connections (as this indicates interest in staying abreast of evolving regulatory requirements).

You will also want to know if the subcontractor has the liability and workers' compensation insurance coverage you require, perhaps adding you as an additional insured. This prequalification may be time consuming, but if it can protect you from a $15 million lawsuit, surely it is worth it.

The prequalification steps needed will vary, depending on the nature and extent of the subcontractor's involvement in your work. Since you could ultimately be held legally liable for any failures on the subcontractor's part, caution is warranted. Don't fail to update old prequalification information, particularly if you are doing work under federal or state contracts that have debarment provisions for employment or safety violations.

These are some suggested items to include if you are vetting the subcontractor yourself (there are also companies that will do this, for a fee). You can play detective, and verify some of this by checking the online OSHA and MSHA databases, as well as checking court judiciary search data, once you learn the jurisdictions in which the subcontractor operates. How much of this information you need may depend on who your client is and how large is the project; you may not need all of this for a subcontractor who is just covering a two-hour training session for you. Generally, the information you may want includes:

- The corporate form of the subcontractor's business, and state of incorporation (if applicable). With this information, you can determine if they are in "good standing" with the government by checking state databases.
- Whether the subcontractor has petitioned for bankruptcy, compromised with creditors, defaulted on a contract, or caused a loss to a surety.
- Whether there are any claims, arbitration proceedings, or judgments pending or finalized against them.
- Contacts for insurance information, as well as information on the insurance policy type and limits, and whether you will be added as an additional insured.
- References from other contractors or clients for whom the subcontractor has worked in the last three years.
- Licenses and certifications held by the subcontractor, and mandated training received by him or her, where it is required for your project.
- Employees and equipment of the subcontractor that will be used in your work. Documentation that the subcontractor will provide its workers with appropriate personal protective equipment.
- Basic information on the subcontractor's safety and health compliance (final and pending OSHA and MSHA citations covering a

five-year period, copies of the OSHA logs and MSHA 7000-1 forms for the previous three years, workers' compensation Experience Modification Rate).
- Copies of the subcontractor's safety programs, policies, and procedures.
- Information on union representation, and safety and health committee requirements, where applicable.
- Documentation on drug-free workplace programs and drug testing requirements, where applicable.

Finally, remember that you may be a subcontractor to a company (or client) who is working on an even larger project. In such situations, you can expect to be scrutinized just as thoroughly as you would study your subcontractors. Therefore, you will be expected to show a good record of compliance with all relevant federal, state and local laws, to carry adequate insurance, to have proof of specialized training or certifications (where required), and to show financial stability and a record free from malpractice claims.

EMPLOYMENT LAW ISSUES

If you decide to hire assistants or other types of employees to help with specific tasks, such as accounting, or to work with you as consultants, you should decide, upfront, if a contract will be necessary. Whether you need a contract depends on the type of relationship you intend to create. Contracts are desirable for temporary contingent workers and subcontractors who will perform ancillary duties for you periodically. If you hire an assistant to work on a permanent basis, no contract will be needed as most workers are "employees at will," but the terms and conditions (e.g., hours, rate of pay) should be agreed upon in advance.

If you're a solo practitioner, you're unlikely to have employment law concerns. But at some point you may find that it is not in your financial interest to spend time running to the post office, handling filing or bill-paying yourself when you could earn more money out on assignments.

Once you hire a permanent administrative aide, bookkeeper or other OH&S professionals, you have become an employer. Depending on your company size, you may now be subject to some or all of the federal laws discussed below. If you want to avoid these complications, use a temporary service, at least to start out. That way, the agency providing the worker is the worker's legal employer, and you will only pay for the services rendered. If you do hire employees, you might want to use professional payroll companies that will compute and submit federal and state tax contributions and corresponding reports (such as W-2 forms to employees), issue electronic payroll to workers, track leave, and handle other necessary HR (human relations or human resources) tasks for a fee. Some have a threshold of a minimum number of employees but, as I recall, I started using such a system when I had as few as four employees.

The typical *employment* relationship outside of a union setting (where terms and condition of employment are dictated by a collective bargaining agreement) is "employment at will." This means that both the employer and the employee are free to unilaterally end the relationship at any time, without cause or advance notice.

However, there are a few exceptions to employment at will, including circumstances where there is an actual signed contract (express contract) or where an employee handbook, policy or other evidence (e.g., an offer letter) creates an "implied contract." Courts may find that an employer must honor such implied contracts, but it is a case-by-case determination based on the facts. There are also commonly recognized exceptions to employment at will based on public policy, such as protection of whistleblowers, or breach of the covenants of good faith and fair dealing (only recognized in some states).

Of course, even if you have an "at will" employee, under federal law, you must never terminate or take other adverse action against a worker, or a job applicant, based on race, color, gender, religion, national origin, age, disability, or military status. Similarly, there can be no discrimination against workers because of their "caregiver" responsibilities to children, ailing family members or elderly parents, or because they filed workers' compensation claims against you, the current employer, or even against former employers. Some state laws also prohibit discrimination based on marital status or sexual orientation. If your company is large enough (50 or more employees), you also can't discriminate against or penalize employees who take a leave of absence under the Family and Medical Leave Act (FMLA).

All of the civil rights laws include anti-retaliation provisions, as do most state workers' compensation statutes and codes. Moreover, while the discussion below deals with federal law, your state may have other legal issues to contend with, such as legalization of medical (or recreational) marijuana, which could create present drug-testing issues, particularly for consultants who seek to work as federal contractors and, therefore, must have drug-free workplace programs in place. You may have state or local laws that prohibit discrimination against employees or applicants based on sexual orientation, or appearance (such as obesity, tattoos, and piercings), even though federal civil rights laws do not cover those areas.

You may find that your state or municipal laws are more protective than federal laws in key respects: for example, in the District of Columbia, age discrimination laws cover any discrimination based on age, not just discrimination against persons aged 40 and older. Even though the federal FMLA doesn't apply until you have 50 or more employees, some jurisdictions may require smaller employers to provide unpaid leave for eligible employees who must take medical leave for serious health conditions, to care for family members with serious health conditions, or following birth, fostering or adoption of a child. Some areas also have more generous leave required than the federal law requires (e.g., while the federal FMLA requires up to 12 weeks of unpaid leave per year, the District of Columbia's analogous statute expands the leave to 16 weeks).

A chart listing the primary federal employment laws that may apply to your business is in Appendix B to this chapter. Appendix C provides links to each state's labor and civil rights offices. Those agencies can provide information about state-specific employment law requirements.

Worker Misclassification Issues

It may be tempting to consider your part-time assistant as a contractor, so that you can avoid the complexity of figuring out (and paying) the employer contribution for payroll taxes, or avoid having to acquire workers' compensation insurance or contribute to your state's unemployment insurance fund, but if you're caught, the consequences can be severe.

In 2011, the U.S. Department of Labor (DOL) launched its "Employee Misclassification Initiative" and entered into a Memorandum of Understanding with the Internal Revenue Service (IRS) to reduce the tax gap caused by misclassification of employees as independent contractors and to improve compliance with federal labor laws.

According to DOL, the misclassification of employees as something other than employees, such as independent contractors, presents a serious problem because misclassified employees are often denied access to critical benefits and protections—such as family and medical leave, overtime, minimum wage and unemployment insurance—to which they are entitled. Employee misclassification also generates substantial losses to the Treasury and the Social Security and Medicare funds, as well as to state unemployment insurance and workers' compensation funds (DOL 2011). Simply put, misclassifying workers as contractors is a federal offense.

> *Simply put, misclassifying workers as contractors is a federal offense.*

One small business with whom I worked had classified its four workers as contractors, and issued Form 1099s to them at the end of the year instead of W-2s. The company was audited in the wake of a fatal accident (because OSHA shares any suspicions of misclassification with its sister agency in DOL, the Employment Standards Administration). Because DOL found that the workers were incorrectly classified, the company was required to pay negotiated penalties to the government and full "back wages" to the workers in the form of "recreated overtime" that the government determined was due.

If you are not sure if you can commit to hiring a clerical or accounting worker for the long term, it may be best to use a temporary agency, where you pay the agency and the agency actually hires the workers, paying their taxes and benefits. If you do hire workers directly, make it clear that they are "at will" employees, which means you can terminate the relationship at any time, without notice and without cause (subject to certain restrictions—for example, you cannot violate public policy by firing someone for serving jury duty—and, of course, you cannot fire the worker for any discriminatory reason).

Make sure that your communications with your employees do not create "implied contracts," where you may have made promises about the duration of work, terms and conditions of employment, or reasons why the relationship could be ended. Often "offer" letters (or emails), employee handbooks, and progressive discipline systems are used against the employer to show that the workers were not "at will" at all, and that they could only be terminated for good cause.

Also remember that "at-will" workers can quit at any time, without notice, which could leave you in a breach situation with respect to completing work for your clients. If a worker absolutely will be needed for a specified period of time, an express contract may be more prudent than an "at-will" employee relationship.

If you find that your work is growing by leaps and bounds, and you need another professional to service clients, a contractor arrangement may work well for you, as long as the IRS "common law rules" are satisfied.

The IRS Common-Law Rules

What used to be known as the IRS "20-factor test" has been simplified in recent years to help employers determine whether an individual can be legally classified as an employee or independent contractor under common law. The relationship of the worker and the business must be examined carefully, and all evidence of control and independence must be considered (IRS 2014a).

Factors that give evidence of the degree of control/independence fall into three categories: behavioral control, financial control, and the type of relationship of the parties:

1. *Behavioral control:* Does the business have a right to direct and control how the worker does the task for which the worker is hired? That may be shown by:
   i. whether your business instructs the worker about how, when and where to work (*Note:* the amount of instruction varies by job. DOL, IRS and courts will look at whether there is sufficient behavioral control of the worker),
   ii. whether you specify what tools or equipment to use, and provide them to the worker), and
   iii. what training you give the worker.

2. *Financial control:* Does the business have the right to control the business aspects of the worker's job? That may be shown by:
   i. the extent to which the worker has unreimbursed business expenses in performing the services for the business,
   ii. the extent of the worker's investment in tools or equipment that may be used outside of your business,
   iii. the extent to which the worker makes services available to others rather than working exclusively for your business,
   iv. how you pay the worker (hourly, weekly, or flat fee for performing project work), and
   v. the extent to which the worker can realize a profit or loss.

3. *Type of relationship*, as shown by:
   i. whether there are written contracts describing the relationship you and the worker intended to create,
   ii. whether your business provides the worker with employee-type benefits (such as insurance, a pension plan, vacation or sick pay),
   iii. the permanency of the relationship, and
   iv. the extent to which services provided by the worker are a key aspect of the regular business of the company.

No single criterion listed above determines the issue; typically, the courts and agencies will look at the totality of the circumstances in making a decision. If you use a bookkeeper who provides the same services to ten other clients, has an advertisement for bookkeeping services in the phone book or on the Internet, is incorporated or does the work from an offsite location, that person would probably be considered a contractor. On the other hand, if you expect the bookkeeper to be at your office five days a week, and prohibit him or her from working for any other businesses, that person would likely be considered your employee.

Note also that whether a worker is your employee or an independent contractor will have an impact on whether your business or the worker is held responsible if the worker violates an OSHA standard while doing work for you. If the person is deemed to be your employee, your business would be cited. If the person is an independent contractor, you could avoid liability, unless OSHA cites you as a "controlling" employer under its multi-employer worksite doctrine (OSHA 1999).

Employment Law 101

In law school, entire semester-long courses are taught on individual employment laws. Volumes have been written full of compliance information for employers about the maze of statutory requirements at the federal level. That doesn't even address the additional, more stringent, requirements that most states, some counties, and many major cities can have. Those may cover even the smallest employers.

You will need to decide whether you can handle the complexities that come with being an employer, both logistically and financially (such as contributing to the state unemployment fund, carrying workers' compensation insurance, and so on). If you will have employees, you will need to develop policies on whether to offer paid leave (which is not federally required but could be required by state law), and on what benefits you will extend to employees. You'll need to develop a discipline policy. It may be useful to hire an employment consultant to help you develop appropriate policies and procedures. Once you have a policy, follow it! This is a defense against allegations of disparate treatment.

Obviously, a detailed discussion of all the employment laws that apply in the United States to employers is outside the scope of this publication. Many consultants may be under the size limits for many of the federal laws, at least until their successful practice expands. Even so, you should be cognizant of the basic requirements and remedies, and at what point those requirements apply to your operation. The chart in Appendix C on state employment and labor regulatory agencies and state civil/human rights commissions provides links, as a starting point, to your local resources. Use them to begin to determine whether more stringent state, county, or municipal laws apply to your business based on number of employees. Of course, regardless of the number of employees, discrimination in employment is improper ethically and as a matter of public policy.

Federal employment laws that could, under certain circumstances, impact your business include:

The Fair Labor Standards Act (FLSA) . . . applies to every business that engages in interstate commerce. . . .

- Fair Labor Standards Act (FLSA, which covers minimum wage, child labor, and overtime compensation issues)
- Immigration Reform and Control Act of 1986 (employment eligibility and identity, etc.)
- Title VII of the Civil Rights Act (prohibits discrimination based on race, color, gender, religion or national origin)
- Americans with Disabilities Act (ADA)
- Age Discrimination in Employment Act of 1967 (ADEA)
- Family and Medical Leave Act (FMLA)
- Uniformed Services Employment and Reemployment Rights Act (USERRA)

Finally, if you are doing business as a federal contractor, you may have additional requirements (depending largely on contract size), including the need for affirmative action plans and drug-free workplace programs.

Do you see why seeking assistance with employment law or using an HR consultant is recommended?

Fair Labor Standards Act

The Fair Labor Standards Act (FLSA) is one of the oldest federal employment laws. Enacted in 1938, it covers minimum wages, overtime entitlements and exemptions, and restrictions on child labor. It applies to every business that engages in interstate commerce and has at least one employee. Interstate commerce is broadly defined and includes using the mails or telephones, or shipping or receiving goods, or crossing state lines in the course of employment.

The FLSA has recordkeeping requirements. If an action is brought for alleged underpayment, if the employer does not have the mandatory timesheet/payroll records, the employee's claim of hours worked will be accepted as fact.

As of 2014, the federal minimum wage was $7.25 per hour, but some states and even counties and large cities have higher minimum wages. The U.S. Department of Labor, or the comparable state agency, will often bring FLSA actions against the employer at no cost to the worker. The worker also has a right of private action to sue the business directly, rather than going through administrative channels. If successful, the worker may be entitled to the back pay/overtime due, plus liquidated damages and attorney fees.

Exempt employees, who are not required to be paid overtime, include: executive, administrative, and professional employees, outside sales employees and employees in certain computer-related occupations (defined in DOL regulations), and commissioned employees of retail or service establishments. But there are fairly technical legal tests on exemption. I handled one case involving a safety and health professional, working under contract, who was determined to be owed significant back overtime pay based on the totality of her circumstances.

Every non-exempt employee is entitled to overtime pay, paid at one and one-half times the employee's regular rate of pay, for any hours worked in excess of 40 per workweek. To calculate the overtime rate for salaried non-exempt employees, divide the salary by the number of hours that the salary was intended to compensate under regular work conditions.

This can be tricky to understand. A common mistake occurs when a biweekly pay period is used. You can't average the hours over the two weeks in the pay period. If an employee worked 80 hours in a biweekly pay period, but worked 45 hours in one week and 35 hours in the other week, that employee would be entitled to five hours of overtime pay for the first week during that pay cycle. A "workweek" is defined by DOL as a period of 168 hours during seven consecutive 24-hour periods, beginning on any day and any hour of the week. There can be no averaging of two or more work weeks.

When in doubt as to how an employee should be classified, consult an HR professional or attorney, as mistakes can be very costly by the time penalties are added.

IRCA and Immigration Issues

The Immigration Reform and Control Act of 1986 (IRCA) makes it illegal for employers with four or more employees to fire or refuse to hire a person on the basis of that person's national origin or citizenship. It also forbids the hiring of people illegally in the U.S. The two agencies most involved with employment issues as they relate to immigration laws are the U.S. Citizenship and Immigration Services (USCIS) agency and the U.S. Immigration and Customs Enforcement (ICE) agency; both are part of the Department of Homeland Security (DHS).

> USCIS Form I-9 ... requires that you verify both the person's identity and his or her eligibility to work in the U.S.

Whenever you hire anyone, you must complete an USCIS Form I-9 "Employment Eligibility Verification" for that person, which requires that you verify both the person's identity and his or her eligibility to work in the U.S (DHS 2013). You need to do this for all people you hire; you cannot request employment verification from only people of a certain national origin or only from applicants who appear to be from a foreign country. An employer who has citizenship requirements or gives preference to United States citizens may violate IRCA. There are exceptions that allow an employer to refuse to hire an alien worker, such as where citizenship is a "bona fide occupational qualification," (e.g., if you are performing work for the federal government on a defense contract where a security clearance is required). If you are doing work where special visas are required for specialized workers, obtaining advice from an immigration law professional is a good idea.

As the employer, you must physically examine the documents your newly hired employees provide to show their identity and employment authorization. The I-9 form has a complete list of the documents that can be used (DHS 2013). They must not be expired, of course.

The main document most people can use to establish both identity and employment authorization is the U.S. passport. A driver's license or ID card issued by a federal, state, or local government agency is the most common document used to prove identity, but it doesn't prove employment authorization. To demonstrate that someone is authorized to work in the U.S., a Social Security account number card or an original or certified copy of a U.S. birth certificate could be used. Those are not the only documents authorized to prove identity and employment authorization; see the I-9 form itself for a full list (DHS 2013).

Title VII of the Civil Rights Act

Title VII of the Civil Rights Act, 42 U.S.C. §2000e et seq., applies to employers who have at least 15 or more employees for 20 or more weeks in the preceding or current calendar year. It prohibits discrimination in any aspect of employment including: hiring, firing, compensation, assignment or classification of employees, transfer, promotion, layoff, job advertising, recruitment, testing, training, benefits, leave and other terms and conditions of employment.

Specifically, Title VII prohibits discrimination based on race, color, religion, national origin, and gender (both quid pro quo sex discrimination and hostile work environment gender discrimination). Currently, sexual orientation is not covered by Title VII (although Congress has considered this repeatedly), but many states do have such bans.

Title VII also bars retaliation against an employee who has complained internally or externally about discrimination, or who has testified in his or her own or another worker's EEOC action. Many states and municipalities have adopted their own versions of Title VII, which often will extend protections to employees and applicants at smaller companies. So you'll need to determine which laws may cover your business.

Statutes that are related to the Civil Rights Act, Title VII, by dealing with gender discrimination issues, which are also enforced by the EEOC, include the Pregnancy Discrimination Act of 1978 and the Equal Pay Act of 1963. The Equal Pay Act requires equal pay for men and women who perform substantially equal work on jobs that require equal skill, effort, and responsibility, and that are done under similar working conditions.

Unlike Title VII, the Equal Pay Act has no minimum number of employees to trigger its applicability, and there is no requirement for an employee to first file a complaint with the EEOC before proceeding to court. The Equal Pay Act has a two-year statute of limitations for filing suit in court. Both back pay and liquidated damages are available as remedies. By contrast, under Title VII, the employee must file a complaint within 180 days of the triggering event with the EEOC, or within 300 days if there is a state civil rights agency with a work-share agreement with the EEOC, and the employee must prove intentional discrimination in order to get anything more than back pay.

Under the Lilly Ledbetter Fair Pay Act, P.L. 111-2, Jan. 29, 2009, signed into law by President Barack Obama, each paycheck that is "unequal," based on any protected characteristic under Title VII, or based on age or disability, constitutes a new violation and restarts the statute of limitations under Title VII.

Americans with Disabilities Act

The Americans with Disabilities Act of 1990 (ADA), Title I, prohibits employment discrimination against individuals with disabilities, those regarded as disabled, even if not actually disabled, and those associated with disabled persons, such as someone with a disabled spouse or child. It applies to employers with 15 or more employees. The EEOC enforces the ADA. The same filing deadlines and remedies apply as under Title VII of the Civil Rights Act.

The types of disabilities covered by the ADA are quite broad.

The types of disabilities covered by the ADA are quite broad. In general, if a disability (physical or mental) interferes with a major life activity for an extended period, it would be covered. This includes conditions that may go into remission, such as cancer or multiple sclerosis, but does not cover temporary impairments such as a broken leg, or normal pregnancies.

To be protected, the applicant or worker must be a "qualified individual with a disability," able to meet all essential job functions with or without reasonable accommodation. The employer does not have to ask the applicant or employee if they need an accommodation; the burden is on the disabled person to make the request. The employer is expected to provide a reasonable accommodation (not necessarily the precise accommodation requested by the individual), unless it would impose undue hardship, on a case-by-case analysis, since what a large company might easily do could be unduly burdensome for a small business.

Reasonable accommodations can include making facilities accessible, restructuring jobs, providing part-time or modified work schedules, and acquiring or modifying equipment. Essential job functions are defined by the employer but it is much better to have a job description that delineates these prior to the onset of litigation!

In addition to undue hardship, other employer defenses that can be used to rebut discrimination charges for failing to hire or retain a worker covered under the ADA include:

- Direct threat to safety or health of others, defined as a "significant risk to the health or safety of others that cannot be eliminated by reasonable accommodation." That can include infectious diseases.
- Job-related criteria, defined as tests, standards, or criteria that are job related or consistent with business necessity (e.g., requiring a Certified Safety Professional (CSP) designation allows you to discriminate against a disabled (or non-disabled) person who lacks that credential).
- Food-handler defense, under which employers in the food service industry can refuse to assign or transfer to a food-handling job any individual who has an infectious or communicable disease that can be transmitted to other in that manner. The U.S. Department of Health & Human Services compiles a list of such conditions annually.
- Religious entities, which exemption permits a church-run employer to refuse to hire a disabled applicant who is not a member of that church.

Age Discrimination in Employment Act of 1967 (ADEA)

The Age Discrimination in Employment Act of 1967 (ADEA), which applies to employers, labor unions, and employment agencies of 20 or more employees, prohibits discrimination in hiring, awarding promotions or benefits, and other employment practices against applicants and employees aged 40 or older. Some state analogs may cover workers under age 40 or may bar any age-based decision making, so check your local statutes.

... Age Discrimination in Employment Act ... claims are increasing in number....

ADEA claims are increasing in number, based in part on the large number of baby boomers (all of whom are over age 40 now) who are staying in the workforce past normal retirement age or who are seeking supplemental employment after retiring from their primary careers.

Often, claims arise after an applicant is told he/she is "overqualified" for a position, or where layoffs that target the most senior workers have the effect of removing those who are older than the retained employees. Even if a worker over 40 is replaced by another worker over 40, discrimination can still be found if there is a significant difference in the respective workers' ages (e.g., the discharged worker is 58 and is replaced by a 42-year-old).

Employer defenses against age discrimination claims include showing that the alleged discriminatory action was taken pursuant to a bona fide seniority system, retirement, pension or benefit system or for a reasonable factor other than age. Having good cause to discharge or discipline an employee is another legitimate defense. Age can also be a "bona fide occupational qualification."

The ADEA is administered by the EEOC, and complaint deadlines are the same as for Title VII. However, complainants do not have to wait more than 60 days before filing suit in court, and they do not have to wait to receive an EEOC "right to sue" letter. The remedies under the ADEA are back pay, attorney fees, and liquidated damages for willful violations.

Family and Medical Leave Act

Although most consultants will fall short of having the 50-employee minimum threshold that triggers coverage under the Family and Medical Leave Act of 1993 (FMLA), some state or municipal laws require similar protections at smaller places of employment. Therefore, a brief discussion of this law is provided for reference.

The FMLA covers employees who have been employed at least one year and have worked at least 1250 hours (for an average of about 24 hours a week) in the preceding year. Employers must provide these eligible employees with up to twelve weeks of unpaid leave in a year to address their own serious health condition, the serious health condition of a family member, or the birth, fostering, or adoption of a child. The employee's group health benefits need to be maintained during that leave. There are limited exceptions to allowing leave, such as one for "key" employees. If the employee's old position is no longer available when leave ends, the employer is normally expected to provide a comparable position.

Military leave and military caregiver provisions were added to the FMLA in 2008.

A "serious health condition" is one that requires inpatient hospital care, or that lasts more than three days and requires ongoing treatment by a healthcare professional, that involves pregnancy, that involves a long-term or permanently disabling health condition, that requires absences for receiving multiple treatments for restorative surgery, or for a condition that would likely result in a period of incapacity of more than three days if left untreated.

The employee is allowed to use intermittent leave under FMLA, where the twelve weeks is not taken in one block of time. The employee is expected to provide advance notice of such leave requests, where feasible, and to provide supporting documentation if requested by the employer. An employee or the employer may choose to substitute accrued paid leave for part or all of the normally unpaid FMLA leave, but the employee cannot take the paid leave and then add on 12 more weeks of unpaid leave after paid leave is exhausted.

Military leave and military caregiver provisions were added to the FMLA in 2008. These allow eligible employees to take up to twelve weeks of unpaid leave during a twelve-month period for "qualified exigencies" associated with the employee's spouse, child, or parent being called to active military duty or being suddenly deployed to a foreign country. The caregiver provisions, which provide up to 26 weeks of unpaid leave rather than the normal twelve weeks, cover employees whose immediate family member (or other family member for whom the employee is "next of kin") is a member of the armed services and undergoing medical treatment, recuperation or therapy because of a military-related illness or injury.

FMLA leave cannot be counted against the employee under a "no-fault" attendance policy. The employer cannot deny the employee taking FMLA leave any benefits, seniority or bonuses as a result of that employee exercising the leave rights.

The FMLA is enforced by the Wage and Hour Division of the U.S. Department of Labor, not the EEOC. An employee who believes his or her rights under the FMLA have been violated has the choice of filing a complaint with the agency or filing a private lawsuit. Lawsuits are subject to a two-year statute of limitations (three years if the violation was willful). Legal remedies include: recovery of lost wages and benefits, actual monetary losses, liquidated damages of two times the actual damages (unless the employer had reasonable grounds for not knowing it was violating the law), and attorney fees and costs.

Uniformed Services Employment and Reemployment Rights Act (USERRA)

The Uniformed Services Employment and Reemployment Rights Act (USERRA) was enacted in 1994, but has become a growing area of employment litigation because of the number of affected individuals returning to the workforce after recent United States conflicts abroad. The law applies to virtually all employers, regardless of size.

USERRA protects workers who are absent from employment because they were called to active military service, provided they gave the employer notice and are absent for a cumulative period of less than five years. The service member must also apply for reemployment within a specified timeframe, which varies depending on the length of deployment.

Employees reemployed after military service are entitled to the seniority, rights and benefits that they had when the service began, plus any such rights and benefits that might have accrued if they had been continuously employed.

Complaints are filed with the U.S. Department of Labor, not the EEOC. Remedies include injunctions, restoration of lost wages, benefits, and legal fees. Liquidated damages are available for willful violations. The employee needs to only demonstrate that the military service was a motivating factor in the decision not to reinstate him or her, not that it was the sole factor. The employer can defend by showing that the circumstances have changed so that reemployment would be unreasonable or impossible, or would cause undue hardship in accommodation, training or effort, or that the initial employment was for a brief, nonrecurring period.

REGULATORY COMPLIANCE CONSIDERATIONS

... if you have formed a corporation, then you and other consultants working for the corporation are probably classified as its employees.

If you want to work as an occupational health and safety or environmental consultant, the last thing you need is to develop a public track record of non-compliance with OSHA, MSHA, or the EPA. These days, the agencies have detailed databases on their websites that detail what you are accused of doing wrong, the proposed penalties, and whether the citations and penalties were upheld. Information about your injury and illness history is also available, and there are even ways to learn the precise overexposures measured when the DOL conducts health sampling of your employees.

An obvious question is whether a consultant even falls under the jurisdiction of these agencies. The answer, of course, is "maybe." OSHA does not have jurisdiction unless a company has employees, so if you have none, and are a sole proprietorship or partnership, you are in the clear. But if you have formed a corporation, then you and other consultants working for the corporation are probably classified as its employees. Moreover, MSHA does not even provide this exception: if you're hired to do consulting work at a mine site, you are a mine operator by definition under the 1977 Mine Act. That act specifically defines independent contractors performing services at the mine as an operator.

At any rate, if one's intention is to be a successful, high-quality safety and health consultant, setting a stellar compliance example is not only the right thing to do, it's a good business practice as well.

As for the EPA, while you may not be generating hazardous waste or spewing clouds of air toxics into the environment as a consultant, you may still have some exposure to prosecution. Years ago, I represented a safety and environmental consultant who was criminally charged for failing to timely report a "spill;" the consultant had reported it to his client, but the client did not report it to the environmental agency. When the blame game of musical chairs stopped, the consultant was the one left standing. Although (thankfully!) he was not convicted, it brought home the dramatic potential consequences of non-compliance.

OSHA does exempt low-hazard employers with ten or fewer employees from some of its injury and illness paperwork requirements (see 29 CFR §1904.1), although they are still required to comply with all other applicable regulations in 29 CFR. MSHA contains no comparable exemptions. Also, remember that more than 20 states run their own state OSHA programs, and a number have additional mine safety programs (MSHA retains concurrent jurisdiction). These may have more stringent requirements than their federal counterparts.

Beyond the obvious safety, health and environmental laws with which you need to comply, when starting a consultancy practice, you will need to see what state-specific regulations govern your enterprise. As an example, the state-based workers' compensation insurance requirement thresholds vary widely from state to state; I learned, when I started my firm in Maryland, that because I had formed an S corporation and was its employee (the only one, initially), I had to purchase workers' compensation insurance to cover myself. Other states do not require insurance unless there are five or more employees. Some states allow owners to opt out of workers' compensation, only requiring employees be covered.

> ... when I started my firm in Maryland, I had to purchase workers' compensation insurance to cover myself.

Failure to carry mandatory workers' compensation insurance or to comply with other state and federal safety, environmental, and licensing regulations, as well as the employment laws discussed above, can trigger penalties but can carry other reputation-based consequences, including exclusion from participating in federal and state contracts (known as "debarment") or even stripping away your professional certifications. For example, Certified Safety Professionals can lose their CSP status for any violation of the BCSP Code of Professional Conduct, which includes having a criminal conviction of a felony, misdemeanor or petty offense for acts done in connection with activities for which the certification was granted.

You will find there are reports and fees that are necessary to file with various agencies just to stay in business. Noncompliance may be noted on the state corporation's public databases, and can thwart your chances of getting work if your company is vetted by a prospective client. Do your homework before falling out of compliance. Once the state issues a notice to you, it becomes part of your permanent record!

LEGAL PRIVILEGE ISSUES

Any discussion about the legal and regulatory issues facing consultants would be remiss if issues of legal privilege were not mentioned. Depending on the scope of your work, you may be serving as a "behind the scene" (non-testifying) consultant in matters that will result in litigation. Or, conversely, you may be retained to serve as an expert witness, with the intent of having you testify on the client's behalf if a matter goes to court. In some cases, you may be retained directly by a company that needs assistance with safety and health training or auditing, and find that you are subsequently on the receiving end of an OSHA subpoena.

> *Depending on the scope of your work, you may be serving as a "behind the scene" (non-testifying) consultant in matters that will result in litigation.*

In recent years, OSHA has been aggressive in seeking even insurance company reports and records, under the theory that these can help when prosecuting the client, as they may document what the client knew, and when they knew it.[1] In one case, OSHA used subpoenas to obtain a third-party safety and health consultant's notes and to compel that consultant to testify in advance of issuing citations against the employer who hired his consulting firm. The work product of the consultant was evidence in supporting approximately $500,000 in penalties against the client.[2]

Therefore, when engaging in litigation support activities, clarify up front whether your role will include being a testifying or non-testifying expert, because everything that a testifying expert reviews in forming his/her opinion in the case becomes discoverable, even if it was a previously privileged document under attorney/client communications or the attorney work product doctrine.

On the other hand, documents shared with or produced by a non-testifying expert through the client's in-house or outside counsel, who has retained the expert and directed that expert to prepare reports or other documents "in anticipation of litigation" (and mark them in this manner), can remain confidential. Where the threat of criminal prosecution is present for a client, such as in a fatality case where a "willful" OSHA violation is alleged, it will be important to privilege as many documents between the OH&S consultant and the client as possible, so that the consultant can be candid in communicating findings and recommendations without creating additional liability for the client, or being used as the star witness against the client! Usually, to develop privilege, it will be necessary to work through either in-house counsel or an outside law firm who will direct preparation of the reports "in anticipation of litigation."

---

[1] *Solis v. Grinnell Mutual Reinsurance Co.*, U.S. Dist. Ct. N.D. IL, No. 11 C 50014, 2011.
[2] *Secretary v. Bianchi Trison Corp.*, 20 BNA OSHC 1801 (Nos. 011367 & 1368, 2004).

Audit reports are a trickier matter because these are often conducted proactively and are not part of an accident investigation or development of a litigation defense. Although OSHA has something of an audit "safe harbor" policy, it is not absolute. While a recent decision upheld the employer's right not to furnish audit reports pursuant to a subpoena, where OSHA was "fishing" for violations but did not have independent evidence of a specific hazard, this is by no means a certain outcome.[3] As shown in the *Grinnell case*, OSHA's right to broadly subpoena audits and other records from insurance companies has been upheld, although the *Grede Wisconsin* case would seem to place some limits. Because different jurisdictions were involved (Illinois and Wisconsin), this area of case law is still evolving.

> *Although OSHA has something of an audit "safe harbor" policy, it is not absolute.*

Therefore, it is critical to communicate to clients that such reports may be discoverable and used against them, especially if they fail to implement recommendations that point to deficiencies in safety, health, or environmental compliance.

Knowing your role is important, determine as quickly as possible whether you are just consulting in a way unrelated to litigation, or will be a testifying expert (in which case what you write or report is discoverable via subpoena by OSHA, MSHA, EPA, or private litigants to show what your client knew, and when they knew it), or whether you will be a non-testifying consultant retained for litigation, through counsel (in which case your work product should be marked as "privileged and confidential"). Getting privilege issues right is critical to avoid inadvertent production of documents that could end up pitting you against your client.

Finally, a word or two concerning record retention. OH&S professionals, in my experience (and including myself) are notorious packrats, because we never know when some report or document might come in handy for training or research. Although there are some who can manage "paperless offices," most of us cannot part with our files. There are methods of offsite and electronic storage that can be explored but, at least in my view, I am more comfortable with keeping hard copies of any mandatory documents (such as payroll and time sheets, or training records) for at least the statutory period plus one year.

> *Clearly communicate with your clients how long their files will be kept and your policies (including any costs) for copies of old files.*

When starting your business, make sure to develop an effective document retention and destruction policy, taking care to meet any statutory record retention

---

[3] *Solis v. Grede Wisconsin Subsidiaries LLC*, slip op., US Dist. Ct., WD-Wis., 2013.

time periods for safety, environmental, training, or employment documents. Clearly communicate with your clients how long their files will be kept and your policies (including any costs) for copies of old files. Manage expectations, such as whether you are maintaining duplicate copies of records for training you provide or audits you conduct.

If your policy calls for destruction of documents following their useful or required lifespan, follow your policy. This is the best way to avoid claims of spoliation of evidence if old records are sought in litigation. However, once you are on notice of litigation, you have an obligation not to destroy relevant materials or you could face obstruction of justice charges. And remember, simply removing a file from your hard drive does not erase it from servers; it can often be retrieved through forensic IT work. Don't write anything down, and don't delete anything without considering the legal consequences.

CONCLUSION

In summary, there are many legal and regulatory concerns associated with any start-up business, but a consultancy in the occupational health and safety or environmental field can pose some unique challenges.

These are the top five things I have learned about legal and regulatory compliance:

1. Put it in writing. Do not rely on handshake agreements with those you work for, or those who work for you. As the saying goes, "A verbal contract is worth the paper it's written on."
2. Laws and regulations are constantly changing. Make sure that you are monitoring the statutes, standards, and regulations that apply to your area of expertise, but also monitor changes to business and tax laws that can have a significant impact on you as a business owner. If you don't have the time to do this, hire a human relations professional consultant, keep a line of communication open with an attorney or tax professional, or join professional associations that will send you timely notifications. In addition to professional safety organizations, national or local chambers of commerce or trade groups related to your area of practice (e.g., construction, mining, or manufacturing) will often issue e-bulletins to help you avoid legal pitfalls. These organizations can also offer valuable networking opportunities to expand your client base.

3. Don't ignore the tax man. Pay your federal, state, and local taxes on time, use professional accounting help if you think you need it, and make sure employer contributions are correctly made for any employees you may hire. If you are retaining employees or contractors, make sure to issue appropriate IRS tax forms for the previous year in a timely manner. It is hard to practice your profession behind bars; the IRS is not shy about putting tax scofflaws in prison.
4. Don't forget that the federal government requires all employers to verify the legality of employees, and obtain their "right-to-work" documentation. This applies to everyone you hire, even if you have known them since childhood.
5. Even lawyers need lawyers and consultants. When starting a business, consultants will be faced with a broad array of tax, legal, and regulatory issues outside of their area of expertise. Don't be afraid to seek professional help; the fees associated with such help are probably tax deductible.

To recap what we've discussed in this chapter, consider the following:

- Will I employ individuals directly, get temporary workers through an agency, or use independent contractors on an "as-needed" basis?
- Do I understand the employment and labor laws that will apply to me?
- Have I chosen the best corporate structure for my intended type of practice (e.g., sole proprietor), or will I work in concert with other professionals who may be suitable partners or corporate shareholders who can share costs and/or liability?
- Do I understand how to draft or review contracts that I will enter into with clients, subcontractors, landlords, suppliers, or employees?
- Will I have sufficient capital to pay for registration fees, estimated taxes, withholding and employer contributions for worker taxes and benefits, insurance (general liability, workers' compensation, and malpractice, as needed)?
- Have I discussed tax and liability issues to thoroughly understand my exposure before committing to a corporate format?

The information included in this chapter may seem complicated and certainly will be thought-provoking, but it is essential to enter business with your eyes wide open. Remember that you don't have to go it alone. There are many qualified attorneys, accountants, tax professionals, human resources consultants and even companies that manage payroll for small businesses, to guide you on your maiden voyage into the world of consulting.

If you approach your business plan with the same due diligence you would exercise in preparing advice for a client, you will be able to master the obstacle course, even if it requires enlisting the sound advice of professionals in the legal, accounting, insurance, or other arenas. My best advice: Don't trust critical legal and compliance decisions to your gut instinct. As Mark Twain famously said, "It ain't what you don't know that gets you into trouble. It's what you know for sure that just ain't so."

Now that you have considered your business plan, finances, corporate structure, and legal issues around having your own business, it is time to bring in work. The next chapters will help you develop your marketing strategy, obtaining and retaining clients.

BIBLIOGRAPHY

Abrams, Adele L. 2007. *Contractor Liability and Risk Management Solutions* (retrieved November 11, 2014). www.browz.com/Content/pdfs/browzwp 20071115.pdf

Abrams, Adele L., et al. 2011. *Legal Aspects of Doing Business in North America*. 2nd ed. Huntington, NY: Juris Publishing, Inc.

Abrams, Adele L. 2012. "Section 5: Workers' Compensation." From Haight, Joel M., ed, *The Safety Professionals Handbook*. 2nd ed. Des Plaines, IL: ASSE.

Black, Henry B. 1991. *Black's Law Dictionary*. 6th ed. St. Paul, MN: West Publishing Co.

Cihon, Patrick J., and Castagnera, James O. 2011. *Employment & Labor Law*. 7th ed. Independence, KY: South-Western/Cengage Learning

Department of Homeland Security (DHS). 2013. *USCIS Form I-9, Employment Eligibility Verification and Instructions* (retrieved November 11, 2014) www.ucsis.gov/sites/default/files/form/i-9.pdf

Department of Labor (DOL), Wage and Hour Division. n.d. Employee Misclassification as Independent Contractor (retrieved November 11, 2014) www.dol.gov/whd/workers/misclassification

Ford, Karen E. et al. 2000. *Fundamentals of Employment Law*. 2nd ed. Chicago: ABA Publishing.

Hill, Darryl C., ed. 2004. "Managing Subcontractor Liability." *Construction Safety Management and Engineering*. 1st ed. Chicago: ASSE.

Internal Revenue Service (IRS). 2014b. *S Corporations* (retrieved November 11, 2014) www.irs.gov/Businesses/Small-Businesses-&-Self-Employed-or-Employee

_____. 2014a. *Independent Contractor (Self-Employed) or Employee* (retrieved November 11, 2014) www.irs.gov/Businesses/Small-Businesses-&-Self-Employed-or-Employee

_____. 2014c. *Sole Proprietorships* (retrieved November 11, 2014) www.irs.gov/Businesses/Small-Businesses-&-Self-Employed/Sole-Proprietorship

Occupational Health and Safety Administration (OSHA). 1999. "CPL 02-00-124, Multi-Employer Citation Policy" (retrieved January 5, 2015). www.isha.gov/pls/oshaweb/owadisp.show_document?p_table=DIRECTIVES&p_id=2024

APPENDIX A

Common Contract Terms

TERM	DEFINITION
Blanket contract	A contract covering a number or group of services or goods for a fixed period of time.
Contract	An agreement by two or more parties which creates an obligation to do or not to do a particular thing, which the law recognizes as an enforceable duty.
Divisible and indivisible	The effect of a breach depends on whether it is "indivisible" (forms a whole, the performance of every part is required to bind the other party) or divisible (composed of several independent parts).
Entire and severable	An entire contract is one where the entire fulfillment of the promise by one party is a condition precedent to fulfillment of the promise (e.g., payment) by the other party. A severable contract is one which is subject to apportionment by either side.
Express and implied	An express contract is an actual agreement by the parties (and may have to be in writing depending on state contract law, types of services, and the dollar amounts involved). An implied contract is inferred by law from the parties' acts or conduct, looking at the circumstances of the transaction. Often, letters, emails, voicemails, or other information are reviewed by the courts to ascertain the parties' intentions.
Force majeure and *force majesture*	Force majeure refers to a scenario where a contract cannot be performed or completed due to causes outside the control of the parties and could not be avoided by exercise of due care. Such circumstances legally excuse performance under the contract. Force majesture refers to "acts of God" (earthquake, flood, storms etc.).
Joint and several	A joint contract is made by two or more promisors who are jointly bound to fulfill its obligations. A "several" contract is one where a party has a legal right to enforce his/her interest separate from the other parties.
Liquidated damages and penalties	A situation where the amount of damages has been ascertained by judgment in the action for breach, or where a specified amount is stipulated by the parties in the contract terms.
Open end contract	A contract in which certain terms (e.g. quantity) are deliberately left open.

TERM	DEFINITION
Parol contract	A contract not in writing, or partially in writing.
Subcontract	A contract subordinate to another contract, made between the contracting parties, on one part, and a third party (the subcontractor). Usually this involves one party to the original contract engaging a third party to perform in whole or part the work included in the original contract.
Unconscionable contract	One in which no sensible person not under delusion, duress or in distress would make, and no honest or fair person would accept.
Unenforceable contract	A contract where a breach has neither a remedy of damages nor specific performance.
Uniform Commercial Code (UCC)	A uniform law governing commercial transactions, adopted in whole or part by all states. It applies to sale and leasing of goods, transfer of funds, commercial paper, letters of credit, and secured transactions, among other types of activities.

APPENDIX B

Federal Employment Laws: Coverage and Scope

EMPLOYMENT LAW	EMPLOYMENT SIZE THRESHOLD	SCOPE OF STATUTE
Fair Labor Standards Act of 1938 (FLSA)	Covers all employers	Sets requirements for minimum wage, child labor restrictions, and overtime compensation for nonexempt workers.
Equal Pay Act of 1963	Covers all employers	Bars discrimination in compensation based on sex.
Uniformed Services Employment and Reemployment Rights Act of 1994 (USERRA)	Covers all employers	Requires reinstatement for most employees who have been absent due to active military service.
Occupational Safety & Health Act of 1970 (OSHAct)	Covers all employers	Requires all employers to provide a workplace free from recognized hazards that could cause death or serious bodily harm; requires compliance with mandatory OSHA standards; bars discrimination against whistleblowers (Sec. 11(c) of OSH Act).
Title VII, Civil Rights Act of 1964, as amended	Covers employers with 15+ employees (except for employment agencies or labor organizations, which have no size limitation)	Bars discrimination in hiring and employment based on sex, race, color, sex, religion or national origin.
Lilly Ledbetter Fair Pay Act of 2007	Covers employers with 15+ employees	Bars discrimination in compensation based on sex, race, color, religion, age, disability or national origin.
Americans with Disabilities Act of 1990 (ADA)	Covers employers with 15+ employees	Bars discrimination in hiring and employment against a qualified individual with a disability, a record of such impairment, association with a disabled individual, or one who is perceived by the employer as being disabled (even if not disabled). Disability must impact a major life activity.

EMPLOYMENT LAW	EMPLOYMENT SIZE THRESHOLD	SCOPE OF STATUTE
Genetic Information Nondiscrimination Act of 2008 (GINA)	Covers employers with 15+ employees	Bars discrimination in hiring and employment based upon an individual's genetic information and family history.
Age Discrimination in Employment Act of 1967 (ADEA)	Covers employers with 20+ employees	Bars discrimination in hiring and employment based upon an individual's age (40 or older). There are certain exceptions for public safety positions.
Consolidated Omnibus Benefits Reconciliation Act (COBRA) of 1986	Covers employers with 20+ employees	Contains provisions for continuation of medical benefits for terminated employees.
Family and Medical Leave Act of 1993 (FMLA)	Covers employers with 50+ employees within a 75-mile radius	Requires job retention and up to 12 weeks of unpaid leave (can be intermittent) for the employee's own serious illness or that of an immediate family member, the birth, adoption or fostering of a child, and for employees who have an immediate family member called up for military service; and up to 26 weeks of unpaid leave to care for an immediate family member who was injured during military service.
Worker Adjustment & Retraining Notification Act of 1989 (WARN)	Covers employers with 100+ employees	Requires covered employers to provide notification 60 calendar days in advance of plant closings or mass layoffs. Notification requirements may vary state-to-state.

APPENDIX C

State Employment Laws Chart

EMPLOYER RESOURCES: STATE LABOR AND EMPLOYMENT OFFICES

STATE	STATE LABOR DEPARTMENT	STATE CIVIL RIGHTS OFFICE
ALABAMA	Alabama Department of Labor www.labor.alabama.gov	Alabama Department of Human Resources Equal Employment & Civil Rights http://dhr.alabama.gov/directory/Equal_Emp_Civil_Rts.aspx
ALASKA	Department of Labor and Workforce Development www.labor.state.AK.us	Alaska State Commission for Human Rights http://humanrights.alaska.gov/
ARIZONA	Industrial Commission of Arizona www.ica.state.AZ.us	Arizona Attorney General's Office, Civil Rights Division https://www.azag.gov/civil-rights
ARKANSAS	Director of Labor www.labor.ar.gov	
CALIFORNIA	Division of Labor Standards Enforcement and the Office of the Labor Commissioner www.dir.ca.gov/DLSE/dlse.html	California Department of Fair Employment and Housing http://www.dfeh.ca.gov/
COLORADO	Department of Labor and Employment www.COworkforce.com	Colorado Civil Rights Division http://cdn.colorado.gov/cs/Satellite?c=Page&childpagename=DORA-DCR/DORALayout&cid=1251614735957&pagename=CBONWrapper
CONNECTICUT	Department of Labor www.CT.gov/dol	Connecticut Commission on Human Rights and Opportunities http://www.ct.gov/chro/site/default.asp
DELAWARE	Delaware Department of Labor www.Delawareworks.com	Delaware Department of Labor, Office of Discrimination http://dia.delawareworks.com/discrimination/
District of Columbia	Department of Employment Services www.DOES.DC.gov	D.C. Office of Human Rights http://ohr.dc.gov/

Employer Resources: State Labor and Employment Offices

STATE	STATE LABOR DEPARTMENT	STATE CIVIL RIGHTS OFFICE
FLORIDA	Division of Regulation http://www.myfloridalicense.com	Florida Commission on Human Relations http://fchr.state.fl.us/
GEORGIA	Department of Labor www.dol.state.GA.us	Georgia Commission on Equal Opportunity http://gceo.state.ga.us/
HAWAII	Department of Labor & Industrial Relations www.Hawaii.gov/labor/	Hawaii Civil Rights Commission http://labor.hawaii.gov/hcrc/
IDAHO	Department of Labor www.labor.Idaho.gov	Idaho Commission on Human Rights http://humanrights.idaho.gov/
ILLINOIS	Department of Labor www.state.IL.us/agency/idol	Illinois Department of Human Rights http://www2.illinois.gov/dhr/Pages/default.aspx
INDIANA	Department of Labor www.IN.gov/labor	Indiana Civil Rights Commission http://www.state.in.us/icrc/2654.htm
IOWA	Iowa Labor Services Division www.Iowaworkforce.org/labor	Iowa Civil Rights Commission https://icrc.iowa.gov/
KANSAS	Department of Labor www.dol.KS.gov	Kansas Human Rights Commission http://www.khrc.net/main.html
KENTUCKY	Kentucky Labor Cabinet www.labor.KY.gov	Kentucky Commission on Human Rights http://kchr.ky.gov/
LOUISIANA	Louisiana Workforce Commission www.ldol.state.la.us/	Louisiana Commission on Human Rights http://www.gov.state.la.us/HumanRights/humanrightshome.htm
MAINE	Department of Labor www.state.ME.us/labor	Maine Human Rights Commission http://www.state.me.us/mhrc/employment.shtml
MARYLAND	Department of Labor, Licensing and Regulation www.dllr.state.MD.us	Maryland Commission on Civil Rights http://mccr.maryland.gov/

Employer Resources: State Labor and Employment Offices

STATE	STATE LABOR DEPARTMENT	STATE CIVIL RIGHTS OFFICE
NEW MEXICO	Department of Work Force Solutions www.dws.state.nm.us	New Mexico Human Rights Bureau http://www.dws.state.nm.us/LaborRelations/HumanRights/Information
NEW YORK	Department of Labor www.labor.ny.gov	New York State Division of Human Rights http://www.dhr.ny.gov/
NORTH CAROLINA	Department of Labor www.nclabor.com	North Carolina has no state "EEOC" office and any workplace discrimination complaints are handled through the federal EEOC field offices in NC. See http://www.eeocoffice.com/north-carolina-eeoc-offices.
NORTH DAKOTA	Department of Labor www.nd.gov/labor	North Dakota Department of Labor and Human Rights http://www.nd.gov/labor/human-rights/
OHIO	Department of Commerce www.com.state.OH.us	Ohio Civil Rights Commission http://crc.ohio.gov/Home.aspx
OKLAHOMA	Department of Labor www.ok.gov/odol/	Oklahoma Office of Civil Rights Enforcement http://www.oag.ok.gov/oagweb.nsf/ocre.html
OREGON	Bureau of Labor and Industries www.Oregon.gov/boli	Oregon Civil Rights Division http://www.oregon.gov/boli/CRD/Pages/about_us.aspx
PENNSYLVANIA	Department of Labor and Industry www.dli.state.PA.us	Pennsylvania Human Relations Commission http://www.portal.state.pa.us/portal/server.pt/community/phrc_home/18970
RHODE ISLAND	Department of Labor and Training www.dlt.state.RI.us	Rhode Island Commission for Human Rights http://www.richr.ri.gov/frames.html

Employer Resources: State Labor and Employment Offices

STATE	STATE LABOR DEPARTMENT	STATE CIVIL RIGHTS OFFICE
SOUTH CAROLINA	Department of Labor, Licensing & Regulations www.llr.state.SC.us	South Carolina Human Affairs Commission http://www.schac.sc.gov/Pages/default.aspx
SOUTH DAKOTA	Department of Labor and Regulation www.dlr.sd.gov	South Dakota Division of Human Rights http://dlr.sd.gov/humanrights/default.aspx
TENNESSEE	Depart. of Labor & Workforce Development www.state.TN.us/labor-wfd	Tennessee Human Rights Commission http://www.tn.gov/humanrights/
TEXAS	Texas Workforce Commission www.twc.state.TX.us	Texas Civil Rights Division http://www.twc.state.tx.us/crd/civil-rights-program-overview.html
UTAH	Utah Labor Commission www.Laborcommission.Utah.gov	Utah AntiDiscrimination & Labor Division http://laborcommission.utah.gov/divisions/AntidiscriminationAndLabor/index.html
VERMONT	Department of Labor www.labor.vermont.gov	Vermont Human Rights Commission http://hrc.vermont.gov/
VIRGINIA	Department of Labor and Industry www.doli.Virginia.gov	Virginia Office of the Attorney General – Division of Human Rights http://www.uy.virginia.gov/Programs%20and%20Resources/Human_Rights/index.html
WASHINGTON	Department of Labor and Industries www.lni.WA.gov	Washington State Human Rights Commission http://www.hum.wa.gov/
WEST VIRGINIA	Division of Labor www.wvlabor.com/newwebsite/pages/index.html	West Virginia Human Rights Commission http://www.hrc.wv.gov/Pages/default.aspx
WISCONSIN	Department of Workforce Development dwd.wisconsin.gov	Wisconsin Equal Rights Division http://dwd.wisconsin.gov/er/

Employer Resources: State Labor and Employment Offices

STATE	STATE LABOR DEPARTMENT	STATE CIVIL RIGHTS OFFICE
WYOMING	Department of Workforce Service www.wyomingworkforce.org/Pages/default.aspx	Wyoming Labor Standards Division http://www.wyomingworkforce.org/job-seekers-and-workers/labor-standards/Pages/default.aspx
GUAM	Department of Labor www.dol.guam.gov	Guam Fair Employment Practice Division http://www.dol.guam.gov/index.php?option=com_content&view=article&id=114&Itemid=623
PUERTO RICO	Dept. of Labor and Human Resources www2.PR.gov/presupuestos/presupuestosanteriores/af2000/ingles/sombrill/trabajo/067.htm	Puerto Rico Department of Labor and Human Resources http://www2.pr.gov/presupuestos/presupuestosanteriores/af2000/ingles/sombrill/trabajo/067.htm
VIRGIN ISLANDS	Department of Labor www.VIdol.gov	U.S. Virgin Islands Department of Labor http://www.vidol.gov/employee_right.php

Questions to ask:

Do you understand what marketing entails and how it can be different for service companies like OS&H consulting firms?

How can you use marketing to even the playing field when you are competing with much larger or established firms?

Can you use social media to your advantage?

How can you network with others as part of your marketing strategy without being annoying?

Do your proposals "seal the deal" or simply get added to the pile?

Chapter 6

Marketing and Sales

BY LINDA TAPP, CSP, ALCM

Linda Tapp is President of Crown Safety and SafetyFUNdamentals®, both in Madison, NJ. Crown Safety, established in 1999, and SafetyFUNdamentals, a spin-off company to develop and provide safety training materials and seminars, have a mission to offer products, services, and programs that are not only technically correct, but that work in conjunction with normal facility operations. Linda specializes in providing consulting services to manufacturing facilities. Along with being a safety consultant, trainer, and speaker, Linda has published several books. She has lived and worked as a consultant in England, Germany, and the Netherlands, in addition to the United States. She is also a past Chair of the Board of Certified Safety Progessionals Marketing Committee and past Administrator of the ASSE Consultants Practice Specialty.

THERE'S A GOOD CHANCE that many current or would-be OS&H consultants have never had a class in marketing because most of us have a technical background. This is what has allowed us to provide consulting services in our areas of expertise. It is easier for larger professional services firms to have a dedicated marketing person or staff. But this is often not an option for individuals just starting out or for small firms. In order to grow your consulting firm, or even just keep business coming in at an average rate, marketing is something you must do. Without marketing, there will be no consulting.

MARKETING

Let's start with the very basics, and look at a textbook definition of marketing. "Marketing is the activity, set of institutions, and processes for creating, communicating, delivering, and exchanging offerings that have value for customers, clients, partners, and society at large" (AMA 2013). This definition covers a great deal of what you do all the time, and it can be a lot of work. Much of marketing is just the way you operate day to day. That includes everything from your branding, reputation, the services you provide, the products you sell, and how you go about doing all of this. Other areas that may seem more like traditional marketing include networking, selling, proposals, Web sites, speaking and writing, publicity efforts, and social media activities. Almost everything you do is related to marketing. All of these activities need to be considered in your marketing action plan.

Changes in Marketing and Advertising

In my opinion, marketing used to be all about advertising; on television, radio, advertisements in magazines, and direct mail. This is not really the case anymore, especially for service companies, such as OS&H consulting firms. When was the last time you decided to make a purchase when you received a postcard or brochure in the mail or read an advertisement? Especially if it was a service, it was probably not recently. It's important to understand how marketing has changed, and how you can use the new marketing strategies to your advantage. As Charles Darwin said, "It's not the strongest of the species that survive, nor the most intelligent, but the one most responsive to change." (CITE??)

Marketing the intangible, such as services, has always been a challenge; this is even more so with traditional advertising. The problem for safety consultants with how marketing used to be done is that information was pushed at you. It was difficult to make sure that your target audience would receive your message. Advertising methods that were popular in the past were often sent to a large group, and were expensive. While some of these methods may still work for large consulting firms, there are better ways to spend your energy, if you are a small firm or just starting out. The marketing information was an interruption, and wasn't very personal.

Branding is the expression of the essential truth or value of an organization, product, or service.

The latest trends in marketing, as described in David Meerman Scott's book, *The New Rules of Marketing & PR*, are largely based on the Internet (Scott 2010).

Marketing in the past relied on creating advertising that would try to get potential clients to pay attention and contact you. To a point, this is still one of the goals of marketing today. The difference is that, in the past, marketing was mostly a one-way street. A safety consultant might have placed an advertisement in the back of a professional journal, and hoped that people needing her services would pick up the phone and call her. Another consultant may have purchased a mailing list, and mailed postcards advertising his services to

5000 people in his region. Again, the consultant was hoping that his postcard was interesting enough to get attention, and cause the reader to make contact.

In the past, the more money you had, the more people you could generally reach. This made it very difficult for small firms or solo practitioners to compete with larger, more established companies. Now, the Internet allows you to perform many marketing activities easily and inexpensively; there is a much more level playing field.

Marketing is a two-way street; consultants will not only push information out in the hope of getting someone to contact them but also pull, by creating valuable material, publishing it for the world to see, and hoping it is strong enough to attract potential clients.

In Gary Vaynerchuk's book, *Jab, Jab, Jab, Right Hook: How to Tell Your Story in a Noisy, Social World*, the idea of providing valuable material over a period of time (what Vaynerchuk calls "jabs") before asking for the sale (the "right hook") is imperative, if you want to be successful in today's world of marketing. If you push a message directly out (a "jab" in the words of Vaynerchuck), it will not be successful unless followed up or preceded by a series of jabs. Pulling clients in is going to take time (Vaynerchuck 2013).

We will cover various types of marketing actions for you to consider. First, we'll jump right in with the things that may seem like basic business operations.

Branding

Day-to-day business efforts affect your branding. In fact, all of the efforts you put into branding yourself fall under marketing. What is your "brand?" In a post by James Heaton on the Tronvig Group's blog on December 20, 2011, "Branding should both precede and underlie any marketing effort. Branding is not push, but pull. Branding is the expression of the essential truth or value of an organization, product, or service. It is communication of characteristics, values, and attributes that clarify what this particular brand is, and is not." The American Marketing Association (AMA) defines a company's brand as the "name, term, design, symbol, or any other feature that identifies one seller's product distinct from those of other sellers" (AMA 2013). The most important part of this sentence for most OS&H consultants is "other feature." As described by Heaton above, this is the "essential truth or value of an organization, product, or service" (Heaton 2011).

However you decide to brand your company is going to determine how you market your company.

What do you want your company to be? Do you want to be the small mom-and-pop consulting shop that services only other small businesses? Or do you want to be (or at least be viewed as) a larger consulting firm that services large multinational firms? Do you want to be known as the best affordable option or as a high-priced/high-value boutique firm? Do you want to be known as the consultant who comes in, and gets his or her hands dirty, or the firm that only takes part at a very high, strategic level? However you decide to brand your company is going to determine how you market your company. "The first rule of marketing—a key to revenue and profitability or growth—is getting your service right" (Schultz and Doer 2009). Getting your service right is all about branding.

Once you understand your brand, you can use it to market. If you have branded yourself as the most experienced construction safety expert with global experience, your marketing materials should reflect your international operations. You could do this by providing international call access codes, and links on your Web site with information in other languages. If your brand is to be the best OSHA training provider in Ohio, for example, you could have a more local feel to your Web site by including driving directions to your office or training locations, or even by having small announcements about how you support other local businesses or community organizations. A contact page showing a phone number with an international access code would not fit in on this Web site.

Looking Professional

One of the first ways to start establishing your brand is to polish the parts of your consulting practice that people actually see. This includes your Web site, marketing materials, and even the way you dress. Does your Web site look professional? Does it have its own domain name? Domain names are inexpensive, and it's not difficult to set up your e-mail address through them. There are many options for getting your own domain name. Some popular domain registrars (companies that are allowed to registrar domain names) include GoDaddy.com, www.1and1.com, and www.dreamhost.com. You simply need to think of a domain name that fits your company, search to see if it is available (this can be done on the same site that you are using to register a domain), and if it is available, pay the fee, and register the name. Costs vary, depending on the domain registrar and the type of domain you register, e.g., .com, .co, .biz.

If you love free services like gmail, you don't have to stop using them when you get your own domain name. Depending on the domain registrar you use, it is very easy to forward your e-mail to the application you currently use. Additionally, you can reply from your same business address and not from the gmail address. Many professionals may argue that receiving an e-mail from consultant@establishedconsultingfirm.com is going to deliver a better impression than consultant@gmail.com (or @aol, @yahoo, or @hotmail). Having the e-mail come from your own domain name makes you appear more established and reputable, not as someone who just decided to go into business yesterday (even if that is the case).

Your e-mail address and your Web site will be on your business card and letterhead, so get this set-up before you spend a lot on these other materials. Along the same lines, some consultants who work from home use a business, and not a residential, address so they appear more established. If you are fortunate enough to have a home address that could also easily be a professional address (such as 123 Main Street or 1000 Buena Blvd), you are in luck. But if you live at 1234 Cherry Picking Lane, this may be a little more difficult; however, since it is getting more and more common for people to work from home, such an address might not raise too many eyebrows. But it is something to keep in mind if your potential clients are accustomed to working with, or actually prefer, large established firms.

Address Options

In this age, where we are not limited on where we can work by geography, and with the advent of online billing and payment, I am not convinced that an actual physical address is necessary on business cards or on a Web site. If you do wish to show a professional-sounding address, and you live on Cherry Picking Lane, there are a few options at your disposal. First, you could get a Post Office box at your local post office, although many people see right through this. In addition, some deliveries can only be delivered to physical addresses. Another option is to sign up with a shared or virtual office center. Often, these centers have a variety of services, from mail holding or forwarding to conference rooms and offices you can use as needed. Another option is to find a local friendly business that may be willing to rent you desk space and let you use its address. Many consultants prefer to work out of their homes, or are on the road most of the time anyway, so paying a lot for rented office space might not be high on your list of needs. Once you get bigger and more established or have staff that needs to work together, you may want to consider this expense.

Appearance and Dress

Finally, how you dress is also part of your branding. The old adage, "It's what's on the inside that matters," does not apply to consulting. Everywhere you go, people are judging you by how you look. Whether you show up at a client in a polo shirt with a logo and khakis or in a formal business suit will not only depend on the type of work you do, but also the impression you wish to make. I once showed up at a potential new construction client in a suit, and my contact said, "You look expensive." We laughed it off, and I did get the project, which that consisted of weekly construction site inspections for the next few years (for which I definitely did not wear a suit).

Know your client. You do not want to show up in a tailored suit with dress shoes at a construction site, but you also do not want to show up in jeans and a white t-shirt. Your outward appearance shows who you are and who you represent, your company.

Publishing, Participating, Targeting and Public Relations

There are four easy and suggested areas you can work with to get started in what you may think of as more traditional marketing: publishing, participating, targeting and public relations. Let's look at each of the above. First, we'll take on publishing.

Publishing

The opportunities to publish are endless. Most professional associations and even many local newspapers are hungry for content.

Safety consultants usually know the importance of publishing as a way of getting their names out. Articles in professional journals, such as *Professional Safety*, and trade magazines, such as *Industrial Hygiene and Safety News* and *EHS Today*, can be great ways to get exposure and showcase your talents to others working in safety, health and the environmental fields. If you market primarily to other safety professionals or to those with safety as an adjunct responsibility, the publications dedicated to safety are great places to submit your work.

Alternatively, if you market to a particular industry, and the person hiring you is more likely to be the head of maintenance or the president of a small construction company, you should consider publishing in trade magazines specific to those industries. If you are an expert in a particular field, you are likely already familiar with those trade-specific publications, and with what your target audience is reading.

Publishing on the Internet can be just as important, especially if you hope to reach potential clients who may not subscribe to, or be members of, other groups. Fortunately, many of the print publications, such as those mentioned above, also publish their content online, so the content receives additional exposure. By publishing online, you and your ideas are searchable by the over two billon people who are estimated to use the Internet (CIA 2014). The opportunities to publish are endless. Most professional associations and even many local newspapers are hungry for content.

If you wish to publish separately on the Internet, and not rely on a publisher of a magazine or journal to post your content, you can do this in several ways. You can write an article, and place it or a link to it on your Web site. You can place your article or other item of value (more on that below) on your blog, if you have one, or as a guest contributor on someone else's blog. In either of these instances, you can post the link on social media sites, such as Twitter or LinkedIn, so interested parties can click back to the material. If you send out an online newsletter or send out marketing e-mails, you can also provide a link to your article.

In addition to articles, you can publish anything that would be of value to your target customer; for example, a checklist, an infographic, a sample procedure, or even a mini-guidebook.

Books, in all forms, also make great marketing tools. Books can make you an instant expert, and can lead to speaking engagements. Book publishing opportunities include everything from free downloadable books to more substantial academic texts. In most cases, being a published author is not going to make you rich, but it will open doors for you. Using books as an additional income stream, as well as being a marketing tool, is a possibility. This idea is discussed more in the "Products" section of this chapter.

Additionally, books make a great alternative to a brochure. Instead of sending a piece of folded paper with company details with your cover letter, you can send along a book, if it's related to the job in question. Or you could send the book, along with the brochure.

Participating

Participating in groups and associations where your potential clients are involved is a great way to build relationships. Relationship building is key to sales, and helps with your marketing efforts. You can participate by becoming an active member of OS&H blogging communities, listservs, professional committees, LinkedIn groups, and on Twitter by just being available to answer questions, share your comments, or provide your views to others. If you set up your own blog, your content will be searchable, so anyone Googling an idea or topic that you write about will be able to find you. To participate in other blogging communities, find other safety blogs that interest you, and follow them. If there is a post or a question that you can comment on or answer, then go ahead and help out. Always remember to provide a way for others to contact you. An excellent discussion on relationship building and using LinkedIn for networking can be found in Chapter 7.

Often, participating can be as simple as forwarding great articles you have read that can help others, although this can be overdone. The key is to be selective, only forwarding content that best represents your company. Your participation is an extension of the services you provide.

Targeting

The ability to target specific groups has become easier over recent years. Previously, the marketing and advertising efforts of small safety consultants were directed towards a large audience: You threw out a wide net, and hoped to catch a fish. If you were a safety consultant trying to get the word out about your services, you might buy a mailing list, and send a brochure or postcard to everyone in a particular geographic area or, if you had a really big budget, to everyone in a particular professional association. Marketing this way often meant that many, many people would see your materials, but also that many of these people would have no interest or need for your services, so your time and money was wasted. The Internet has made it much easier to target specific niches, or even specific people.

Most niches have an online presence, such LinkedIn groups or Twitter lists. Engage with these groups, and their members will know where to turn for help. For example, if your target audience includes industrial hygienists, you can join any of the many industrial hygiene groups on LinkedIn. Not only will staying current with comments posted by others alert you to hot topics or nagging problems in that field, but responding to some of the comments will also provide an opportunity to share your expertise.

There are LinkedIn groups for just about every area of specialty; everything from Asbestos Professionals to Zoo and Aquarium Safety. Join the groups that apply to your business, and get to know the members. Once you join a group, you can view the members. There is more information on social media later in this chapter.

E-mail as Targeted Marketing. If you have been able to build your own mailing list of interested people (an e-mail list versus a list based on physical addresses), you have a much better ocean where you can throw your net. How do you build this list? You will want to add all of your clients and OS&H contacts for starters. But that is not likely to get you to the size of group that you would like. A great way to do this is to offer something free online in exchange for an e-mail address, and permission to contact them in the future. If, for example, you offered a free guide to excavation safety, and your ideal client is in construction, you will be building a pool of potential clients in the niche you service. You could also offer free webinars in exchange for contact information.

Webinars and free downloads showcase your talents, deliver value to your target audience, and fill your list with a targeted client base.

If you want to offer free downloads, there are many ways to do this. If you set it up right, you will need to do very little. There are services that, for very little money, will let you upload your free product, and then allow others to download it in exchange for whatever information you specify, all the while collecting information like e-mail addresses; Ejunkie and Clickbank are only such services.

When you use such services, they will provide you with the html code that can be added to a Web site, which will then lead people clicking on the link on your Web site to the free downloads. Alternatively, the service will provide a simple link that you can share on social media, on correspondence, and in e-mail marketing pieces.

In addition to collecting target information for targets that have self-identified as being interested in what you have to offer, you are also providing materials that may keep your company name in front of buyers, if the item is something they can use often. Also, if they feel the material is really valuable, they are more likely to share it with others within their company and elsewhere, thus expanding your reach. Vaynerchuk, a marketing expert, believes that you need to deliver high quality content, not just once, but multiple times before asking for business (Vaynerchuk 2013). Providing free downloads of material designed with your target audience in mind is one way to do this.

You can also use this list as a way to stay in touch. E-mail newsletters, announcements of upcoming speaking engagements, and invitations to webinars are all things you can send out. Keep in mind that just because something is interesting to you, it may not be interesting to your readers. If you start to fill their inboxes with information they cannot use, they will either unsubscribe or send your e-mails directly to spam folders.

Personally, I have over 7000 names in my e-mail distribution list. I have built this list by offering free downloads of safety training materials, and by informing audience members at presentations I have delivered for which they can also sign up. I use this list to send out occasional e-mail newsletters. Many companies, such as Constant Contact and Mail Chimp, make this very easy to do.

Some experts believe the success of e-mail marketing is decreasing. When I first started sending e-mail newsletters in 2006, the newsletters generally had an open rate anywhere from 35%–50% or higher. The open rate is the percentage of e-mails sent that are actually opened. In the past few years, I have seen much lower open rates. This may be due to much stricter spam filters, some of which send anything that comes through e-mail marketing companies, such as Constant Contact, directly to spam folders. It may also be because there is so much other competition in the way people receive marketing information online.

Public Relations

Public relations, as a marketing tool, could fill an entire book. It's often confused with publicity, but the two are different. As Seth Godin, author of 14 books and a very popular marketing blog, stated (Godin 2009):

> Publicity is the act of getting ink. Publicity is getting unpaid media to pay attention, write you up, point to you, run a picture, make a commotion. Sometimes publicity is helpful, and good publicity is always good for your ego.
> But it's not PR.
> PR is the strategic crafting of your story. It's the focused examination of your interactions and tactics and products and pricing that, when combined, determine what and how people talk about you.

Why are public relations and publicity so important? Whenever someone else says something positive about you, it is going to carry more weight than if you said it yourself. You may have a beautifully designed marketing brochure that talks a lot about all of your wonderful services, your impressive background, and your list of Fortune 500 clients, but if a newspaper mentions your name and company, and includes a short quote from you, that will go farther than your brochure. Additionally, when you appear quoted in a magazine or newspaper, you gain instant expert status. Potential clients may think, "If the newspaper trusts this individual enough to print what they say, then I should, too." If you do start to get mentioned in a few places, always provide links to these articles on your Web site. Don't be afraid to share them.

One of the best free strategies to getting noticed in your field is to sign up to be a blogger for any of the industry leading OS&H magazines. When you are accepted, they are placing their reputation on the line for your work, and you are representing the quality of theirs. In the end, it is a win-win for everyone, including your clients. All you have to do is send the magazine's editor a note expressing your interest. Things will flow from there. More on blogs will be discussed later.

Public relations is not just getting mentioned in the media. If you take the phrase literally, it means your relationships with the public. As a safety and health professional, you have a lot of unique skills that most of your neighbors

> *Publicity is the act of getting ink.... But it's not PR.*

do not. Can you use these to help out neighborhood groups? Maybe the local volunteer fire department could use some free safety and health training, or the Boys and Girls Club needs help putting together a new safety committee. All of these events not only give back and build your relationship with the community, but also provide a form of marketing.

The Press

Press releases used to be the way you would get yourself noticed by the media. You had to learn the proper format, write an enticing headline, and then try to get the attention of the reporters or writers so that they wanted to follow up with you and then promote you and your story. In the past, these were only minimally effective for small business owners; now, they are even less so. It is difficult and either time-consuming or expensive (if you use a wire service) to distribute them to the appropriate reporter or writer. Additionally, many reporters get dozens, if not hundreds, of press releases a day. It is very hard to get noticed.

Reporters are more likely to start the search for interesting information, stories and experts online. Will they be able to find you? In most cases, they will not be searching for your name, but for a particular topic. If they are looking for an expert to quote on a recent disaster, and you specialize in emergency preparedness, will they be able to find you?

You have a better chance of getting noticed by the press if you focus your efforts on tying into trending news. Twitter and Instagram are two places they look, through the use of hashtags. Hashtags are discussed more in the social media section, but are basically a way to tag your post with a particular word or phrase. Hashtags included in Twitter posts, called tweets, are always preceded by "#." When breaking news occurs, people directly involved, and those looking to add their own opinion, will post something and include a related hashtag.

For example, many posts related to an Amtrak train derailment were given the hashtag #traincrash. Some were given several, including #Amtrak, #metronorth, and #railsafety. If you are a consultant who specializes in railroad safety, you could comment and include these hashtags. Then reporters could find you when they search these hashtags as part of their reporting efforts.

One way to jump on trending topics is to use the comment section of news sites. If a fire broke out, and the story shows up on the Web page of a newspaper, add a comment that starts with a statement of your expertise. For example, "As a safety professional with over 20 years of experience, I feel that...." If a reporter is looking for an expert, you will have just planted yourself firmly in front of him or her, as well as in front of others who are interested enough in the topic to read through the comments.

A word of warning: Be very careful if you choose to criticize others in your comments. It is unlikely that you, or the public in general, have all the facts of what happened and the causes, so proceed with caution.

Social Media

There are many platforms online that you can use to showcase your talents and your company. What's available grows every day. In fact, there are probably more opportunities to market your company online than there are to market yourself off-line. Some areas you might consider include Web sites, blogs, Twitter, LinkedIn, YouTube, and Facebook.

Web Sites

In my experience, almost every OS&H consulting firm has a Web site. These range from simple, one page, do-it-yourself Web sites to multi-page, mammoth sites full of resources, created by professional designers, and maintained by webmasters. Whatever you have for a Web site, the key is that people can find it and, once they do, that it provides what they need in a professional way. Even with all of the new and ever-changing social media sites, "search engines remain the primary source for research for customers close to buying a service or product" (Zarrella 2012, 40). In this day and age, companies are expected to have a Web site. If you do not, you may not be taken seriously, or you may be passed over by someone looking for services that you can provide.

Many Web sites are actually built on blogging platforms.

Zarella, who is a social search and viral marketing scientist, found out something very interesting in his research. He asked people if they believe the Web sites that appear first in a search are most trustworthy than those below. More than half the people said this is the case (Zarella 2012, 45). What does this means if you use your Web site as your primary marketing tool? If your company's Web site does not appear at the top or at least very near the top of search results, your consulting firm will be seen as less trustworthy than those that do. Getting to the top of those search results is a field called search engine optimization (SEO).

SEO can be complicated, and it changes all the time. You might have content and settings on your Web site one day that will get you near the top, but then the search engines, such as Google, change the algorithms used to rank search results, and you are no longer where you were. If you are a large company, you might want to hire outside help to optimize your Web site for search. In his book, *The Science of Marketing*, Zarella says that it is better to spend time creating great content, and then share that in social media (Zarella 2012). Of course, you can take on the task of learning SEO on your own, and applying it to your Web site. But be prepared for a time-consuming task that will need to be repeated often. If you take Zarella's advice, and focus on creating great content, blogs are often the platform used for posting and sharing it.

Blogs

In *The New Rules of Marketing and PR*, David Meerman Scott nicely describes blogs as "... basically just a website.... a special kind of site that is created and maintained by a person who is passionate about a subject and wants to tell the world about his or her area of expertise" (Scott 2010, 59). When you see "maintained by a person who is passionate" and someone who "wants to tell the world about his or her expertise," you can see how blogs are a great match for OS&H consultants. It is estimated that there are over 181 million blogs around the world (Nielsen 2012). Many Web sites are actually built on blogging platforms. It is often very hard to tell the difference.

One of the interesting things about blogs, and the Internet in general, is that you are not limited to just your geographic area, or even your own country. People love to share useful content. In fact, one study showed that the majority of people who share things do so because they want to help others (Berger 2013). If you write a blog that has interesting and helpful material, then you are putting content out there that is both searchable, and something that others will share on your behalf.

Blogs used to be a bit more complicated. Although many free services will let you blog easily, the downside is that you will generally have the blogging application's name in your blog domain name. If you truly want to make it your own, set up a blogging account, and either pay the blogging platform for your own domain, or set up a domain name through a company like GoDaddy or NetworkSolutions for about $10 a year. Then forward the domain name to your free blog site. When you do this, you can set up "masking." That means that when the web address is redirected, visitors will only see the web address they typed in and not the web address of the page to which it was directed.

I use it [Tumblr] when I need a place to quickly publish something, since it provides me with a link to share on other social networks or even in e-mail marketing pieces.

Some of the main free blogging sites include Wordpress, Blogger, and Tumblr. Many people use Tumblr for images, or for sharing content they found that was created on other Tumblr blogs. You can use it however it suits your needs. You can easily write your own short or long blog post or share an image or video, or simply a link to someone else's content. I would not set up a Tumblr blog with the hope of being found there by someone searching for safety consultants. I use it when I need a place to quickly publish something, since it provides me with a link to share on other social networks or even in e-mail marketing pieces.

For example, say you have a traditional Web site managed by a webmaster. If you want to upload forms, checklists, or articles for example, you could send these to your webmaster to upload to your Web site. Depending on how sophisticated your site is, it may have to be hosted somewhere. Alternatively, with Tumblr, you could post it yourself on this very simple sharing site, and then share the link. If you don't like having "tumblr" in your page title or link, you can set up the site using a custom domain by following the instructions on the Tumblr site.

Of course, Tumblr is not the answer for everyone; it's only one of many options available. Wordpress and Blogger have been around much longer, and offer more options. Just enter "reviews of free blogging sites" into a search engine, such as Google, and you will see many options, as well as some expert opinions.

In many instances, blogs have replaced traditional Web sites. I personally do not see any advantage of having a traditional Web site over one based on a blogging platform. You can make a blog look just like a Web site. The great thing about blogs is their ease of updating. Many Web sites require the use of a webmaster for updates and changes. With a blog, the content, format, and even the design can easily be modified by an individual with no programming or web design experience. Blogs are an especially good option for consultants just starting out on a limited budget. I'm not saying that you should forget about using a web designer, especially if you have no interest in learning about good Web site design and SEO, but am suggesting that you keep your options in mind.

To make sure your blog is a marketing tool, make sure you have it set to "public" so the content is searchable. Also be sure you let people know about it. You should definitely add it to your contact information at the bottom of your e-mails. You may also want to add the blog address to your business cards.

Twitter

Many people use blogs and Twitter together. Actually, Twitter is just another type of blog. Since Twitter is only limited to 140 characters, online marketers will often write a lengthy blog post and then post a few key words of that post, and the link to it, to Twitter. If you get really into this, there is software that tracks how many people shared your content or clicked through to your blog post. If you gave your company Web site or product information on your blog, you can also track how many visitors followed through to check out your company.

Twitter has taken off. A large percentage of adult Internet users have accounts, and the user base has increased significantly (Brenner and Smith

2013). There are hundreds of millions of users in the United States and worldwide (Vaynerchuk 2013). Even if you are still not convinced that it is just a bunch of teenagers posting about what they ate for breakfast, these numbers should make you sit up and take notice. While undoubtedly there are many people using Twitter for personal use, there is a real science to using Twitter for business, if you want to put in the time and effort.

Twitter is difficult to use as a marketing strategy, but many, many businesses are trying to do just that, and many do it very well. You can try to engage in conversations with potential clients on Twitter. However, this is unlikely to build your reach; instead, focus on gathering and sharing as much useful information as possible (Zarrella 2012, 57). This will help you to build Twitter relationships that may one day result in paying clients. People like to do business with people they know and like. Sharing your knowledge on Twitter is one way to do that.

> *. . . it is important to have a Twitter presence, even if you can't commit to using it as a primary marketing method.*

When using Twitter, business benefits are created through three elements: targeted communications, meaningful content, and authentic helpfulness (Schaefer 2012, 15). Interested Twitter "followers" are important to have if you are going to be able to use Twitter for targeted communications. If you tweet about something safety related, and no one in safety is following you, you are wasting your time.

Once you get involved in Twitter, you will want to start building an audience. Often, unless you are a rock star or VIP, that means you need to start following others in whom you are generally interested. Very often, when you follow another person interested in OS&H for example, that person will follow you back, as well as that person's followers; in that way, more people with similar interests will follow you. Of course, you will also get a lot of people with no connection to OS&H at all or even the slightest interest in it following you because they hope that you will reciprocate and follow them. If you have irrelevant followers, you don't follow them back, so then they will unfollow you.

As mentioned above, there is a real science to using Twitter most effectively. That science is too detailed to cover in this limited space. I would suggest that you read what experts in Twitter marketing have to say, then decide for yourself how much effort you can put into this. Suggested resources can be found at the end of this chapter. I think it is important to have a Twitter presence, even if you can't commit to using it as a primary marketing method.

It is important to tweet meaningful content if you want anyone to pay attention to your tweets. When many people think about Twitter, they think about the tweets which only provide information that is irrelevant to most people except a few close friends. When you tweet something for your business, ask yourself if a potential client or colleague would care about the information, or share it with others. If not, don't tweet it. Following other people on Twitter who post what you are interested in, and then "retweeting" (forwarding) that information is one way to share meaningful content with your followers.

Because Twitter limits you to 140 characters, sharing meaningful content is difficult, so many valuable tweets provide a link to a longer piece, very often a post on a blog or Web site. If your followers "retweet" (share with their followers) one of your tweets, they are suggesting you to their contacts, which can lead to more blog or Web site visits, and possible contact with potential clients.

Being genuinely interested in helping other people and sharing what you know is a way of providing authentic helpfulness. OS&H professionals, by our very nature, enjoy helping other people, and sharing our knowledge of safety. If you see something on Twitter that catches your eye, reply to the original source, comment on the blog it came from, or add a comment, and share with your followers. There really are endless opportunities to be helpful.

Since many of your potential clients are extremely busy people, if you see something of interest, especially something that may not be in mainstream publications, then tweet that link. Adding a few words of your own stating why you think it is tweet-worthy is also helpful. For example, if your target audience consists of Human Resource (HR) professionals, and many of your followers work in HR, sharing news about an updated OSHA standard or safety tips for a particular activity could be valuable information that they might not see elsewhere.

Some companies choose to block some social media Web sites. A recent study (Richter 2013) found that only one in five companies block Facebook, and less than that block Twitter, YouTube, and others. Additionally, with the use of smartphones, many people visit these sites primarily on their phones and not on their workplace computers. The bans don't always affect who will get to benefit from your efforts.

The bright side is that as more and more government agencies, including those that regulate OS&H, develop a substantial Twitter presence, and as many organizations learn how social media sites, like Twitter, can be used in emergency response situations, companies will understand the value that social media can have in the workplace, and will hopefully allow more social media use at work.

With any type of social media, it will take some time for many people and companies to catch up. Depending on your ideal client, your targets might not be on social media. So why bother? Many people, including myself, believe that social media marketing is the way of the future. Even by just dabbling in the different options available, you can get a jump start on the learning curve and your competitors. You can get on the train early and get a good seat, or wait until it leaves the platform, and then sprint to catch up. It's up to you.

LinkedIn

According to Jeff Gitomer in *Social Boom*, LinkedIn has more than 85 million members. Executives from all Fortune 500 companies are LinkedIn members (Gitomer 2011, 81). Most people in business are familiar with LinkedIn, although many people feel it is only best for job-hunting. LinkedIn has become a popular tool for recruiters and employers to use when hunting for job candidates. Along the same lines, potential clients can search for consultants through LinkedIn, so you need a LinkedIn profile that is complete, showing your strengths and capabilities. When I have needed subcontractors to work on locations out of my area, I have used LinkedIn to find them.

I have approximately 1700 LinkedIn contacts, with most of these sorted into lists. If I need to find a subcontractor or expert in a particular area, I can search those lists. If I find particular experts on LinkedIn to whom I am not connected, LinkedIn will show me if I am connected to them through mutual friends. I can then contact the mutual friends and ask for an introduction.

If I am meeting with a potential new client, I will always do some research on that person beforehand, if I do not know him or her. LinkedIn is a great way to do that. If my LinkedIn search shows that the potential client and I have a mutual contact, I can reach out to the person that I know, and gather information about the potential client. My contact might also be able to reach out to the potential client directly, and either make an introduction or recommend me ahead of the meeting. As said by Mark Zuckerberg, "Nothing influences people more than a recommendation from a trusted friend."

Trying to attract contacts and interest within LinkedIn is also possible. By providing information on LinkedIn, you can share helpful information just as you would on other social media platforms. If you post something to your blog or post a PowerPoint presentation to Slideshare, you can share the link very easily on LinkedIn for your contacts to view it. Targeting clients with LinkedIn may not be as popular as Twitter or Facebook, but it does provide a unique opportunity, as there is much less action to distract from what you are trying to accomplish (Zarrella 2012, 44).

LinkedIn is also a great way to stay in touch with your clients. Many people update their LinkedIn profiles when they change jobs; these will appear in your LinkedIn news updates. Not only is this is a great opportunity to reach out to your client, and congratulate him or her on the new position or promotion, but it is also an alert to update the contact information in your files so you can keep in touch. As mentioned earlier, further details about how to use LinkedIn to build a consulting business can be found in Chapter 7, "Networking."

Facebook

If you are going to use Facebook for business, set up a Facebook page for your consulting firm, which makes it easier to keep your personal activities separate from your business activities. Some people feel that, in order to be authentic and build deep relationships with clients, your professional self should be the same as your personal self, and the two should not be separate. This is your decision; I like to keep at least some separation between the two.

Facebook pages are like separate accounts you set up where you can have a community of people who "like" your page. When they "like" your business Facebook page, they see whatever updates you post on this page but not on your personal Facebook page. Since many OS&H pros do not have access to Facebook in the workplace, these pages may be visited only during non-work hours or not at all.

To get people to "like" your page (which is similar to someone asking to subscribe to your e-mail updates), you can invite them; then, they have to take the steps to "like" it. The key to getting people to do this is to provide valuable content that people will want to share and comment on. In *Social Boom*, Jeff Gitomer gets it right when he says, "Facebook's 'page' term is a misnomer. It should be a 'community' where all of your customers, your prospective customers, and even your vendors would find you as the focal point for information dissemination" (Gitomer 2011, 66).

> *. . . one out of every five page views in the United States is on Facebook.*

I would suggest that you approach Facebook as a marketing tool, much the same way you approach Twitter. It is a hugely popular social media site, with over 680 million active users. If you have potential clients there, and it is likely you do, you should consider having a presence, since one out of every five page views in the United States is on Facebook. Considering how often so many people are on Facebook, isn't it worth it to you to give your company a presence? With a blog or website, your potential or existing clients will have to type in that web address in an effort to find you. With Facebook, the same people are there anyway. As they scan through their newsfeeds, they will likely see your posts and, if those interest them, they will click through.

Facebook appeals to young and old, men and women, and people from every possible demographic. Professional marketers see it as a legitimate marketing tool. As a social media marketing expert states, "Only the most stubborn holdouts . . . question whether their customer is actually on Facebook and whether it's worth maintaining a presence there" (Vaynerchuk 2013, 30).

Personally, compared to other social media platforms, I have only recently attempted to market on Facebook in a beta-test fashion, and I have about 200 "likes" on my business page. I use this page to make announcements or offers that I think my target audience will like. Recently, I ran a ten-week contest, which I also promoted elsewhere. The contest did result in increased sales. The contest was photo-based, so Facebook was the perfect place for it. I like that the individuals who "like" my page can ask a question for others to see, and that my answers are available to everyone. I was also surprised that several people posted unsolicited praise for my company. Testimonials are priceless; the value of these alone is worth maintaining, and worth the effort of trying to expand the number of "likes" on the page.

> *Be careful not to dilute yourself too much. Focus your resources on where your clients are, and the return on your time investment will be higher.*

YouTube

YouTube, home of the online video, is another extremely popular site. On YouTube, users can upload, view, and share videos with a select group of people or with the world. More than 1 billion unique users visit YouTube every month.

How can you use YouTube? Again, the idea is to create valuable content that you can share with clients and potential clients, as well as to increase the materials that you have searchable on the web. You could record "how-tos," summaries of presentations or even entire presentations, introductions about yourself, your firm or a product, a tip of the week, or almost anything created by your imagination. An effective strategy to use on YouTube is to create one-minute, energetic videos that leave viewers wanting more. Once you have these uploaded, you need to share the link on other sites and with your contacts.

Other Social Media Sites

There is a trend towards visual marketing. Although sites like Instagram and Pinterest are extremely popular, they are not widely used in the OS&H community yet. It wasn't that long ago that the three of the biggest social media outlets (YouTube, Twitter and Facebook) were scoffed at by most OS&H professionals. As this same group realized that these sites have real benefits and are not just for teens or for irrelevant updates, more and more OS&H pros can be found on these sites (Johnson 2012). At the Professional Development Conference (PDC) of the American Society of Safety Engineers (ASSE) in June 2013, there was a noticeable increase in the use of social media during the PDC by OS&H professionals. (Walaski 2013a and b). For this reason, it is a good idea to keep an eye on sites like Instagram and Pinterest, so when these and other similar newer sites become widely used for professional services, you will be able to easily jump on board.

Instagram is a place where you post photos. Those who choose to follow you can see, like, and comment on what you post. Instagram also allows you to provide a hashtag for your photo. One marketing professional told me that it is a place where reporters will go to search, by hashtag, for content.

With Instagram, you cannot easily share content that you like with others, so word-of-mouth marketing is limited. The key to marketing with Instagram is to post photos that have a hyperlink to your Web site or product page. If your OS&H consulting company is primarily a service provider, it might be difficult to find photos related to your work. A few ideas would be a photo of you speaking or providing training, a blank form such as an inspection report that you are willing to share, or even a photo of personal protective equipment (PPE) that links back to an article on your Web site.

While I don't think that Instagram is the best place to spend your marketing time right now, I like the advice of Gary Vaynerchuk, "Learn to make Instagram work for you—it will be your gateway to the next generation of social users"(Vaynerchuk 2013, 137).

Pinterest is the other new weapon is the social media kit of marketing professionals. Pinterest grew 379,599% in 2012. As of July 2013, it had 70 million users. Visit Pinterest and search something related to safety or safety consulting, and you will see what is already being done by others in the field. I have a lot of training material I could post on Pinterest in the hope that someone searching for information on PPE training, for example, will find something I pinned (the Pinterest term for posting something), follow through, and contact me. As with Vaynerchuk's advice on using Instagram, get your feet wet, and be ready when this takes off.

Be careful not to dilute yourself too much. Each of these social media sites takes time to learn and update. Focus your resources on where your clients are, and the return on your time investment will be higher.

Speaking and Writing

Speaking and writing are two of the best ways to get your name out there. I have always had at least one potential client contact me, or at least one book purchased, whenever I have had something published or given a presentation. Even articles written by someone else that mention me or my company usually result in potential client contacts, or at least a few sales of my products.

Speaking can be a part of your moneymaking activities, or it can be something you do for free to gain exposure. While it is great to get a paid gig, this can be difficult, especially if you are just starting out, with so many other consultants willing to speak for free. Some safety consultants are paid professional speakers, and some are even Certified Speaking Professionals through the National Speakers Association (NSA). More often than not, though, I have found that NSA members speaking on safety are not safety professionals, but work in adjunct areas with some connection to safety or security. If you speak as a volunteer, you probably will not be paid, or you may be given a small honorarium. For example, when you speak at the ASSE's Professional Development Conference (PDC), your registration fee for the conference is waived, either fully or in part.

Often, speaking engagements must be pursued and scheduled months in advance. In the case of ASSE and the American Industrial Hygiene Association (AIHA), proposals are due almost a year before the conferences. You should have your presentation idea in mind, and be prepared to commit to a date many months away. However, if you are selected and agree to speak, but then back out because you have a client engagement, you probably will not be selected to speak again.

If other OS&H professionals are your target customers, then speaking at large national conferences, such as these, are great places to put in your time and energy. If, instead, you provide OSHA-mandated training to construction firms in your area, it would be better for you to present at conferences where these targets are present. If you know your potential customers, you should know or ask them if they attend any conferences or local meetings. Once you have that information, contact the group and ask if they would be interested in having you speak.

I have found that word of mouth leads to many speaking engagements. I recently landed a speaking engagement because someone saw a "tweet" of mine, followed it back to my Web site, and then thought I'd be a good addition to their speaking lineup. While this speaking engagement will be unpaid, it will be worthwhile for the exposure to many potential customers.

How to Maximize Your Public Speaking Efforts

In almost all instances, it is unprofessional to sell your services while you are delivering a presentation sponsored by another party, and many groups have outright rules against it. In addition to sharing your knowledge, you are most likely donating your time to speak in order to make contacts and gain exposure. How can you make the best of it? Make sure it is very easy for attendees to contact you after the presentation. You can provide your contact information by including it on slides (although providing this

I have seen too many speakers who quickly escape after they wrap up their presentations.

on every slide may make the slides cumbersome to read), on one slide at the beginning and/or end, on hand-outs or free takeaways you provide, and, of course, on business cards.

Additionally, make sure you are accessible. I have seen too many speakers who quickly escape after they wrap up their presentations. If you have a plane to catch after your presentation, plan accordingly, so you can hang around and talk for an hour if need be with a prospective client. If another speaker is coming into your speaking area to set up for another session, move yourself and your business cards outside the room, so you can continue to have conversations as long as necessary.

When you present, give attendees hand-outs or copies of your slides before or during your presentation. This may cause people to leave early or spend more time reading your materials than listening to you, so it is often better to offer to send out materials after the presentation in exchange for a business card. Most people will appreciate not having to carry extra materials. Ask people to contact you if they want your materials, though this isn't always the best route, since (1) they are either likely to get too busy or forget to contact you once they get back to the office, or (2) they will lose your contact information. By collecting their business cards, you have a way to stay in touch, and a way to make sure they get the materials at a later time.

Always have an introduction written for yourself, and be ready to provide it. This is another way to maximize your speaking efforts by assisting the person introducing you. If you do not pay attention to this yourself, you may end up having someone stand up, and read bits and pieces from your resume to the audience. If this happens, you will "lose" your group before you even start. While some very academic audiences may wish to hear about every degree and certification you possess, most people just want to know what's in it for them.

If you cannot sell during your presentation, have the person introducing you briefly describe your services and products and, if you like, your success; it's better if it comes out of someone else's mouth instead of your own even, if you told that person what to say. If you think it's really important that the group knows your background, be brief. Provide a hand-out with a page all about yourself if you think it would be helpful. Keep in mind that the group you are speaking to probably doesn't care too much about what you have done in the past; it's all about what you can do for them now.

Repurposing Content

With a little pre-planning, you can repurpose your content, which is one of the best things about a speaking engagement. If the organizer tapes you and provides you with a copy, get that presentation transcribed so you have it in writing. If they don't provide this service, taping yourself is easy enough. Turning your into an article, a series of blog posts, or even an informational booklet is relatively easy, with a little tweaking.

If your presentation is long enough or if you have a collection of these transcribed presentations, you can even make them into an e-book to be offered online for sale or even for free. Selling or giving away items such as e-books online allows you to grow your contact database: for every download, you will collect the contact information of people who are specifically interested in your topic. With all marketing of this type, it is important to ask permission to contact them in the future or to make a statement that ensures they know that by requesting and/or downloading your e-book, they are agreeing to receive future correspondence.

If you have taken your transcribed presentation and submitted it for publication anywhere, such as a trade journal, professional magazine, local newsletter or newspaper, once it is published, you are again marketing to a wider audience. If you have a Twitter account, you should post a link to the online version of the article. If you have a blog, make sure you provide a link there as well.

Create and Market Your Own Seminars

In addition to speaking for others at conferences and meetings, you can also create and market your own seminars. Seminars can be a lucrative business on their own, in addition to being a great way to market. Look at the number of seminars and webinars offered by professional associations, trade magazines, and training companies within the OS&H arena, and you will quickly see how popular they have become. Seminars can be a simple speech, a hands-on workshop or a multi-day training class. The secret to success from seminars, both professionally and financially, is to master both the "front end" of the business and the "back end" (Karasik 1992, 7).

The back end involves everything necessary to get bodies in seats.... If you don't do well on the back end, there will be no front end in the future.

The front end is the actual presentation. Having a high-quality program that is organized and provides tons of valuable content is the first step in being successful. Your speaking and audience management skills must also be top-notch. The information you present, and how you come across, will determine how well people speak of you after the presentation, and how likely they are to recommend you and your company or products.

The back end involves everything necessary to get bodies in seats. It is all of the effort needed to get the word out about your seminar, get people registered, and collect registration fees. If you don't do well on the back end, there will be no front end in the future. If you do not have an assistant, recruit one or two people to help you with the logistics the day of the seminar. This could be as formal as placing an advertisement for help or asking a stay-at-home parent with administrative skills to work with you for a day. Just remember that, whoever is helping you on that day will also be a reflection of you and your consulting firm.

"Back-of-the-Room" Sales

If you have ever attended a seminar delivered by a professional speaker, chances are that speaker was benefitting from "back-of-the-room" sales. Many seminar speakers make just as much, if not more, from the products they sell during breaks, and after the session.

To add this type of revenue stream to your consulting business, you need some products to sell, which be yours or those produced by other people, or a combination of both. If you are speaking on safety leadership for example, you can offer books on leadership that you recommend during your seminar; however, to make money, you will most likely need to make a deal with the publisher of the book to allow you to purchase a few copies at a reduced rate, with a buy-back option for unsold books. Since this gets a little risky, it is probably not something you want to try your first time out.

Creating your own products and selling them is a safer bet. Think about what would really be useful for your clients. If you can find out their greatest needs, you can create something they will actually want. Products can include e-books, paperback or hardback books, DVDs, audiotapes, customizable Power Point presentations, checklists, workbooks, or recordkeeping systems. The possibilities are endless. As stated by Seth Godin (2005), "Don't find customers for your products, find products for your customers."

To offer back-of-the-room sales, you are going to need some help. You will probably have that already if someone was present to help with registration of attendees. It is important not to fall into the habit that some professional motivational speakers have of talking about your topic only to a point, and then directing the audience to your products to get the rest, and usually the most beneficial, information. It is more important to deliver valuable information in your seminars than to sell a few books.

To conclude this section, here are the top five things I have learned about marketing:

- Marketing activities are an ongoing process, not just something to work on during slow times.
- Marketing your OS&H firm can be costly, especially if you use traditional methods.
- Marketing to too broad of an audience wastes time and effort.

- The general OS&H population is not overwhelmingly using social media for business (yet).
- Who you know can be far more important than what you know.

SALES

There are more than two million books about sales available on Amazon. These have titles like *Spin Selling,* *Unselling,* and *Snap Selling,* and could easily overwhelm and confuse you. To put it simply, selling occurs when you need to convince someone else to buy what you have. This could be a service, a product or even an idea. Marketing and sales go together. Your marketing, your Web site, and especially your testimonials and references are selling for you. Simply put, marketing is everything you do to reach potential clients, and sales is the process of getting those potential clients to buy what you are selling.

When I first started consulting, I took a lot of sales classes and read a lot of sales books. I always felt very uncomfortable in these situations because I felt like these classes were teaching me to convince people to do something they might not necessarily want to do. I took an entire class on cold-calling. Cold-calling is when you pick up the phone and call a total stranger to try to get him or her to buy from you or to at least set up an appointment to see you. The calls you get from strangers around dinner time usually fall into this category. I had never realized how many tricks there were to getting by the "gatekeepers" (those assistants in charge of keeping nuisance calls away from their bosses). I not only learned how to trick the gatekeeper, but also how to make "warm calls," how to get appointments, and how to use body language to get the sale. While I am sure parts of these lessons are helpful when applied elsewhere, I quickly abandoned my efforts at the traditional cold-calling techniques. As Peter Drucker said, "There is no doubt that if marketing were done perfectly, selling, in the actual sense of the word, would be unnecessary" (Cohen 2008, 98).

Referrals

In *The Consultant's Calling,* the author Geoffrey M. Bellman (1990) states that he tries "to create a world in which my knowledge of the marketplace and its knowledge of me brings appropriate clients to me, asking for my services and eliminating the need for me to knock on their doors offering my services." I believe this is the ideal way to sell.

The "knowledge of me" clause in Mr. Bellman's statement above can be greatly helped by building up what John Jantsch calls the "referral engine."

The subtitle of Jantsch's book, *The Referral Engine*, is "Teaching Your Business to Market Itself," which is an especially good idea if, like many consultants, you are trying to do all of the marketing, bookkeeping, networking, and the actual consulting work yourself. Referrals are priceless. The old adage, "it's not what you know, but who you know," is never more true than in the world of consulting. Many would-be consultants come out of industry or government with 20 or more years of OS&H work experience on their resumes, but very little in the way of connections, especially if they were not involved in groups like ASSE. Unfortunately, all of the technical knowledge in the world is not going to get you consulting work. It's all about who you know and who knows you and, more importantly, getting those people who know you to refer you.

You might be thinking, "Why would a competitor recommend me?" I believe that it is because we all like to be helpful, especially to people we know, like, and trust, and also because it builds a relationship in which others will feel comfortable sending work back to you. The goal of OS&H consultants is ultimately to help people stay safe at work. If you can do that by referring potential clients to someone else when you can't provide a service, you are working towards that goal.

> *Many consultants start off thinking they can and will do everything for everyone.*

You can help other consultants and past clients to provide referrals by having a "core talkable difference." In *The Referral Engine*, Jantsch (2012) states that, "the first step in the design of your referral system is to unearth the simple, remarkable difference that is your chief competitive advantage." You need to realize what makes you and your consulting firm special so that others will be able to refer you based on this difference. Jantsch (2012) further explains that, "talkable differences must be original, real, and compelling." Think about what sets you apart; if there is nothing, take action to differentiate yourself, so your past clients and colleagues have an easy way to remember and refer your services.

When I was first starting out in consulting, I met a stranger at an ASSE networking event and, after chatting awhile, he invited me to send my resume to him. I initially had no idea who this person was, but when he handed me his card, I saw that he was Vice President of OS&H for a global organization. Obviously, I followed through; within a few months, I had several OS&H professionals from various plants contacting me with possible project opportunities. In this case, the referral was key. None of these new clients really knew anything about my expertise, only that someone they respected had recommended me. Persuading contacts, past employers, friends, family, and even competitors to recommend you are skills that you must learn as they are vital to your success.

Referrals may happen by chance, or they can be the result of a planned strategy on your part. By identifying your ideal client and sharing that with your current and past clients, you are making it easy for them to introduce you to the most promising prospects.

Many consultants start off thinking they can and will do everything for everyone. When you are living off the fees from your last project, this can be tempting, but don't go down this path. As much as you would like to, you can't be all things to all people. Your ability to send others away or to another consultant when you can't do the work yourself will show that you are a professional, willing to take on projects only when you can truly help the client. In turn, the consultants to whom you refer business will hopefully reciprocate. You want to have this conversation with other consultants even before a situation comes up. If you know exactly who your perfect customer is and conversely, who it is not, you will be able to develop a meaningful referral strategy.

Jantsch has a great way of describing how referrals can be a major part of your marketing strategy; he states (Jantsch 2012, 61):

> In traditional business models, marketers generally go out and hunt for customers. They do it with advertising; they do it with sales pitches; they do it with trade shows and networking efforts. In a fully functioning referral marketing system, the emphasis has moved from finding to being found, creating valuable content, engagement, and interaction where the ideal prospects are already looking.

Even if your potential client base does not consist of other safety professionals, it is still very important to have other safety professionals in your network. If an ASSE colleague, for example, has a local company call him for help with a project in which he does not have experience, that other safety consultant needs to know to whom he can refer the work. Even if other OS&H professionals are not your targets, their referrals from non-OS&H people will be invaluable.

For example, I volunteer with a Boys & Girls Club in my area. The club is planning to provide active shooter training to its staff. I do not provide this training, and I know very little about it. Fortunately, I do know a colleague I met at a safety conference, and subsequently worked with on a volunteer committee, who can help them. While this colleague may not ever have marketed his expertise to my local Boys & Girls Club, I can confidently refer them to him, and hope it's a win-win situation for both parties.

Many of my past clients have not been OS&H professionals and often, there is no OS&H presence at all in the workplaces where I provide services. These clients usually find me by first searching online for safety consultants in their areas. Other times, an article I have written or been mentioned in gets picked up by another trade journal not related to OS&H. For example, an article I once wrote on PPE got picked up by a metalworking magazine. One of the readers of that magazine saw the credits, which included my city and state, and since I was close, decided to contact me. This led to a small consulting project with a company, and an industry for that matter, that I would never have thought to approach.

Reputation Management

It is great to be talked about, but not for the wrong reasons. In this age of online reviews, it is very easy for an unhappy client, or even a disgruntled competitor, to put a ding in your reputation. Reputation management is an area that will need your attention if you hope to be an effective marketer of your OS&H consulting business. Before, if a client wasn't happy with you, there were probably a limited number of colleagues he or she would tell about it. Now, complaints or comments about companies are commonplace through social media, such as Twitter. Other extremely popular Web sites, such as Yelp, Angie's List, and TripAdvisor, are set up for customers to provide reviews.

While there are very few safety consulting firms, if any, being reviewed on sites such as Yelp or Angie's List at the moment, all it takes is one client to add you and comment. You may be thinking that you have nothing to worry about, since you only do great work. Unfortunately, the reality is that some clients don't know what they want (or need), and may not understand the value of what you have provided. As a safety professional, and as the creator of the work, you are, of course, going to be biased. Another safety professional as a client may be particularly critical, especially if that person was not in favor of using a consultant in the first place, but was told to do so by a boss who realized that he or she did not have the necessary experience or skill set for the project. A client that is not in OS&H may not realize that what you provided or recommended is required by law or is best practice, and may criticize you for that. This seems like a no-win situation. Fortunately, I believe this kind of unjust reaction occurs very infrequently. I only point it out so that you are aware of how someone could possibly publish negative feedback about your services.

Reputation management is an area that will need your attention....

If you create and produce products in addition to services (which I highly recommend), then you also have to think about how bad reviews of your products affect your reputation. If you have a product on Amazon, it is very easy for the purchaser to provide a review, which you cannot edit. If an old colleague, still stuck in the corporate world, is jealous of you for having the courage and skills to venture out on your own, he or she could easily affect your product sales with one bad review. Since Amazon allows users to post a review and only provide their Amazon name, they can do this pretty much anonymously.

The easiest and most inexpensive way to check on your reputation online is to Google yourself. Don't forget to use all variations of your name. You also want to Google your company name to see where it pops up. Whenever I Google myself, I always find a mention or two that I did not know about. Luckily, these have all been good. I have also discovered a few attempts by people to use my content without permission. To help aid in this process, you can set up "Google Alerts" that will notify you every time certain key phrases or your name appears on the Internet. This can be an effective way to stay on top of things; however, if you have a common name, like Joe Smith, you are likely to get a lot of hits on people that are not you.

If you are really serious about reputation management or think you may really have an issue, there are firms that will help you track your online reputation for a fee. Just search "online reputation monitoring," and you will find available providers and applications.

Another way to attack reputation management head-on is to be proactive about disseminating good things about you and your work. After something bad has happened, this becomes especially important, and is a method often used by large companies. If you have never made any contributions to the Internet, and your name suddenly receives negative press, then that is all that will be seen when someone searches for you. If you have posted online articles, comments on blogs, won awards, and so on, then these links will also appear. If someone ends up reading something unfavorable online, all of the good information will appear as well.

Finally, take the same advice you should be giving your teens and college-age kids: Don't post anything that you would not want to see on the front page of a newspaper. Even if you keep your Facebook® account for personal use and never share it with professional contacts, your photos and comments may still find their way out to a larger audience. Many people do not fully utilize the privacy controls available on those sites. Anyone Googling their name can find their latest party pictures, political rants, or worse. Prospective clients may change their mind about hiring you when they see something that you thought was private. If you are going to provide a controversial comment or opinion on your own or on someone else's blog, think about what you really want to accomplish by doing so. There are consultants of all types who make their living being contrarians, but I don't think is the right path for everyone.

> *The easiest and most inexpensive way to check on your reputation online is to Google yourself.*

The Sales and Marketing Funnel

One way I like to approach sales and marketing is with the funnel system. If you picture a funnel in your mind, the top is very wide, and the bottom is very small. Marketing, as well as the products and services you provide, can be thought of as a funnel. Using the funnel as part of a marketing and sales plan, you would try to reach as many potential clients as you could (the top of the funnel) by providing something free or at a very low cost. As you move down the funnel, you have a smaller and smaller pool of potential clients, but also higher and higher value products and services. For example, you might offer a free OSHA-type inspection form at the top of the funnel. You could then target the group responding to this offer, since you know they have an interest, and offer them a one-day basic training class on inspection techniques. You might also offer a full day of your time on site, followed up by a written report. Next, you might offer to provide a comprehensive inspection and follow up for multiple sites over the course of a week.

Obviously, the cost of each of these items increases and at the same time, the number of participants goes down. Eventually, you should be doing a few very high-value jobs or selling a few high-priced products to a select group of people. To illustrate, say you have a hundred clients paying you $1 for the basic form ($100 total revenue), fifty clients paying you $10 for a one-day class ($500 total revenue), and ten clients paying you $100 for a comprehensive inspection and follow up ($1000 total revenue). If you tried to get these ten high-value clients from the get-go, it would not be impossible, but it would not be easy either. When you use the funnel as a marketing and sales method, you are first building a large pool in which to market, instead of trying to sell your high-value items to the entire OS&H world.

The funnel as a marketing tool basically means that you offer something basic to a large group with the hope of moving a percentage of each group down your funnel. At the top of the funnel, you have more mass marketing. While not everyone out there is a potential client at this level, many companies could use this service, and equally as important, you could provide it. As you move down the funnel, you are narrowing your audience, based on your abilities and the needs of your target population. For example, if you are a solo consultant or part of a small firm, marketing a multi-site, long-term inspection program might not be realistically feasible for you or something that you would want to take on. Not only would you have to hire or subcontract additional staff (which has risks of its own), but you would also be giving up your ability to market and service other existing and new clients.

Another benefit of the funnel method is that you are offering "just a taste" of your services. Allowing potential clients to "try before they buy" is a great way to market yourself. Allowing someone to listen in on a free teleconference is not going to cost you any extra money if you are already holding the teleseminar.

Networking

Chapter 7 discusses networking in greater detail. Networking is one of the best marketing methods because, if done correctly, it is sincere, provides value to others, is inexpensive, and can provide a great return on investment. Good old-fashioned networking, or "pressing the flesh," is very effective in building relationships. That's why attending conferences, such as the ASSE's annual professional development conference (PDC), is very important for OS&H consultants. I know many consultants who do not regularly attend. When you work for yourself and have to pay your own way, it might make you think twice about attending but, in reality, attending should be automatic. Sure, you will be out of pocket for your registration, travel, and meals, and you will probably not be able to get any billable work done while you attend. But the opportunity to meet many, many potential clients, as well as to get you and/or your company's name out, should not be undervalued.

Online networking is very easy, may be effective, and sometimes, might be the best option available to you. The best thing about online networking is that it can be done anytime, so you are not missing work time if you plan it out well. You can network online any time of the day or night (if you are thinking that you have no intention of working after normal business hours, you may want to reconsider your choice to be an OS&H consultant). There are some ways to manage this. The easiest is to use a service that allows you to schedule your online activities and participation.

If you use e-mail marketing, you can pick the time your e-mails are delivered. If you want to be involved in the Twittersphere, you can schedule tweets to post at a later time. There are applications, such as Hootsuite and Sendible, which will allow you to post to just about every social media site on a pre-determined schedule. Of course, the idea of online networking is to have a two-way conversation. You will have to make time to respond to any replies you get, but this is just part of running a business.

Follow-Up

With online networking, as well as in-person networking, follow-up is critical. If you leave a conference or dinner meeting with a pocket full of business cards, and never do anything with those cards, your networking efforts and the effort it took to collect those cards are totally wasted. Follow-up is a key part of building relationships through networking. One of the first marketing books I ever read was *How to Swim With the Sharks Without Getting Eaten Alive* by Harvey Mackay, an envelope salesman turned motivational speaker. This book makes a very important point about building relationships (Mackay 2005).

Harvey would always find out what outside interests and needs his clients and potential clients had, so that he had an excuse for following up. For example, if he was making a sales call in someone's office, he would notice any photos, awards, certificates, diplomas, trophies, or desk decorations that might help him to learn more about the person. If he noticed a photo of a family or pet, he would ask about them. If he saw a diploma on the wall, he would ask about the college. If he learned that the potential client was a particular sports fan, he would make a note of that too. He was very observant of everything around him, and would make notes about each client after he left the meeting.

Now if Harvey just kept that information scribbled on the back of a business card or in his portfolio and never looked at it again, it was a waste. Instead, Harvey would keep his eye out for anything that might interest the client, and pass it along with a short note. Back in Harvey's day, this could be a newspaper article, a page torn out of a magazine, or even a page of a catalog. This was Harvey's way of building the relationship, and providing value to the client or potential client, even if he didn't get the sale.

In today's world, it is much easier to follow up. You can use a variety of computer applications, or even simply make a note on your calendar on a future date, with instructions to follow up with a particular person about a particular topic. It is very easy, and takes very little time to forward a link, a web page, a blog post, or a video when you know it is something that someone else is interested in. It literally takes a minute or less.

It might sound like a lot of work but it is really very easy. When you are sitting around watching your favorite television show or sports team on a Sunday afternoon, you can multi-task (a useful skill to have when you are a consultant), and set up your follow-up networking activities for the week.

For starters, you can set up a Google Alert (free), particularly if the potential client has a really unusual interest. If the prospect has an unusual breed of dog, you could set up an alert for that type of dog and, when you receive an alert that might interest that person, you can easily send it along. Similarly, you can search for certain key words in Twitter, and you will quickly find a lot of links related to that topic. Pick a good one, and send it along. There are many programs that will allow you to send an e-mail at a future date and time. If finding content and forwarding it were any easier, the computer would do it for you. Considering Harvey had to cut something out, attach a note, fold it, put it in an envelope, address it, add a stamp, and take it to the post office, and he managed to do it every day, you can do it too. Try setting aside fifteen minutes a day to do this type of follow-up or spend an hour or two on the weekend searching for good content, and setting up a schedule to send it out. Once you get the hang of it, it's easier than you think.

Another advantage of follow-up networking is that it keeps you and your name in front of the client. Even if you did not get the project, or you did and haven't worked for the client for years, you may be surprised at how often the client just happens to reply that he or she has a need that you may be able to help with. Our clients and potential clients are extremely busy. They might know they need help with something but just haven't had the time to dig out your contact information, and take the time to call or e-mail you. By just "checking in" with a friendly e-mail or by forwarding something of interest, you will stay in front of them, and make it easier for them to send a project your way. If a potential client mentions a problem, even if it's something that you can't help with, take some time and research it for them, and pass it along. Instead of being seen as just a safety consultant, you will be a valued contact who can make their lives easier. If you build this type of relationship, you will have no trouble getting clients and prospective clients to take your calls.

Marketing Plans and Research

After reading about all of the ways you can market your consulting firm, you may be anxious to start. Before you start, it is wise to develop a marketing plan so you can focus your attention where it's needed and be able to measure your results. Once you are established, you will probably want to devise a different marketing plan for different market segments. If you are a new consultant, the following guidelines for a basic plan should be good to get you started. Traditionally, you would follow the "ready-aim-fire" approach, which means: (1) do some market research, (2) develop strategies that align with the kind of clients you are trying to attract, and how you think you can best reach those potential clients, (3) consider the expenses involved, and (4) start. Alternatively, you could "fire" first. In this age of online and social media marketing, it is very easy to quickly test some of the many options available to you. If you choose the traditional, more planned method, you will still be doing bits of the latter, since with all of your marketing, you are going to be trying things out, revising them, and determining the level of success, and then adjusting your plans from there, and you will be doing this continuously.

> *The most important step in the traditional marketing template is research.*

In *The Marketing Plan Template*, by Chris Gattis & Felica Sparks (2011), the authors provide a basic template, along with an explanation for each section. The following template includes their basic template, plus sections I added to correlate with the ideas presented in this chapter.

Section 1: Market Research
    Industry
    Competition
    Potential clients for services
    Potential purchases of your products

Section 2: Marketing Strategy
    Unique Sales Proposition (USP) or "core talkable difference"
    Brand
    Products or Services
    Promotion Goals

Section 3: Action Plans
    Advertising and Promotion
    PR Campaigns
    Networking
    Speaking and Writing
    Social Media
    Putting it to Work

Section 4: Monitor

The most important step in the traditional marketing template is research. Market research is something you probably already did when you decided to start your consulting firm (see Chapter 2, "Business Plans," for more information). You should already have a pretty good understanding of your industry, your competition, and who you think your ideal clients would be.

Once you have done all of your research, you need to develop a strategy. Merriam-Webster's Dictionary (2014) defines strategy as "a careful plan or method for achieving a particular goal usually over a long period of time." What is your plan? Where do you start? As shown in the above template, you need to first identify your "core talkable difference" as described in the "Referrals" section above.

The third section in Gattis and Sparks (2011) marketing plan template covers the action plan. The action plan will cover everything previously mentioned in this chapter, from networking to social media. For many people, this is the most enjoyable part of marketing.

Your action plan will consist of the tactics you will use to track your target audience. The tactics you choose should be based on your goals, budget, time frame, and most importantly, your audience. If everyone is raving about the value of Pinterest as a marketing tool, it does not mean that your potential clients use it (or have even heard of it). While many social media platforms might be great marketing tools for the masses, using only those methods to market will be a disaster if your potential clients never use them.

As OS&H professionals, we are used to measuring results, and then returning to the plan to tweak it as necessary in an effort to improve results. In Section 4 of the template, you apply the same reviews and monitoring to the action plan as you would to a traditional safety program or accident reduction plan. Monitoring the results is an important step in determining what you should do more of, and what you should do less of.

Putting It All Together

One way to develop and maintain your plan is to use a spreadsheet. You will want to include the how, what, why, when, cost, and metric for each item in your plan. For each tactic you try, you will need a separate mini-action plan for it. For example, if you use a traditional magazine advertisement as one of your tactics, you will need a mini-action plan for the ad. For each of your tactics, you may want to have a separate spreadsheet that further breaks down the details associated with implementation of that tactic.

The final step, and part of your spreadsheet, would be the monitor and measure aspect of your marketing plan. If, in your original goals, you specified that, in one year, you wanted to gain 100 new contacts from your new Facebook page, and you wanted ten of those to turn into paying clients, how did you do? Did your Facebook page perform as expected, worse than expected, or better? The original goals you had when putting together your marketing plan should have been in the standard format for a good goal; that is, they should be SMART (specific, measurable, attainable, realistic and timely). If your goals include all of these things, you should not have a problem determining if they were successful.

Table: Sample Action Plan (To Be Updated Regularly)

Six-Month Marketing Action Plan for ABC Consulting Firm: July–December [Year]

	Specific Tactic	Time Frame	Cost	Outcome	Notes	Repeat
Advertising	Ad in local ASSE Chapter newsletter	Sept. to Dec.	$200	1 new client	Increased name recognition Can't really be measured	yes
	Redesign company Web site	July	$40 and time	18 new subscribers		yes
	Maintain sales site for OS&H Guidebook	July	$40 and time	70 sales	Approx. $1500 profit	yes
Promotion	none					
PR/Publicity	Participate on YWCA Safety Committee	Sept. & Nov.	Time only	Helping community		yes
Networking	Attend 3 or more ASSE or AIHA dinner meetings	Sept., Oct., Nov.	$150	2 referrals		yes
	Attend regional Professional Development Conference (PDC)	Oct.	$295	8 new contacts	1 very likely to result in a project	yes
Branding	New business cards	Dec.	$175	Not measured		No (not for awhile)
Participating	Add 10 new posts to blog	Sept.	time	25 new blog subscribers		yes
	Comment on 5 other blogs	Sept.	time	Not measured		
	Minimum of 50 Twitter® Updates	Sept.	time	63 new subscribers to ezine/blog		yes
Speaking	Speak at Chamber of Commerce Dinner Meeting	Oct.	time	Name recognition only	Ideal clients not in this group	No
	Submit proposal to speak at ASSE PDC	July	time	Unknown yet, but from past years, new contacts can be significant		Yes
Publishing	Write article for Practice Specialty Newsletter	Aug.	time	3 new contacts		yes
Product Development	Create and publish free e-book online	Sept.	$20/month	790 new subscribers to e-zine; 70 sales of Safety Guidebook		yes

Below you will find additional ideas for tactics. These tactical ideas are not for every consultant. Whether you should use them depends on your potential clients, your budget, your product or services, and the amount of time you have on your schedule.

Ideas for Specific Marketing Actions

The possibilities for marketing your consulting practice are endless. Many of the following ideas are low-cost options so, with low risk, you can experiment to see what works for you and your specialization.

- Place an advertisement in *Professional Safety* or other professional OS&H journal
- Write a letter to the editor of a OS&H publication or publication for the general public, commenting on a particular article or news shared in the publication
- Regularly comment on a OS&H or other blog where you can share your expertise and/or where your potential clients can benefit from your knowledge
- Join a committee where you can use your experience and/or make valuable contacts
- Get nominated to a board that will give you exposure to other OS&H professionals or to potential clients
- Sponsor an event at a conference where you will gain exposure or help increase your company's name recognition
- Pay for event "goodies," such as tote bags, pens, etc., that are likely to be saved by attendees, and thus provide a way to keep your company name in front of potential or existing clients
- Run a contest that will attract potential clients to your Web site or blog
- Offer a free OS&H helpline for existing or potential clients
- Write an article that showcases the expertise that your OS&H consulting firm can offer, and submit it for publication in a professional journal, trade magazine or even online
- Write a "how-to" article or list that you can share on social media or with your e-mail list. Make it easy for those who receive it to share it with others
- Include contact information on everything you have or do that reaches your potential targets, such as all paper products, digital presence, presentation materials, phone messages, and even company vehicles, if you have them

- Wear company-branded clothing that reflects the image you would like to convey
- Speak at conferences and local meetings that your potential clients attend
- Provide seminars and workshops, for free or for a fee, on topics that are related to the consulting services you provide
- Find networking events that potential clients, or people who can refer you to potential clients, attend
- Use Google Adwords to attract potential clients to your Web site
- Develop a professional Web site that conveys your image and your services in a way so that even non-OS&H professionals can easily find the information they need
- Have cohesive marketing materials so that the same logo, colors, fonts, etc., are used everywhere
- Direct market (such as direct mail, e-mail campaigns, or telephone solicitation) to targeted groups that you have identified as being individuals or companies with whom you would like to do business
- Offer samples of your work that will lead others to want to do business with you
- Deliver webinars for other organizations where the members of the organization are people that could benefit from your consulting services
- Become active with social media (this is low cost but can have a high time requirement, depending on strategy) including Facebook pages, Twitter, LinkedIn, blogs, YouTube, Slideshare and podcasts
- Create press releases tied to holidays, seasons, and current events that are related to services your firm can provide
- Volunteer or provide services pro bono, where you will not only be helping others but where your work will be seen by potential clients
- Teach (or guest lecture) at a community college where the students could be, either now or in the future, paying customers
- Write a book that will be of interest to potential clients
- Create a free e-book that will be of interest to those in a position to buy your services, or refer you to others who can
- Collect reference letters and testimonials from satisfied clients, and share those in your marketing materials, including on your Web site

Of course, there are many other benefits to many of these marketing ideas (such as sharing your expertise with others who may not have the funds to hire a consultant or who may not even realize they need your services) but since we are talking about marketing here, the above list focuses only on the marketing aspects of these activities.

Proposals

If all of your marketing efforts have paid off and you have been asked to submit a proposal, make the most of this opportunity to continue marketing your company and increase the opportunity of getting the work.

Most purchase decisions are made in 2.6 seconds (Fisk 2006, 229). With respect to the proposal, this could be the amount of time it takes for the clients to locate your price if they are only interested in the cost, or it could be the amount of time it takes them to disregard a poorly written proposal. To make sure the proposal you struggled with for hours or days does not go unread, it needs to be professional, easy to read and understand, and provide information that will help you get the project.

The theme of your proposal should be your customer value propositions (CVPs). "CVPs are the centerpiece of operational marketing that is focused, differentiated, and engaging. Propositions focus on what matters to customers: they are high-level, benefit-driven themes or promises delivered by products and services, functions and processes that enable the benefits to be realized" (Fisk 2006, 230). Your CVPs should change and evolve; don't reuse proposals for different potential clients, for different industries, or for different years. What may have been important five years ago might be very different today. Readers are going to pay attention to what is important to them, not to what you think is important.

Often, a consultant will get a call asking for a proposal for a particular service. Do not succumb to the temptation to immediately put something together or, worse yet, simply tweak a boilerplate proposal you have ready to go, and send it out. The reason not to do so is that it is highly likely that the potential client is calling not only you but a number of other consultants, asking for the same thing. When that potential client receives all of these proposals, he or she is going to be looking for one thing (price) and your goal should not to win jobs because you are always the low bidder. You should want to win jobs because your individual skill set and personality are the best fit for that client's needs.

Your goal should be to get in front of that potential client, even if it is just for a 15-minute meeting. . . .

Obviously, you can't gauge what a client really needs or wants simply from an initial phone call. I once heard that "people buy from people they like," and I have found this to be true. Your goal should be to get in front of that potential client, even if it is just for a 15-minute meeting, so that you can let the potential client meet you, and see what you are like in person. This is also an opportunity to get a better understanding of what the potential client is really looking for or needs (since, many times, it is not what they think). You could try to do this over the phone, which is acceptable in the absolutely worst case scenarios but it is not the best option. What if the client is a plane ride away? Do you make the trip? If winning the job could result in a significant project, then take that flight. If winning the project would just about cover your travel expenses, you might want to still consider making the trip, if the proposed project could lead to bigger and better things, or if the potential client is in an industry you have been trying to break in to. If you do push for a face-to-face meeting and get it, you are likely the only consultant doing this. By making the extra effort, you will be remembered.

After I had been consulting about a year, I decided to take a chance and fly twelve hours to discuss a potential project with a large chemical company. It involved travel with multiple connections, further complicated by a snowstorm. I was a sole practitioner and the other consultants trying to get the work were from much larger firms. When I finally arrived on site, I found that the site management group had changed their minds that morning at a staff meeting, and decided to go in a different direction. They asked my opinion on how they should approach it. Although my carefully and thoughtfully prepared proposal packet was now pretty much useless, I was able to think on my feet, and offer them a great option for their program. By sitting down with them, and discussing what they really needed versus what they thought they needed, they could see my creativity and flexibility first-hand (two things very hard to convey in a written proposal). I was able to follow up with a new proposal that truly identified what they needed. As a result, I was rewarded with a six-figure contract. My travel time, door to door, was a little over 20 hours, but in the end, it was worth it.

What does all this have to do with marketing through proposals? Proposals should be fluid, not boilerplate. Proposals should be a formality after you pretty much have the job in the bag. In addition to the list below, proposals should be an extension of your marketing efforts and should further cement in the buyer's mind that you are exactly the right consultant for the job. In *Million Dollar Consulting*, Dr. Weiss sums up nicely the purpose of a proposal:

The theme of your proposal should be your customer value propositions (CVPs).

- A summation of conceptual agreement between you and the buyer
- A template that will govern the boundaries of the proposed project
- A formal contract (when signed) that protects you and the client
- The reference point for details as the project unfolds (for example, it can be shared with other key people in the project) (Weiss 2006)

Offering Options

Alan Weiss has written over 25 books on consulting, marketing, speaking and other business topics. By listening to a lot of what he has to say, you can gain some valuable insights, and get some great suggestions to apply to your practice. Keep in mind that not every suggestion is right for every consultant; decide for yourself what you want to try. One of the best things I learned from Alan Weiss with respect to proposals is the use of alternatives.

It can be highly beneficial to offer alternatives in your proposal.

It can be highly beneficial to offer alternatives in your proposal. When I received a proposal while I was still in the corporate world, one of the first things I did was look for the price, which was usually on the last page. Although price shouldn't be the determining factor, often it is. When you provide alternatives in your proposals, you are moving away from a yes or no answer to a "yes, and this is how I'd like to proceed." As Alan Weiss states, in *Million Dollar Consulting*, "The Choice of yeses psychologically moves the buyer from the binary question of 'Should I?' to the pluralistic question of 'How should I?' This nuance, when used adroitly, will increase the likelihood of your proposals being accepted—and at higher fees—by at least 50 percent" (Weiss 2006).

Let's review how you can do this. A potential client calls to ask for an evaluation of the guarding on a particular machine in his shop. Think about a good, better, and best solution for the perceived need. After meeting with the client and taking a quick look at the machine in question, you should be able to easily think of these three options. In your proposal, include a paragraph, titled something like "Investment Options" or simply "Alternatives" An example follows:

> *Option 1:* Perform comprehensive evaluation of the machine guarding on XYZ, and provide a written report, including recommendations for improving the safety of the machine, if any deficiencies are found. Price: $$$

> *Option 2:* Perform comprehensive evaluation of machine guarding on *all* machines in the Maintenance Shop, plus a written report including recommendations for improving the safety of the machines, if any deficiencies are found. The report will include a searchable spreadsheet identifying all machines in the Maintenance Shop, the type of guarding present, the status of the guard, and a suggested maintenance schedule. Price: $$$

> *Option 3:* Perform comprehensive evaluation of machine guarding on *all* machines in the Maintenance Shop, plus a written report with

searchable database including recommendations for improving the safety of the machines, if any deficiencies are found. Additionally, a half-day follow-up training session will be delivered on site for up to 20 employees, covering the basics of machine guarding safety (allowing future evaluations to be done in-house), recommended engineering fixes, and an overview of maintenance procedures to keep the guards functioning as designed. Price: $$$$

The client may not have realized that all of his machines were going to need to be evaluated, and may not have realized that, with training, his people could do this in-house. By providing the additional options, you are providing additional value.

Include Outcomes

In addition to providing alternatives as described above, you should include additional components of a proposal. If you are going to use a signed copy of the proposal as a contract, you need to make sure that the objectives and outcomes are very clear. With outcomes, you need some way to measure whether or not the project was successful. Some government contracts ask you to supply metrics up front; this is a good practice to get into.

Outcomes can be deal breakers and often, they are left out of proposals.

Outcomes can be deal breakers and often, they are left out of proposals. People tend to focus on the inputs, which, by their nature, are much less risky. For example, your proposal might say that you will provide training to 25 employees. That's nice, but what is the outcome? Compliance with an OSHA standard or measurably improved behavior or compliance with respect to the training topic? Stating the outcomes expected from your consulting work is harder to do, with a lot of things outside your control. You may need to use "if/then" statements if the outcome depends on the client or others as much as it depends on you (Turak 2013). For example, you could say, "If all 25 employees attend training and pass the final exam with a score of 90%, and if the floor supervisors enforce the lessons learned in training, then the number of near-misses is expected to decline by 75 percent." Do you get the idea? It's not always necessary to use "if /then" statements, but if you really feel you cannot commit to an outcome in your proposal because there are too many other variables at play, you may want to consider using them.

Your Approach

You also need to describe how you will do this work, and how much time you will need from the site management and employees. If no one is available to help you collect data, tour the plant, schedule training time, and allow trainees to attend sessions, your project will fail before it even starts. The project timing—not just what you will need from the client, but also when you can expect to start and end the project—is also important to include.

If the client comes back to you and says they really like you but the cost is too high, you can refer them to your lower option. If they are balking at that option, they probably didn't fully grasp the value of what you were proposing (or more likely, you didn't do a good enough job conveying it). You can choose to either stand your ground or lower your price. This is a personal decision but, keep in mind, if you stand your ground, you may still get the work at the price you want. If you lower your price, you should take out some of the deliverables; this should be a new, revised proposal. Do not lower your price, and give them the same thing you were going to do at a higher cost. If you hired consultants to help you in your business, and they lowered their price for you, would you trust them in the future? For every additional project you gave them, you would be wondering if they would really do it cheaper and, if so, whether their original price was an attempt to take advantage of you. You hope all of your projects lead to future projects; for that reason alone you do not want to set the precedent of lowering your price.

Separate from your implementation alternatives, make sure you address how travel, expenses, payments, cancellation clauses, and other money factors will be handled. Don't get stuck funding your cross-country plane travel because you forgot to include it in the proposal. Speaking of travel costs, build these in to the project cost, especially if you are quoting a flat project fee, and the cost of travel is fairly defined.

Cancellation Clauses

The mention of cancellation clauses here might be the first time you have thought about what you would do if the client asked to cancel the project after the work began, or even before but after the contract was signed. Depending on how comfortable you are with the various options available, you need to describe exactly what your requirements are with respect to cancellations. Alan Weiss provides a sample clause in his book, *Million Dollar Consulting Tool Kit* (Weiss 2006, p. 33):

> This project is noncancelable for any reason. However, it may be postponed, delayed, and/or rescheduled without penalty or time limit, subject only to mutually agreeable dates and times. All payments must be made per the existing payment schedule in this agreement.

Proposal Template

The Appendix is an example of a proposal template. You may or may not want to include all of these sections discussed below in every proposal.

Cover letter: The cover letter briefly summarizes how the contact and the project came to be, plus provides contact information. The cover letter should be on a separate page from the actual proposal.

Title Page: This should specifically describe the work to be done and the specific location. It should also include the date the proposal was submitted, plus how long it is valid. You would not want someone sticking your proposal in a drawer, then pulling it out two years later, expecting you to honor the same prices.

Scope of Work: This is where you describe what you will and will not do. Each different task should be a separate paragraph. You should provide sufficient details to explain what will be covered, but you need to be careful not to give away so much information that the potential client can go and do the job in house or share your scope with a competitor. Even though the sample cover page In the Appendix prohibits the potential client from sharing your proposal with a third party, this does not mean it won't happen.

Photographs: Depending on the type of project, you may need to discuss photographs with the client. In particular, specify who will take them, who will own them, and the requirement for model releases before using them in the future.

Costs/Investment/Prices: You can call this section whatever you think is best for your client and type of project. I almost always use only a lump-sum project fee and not an hourly rate (reflected in the sample proposal that follows). If you use an hourly rate, you would need to modify the wording.

This is also the section where you can provide alternatives or "investment options," as described above. If you are submitting travel costs separately from the project fee or hourly rate, you would need to break those down here as well. If you do not have an exact amount, and this is likely if airfare is involved, you can state what class of airline ticket you will purchase, and a not-to-exceed value.

Terms and Conditions: In this section, you need to be specific about your billing and payment requirements, including whether any deposit is needed, or if the client needs to provide any supplies. If you use a cancellation clause, as described above, it would be included here. You can also use this section to reiterate the expiration date of the proposal that you stated on the cover page. If you offer a money-back guarantee, you can include it here as well.

Timeline: Be specific about when you can start the project, how long you expect it to take, and when a final report or project can be expected.

Agreement of Contract: A proposal becomes a legal document when both parties sign it (Weiss 2006, 27). I prefer to use my proposals as documents that will become the contract for the job. If written correctly, I have found a signed proposal will serve this purpose well. Contracts are discussed in detail elsewhere in this book.

If you plan to use a signed proposal as the contract for the project, you should include a section titled, "Acceptance" at the end of your proposal. The following wording is provided in Alan Weiss's *Million Dollar Consulting Toolkit* (Weiss 2006, 32).

Your signature below indicates acceptance of this proposal and the terms and conditions herein. Alternatively, your initial payment per the terms above will also represent acceptance of this proposal.

Please check the option you prefer: ____#1   ____#2   ____#3

For (your company):   For (client):

Signature:_____   Signature:_____

Name:_____   Name:_____

Title:_____   Title:_____

Date: _____   Date: _____

Statement of Qualifications: In this section, you can provide a brief summary of each of the proposed team members, and offer to provide a full resume upon request. If you will be using subcontractors on the project, you can mention that here or simply refer to the proposed project team as "(Your Company) Representatives" on site. You can provide three different sections under your Statement of Qualifications. First, your corporate background would give a few sentences about your company, when it was founded, by whom, a mission statement, and maybe an accomplishment type of statement, such as "XYZ Consulting has worked with (specify number) of Fortune 500 firms and in locations across America (or the world)." If you are a new consultant, and perhaps just came out of the corporate world, you could say, for example, "For # years, Jane Consultant has trained over 1,000 people on machine guarding."

After "Corporate Background," you may want to include a brief summary of clients. Of course, you should get permission from these clients if you are going to refer to them by name.

The third area under "Statement of Qualifications" can be a description of the project team. Here, you can list the specific names and qualifications of individuals who would work on this project.

Testimonials: Finally, we get to the end, and to one part of your proposal that you may be able to copy, at least in part, from one proposal to the next. Testimonials from past clients, with full names included, are an incredibly good way to demonstrate your value to the potential client. It is important to get into the habit of asking for, and collecting, them for use in future proposals. If you are just starting in consulting, look through your past performance reviews for great statements about your work ethics, technical ability, the way you work with others, or your ability to handle large projects. Then include these, attributed to the person who wrote about you.

Testimonials, which can also be used as references, are extremely valuable. To get them, you will usually have to be proactive. The best time to ask for these is as soon as a project is finished. If you have any kind of closing meeting at the end of a job, no matter how small or big the project, be sure to ask the clients if they were happy with the work and, if so, would they please write you a short testimonial. It doesn't have to be something formal on company letterhead; make sure they understand that a quick e-mail is fine. If they prefer, you could also offer to make a few notes, based on the positive feedback they just gave you, and offer it to them to review and sign. You may even have some clients tell you to just write it yourself. If that is the case, you can summarize any positive feedback they have given you, and send it back to them to review, edit if necessary, and sign.

> *Testimonials from past clients, with full names included, are an incredibly good way to demonstrate your value to the potential client.*

REVIEW QUESTIONS

1. Are you ready to market?
2. Have you identified what makes your OS&H consulting firm special and how you can use that to an advantage? Can you do a good job of communicating this?
3. Do you have the skills you need to develop and/or maintain a professional online presence? How will you do this? If people Google your name or company name, where will they find you?
4. How can you connect with current and potential clients in person and online? What are five ways you could take steps to connect with new clients right now? How will you manage and use the contact information that you collect from potential clients? What can you offer? How can you stay in touch?

5. Have you thought about a sales funnel? If so, what products could you develop and offer at every level? What do you need to develop these products and bring them to market? Where can you market them?
6. What is your branding and what does it say about you? What changes do you need to make to ensure that your marketing materials and even the way you present yourself correctly convey the type of OS&H consulting firm you are?
7. Can you develop a proposal that stands out from the crowd? How will you do this? What will make your proposal unique?
8. What are the top 10 marketing tactics you will implement? How soon can you get these in place? What is your timeline for monitoring how they perform?

In this chapter, you learned about marketing and sales concepts and actions. Chapter 7, "Networking," will focus on how to effectively grow a network that fosters powerful relationships towards the goal of creating a fruitful and sustainable business.

BIBLIOGRAPHY

American Marketing Association (AMA). 2014. "Dictionary" (retrieved December 8, 2014) www.ama.org/resources/Pages/Dictionary.aspx

Bellman, Geoffrey M. 1990. *The Consultant's Calling: Bringing Who You Are to What You Do*. San Francisco: Jossey-Bass.

Berger, Johnathan. 2013. *Contagious: Why Things Catch On*. New York: Simon & Schuster.

Bond, William J. 1997. *Going Solo: Developing a Home-based Consulting Business from the Ground up*. New York: McGraw-Hill.

Brenner, Joanna, and Aaron Smith. 2013. "72% of Online Adults are Social Networking Site Users" (retrieved December 8. 2014). www.pewinternet.org/Reports/2013/social-networking-sites/Findings/Twitter.aspx

Central Intelligence Agency (CIA). 2013. "World Factbook" (retrieved December 8, 2014). https://www.cia.gov/library/publications/the-world-factbook/fields/2153.html#xx

Cohen, William A. 2008. *A Class with Drucker: The Lost Lessons of the World's Greatest Management Teacher*. New York: Amacom.

Dunn, Nina. 2013. "A 5-Step Guide to Free Publicity" (retrieved December 8, 2014). http://upstart.bizjournals.com/resources/executive-forum/2013/09/24/a-5-step-guide-to-free-publicity.html?page=all

Fisk, Peter. 2006. *Marketing Genius*. Chichester, West Sussex, UK: Capstone.

Gattis, Chris, and Felica Sparks. 2011 *Marketing Plan Template: Writing Marketing Plans for Small Business*. Huntsville, Ala.: Blue Point Publishers.

Gitomer, Jeffrey H. 2011. *Social Boom!* Upper Saddle River, NJ: Financial Times/Prentice Hall.

Godin, Seth. 2005. *All Marketers Are Liars: Power of Telling Authentic Stories in a Low-Trust World*. New York: Penguin Group.

Godin, Seth. 2009. "The difference between PR and Publicity." www.typepad.com/services/trackback/6a00d83451b31569e2011168a4b0ad970c

Jantsch, John. 2006. *Duct Tape Marketing: The World's Most Practical Small Business Marketing Guide*. Nashville: Nelson Business.

Jantsch, John. 2012. *The Referral Engine: Teaching Your Business to Market Itself*. New York: Penguin Group.

Johnson, Dave. 2012 *Not yet! Social media doesn't interest most safety pros* (retrieved December 8, 2014). www.ishn.com/articles/not-yet-social-media-doesnt-interest-most-safety-pros-

Karasik, Paul. 1992. *How to Make It Big in the Seminar Business*. New York: McGraw-Hill, 1992.

Lacombe, Mary-Eve and James Heaton 2012. "10 Short-cuts to Marketing Success" (retrieved December 8, 2014). www.infor.tronviggroup.com/10-shortcuts-to-marketing-success

Mackay, Harvey. 2005. *Swim With The Sharks Without Being Eaten Alive: Outsell, Outmanage, Outmotivate, and Outnegotiate Your Competition*. New York: Harper Collins.

Marketing Accountability Standards Board (MASB). "The Common Language Project" (retrieved December 8, 2014). www.themasb.org/common-language-project/

Nielsen. 2012. "Buzz in the Blogosphere : Millions More Bloggers and Blog Readers" (retrieved December 8, 2014). www.nielsen.com/us/en/newswire/2012/buzz-in-the-blogosphere-millions-more-bloggers-and-blog-readers.html

Otte, Miriam. 1998. *Marketing with Speeches and Seminars: Your Key to More Clients and Referrals*. Seattle, WA: Zest Press.

Richter, Felix. 2013. "1 in 5 Americans cannot Access Facebook® at Work" www.statista.com/topics/751/Facebook/chart/1483/websites-blocked-by-us-employers/

Ries, A., and Trout, J. 1994. *The 22 Immutable Laws of Marketing*. New York: Harper Collins.

Schaefer, Mark. 2012. *The Tao of Twitter; Changing Your Life and Business 140 Characters at a Time.* New York: McGraw-Hill Companies.

Schultz, Mike, and John Doerr E. 2009. *Professional Services Marketing: How the Best Firms Build Premier Brands, Thriving Lead Generation Engines, and Cultures of Business Development Success.* Hoboken, NJ: John Wiley & Sons.

Scott, David Meerman. 2010 *The New Rules of Marketing and PR: How to Use Social Media, Blogs, News Releases, Online Video & Viral Marketing to Reach Buyers Directly.* Hoboken, NJ: John Wiley & Sons.

Taylor, Gabriela. 2012. *The Ultimate Guide to Marketing Your Business with Tumblr: Using Tumblr to Leverage Social Buzz and Develop a Brand Awareness Strategy for Your Business.* [S.l.]: Gabriela Taylor.

Turak, August. 2013 "How to Write a Plan or Proposal That Rocks" (retrieved DATE?) www.forbes.com/sites/augustturak/2013/02/18/how-to-write-a-plan-or-proposal-that-rocks/

Vaynerchuk, Gary. 2013. *Jab, Jab, Jab, Right Hook: How to Tell Your Story in a Noisy, Social World.* New York: HarperCollins

Walaski, Pam. 2013a "Live From Safety 2013: Safety 2013 Goes Social in a Big Way." (retrieved January 21, 2014). http://ehsworks1.blogspot.com/2013/06/live-from-safety-2013-safety-2013-goes.html

Walaski, Pam. 2013b "Social Media: Powerful Tools for SH&E Professionals." *Professional Safety*, April 2013 (40-49).

Weiss, Alan. 2013. *Million Dollar Consulting: The Professional's Guide to Growing a Practice.* New York: McGraw-Hill.

Weiss, Alan. 2006. *Million Dollar Consulting Toolkit: Step-by-step Guidance, Checklists, Templates, and Samples from the Million Dollar Consultant.* Hoboken, NJ: John Wiley & Sons.

YouTube. "Statistics" (retrieved December 8, 2014) www.YouTube.com/yt/press/statistics.html

Zarrella, Dan. 2012. *The Science of Marketing: When to Tweet, What to Post, How to Blog, and Other Proven Strategies.* Hoboken, NJ: John Wiley & Sons.

APPENDIX: SAMPLE PROPOSAL

Needs Assessment and Development of OSHA Compliance Plan for the DEF Department of Company XYZ

OS&H Consulting Firm
Date Submitted: May 3, 2014

This proposal is confidential and may not be disclosed to any 3rd party without the prior written consent of OS&H Consulting. This proposal is valid 60 days from the date submitted.

Scope of Work

Basic Safety and Health Needs Assessment of the DEF facilities completed by 2 certified professionals over the course of 1 day. This assessment is expected to take 4–8 hours. This will involve a walk-through of the facilities (preferably escorted by a XYZ representative) to make observations as well as informally interview experienced employees on current safety and health practices.

Written OSHA Compliance Plan will be completed after visiting the facilities and comparing the hazard exposures to current OSHA requirements. We will also research the most common OSHA citations that are issued to this type of industry (name) and determine if the XYZ facilities are especially well prepared in these areas. We will develop a written plan based on our findings that can easily be used by XYZ on a yearly basis when conducting inspections. *Note:* as new OSHA regulations are issued or existing regulations revised, the OSHA compliance plan may need to be updated.

Photographs

Photographs are useful in evaluating health and safety issues during and after the needs assessment. OS&H Consulting will abide by any restrictions or policies regarding the taking of photographs at XYZ facilities. If this practice is prohibited by outside contractors but not by XYZ representatives, OS&H Consulting suggests that a camera be available for use by the XYZ representative who will be available to OS&H Consultants during the assessment. In this case, all photographs would be available for review but would remain in the custody of XYZ.

Investment

Sample 1 (simple and straightforward):

As stated in our cover letter to this proposal, we will have two certified individuals review operations at the XYZ facilities to complete a safety and health needs assessment as well as to develop a detailed written OSHA compliance plan to be used by XYZ for $xxx. There will be no additional expenses billed. Any additional work that may be requested of OS&H Consultants will be handled through a separate proposal.

Sample 2 (Options):

Option 1: Perform a Basic Safety and Health Needs Assessment. The Safety and Health Needs Assessment will be conducted by walking around the DEF facilities to assess compliance with OSHA regulations. Employees will also be interviewed. A written summary will be provided at the end of the day. Price: $$

Option 2: A Basic Safety and Health Needs Assessment will be conducted as described in Option 1 plus a written OSHA Compliance Plan will be prepared after visiting the facilities and comparing the hazard exposures to current OSHA requirements. The written plan will be based on our findings and can easily be used by XYZ on a yearly basis when conducting inspections. Price: $$$

Option 3: A Basic Safety and Health Needs Assessment will be conducted and an OSHA Compliance plan will be completed as described in Option 1 and Option 2 plus a 4-hour training class, providing an overview of OSHA regulations and the new written compliance plan, will be provided to all DEF hourly workers. Price: $$$$

Terms and Conditions

Note: the sample below is for a proposal based on a project and not an hourly fee.

Our fees are always based upon the project, and never upon time units. That way you're encouraged to call upon us without worrying about a meter running, and we are free to suggest additional areas of focus without concern about increasing your investment.

Invoices will be submitted monthly and payment is expected within 30 days.

Timeline

We are available to conduct the onsite safety and health needs assessment immediately upon XYZ's return of this signed Proposal. Once this initial phase is completed, we will have the draft OSHA Compliance Plan to you within 1 week of our visit. If the wording contained in the draft plan is acceptable to you, we will issue the final plan as soon as you approve it. We will be continually available to you in the future to answer any questions you may have about the plan or its implementation.

Corporate Background

OS&H Consultants is a consultancy specializing in manufacturing industries. Sarah Safety is a recognized industry leader and founded OS&H Consulting in 1980. It is OS&H

Consulting's mission to work with clients as partners in developing and maintaining cutting edge solutions to safety and health challenges in the workplace.

Clients

OS&H Consulting's clients come from the pharmaceutical, heavy metal, chemical, wood, plastics and glass industries throughout North America.

The OS&H Consulting Team

If OS&H Consulting is selected to provide safety and health consulting services for the XYZ DEF facilities, the following individuals would be part of the OS&H Consulting team.

Project Manager/Principal Consultant:	Sarah Safety, CSP
Director of Industrial Hygiene/Environmental Specialist	Irene, IH, CIH

Detailed background information on each of these individuals is included with this proposal.

Testimonials

Samples:

"OS&H Consulting has been instrumental in helping QRS Company to reduce their injuries as follows: LTAs were 84 in FY 2000, 38 in FY 2001 and 10 FY 2002. The LTA Rates have been reduced just as dramatically from FY 2001 4.31 to FY 2002 1.94. All the other QRS locations are in the process of adapting the many programs and guides that were developed and implemented at the Circle City location by OS&H Consulting. Sarah Safety, CSP, has done a Herculean job of supporting ABC Company and assisting us in instituting many innovative and successful programs."

Joe Safety, CSP
Safety Manager, QRS Company

"Sarah Safety was incredibly knowledgeable, competent and self-motivated. She knew what issues needed to be prioritized and was very innovative in the way she addressed problems. She gained the complete trust and support of the employees with whom she worked—from hourly employees up through senior management".

Irene, IH, CIH
Director of Global Training, 123 Company

"While employed as a consultant for ZZZ Pharmaceuticals, OS&H Consulting Inc. was responsible for ensuring that the site safety program was compliant with all state and federal regulations. They maintained the site's Emergency Response Plan in addition to our Hazcom, Ergonomics, Back Safety, Fire Marshal & Contractor Safety programs. Additionally, they developed and provided exceptional training to site staff on all these programs. The OS&H Consulting Inc. team was always available to answer/investigate any safety related questions and always provided this support in a very professional manner."

William K.
Manager, Security & Safety Operations
ZZZ Company

Questions to ask:

What are my philosophy and values with respect to networking?

How do I want to be perceived by others with respect to networking?

What is my overarching networking strategy?

What tools do I need to be a successful networker?

What are the associated networking approaches for building and developing my business? And of these, which ones do I currently want to work on versus put off until later?

Chapter 7

Networking

BY KATHERINE HART, Ed.D.

Katherine Hart is the President of ClearVision Consulting, Inc., a global company based in Alameda, CA, which specializes in accelerating organizational effectiveness and improving human performance.

Katherine worked for 20 years as an internal corporate consultant, promoting and advancing employee safety and health and implementing enterprise-wide change efforts. Her dream of being an external consultant was realized when she founded ClearVision Consulting in 2005 to promote the untapped potential of people within business.

Katherine ardently supports the field of safety and health by educating, coaching and mentoring those in the profession. Her reason for writing this chapter was to share her experiences and enable others to realize their dreams of being successful external consultants.

THE VERY WORD NETWORKING sends chills and thrills down the most successful consultants' spine. There are those out there who love the very word, and those who equate it with a used car salesman wearing an offensive polyester suit. Many eschew the term, using descriptions like "relationship building," "managing my portfolio of contacts" or simply "filling the pipeline." None of these descriptors is wrong. All of them describe some aspect of the networking process.

Regardless of the term used, whether you're a beginning or seasoned consultant or you dislike being social, networking is a necessary part of consulting. Being a consultant requires that you continually expand your sphere of influence and contacts to develop your business. To accomplish this, you will need to put yourself out there to make connections, and to share with people who may not know who you are, what you do, and what you're looking for. All of that is summed up in one word: networking.

The purpose of this chapter is to talk about the reasons, strategies, processes, and tactics for successful networking. Many of you may have learned early on that having a cadre of people to go to ask questions, gather new information, or just commiserate with makes the job and profession much easier to navigate. For those of you who are outgoing or extroverted, it may seem natural to want to connect, and be at the center of human interaction. For others, it takes more work and effort to stretch beyond the confines of a few close friends.

Regardless of your personality, networking is a game changer to you as a consultant. In some instances, it may mean the difference between being a successful business owner versus simply eking out an existence. This point was brought home to me full force during my first year of business. Prior to starting my consulting business, I had thought of myself as a pretty good networker. An extrovert by nature with a friendly demeanor, I had worked, over the years, to build a healthy contact list of close friends and colleagues with whom I could connect without a moment's hesitation.

Early in my professional career, realizing the need for continued personal growth and development, I joined several professional associations. While I didn't spend too much time actively reaching out to people, I did make the time to attend local American Society of Safety Engineers (ASSE) chapter meetings and professional development conferences to stay current on the latest topics.

My game-changing event happened when I was attending a national Organization Development Network meeting. I was standing next to a close friend, the interim senior director for organization and development at a Fortune® 100 company. We were talking about who knows what topic related to the conference. At that moment, he excused himself to take an urgent call, but asked if I could wait a few minutes so we could continue our conversation. Standing next to him, I heard fragments of, "I don't have the time," and "Yes, I will find someone to help you." He turned around, looked at me, lowered the phone, and asked, "Are you available next month to lead a leadership retreat?" My immediate answer was "Yes!" He then handed me his phone and said, "Good, let me introduce you to Steve, our senior director in charge of HR technology." A month later, I led that retreat. Eight years later, that organization is one of my top-grossing clients.

That day changed my whole outlook with regards to networking. Networking was no longer just a contact list of people on whom I could call. Networking was about who I knew, who knew me, what I could do for them, what value or services they knew I offered, and would they refer my services. It was then that networking became a core part of my business. The actions and follow-up taken as part of networking have served to contribute to my success as a business consultant. And, while I may not always be standing right next to that serendipitous contact, I could be at the top of someone's mind who needs my services. Today, networking is such a core aspect of my business that I can't imagine not networking.

I learned many things along this journey, some very helpful, and others rather painful. Throughout this chapter, I will take the opportunity to share this wisdom and lessons learned. And, while I think many aspects of networking are skills that a consultant builds on as part of his or her repertoire, I also believe many aspects are very personal and contribute to what and how you want to be perceived. Call it the science and art of networking.

As you read this chapter on networking you will find quite a few similarities to those of the previous Chapter 6, "Marketing and Sales." Many of the tools and concepts apply to both. However, the purposes are rather distinct. Marketing is the ability to brand yourself, your company, and build momentum for the products and services you have to offer to prospective clients. This chapter on networking builds on the concepts and practices of marketing, while adding the nuance of building and developing relationships to obtain and offer referrals, find services for your own business, and continual your personal learning and development journey.

REASONS FOR NETWORKING

Over time, I have compartmentalized the reasons for networking into three areas: (1) external business development, (2) internal business development, and (3) personal development. Knowing and understanding these three up front will help later in the chapter when we talk about goals and strategic planning. You will be able to decide where you want to focus your networking energies to make the best use of your time and other resources. As a consultant, maximizing the use of your time can make or break your business. And finally, when you are knee-deep in a project, and feeling like the last thing you want to do is to go out and attend a networking event, these reasons can serve as motivators for taking advantage of and following through on your networking activities.

> ... networking ... may mean the difference between being a successful business owner versus simply eking out an existence.

External Business Development

External business development focuses your networking attention on meeting and being introduced to prospective buyers of your services or future clients. You may either meet them directly, such as at an event they attend, or indirectly, through other people. These other people may work directly for a current or prospective client as employees, provide outside consulting services to them, or just be at the right place and time to provide a referral. Either way, these are all opportunities that enable you to meet and get in front of potential buyers.

Another part of external business development is providing support and assistance for clients already using your services. Once you have a client, you can be helpful and supportive to them in many ways, such as recommending service providers outside of your area of expertise. The more services and opportunities you have to get in front of your clients, the more they will remember you, and ask you back to support them with other ongoing work. This requires a disciplined strategy for continually meeting, connecting with, and updating your listing of service providers outside of your specific field for client referral.

As an example, I had been called by a client to support its effort in filling the safety position at the plant. The leadership team wanted to improve their safety and health program by hiring a safety professional, which they had not done before. We worked together to identify the scope of the job and to develop a job description for the type of person they were looking for. As part of the project, I was able to recommend three different recruiters who specialized in hiring safety and health professionals. One of them was eventually selected to support the recruiting effort. I was able to provide this service because of my networking relationships with these recruiting firms, developed over a number of years.

Another example was shared by a colleague. You have a client with whom you are working to design and implement a hearing conservation program. Your services do not include providing protective equipment or audiometric services. If you have a network of vendors and suppliers that do, you can either refer them or incorporate them as part of your proposal for services. Additionally, those vendors and suppliers that you recommend will be more open to referring you to their clients.

As part of your networking related to external business development, continually think about what additional client needs that you could address through your networking connections. If you find a new vendor or supplier that will benefit your client, make a special point of brokering that introduction. Your brokering activity may span from a simple electronic introduction to coordinating a face-to-face meeting to introduce the two of them.

> *... external business development is providing support and assistance for clients already using your services.*

One activity that works for me is to tell clients that I will be attending a networking activity or event that I think might be relevant to their business. Why do I do this? Because I can offer to perform research for them or seek out other problem-solving solutions on their behalf. This action saves my clients time, and time is a valuable resource. It also helps me secure a target for types of service industries and people to meet.

At the very least, I may be able to offer valuable information after the event. This also gives me a reason to connect with vendors at the networking event. As an added bonus, I may learn of other opportunities where my services might be needed.

Internal Business Development

Internal business development involves the growth and extension of your consulting practice and business. Whether you are first starting out or have been a consultant for a while, you continually need to look for people and resources to supplement the services you offer, and help you build your business. A partial list of reasons related to internal business development includes:

- Finding full-time or part-time employees or subcontractors, sometimes called associates, to help you deliver services to a client. Several of my current associates are professionals I met while volunteering to host a regional conference. I had the opportunity to work side by side with them under very stressful conditions, and really got to know them. Because of this opportunity, I knew their reliability, skills, capabilities, and the values they brought to their work. It took about two years until I found the right client fit to bring them in.
- Identifying vendors and suppliers to supplement your own business needs. I met my web designer when I attended a local chapter meeting for the National Speakers Association®. Asking whom they use or recommend at every networking event is a great opportunity. And don't be shy about recommending others who are doing exceptional work for you. This is all part of the networking web of connections.
- Discovering individuals who are looking for subcontractors or willing to forge strategic alliances. Just as you may be looking for subcontractors to use in your business, there may be individuals who are looking for subcontractors to supplement their business.

Strategic Alliances

Opportunities abound when strategic alliances are fostered. I didn't fully understand the benefits or what to look for in strategic alliances and, in hindsight, I wish I had spent more time cultivating this strategy earlier in my business. For that reason, here is some additional information about strategic alliances.

Strategic alliances are quasi-partnership relationships, though not legal partnership entities, which offer the opportunities to work with other firms (typically larger in size) to service clients. Unlike subcontractors, you treat these relationships as equals coming together to join forces. In his book *Million Dollar Consulting*, Alan Weiss defines these as "a reciprocally beneficial relationship in which the smaller firm obtains access to larger markets and organizations and the larger firm obtains specialized expertise and/or situation help in a cost-effective manner" (Weiss 1992).

In beginning to think about strategic alliances, you need to first be clear about what your business is all about. Yes, you are a safety and health consultant. But what is your niche? What types of businesses do you serve or prefer? Are there specialty services that you don't offer, but in which your clients would be interested? Maybe you are skilled at implementing hearing conservation programs, but don't offer audiometric testing. This might be an opportunity to find a strategic alliance partner. Other opportunities arise when you are a solo or boutique consulting firm that specializes in a particular service or industry. Joining resources with a larger firm benefits both of you. As an example, perhaps you are nationally recognized as having expertise in a specific hazardous material unique to a particular industry. Identifying larger firms that service bigger companies in your industry, but don't have this expertise, would be a potential opportunity.

Strategic alliances . . . offer the opportunities to work with other firms (typically larger in size) to service clients.

Strategic alliances are relationships that don't typically happen quickly, but take time to build and cultivate. You both need to feel comfortable about what the other has to offer. And you both need to be clear on:

- how you will collaboratively work with the client
- who takes the lead on proposal writing and project implementation
  who is responsible if something doesn't work or isn't successful
  how the money from the work is to be divided
- the parameters about follow up and selling future services to the client

I have made use of two specific types of strategic alliance opportunities, which I would recommend for consideration:

1. ***Complementary Process Partners:*** Relationships where you have complementary services, knowledge or products that would be better merged together to meet a client's needs. For example, I met a woman at a networking event whose business was focused on long-term disability. At the time, I was writing a proposal for a client to develop job function analyses. I realized the extent of possible services for this future client could be expanded if a long-term disability component was included. We went in together on the proposal, and won the contract.
2. ***Technology Partners:*** You may offer a service, but need a specific technology or system hardware to support it. For example, I have a proprietary manager effectiveness survey that required a technology

platform to administer. I have a technology partnership with a larger firm that provides the behind-the-scenes technology system to support the survey. Because this is more sophisticated than an online survey, such as Survey Monkey®, I spent some time interviewing technology firms to identify which would best meet my company's needs. I then did a small test project with them to ensure they were the best fit. When working with a technology firm, you will need to determine up front whether their team will also provide the interface between the user and the technology. In my case, the partner only provides the technology, and I've brought in other people with statistical and database knowledge and skills to interface with the technology partner.

Personal Development

The final reason to seek networking opportunities is to develop and grow your own knowledge base. Being a consultant, as opposed to an employee, means having to work a bit harder to stay current and relevant in a world that is continually shifting and changing. Some of you may have worked for bosses who brought classes or training opportunities to your attention. Others may have been employed by large companies, where knowledgeable co-workers served as ready resources, corporate libraries offered access to materials, and learning and development departments recommended courses for soft-skill enrichment.

Not having these advantages means you are responsible for deciding what classes you need, and identifying where to take them. Over the course of starting my business, I have taken classes on software technologies, business planning, growing a speaking business, marketing and sales, and social media. These classes are above and beyond those relevant to staying up on my areas of expertise. Almost all of the classes were either recommended by professionals within my network or discovered during networking events.

Another reason for networking for personal development and growth is to identify mentors, coaches, and people with more experience or knowledge who can show you the ropes. Being a consultant means you are going to be faced with many of the same tasks and challenges that a large business deals with, but there are fewer of you to tackle these efforts. You may decide to hand over some of these tasks, like inputting bills and receipts, to qualified professionals, such as a bookkeeper. Others, such as marketing and sales, you may want to keep in-house. So, you may need to not only increase your skills and abilities, but to make behavioral changes that are difficult.

Certainly, you can read books and take classes. You can also talk with a mentor who has experienced and successfully dealt with the same or similar challenges that you are experiencing. If there are specific behavioral changes that you need to change quickly or that are ingrained, you may want to consider a coach. Just like professional athletes and executives who hire coaches for development, this is another resource to consider. I have found my mentors and coaches through connecting with other people and asking who they use.

You never know the extent of people's talents, knowledge, or connections that you will encounter while networking. As an avid networker, work diligently to ask questions, be curious, and learn what others have to offer. These relationships can help you grow and develop both yourself and your business.

Exercise: Clarifying Your Reasons for Networking

Take this opportunity to think about your reasons for networking. Be clear on the types of resources, support, or connections on which you want to focus. This information will help you decide on where to focus your time, the right associations for your consultancy, and your goals for the networking process. Once you complete this worksheet, revisit it on an annual basis, as your business needs will evolve and change.

1. *External Business Development*
   - Describe your ideal clients. Ask yourself the following: What are their interests? Where might they be hanging out? What associations are they a part of? Which events would be useful to attend to connect with them? (Refer to the marketing and business plan chapters for some of this information.)
   - What types of service providers might benefit or augment the work you already provide for your clients?
   - From your past experience, what types of questions, information or referral sources did your clients typically ask for or need?
2. *Internal Business Development*
   - What types of individuals (i.e., skills, knowledge, and experience) do you need to recruit as associates, subcontractors, or employees to grow your business?
   - What types of vendors or suppliers are you looking for to support, grow, and develop your own business?
   - Who are advantageous strategic partners for you to connect with and get to know?

3. *Personal Development*
    - Identify two or three areas of development that you are interested in pursuing. Based on those, what courses or events do you want to attend to explore or expand your development?
    - What business knowledge or experience do you want to seek out or find in current or future mentors to grow yourself or your business?
    - What behavioral changes or future development, either short or long term, do you want to explore? What type of coach might help fulfill this need?

Take the time required to answer these questions. They are the basis for your networking outreach. Once you recognize and understand your reasons for networking, consider your overall philosophy and strategy for networking.

NETWORKING PHILOSOPHY

Of all the things you can do in networking, being clear on your personal philosophy for how you want to network, and how you want to be perceived as a consultant, are of primary importance. I believe this is what separates the good consultants from the extraordinary ones. There are those who network and are very specific about why they network, what they want to get out of the relationships and, most importantly, what they are willing to give back. There are others who just fall into consulting, and somehow meander along the journey of networking without a clear idea of what they want to accomplish. And then, of course, there are those who are just out for themselves. They use networking to get ahead and satisfy their own personal gains, without caring about those with whom they interact.

Let's face it, networking is a relationship activity, and the business benefits it can generate are tremendous. But you need to decide what kind of networker you want to be viewed as right from the start. I recommend adopting a networking philosophy early on that matches how you want to be perceived by others.

Mine, even before I went into consulting, was to follow the golden rule of, "Do unto others as you would have them do unto you." In his book *The Ultimate Consultant: Powerful Techniques for the Successful Practitioner*, Alan Weiss talks about a "give-to-get" philosophy (Weiss 2001). Jeffrey Meshel and Douglas Garr, in their book, *One Phone Call Away: Secrets of a Master Networker*, shares that networking at its deepest level is "about giving something of yourself" (Meshel and Garr 2005). A colleague I know sees herself as a connector. She finds joy being able to match people with those who can help and support them.

Whatever your philosophy around networking, take a few minutes now to deliberately answer the following questions:

- As a consultant, how do you want to be perceived by your clients, close friends, colleagues, and those you have never met?
- What do you want to be known for, in terms of relationship building and reaching out to others?
- What behaviors can you exhibit with each person you meet that demonstrate your philosophy towards networking?

One of the ways I want to be known is as someone who has a genuine interest in others. The behavior I adopted early on in my networking journey to distinguish this characteristic was to ask questions that would make the other persons feel comfortable about opening up and sharing about themselves. So, in addition to the basic question of "What do you do?" (I will share later in the chapter how to answer this), I will ask questions such as, "How did you get started in that career path?" or "What is the biggest challenge (or success) you are experiencing as a business owner?" These types of questions help me discover something about the other person.

When I meet someone whom I categorize as a good networker, very interested, and asking me a lot of questions, I will take the opportunity to say something like, "I realize I've talked quite a lot about myself. What brought you to this event?" So my question to you is: What actions and behaviors will you adopt to show genuine interest in those with whom you are networking?

Since networking is such a relational activity, to fully participate and reap its benefits, it helps if you can stand out as an interesting person, conversant, and knowledgeable about a variety of topics and interests. If you enter networking as Johnny One Note, people will quickly learn to avoid you at the next meeting.

At one meeting I attend regularly, one of the attendees has a passion, bordering on obsession, about his dog. Regardless of the conversation topic, whenever he joins in, he shares the latest escapade of his dog. In all of the conversations I have had with him, he appears to have nothing else to talk about. I once asked him what he thought about the results of a local election on the city's economy. And, can you believe it, he immediately launched into the latest doggie escapade. Even as a former dog owner and lover of animals, whenever I see him approaching, I immediately cross the room to avoid contact with him.

Here are a couple of suggestions to establish yourself as an interesting person, having the ability to talk about a variety of topics. Be knowledgeable about your local area. Read the local newspapers, and be conversant about the current hot topics. Subscribe to some form of national paper. My favorite is the *Wall Street Journal*, but there is also the *New York Times* or *Business Times*. Another way to stay in touch with both national and international news is through electronic news aggregation services. These will let you scroll through headlines of what's happening in the world at large, business, technology, fashion, and so forth, to get key highlights and bite-sized articles.

Of course, you will need to read and stay up to date on professional safety and health topics. But don't stop there. Read articles and books on a variety of other topics and interests, both personal and professional. My go-to for business is the *Harvard Business Review*. My mother collects *Fortune* magazine to share with me. And my mother-in-law shares her *People* magazines with me. You never know when a topic on a current celebrity action will spark someone's interest. If you want to expand your reach and begin networking globally, a good magazine to read is *The Economist*.

Regardless of how hooked or passionate you are about your consulting business, be sure to keep yourself involved with outside interests. Whether it is the local theater, art, history, or supporting local community activities, don't forget those outside interests. I learned this lesson the hard way.

When I first started my business, I dedicated myself to making it successful. I spent so many hours working on the business that I almost lost my sense of self and identity. It took a pointed comment from my mother, who said, "Don't you have anything else to talk about except your business?" That comment stuck the mirror in front of me, and I realized I had become too engrossed in what I was doing, and had forsaken activities that brought me pleasure.

Reevaluating my priorities, I vowed to schedule time for non-work activities, such as singing in a church choir, reading for pleasure, and volunteering for non-profits. Doing so not only made me happier, but also expanded my repertoire of conversation. Regardless of how much time you need to spend on your business, don't forget to have outside interests and activities. When you do, people will want to talk with you, and get to know you. And that will, in turn, grow and expand your business.

NETWORKING TOOLS

While you can network at any time and with anyone, if you want to leverage your connections to the utmost, it helps to have done some preliminary work and effort to get your networking tools in place. These tools will also support your overall marketing efforts. Many of these you may have learned about in the Chapter 6, "Marketing and Sales." As you review them, think about how they can also be used from a networking perspective.

Elevator Pitch

> When I started my company, I made the mistake of thinking that the elevator pitch was all about me and what my company did.

This is the most important tool in your networking toolbox, and one that can be changed at will to fit your changing business outlook. The name was based on a person's ability to pitch to a prospective client while traveling from one floor to another during an elevator ride. For networking, you are not trying to sell to a client, but quickly engage someone to understand your business and learn about theirs. As you read the remaining section on the elevator pitch, relate it to the previously defined reasons for networking: external and internal business development, and personal development.

Prior to becoming a consultant, I worked for large corporations. I found it easy to talk with others simply by stating what company I worked for, and then talking about that company. Whenever asked, "What do you do for a living?" I would respond that I worked with company leaders to ensure employees go home at the end of the day without getting hurt. Questions would then follow, such as "How did I do that?" and "What was the toughest part of my job?"

When I started my company, I made the mistake of thinking that the elevator pitch was all about me and what my company did. My good fortune was to have a friend who shared, "Kathy, I used to love your opening when you worked internally. It was provocative, and people asked you all sorts of questions, which you could then focus on them. You need to do the same about your business." She was right.

My new mantra about an elevator pitch: Use provocative language to attract attention. Rather than selling your business from one floor to the next, spark interest, so the other person asks questions about what you do. My new pitch, based on the changing aspect of my business: "I work with leaders to dramatically accelerate their organizational effectiveness and improve human performance." When asked: "How do you do that?" I respond, "Share with me an issue your company is dealing with, and I'll share how I worked with a client to address it."

The result is that we now have a conversation going on. And, by the time I reach the other person's floor, his or her comment is: "Can you get off here a few minutes, and let's talk, or give me a call so we can connect, and I can learn more?" So, how can you be provocative when you deliver your elevator pitch? By focusing on the results your services provide and not your methodology.

Think about what you do in terms of the value you provide for clients, and how to get others talking about what they do. Don't focus on the tasks that you accomplish, but the results you obtain for your clients. Maybe your work decreases their injury rate. Perhaps you galvanize senior leadership by clarifying responsibilities around safety. It may help to write at least a half dozen or so of these down.

Another way to pull this listing together is to call some of your current clients or former colleagues and ask them, "When I worked with you, what results would you say I achieved?" Pull it together in one provocative sentence. Two sentences are the maximum, and often overkill. Remember, this is all about the high-level results you offer to clients.

Once you have your sentence, practice saying it in the mirror with a smile and enough passion that it will knock anyone's socks off. Here's the reality I learned years ago, regardless of what you say: If you have a smile, passion, and enthusiasm in your voice, people want to talk with you. They'll ask you something just to learn why you are excited. And that's what you want, interest in what you do.

Another way to practice is to try your sentence with family members and friends, particularly those who know what you do. Ask them if your sentence inspired them to want to ask you questions, or was it completely boring? Use their input to keep refining your message. Then practice it with a group of people you don't know, such as at an out-of-town Chamber of Commerce meeting. You want your sentence or two to be provocative enough that people ask you questions about what you do. Questions mean that you have their interest.

Provocative Questions

If you are a brilliant conversationalist, then you may not need this tool. However, I have yet to meet someone, me included, who couldn't do with a few back-pocket, provocative questions. Once you deliver your elevator pitch and have people asking questions, you need to figure how to quickly get them talking about themselves. Remember, a key part of networking is a "give-to-get" philosophy; helping others so they will, in turn, help you. While you want people interested in asking you questions, they will quickly get bored if the conversation is all about you, and you won't find out how you can help them. The dilemma is that many of us are interested in talking about ourselves. It makes us feel important and worthy to be asked questions.

The very act of networking as a consultant is about engaging people and getting them to talk about themselves. Remember that you are networking for a variety of purposes. And you can't accomplish those purposes unless you are learning from the other people if they have a need for your services, what they do, what's important to them, and so on. So, here's where having a few provocative questions readily available can help.

These are open-ended questions that let you immediately establish rapport, and find out about the other person. A few that I use when wanting to find out if there is a client fit are:

- What is the thorniest challenge/biggest hurdle that your business or clients are facing right now?
- What keeps you awake at nights?
- What are you most proud about that you have accomplished in the past year?

If I am trying to learn more about a person, to determine if that person might be a potential fit as a prospective associate, I ask:

- How did you know that you wanted to be a (fill in the blank)?
- How do your clients get a sense for your passion when working with you?
- What was your most successful client engagement?

If I am trying to learn whether this might be an individual with whom I want to pursue a strategic alliance, I ask:

- What does your firm do that adds value to clients?
- What makes you unique among firms that offer your services?
- When you first established your business, what values carried you through the tough times?

The questions are designed to dig more deeply into each person's background. I am curious, and want to learn what's important to them. It also quickly informs me whether I want to continue the discussion, and get to know them better. If I do, then I can figure out what I can offer or share with them to help them out.

Information about You and Your Company

As part of Chapter 6, "Marketing and Sales," you learn to create materials that describe your company, the services offered, testimonials received, and case studies of work previously done. You also should create a one-page bio about yourself. All of this is very important to incorporate as part of networking.

In addition to the above-listed items, develop a brief paragraph that describes the results you obtain for your clients. It's something that synchronizes your elevator pitch, with a few additional sentences that share results achieved. This is text you can use as part of electronic networking and introductions, which is described later in this chapter.

Database to Track Contacts

You will need to have a method to track your networking contacts. In addition to maintaining the basic personal data found on a business card, I track the following:

- where and when I met each person,
- what type of information I may have shared with them,
- what clients they may have referred me to or contacts shared,
- what special interests they may have, and
- other useful information, such as family, awards received, food allergies, favorite restaurants, etc.

The tracking system you select can be a simple spreadsheet or a fancy database with lots of bells and whistles. There are many different tools on the market, some free and others quite expensive. These tools can pull double-duty for your marketing and sales efforts, such as tracking prospective client meetings and proposals submitted, or can be kept separately. I have found that the more integrated you make this, the better off you are. As for me, I use the "Contact" function of Microsoft Outlook and find it serves most of my needs, along with synching very nicely with my phone.

Regardless of what you use, you will need something that will allow you to categorize people into various groupings for easy access and sharing of information. In addition to Microsoft Outlook's Contact function, I use LinkedIn as a resource to electronically track people. LinkedIn® has a built-in function that allows me to download contacts into a spreadsheet, which I then upload to an e-mail newsletter service that publishes my monthly electronic newsletter. The more you can integrate the resources and tools you use for both marketing and networking, the better for your consulting business.

Business Card Sorter

Many different tools on the market will sort and scan your business cards, including the old fashioned Rolodex. I still know people who rely on this tool. Prior to availability of various electronic apps, I hired my neighbor's high school son to type the information into a spreadsheet, and then upload it into my Contacts folder.

I now have a smart phone application, which allows me to take a picture of the card and export to a spreadsheet. Then I can add the categories, and label the people as I desire. There are several business card applications on the market you may want to consider.

Use something that easily lets you sort your business cards, and upload them into whatever database or tool you are using to track. A word to the wise: Keeping a lot of business cards around when you have no idea how you know the people listed on them, where you met them, or why you ever took their cards is a lot of stress and worry you don't need. Unless you can associate those people with some activity or reason for having the cards, take those cards and toss them. Later on, we will talk about how you can make the most effective use of business cards when you first receive them.

Business Cards for Yourself

Speaking of business cards, you need to have one for both marketing and networking purposes. It is a tangible document, albeit small, that lets someone know who you are, and what you do. At the very least, your card should include your company name, your name, title, Web site, e-mail address, mailing address, and phone numbers. There is quite a lot of discussion in this electronic age about whether to include a mailing address. My answer is: How can I send you specialty notes or cards to stay at the top of your mind? Additionally, have you ever met someone from a large company or corporation who didn't have a business address on the card?

Whether you are a solo practitioner or a smaller boutique firm, you need to have a mailing address. If you work out of your home, and don't feel comfortable using that address, then establish a Post Office box you can use.

Many people identify a company tagline, and include that on their card. A tagline is typically three to five words that describe what you do or offer in a way that makes you memorable to others.

Some people like to list the services they offer on the back of the business card, which is fine. However, make sure you have room on the back of the card for you to write down information or for someone else to do so. I can't tell you how many of my cards I have used, when someone doesn't have his or her own card, to capture that person's name, e-mail, and phone, and to be able to follow up later.

My cards have a clean glossy front, which makes it sturdy and professional looking, with a smooth (not glossy) backing that can be written on. I don't use my picture or lots of additional text on my card. A portion of my elevator pitch,

"Accelerating Organizational Effectiveness," is written under my company name, to help people remember how I introduced myself to them when we first met. Having worked in the corporate arena for so many years, I wanted a professional-looking card that conveyed simply what I did, and had all the pertinent information. Think about who your clients are, how you want to be perceived by them, and then create a business card that mirrors that type of image.

In addition to business cards, I have printed note cards and matching envelopes. "From the desk of Kathy Hart" is on the front of the note card. My company's logo, with my tag line "Accelerating Organizational Effectiveness," is in the lower right-hand corner. I chose not have my address or contact information on the note card, but I have seen others with it included. However, I do have my address and Web site address on the envelope.

NETWORKING OPPORTUNITIES

As a consultant, you need to begin looking at your life from a holistic perspective, as opposed to divided into segments of business, personal, church, associations, and so forth. Unlike employees, who separate personal from professional, as a consultant you never know when you might connect with someone that will eventually become a client, provide a referral for a client, work for you as an employee or subcontractor, or be a strategic alliance partner. Hence, you always need to consider yourself networking, regardless of the activity in which you are involved.

That doesn't mean you immediately start talking about business, but when someone asks you what you do or if you discover a business opportunity to support them, then by all means follow through. An example of this: My husband and I were at a church retreat for couples. The weekend was designed to get to know your partner better, to connect and learn from other couples, and to learn from a marriage family therapist leading the workshop.

My husband and I were in conversation with another couple during one of the mini break-outs. The wife shared that she was frustrated with a remodeling project on their house, and how it was causing friction. As we learned more, I realized that part of the problem was that the contractor had never laid out a project plan for them. The couple didn't know what to expect from their contractor. Last-minute requests were leading to internal strife.

My husband shared how I, the goal-oriented one in our family, compiled a preliminary project plan for our last major remodel, and used it to ensure alignment between ourselves and our contractor. After the retreat, I sat down with the wife, and created a draft project plan for her house remodeling, so she and her husband could be more aligned with their own contractor.

I thought this had nothing to do with work, until later when I was called by the husband. He wanted to know what I did, and then asked if I could pull together a proposal for training his team on project management. That's just one example among many that brings the point home: Regardless of where you are, you need to be networking and looking out for those nuggets of opportunities.

Understand that networking is all about interacting with people, whether those people are individuals or in groups. I suggest that you start at the individual level, and identify all those within your sphere of influence, and how you are connected with them. Then expand your reach to think about the groups you are involved in, and the opportunities to network there.

Spheres of Influence

One of the best activities I ever did, and still go back to refresh, was to document all those people I knew in my personal and professional life. I called the activity my spheres of influence, to help me think visually of all those people I know and connect with in my life. I started thinking of the concentric circles that comprise my life: family, close friends, neighbors, past colleagues, acquaintances, church, and professional associations. The names of your concentric circles may be different from mine, but the effect is still the same. Begin to identify them.

For each concentric circle, identify the people you know. As mentioned earlier, you might want to use some type of spreadsheet to do this, if you don't already have them in some type of organized and categorized manner. This becomes quite a list of people that comprise your sphere of influence. We are going to do a couple of things with this listing.

First, extract from that list a group of people that you will consider your top 50. These top 50 are people about whom you really care, who care about you, and who are invested in mutual support with you. To select them, ask yourself these questions when reviewing your master list of the people you know:

- Do you have a good relationship with them? If you called them or they called you, would you want to help each other to achieve your individual goals?
- If you intimately knew about their business, would you be willing and able to refer them to possible clients or at least to people who might introduce them to clients?

- If they intimately knew about your business, would they be willing and able to refer you to possible clients or at least to people who might introduce you to clients?

Once you have your listing of 50 people, you can employ the 1E:2P strategy. "1E" stands for once a month electronically, and "2P" stands for two people on a personal basis. Here's how it works.

Once a month, reach out to those people, using some type of electronic communication. It may be a monthly newsletter, though you may already be providing this to those in your overall contact list. Other offerings could include a book review that would be of interest, a white paper that you have received or written, or some other information that would be useful for them. In addition to the offering, write an e-mail that shares what you are working on, referrals you are looking for, or other opportunities to help and support your business. Be sure to include that you are interested and willing to do the same for them.

When you are networking, ... you have to be willing to ask what they can do to help you.

Make the effort to stay in front of them electronically once a month. Can you do this more often? Certainly, some people I know share weekly updates. When you talk with these people, ask them their preference. For me, providing a monthly electronic communication with this group of 50 people seems to work the best, especially for consistency's sake. Figure out what will work for you and your overall schedule.

The next part is more personal, hence the "P." Pick two people every day from your top 50 list to personally contact by phone. My age may be showing here, but I think the phone is much more personal, and makes the point of saying you were worth the time to pick up a phone, leave a message, and I want to know how you are doing. You may have a goal in mind, such as scheduling a lunch, sharing a story or contact, or maybe just checking to learn how they are doing, and what's going in their personal and professional lives. This exercise of reaching out probably takes about 15 minutes, maybe longer if you haven't been in touch for a while.

You may cull this list over time or add people to it, but these become the core go-to people in your personal network. Because they get to know you so well, they will always be looking for opportunities for you, and you'll be doing likewise for them. When I go to new networking events, these are the people I ask to join me or share the networking opportunity.

A word of caution that I have learned from my 50 close contacts: In addition to staying in touch and helping them, you also need to be specific about what you are looking for. I remember once, when I was having a conversation with one of my top 50 people, I mentioned that, while I loved reaching out to people and helping them to be successful, I sometimes wished they would reach back. My friend looked at me and smiled, then said something profound, "How can I help you when I don't know what you're looking for? What can I do for you?"

It seemed so simple, and it made a lot of sense. When you are networking, you absolutely need to focus on what you can do for others. At some point, though, you have to be willing to ask what they can do to help you. If you don't, then many people, like my friend, will wonder what you need. Some will ask, but others may be too shy, not feel comfortable or just may not think to ask. As someone told me, my propensity for always helping others was getting in the way of my networking. So don't be afraid to ask for what you want, while you are trying to determine how you can help others be successful.

Now that you have your list of 50, take another look at your sphere of influence people. This time you are examining the list with an eye towards other opportunities. When I was starting my monthly newsletter, I used my listing to populate my monthly newsletter mailing list. I sent an e-mail letting them know I was starting a monthly newsletter. They could easily opt out, but I hoped they would receive the first issue, and provide me with feedback. Many of them did, providing very valuable feedback, and many started sharing that newsletter with others.

One of the best activities I ever did, and still go back to refresh, was to document all those people I knew in my personal and professional life.

Another time, I used the listing to communicate with those in my church network. Over the course of my lifetime, I have belonged to several different churches, and maintained many of those contacts. The reason I was reaching out was that a colleague of mine, a psychotherapist and marriage counselor, had asked for connections to those involved in the church community. We agreed I would send out an e-mail to my church contacts offering a one-time, one-hour free use of his services in exchange for offering a referral. According to my colleague, many of his clients were referred by people who attended church.

The results of my e-mail communication, I believe 20 or so people responded. Several of them got back in touch with me, letting me know they had lost my contact information and were grateful for the follow through. The point here is to continue to mine those connections for opportunities to stay in front of people, though on a somewhat less frequent basis than your top 50 list.

Professional and Trade Associations

Belonging to professional and trade associations is a must. Professional associations consist of people from a common profession, and trade associations consist of companies in a particular industry. Paying to belong to associations is often a shift for those entering consulting, especially if a former employer may have paid for these memberships. While the initial outlay may be a shock, the benefits of association membership are well worth the cost.

Once you realize you need to be responsible for paying for your own professional and trade association dues, the question you should be asking yourself is how many and what types of organizations should you belong to. This is difficult to answer without some thoughtful consideration, based on your business needs, and what you want to accomplish.

Many of you who purchased this book are already members of ASSE. As professionals in the occupational safety and health (OS&H) field, it just makes sense (and cents) to be associated with the world's oldest and most trusted professional association for global occupational safety professionals. For the money, you simply can't go wrong in using ASSE as your go-to professional organization.

However, ASSE should not be your only association outreach. My recommendation is to belong to at least three to five organizations in any given year. Consulting colleagues that I know recommend more, but I am not sure how many of them are actively involved, attending the meetings, and actually reaping the benefits of those memberships. I do know one consultant who is a member of 15 associations. She firmly believes that membership has helped drive her business success. Let me make it clear here: When I talk about belonging to an organization, I mean you have paid the membership dues, have your name available on its Web site, actively attend meetings, receive and read the regular materials from it, and actively participate or volunteer to support the group in some capacity.

A bigger consideration than the number of associations is to have a plan about the right mix of professional and trade associations to join. Realize that there is a host of associations that might be right for you, depending on your business model, target market for clients, and outreach opportunities. There are many ways to learn which trade and professional associations are available to you. Ask other consulting colleagues what associations they have belonged to, what ones they currently belong to, and what were the deciding criteria. You can purchase or reference the *National Trade and Professional Associations of the United States Directory* for a complete listing (AssociationExecs.com 2014). Most local libraries have at least one copy. Use the Internet to investigate associations based on your areas of interest.

Joining a Chamber of Commerce in your area is a great opportunity to learn from other business professionals and to ask what professional and trade associations they belong to in the local area. Depending on the Chamber, they may offer business classes and other educational resources. Early on, I joined my city's Chamber of Commerce, and attended several Chamber events throughout the San Francisco Bay Area. I discovered that the primary attendees were typically smaller businesses, similar to mine. This was very helpful for personal and internal business development, but not so much for external business development, since my target market is large corporate companies and larger mid-size companies. Hence, this is the reason you need to keep evaluating association memberships, both for your marketing and networking needs.

The other caveat is that Chamber memberships differ significantly by geographic region. Larger cities may have multiple Chambers. Check out the local Chamber meetings in your area. Get to know people and determine if there is one Chamber group that might be especially helpful. You can typically attend three meetings without having to make an immediate decision about membership. Many will let you attend meetings, as long as it's sporadic enough, without joining the organization for up to a year.

As a woman entrepreneur, I was interested in finding other women professionals with whom I could network. I tried several associations, from eWomen Network, East Bay Women's Network, and the National Association of Women Business Owners (NAWBO). All of them offered something different, and the connections were very helpful. When I was just starting out, NAWBO offered an opportunity to connect with women professionals who were more skilled and knowledge about running a business. I learned a lot from them and, as mentioned, still have some close friends from the group. I was able to connect one of the speakers featured at a NAWBO meeting with my ASSE colleagues when we were searching for a symposium speaker to provide a forward-thinking perspective on the future of businesses in a down economy.

Each year, I reassess the organizations in which I am an active member. This typically occurs after I have pulled together my strategic plan for the year, identifying where I want to focus the business, and what I want to achieve going forward. For example, maybe I want to expand my outreach into a particular industry, such as biotechnology. I will then identify, through friends, colleagues, and research, what associations exist for biotechnology in my geographical area. I will examine both national and local organizations. I will research via the Internet when they meet, where, and the focus of the organizations, including their purpose. During the course of the year, I will attend at least two to three meetings to check out the groups. Using this method, I will then decide on one group that works the best for me.

A close friend and colleague of mine, Pello Walker, who is President of Daily Digital Imaging is a highly respected sales and marketing consultant in the San Francisco Bay Area. I asked him what criteria or set of guidelines he used when deciding whether to attend an organizational event or join an association. He shared with me the following:

1. Is my target market in attendance?
2. Does the association allow affiliates to attend? Some professional associations have membership categories that allow vendors and suppliers to join.
3. Are there at least 50 people in attendance at each of the events?
4. Is there a governing Board?
5. Do I have the opportunity to join the Board should I choose to?
6. Can I speak at the general meeting should I choose to?

Other associations focus on providing referrals or leads for different types of businesses. They are referred to as leads groups. Typically, they meet once a week, and the group is very careful to have a diverse mix of small business owners. One of the many criteria is that no two of the same business can join a leads group, as they would be competing against each other in the meeting. The expectation is that you will take the time to get to know the fellow business owners in your group, and learn what types of leads or referrals are best for their business. Each week you are expected to bring several leads or names of possible client connections to share with your fellow colleagues. In return, they do the same for you. One caveat with a leads group: Most of the businesses are targeting specific business sizes. Check out a few to see if they might fit into your overall strategic business plan for expansion. More importantly, determine if the people attending are ones you want to refer clients and connections to and vice versa.

In addition to looking at associations for client outreach, assess them based on your developmental needs. As a consultant, there are myriad skills you will need to continually improve upon. Identifying what skills or personal development you want to work on throughout the year also helps to identify suitable associations. Let's say you decide you want to improve your public speaking ability. You will want to research associations that help people improve their public speaking abilities; the most likely would be Toastmasters International. On the other hand, if you want to develop your skills around promoting and selling your speaking talents, you may want to consider The National Speakers Association.

Many of the associates I have working for me I met volunteering for an organization..

Networking is all about the relationships you build with people. One of the best ways to build those relationships is to be personally involved with and working with people. You can do that by volunteering with associations. Whether you take on a small task, such as checking people in at the reception door, or a much bigger task, like chairing a committee, rolling up your sleeves and demonstrating your talents are some of the quickest ways to be noticed, make connections, and be remembered by others. Working side by side with someone offers a great opportunity to suggest a coffee or lunch date to get to know each other better. Many of the associates I have working for me I met volunteering for an organization. Working with them afforded me the opportunity to see them in action, learn if they were dependable, and identify their skills and strengths.

Professional Electronic Connections

Technology has opened up the cyber pathways to ever-burgeoning opportunities for connecting with each other, and it invites us to explore and consider other available tools for use. In his book *Diffusion of Innovations*, Everett Rogers describes an adoption/innovation curve. On the one side are innovators, first in line to try new innovations. On the opposite side are the laggards, resistant and typically the last to use new and innovative ideas (Rogers 1963). Whether you are an innovator, laggard or somewhere in between, electronic tools abound to help you take advantage of networking opportunities. The easiest way to ease into the range of electronic networking is to participate in a professional networking site, such as LinkedIn®, which enables easy access to trusted colleagues through the establishment of a profile page. As you read the next section, think about how you can use this tool, which was mentioned in Chapter 6, "Marketing and Sales," to enhance your networking outreach.

The LinkedIn site has several hundred million members in hundreds of countries and territories. A new member is added to LinkedIn every second. For those new to professional networking sites, the first step is establishing a profile page, which is typically available free of charge to anyone. Costs apply only when you want to expand your use of the site's marketing and promotion tools. From a networking perspective, I have found the nonpaying services perfect for my business.

If you already have a profile, expand that by joining professional groups with interests common to your own. Most of the practice specialties within ASSE have their own LinkedIn® groups available for you to join. If you are further along in your exploration, you may want to think about either starting a discussion within your group on a topic of interest, or at least contributing to one.

To take advantage of the electronic power of networking and make the service work for you, reach out and invite people to join your network. LinkedIn® has made it very easy to send out generic invitations to those with whom you want to connect. As an avid networker, focused on building relationships with people, I will share that I do not use that function. I have a tailored message that I developed several years ago. The text is as follows:

[Name]: Enjoyed meeting you at [ ]. I am reaching out to connect electronically with you via LinkedIn. I am interested in learning how we might be able to support each other to grow and develop our businesses.

It's very simple, but helps to remind people how and where we met. When reaching out to someone I have not talked with in awhile, I will still provide a reminder of how we met, and know each other. The more personal the message, even providing a memory jogger when needed, the more likely people will be to accept your invitation. Using this philosophy, I've found that those I reach out to almost always accept my invitations.

As for accepting invitations, I am a bit more selective. I will accept invitations from nearly everyone in my profession of safety and health or organization development. I will be a bit more cautious about those I don't know at all or who weren't referred to me by someone. Many people automatically accept all invitations, and that's fine for them. As for me, I check out how we might know each other, and what LinkedIn connections we have in common. I try to get to know the other person.

If I am at a complete loss as to why they are reaching out to me, I will take the time to send a response, but not immediately accept their invitation to connect. If they respond and indicate why they want to connect, then I will accept. If I receive no reply, then I will typically delete the invitation. Several years ago, when I first began to use LinkedIn, a colleague of mine had her LinkedIn acccount spammed. Since that time, I have been very leery about accepting invitations when there are no connections, personal or otherwise.

One of the features that I especially enjoy is the ability to download a spreadsheet with all my contacts. I have found this useful when collecting contacts to add to my monthly newsletter, as well as tracking people whom I want to get to know more personally. Another feature offered is the development of a company profile. While I have taken advantage of this service, it is more for marketing purposes than for networking.

BEFORE, DURING AND AFTER A NETWORKING EVENT

This section introduces a step-by-step guide to share what to do before, during, and after a networking event. Especially for those of you who are linear thinkers, it helps to know what to expect and plan for right from the start. I used to think I was a terrific networker. After starting my business, I realized that I needed to be more strategic and thoughtful about how to approach this. Once

I did, it became a lot easier, and actually more fun than it had been in the past. It also magnified the benefits of what I could offer, without making me feel overwhelmed. Certainly, you may be attending for marketing purposes as well, so be clear from your networking needs what you want to accomplish.

Before the Event

You can do quite a lot of preparation to be ready for any type of group networking event. Especially if you have never attended before, research on the Internet to find out what the group itself is all about. What is its purpose? Who is likely to attend? Call the meeting organizers to learn more about the event. Ask them if an attendee listing can be provided ahead of the event. Find out if the organizers will be attending, and, if so, would they be willing to introduce you to a few people once you arrive. At the very least, this provides you a person with whom you have already established a warm connection.

Ask what type of dress attire is typically worn at the event. Is it business formal or business casual? Certain industry gatherings, such as banking, law practices, and financial, are known for dressing business formal, while other industries, such as technology, biotechnology and construction, are known for dressing business casual. In her book *How to Work a Room*, Susan RoAne recommends wearing some type of conversation piece, such as a tie, stick pin or brooch, scarf or necklace (RoAne 2007).

Be clear on the reasons why you are attending the event. I will often write down one or two key objectives I want to accomplish by attending the event. Some questions to ask and answer as part of the event preparation:

- For what reasons, external or internal business development, or for your own personal development, are you attending?
- What do you hope to get out of the networking event?
- What one or two goals do you want to accomplish during the event?
- If you are trying to determine if this group is a good fit for you, what criteria will you be using?

Find out who is hosting the event. For example, maybe the event is sponsored by the local Chapter of ASSE, but a company is hosting the meal or the site. Try to find this out ahead of time, so that you can take the opportunity to introduce yourself during the meeting, and thank the company's representative for their company's generosity.

Research the speakers and learn something about them by accessing their Web site, or referring to an electronic profile they may have. If the topic is unfamiliar to you, do some research to become more familiar with it. Determine if there are questions you want to know about this topic. Bring them, and if someone else does not address them, be ready to ask questions during the session. As a speaker myself, I welcome the opportunity to respond to questions from the audience. It shows they are interested in what I had to say, and enables me to cover additional information that could not be part of the original presentation.

Send out invitations to fellow consultants or clients who might be interested in attending the event with you. Offer to carpool on rides. Carpooling offers a tremendous opportunity to connect more intimately with fellow colleagues or clients, spending time getting to know each other on a different level. Find out ahead of time if there are certain people your colleagues or clients would like to meet, or information they would like receive during the event. You can bring those up in conversation during the event. I find it's easier to engage people when I have a variety of topics or information I am trying to research at an event. Share with fellow colleagues or clients who might be attending what you are looking for and with whom you would like to connect.

I learned a practice from Patricia Fripp, a nationally recognized professional speaker from The National Speakers Association who speaks on topics related to selling. Patricia will often invite a fellow consultant to accompany her to networking events. Before the event, they will agree on how they want to introduce each other to people. When they go in and start connecting with people, they will introduce each other to the grouping, using the previously agreed-upon introduction.

Initially, I thought this was a little too presumptuous. However, always willing to try new behaviors, I tried with another consultant friend of mine. We both focus on organizational effectiveness. His focus is on strategic planning, while mine is on implementation and change management. Pretty quickly, we realized we could speak more eloquently about each other then we would ever do for ourselves. It is now a practice I try to incorporate as part of my pre-event planning.

During the Event

Arrive on time. When you arrive on time, or even a few minutes early, you have the opportunity to get acquainted with the space, determine how everything is set up, and decide how you want to position yourself. Another incentive for arriving on time is the chance to talk with the registration people before the venue becomes crowded. Some of them may be management staff from the association, while others may be volunteers, active with the association. I have found many to be very helpful with providing introductions to people I want to meet.

Now is the time you want to start connecting with others. Remember, it's all about them at this point. It may be easier to approach those who are standing alone. Use open body language, some smiling (or at least don't frown), and show an openness to listen to others. Wear your nametag on the right side of your body. It is easier for people to make eye contact with your name. Use the information from nametags as a conversation starter.

I have been asked if you should have a drink in your hand or not and, if so, should it be alcoholic? What about eating food? I typically will wait until I'm seated to have anything to drink or eat. The negative first impression I would make spilling my drink on myself (or someone else) just isn't worth it to me. And while I adore wine, at networking events I will only have club soda with lime. I am there for business, pure and simple. My focus is finding out what other people need, and accomplishing my networking strategy. As for food, I will typically eat prior to going, so I don't arrive hungry. Focus on connecting with people, and skip the stale pretzels, chips or carrots. If it's a sit-down meal, then I may take a few bites, and eschew the remainder.

Okay, so you are talking to someone, and want to get better acquainted. What do you do? First, dig into those questions you developed beforehand, and ask them of people you meet. What brought them out to this function? What are they hoping to learn, or with whom do they want to connect? What makes each day exciting for them, or what led to them getting involved with this career? Find out something that establishes some type of common ground with them, and share that with them, but always bring the conversation back to them.

Let's say the person you are talking with mentions he or she is in the process of remodeling their home. If you have also remodeled your home, your comment may be something like, "Having remodeled our home a year ago, I am curious, what is your most memorable experience?" This is a helpful conversation starter. It lets him or her know you have something in common, and that you are interested in the experience from that person's perspective. Think about that in contrast with this type of response, "Having remodeled our home a year ago, I found it very frustrating. Let me explain why." Now you have just dominated the conversation, leaving little room for the other person to add or participate.

While you are getting to know the person, finding out what you have in common, also learn if there is something that you can help with or support. Maybe, as part of the remodel, they are looking for a painter. Do you know a good painter? Offer to provide that contact information. Once I am clear there is a contact they want me to share with them, I will follow up by finding out if they would like to me to make the introduction or just provide the contact information. Some people appreciate an introduction, while others may say no.

Now enters the habit that separates networkers from non-networkers. Non-networkers will say, "Absolutely, I'll share that information with you." But they do not write anything down, and walk away, completely forgetting that they promised to provide the contact. Avid networkers will ask for the person's card, and write on the card the information they just agreed to provide. If cards have already been exchanged, then this information is written down on the back or front of the card. I will also write down comments like "remodeling house—expected completion in the next three to four months."

Another tidbit I have found helpful when agreeing to share referrals: I will close with letting the person know he or she will receive an e-mail from me the next day (or whenever), and the subject line will say: eIntro from Katherine Hart. I have found that setting the expectation ahead of time of what they will receive from me, and by when, keeps the agreement very clear.

My goal at the end of any networking event is to walk away with two to three cards of people who were attending. I used to walk out with a stack of cards, but then went into overdrive trying to follow up. Once I learned that more is not necessarily better, I focused my interactions on just a few people. Based on my interaction, and questions asked and answered during a conversation, if I don't think I will want to spend time getting to know a person, then I won't typically ask for a business card.

I do not agree with the concept of exchanging business cards for the sake of the exchange. If people thrust their business card upon me, which sometimes happens, I certainly won't refuse to take the card. Yet most likely, unless there is some compelling reason I want to get to know them better, I will get rid of those cards. Having a stack of business cards piling up on my desk for people I don't remember, and won't necessarily follow up with, will only add clutter to my desk. And if there is someone I should have connected with, serendipity will typically bring us together at a future event.

While I'm meeting people, I will take the opportunity to introduce them to others I have already connected with in the room. Let's say I learn from a conversation with someone that she just recently moved to the area. I will try to find out where she moved from or what new area she has located to.

Based on that information, I will try to introduce her to someone in the room who may have something in common, such as living in the same area. My philosophy is the more I can connect others, the more value I can provide for them. Adding value is my ultimate networking philosophy, and helps me to be remembered by others.

At the close of the event, just before you leave, take the opportunity to say "thank you," just as though you were at someone's home. Thank the speaker for his or her time. Most of them are doing this for free or for a small stipend. Recognizing them makes a lasting impression.

Thank any sponsors that are there, as well as the staff or volunteers who checked you in at the door. I remember one event I attended where I took the opportunity to thank the team of people who were checking everyone in. The next day, when I was following up with one of the guest speakers, I discovered the registration person from the event was the speaker's gatekeeper. My call was immediately put through to the person I was trying to connect with.

After the Event

Now the real work of networking begins. If you use a professional networking site, this is an opportunity to follow up with each card you have. Send a greeting from your professional networking site, let them know how much you enjoyed connecting with them, and ask for an electronic connection.

Follow up on the requests you wrote down. If you said you were going to share the name of a referral, do so. If the people asking for the referral information asked me not to share their name and contact information, then I will simply ask that they be sure to let the person know how they received their contact information. If I am connecting two people with whom I thought there might be a common connection, then the subject line of my e-mail will display: eIntro from Katherine Hart. That way they are both expecting this e-mail, it won't go into spam, and I have gotten my name out in front of them.

Within a week, I will also follow up with a written note card sent to people I met at the event. These may or may not be the same people I have already communicated with electronically. The message is handwritten, with a reminder of how we met, the event, and why I enjoyed meeting them.

Within a week or two, I will follow up with a call or e-mail to learn if they would like to connect on the phone or in person to get to know each other even better. Each follow up is a connection to deepen the networking relationship.

In addition to the actions outlined above, the following provides a comprehensive list of "do's" to help you remember how to make the most of networking events.

Do remember to:

- Obtain a listing of attendees prior to attending the networking event.

- Be clear on what your objectives will be from attending the networking event.
- Know what the dress code is for the networking event, such as business formal or business casual.
- Research the speaker and topic.
- Invite others to attend, whether they are fellow consultants or clients who might be interested in the topic.
- Arrive on time.
- Relax, be yourself, and keep your ego in check.
- Wear your name badge on your right side.
- Smile, and practice body language that is open to meeting others, such as eye contact and reaching out to shake hands.
- Focus on how you can give to others, such as offering an introduction, recommending a good book, or an article of interest.
- Start your conversation by asking them provocative questions that encourage them to talk about themselves, and what's important to them.
- Refrain from starting the conversation with the standard, "What do you do?" Try something more distinctive like, "What interests you about the topic our speaker is sharing tonight?"
- Take the initiative and be inclusive, welcoming others to join in the group with whom you are talking.
- Ask for a business card from people with whom you want to follow up and connect. Take the time to write down what you will do for them, and information learned about them on the card.
- Always have a pen with you.
- Keep your hands free, so you can write down information.
- Have fun.

NETWORKING: PUTTING IT ALL TOGETHER

I'll close this chapter with five foundational guidelines that, if practiced consistently and authentically, will nurture your ability to build and use networking to advance your consulting practice.

First, make networking a priority. It takes work, time and patience. As a consultant, you will be busy with many competing priorities. Ensure you take time to pick up the telephone and reach out to others, schedule time on the calendar for virtual or face-to-face meetings, and follow up on those individual connections.

QUESTION: What actions can you do to promote networking as a part of your business success?
- Daily
- Weekly
- Monthly
- Annually

The second foundation is to focus on the other person, and actively care about him or her. Building relationships and networking is primarily about others, and what you can bring to their success. It is your willingness to listen and learn about what's important to others, taking the time to discover their thoughts and feelings, and just being there (virtually or in person) for them. What you give in any relationship will be returned tenfold in ways you never imagined possible.

Step forward, be brave, and the world of networking and relationship building will reveal itself to you.

QUESTIONS:
1. What is your networking philosophy?
2. How will this philosophy govern the expansion of your consulting practice?
3. How will you use this philosophy to govern your actions when engaging with others?

The third foundation is to ask questions and actively listen, whether it is listening for the nuances typed into a message or for the actual words being shared. Both are important. The underpinnings for effective listening are the willingness and ability to hold multiple frames of thought and reference. That means you think about both the perspective you bring to the relationship, as well as the perspectives made known to you by other people. You may agree with some of them and not agree with others. Either way, offering the invitation of listening, and asking questions to probe for understanding builds your networking credibility.

QUESTIONS:
1. How do you present yourself when networking, both in dress and attitude, that invites people to connect with you?
2. What actions do you take to show you are interested in learning about them and their business?
3. Have you developed provocative questions to ask when you meet new people?

The fourth and fifth foundations are linked: Make connections, and take the lead. Making connections requires that you use any of the various ways to connect with others, individually and as part of professional associations, then take action as a result of connections you made. Actions can be as simple as sharing contacts, following up on a request, or sending needed materials. Taking the lead recognizes the responsibility that each of us has for building our networking relationships. It doesn't just happen by taking a back-seat approach. You actually have to get into the driver's seat, and make the first move. Relationships won't just happen; they must be initiated, and nurtured along.

The reality is that it is much easier to grow successful existing client relationships than it is to continually bring in new clients.

They take personal energy and effort. Be the one to ask the first question or initiate the topic. Step forward, be brave, and the world of networking and relationship building will reveal itself to you.

QUESTIONS:

1. What actions are you taking to be an interesting person, with something to offer to others?
2. Do you plan time into your consulting schedule to attend events, and meet with other professionals?
3. Once you connect with people do you identify ways you can follow up, and provide them a resource or referral?

In the last chapter, you learned about marketing concepts and actions, which was then expanded into how to integrate networking opportunities in this one. The next chapter will focus on how to retain clients once you have secured them, as well as developing successful client-consultant relationships. The reality is that it is much easier to grow successful existing client relationships than it is to continually bring in new clients. While you will need to do both, not just to diversify your client base but for other reasons (e.g., internal and external business development, and personal development), focusing your efforts on retaining clients will likely offer a healthier work-life balance.

BIBLIOGRAPHY

AssociationExecs.com. 2014. *National Trade and Professional Association Directory*. Bethesda, MA: AssociationExecs.com.

Daoust, Bette. 2005. *Networking: 150 Ways to Promote Yourself*. Pleasanton, CA: Blueprint Books.

Meshel, Jeffrey W. and Douglas Garr. 2005. *One Phone Call Away: Secrets of a Master Networker*. New York: Penguin Group. 2005.

Phillips, Jack, Ph.D. 2006. *How to Build a Successful Consulting Practice*. New York: McGraw-Hill, Inc.

Port, Michael. 2006. *Book Yourself Solid: The Fastest, Easiest and Most Reliable System for Getting More Client Than You Can Handle Even if You Hate Marketing and Selling*. Hoboken, New Jersey: Wiley & Sons.

RoAne, Susan. 2007. *How to Work a Room: Your Essential Guide to Savvy Socializing*. Rev ed. New York: William Morrow.

Rogers, Everett M. 1963. *Diffusion of Innovations*. 4th ed. New York: The Free Press.

Weiss, Alan. 2001. *The Ultimate Consultant: Powerful Techniques for the Successful Practitioner*. San Francisco: Jossey-Bass/Pfeiffer.

Weiss, Alan. 1992. *Million Dollar Consulting: The Professional's Guide to Growing a Practice*. New York: McGraw-Hill, Inc.

ADDITIONAL RESOURCES

American Society of Safety Engineers (ASSE): www.asse.org
eWomen Network, Inc.: www.ewomennetwork.com
LinkedIn: www.linkedin.com
National Association of Women Business Owners (NAWBO): www.nawbo.org
National Speakers Association (NSA): www.nsaspeaker.org
Toastmasters International: www.toastmasters.org

Questions to ask:

How will I use my personal brand to build client loyalty and retention?

How do I ensure from the beginning of the client-consultant interaction, even before signing the contract, that I am focused and designing my actions for both my and my client's success?

What is client engagement, and how will it figure into the work I do for clients?

What client actions and behaviors do I need to be attuned to and aware of, so I can be flexible to support both myself and my client's growth and development?

How will I know and prepare for the transition of past client relationships?

CHAPTER 8

Client Retention: How to Develop Successful Client-Consultant Relationships

---

BY KATHERINE HART, Ed.D.

Katherine Hart is the President of ClearVision Consulting, Inc., a global company based in Alameda, CA, which specializes in accelerating organizational effectiveness and improving human performance.

Katherine worked for 20 years as an internal corporate consultant, promoting and advancing employee safety and health and implementing enterprise-wide change efforts. Her dream of being an external consultant was realized when she founded ClearVision Consulting in 2005 to promote the untapped potential of people within business.

Katherine ardently supports the field of safety and health by educating, coaching and mentoring those in the profession. Her reason for writing this chapter was to share her experiences and enable others to realize their dreams of being successful external consultants.

ACCORDING TO THE Small Business Administration (2012, 3), over 50 percent of small businesses survive the first five years, and one-third survive ten years or more. The reasons for small business failure encompass a great many things, depending on the size of business, what is being sold, and type of industry. Weighing all that, I believe there are four primary reasons that service-oriented businesses do not survive:

1. lack of experience or knowledge,
2. lack of capital or growth,
3. competition, and
4. growing too quickly.

To some varying degree, it is my contention that the ability to retain and build successful client-consultant relationships affects all four of these.

Clients who are satisfied and become avid fans will continue to want to work with you. They will also tell their friends and acquaintances about you, which will increase your ability to grow. As you actively listen to, observe and become attuned to what your clients are experiencing, you will quickly realize the additional services and products they need to be successful. You can then adapt and develop your service or product offering to meet those needs. These actions will enable you to remain competitive. Over time, the result of building sustainable client-consultant relationships engenders goodwill and affords greater tolerance for mistakes, and correction of those mistakes during the course of that relationship, which compensates for any lack of experience and mistakes you made by growing too quickly.

Too often, consultants focus on getting those first few clients without thinking ahead and wondering how they are going to convert those initial clients into future clients. Many of the insights shared in this chapter are personal challenges that I had to persevere and overcome to turn them into victories. My goal is to provide you with thought-provoking material that can be applied, starting with your first client and used with successive clients. (*Note:* This is more probably after a year or so in business, but realizing this upfront will help you be forward thinking.)

CLIENT RETENTION: YOUR BRAND AND REPUTATION

According to Alan Weiss (2002, 1), "A brand is a recognition factor. It creates awareness in people's minds that you (or your firm) represent a particular quality in a certain area. It is a marketing force worth billions of dollars." And while you can read more about how to build your overall brand as part of your marketing strategy in the chapter on marketing, the focus here is on your brand as a component of your reputation. Brand is how you want your clients to talk about you. What do you want to be known for by them? How do you want them to remember you when you are not at their site or once you have finished the engagement with them? Do you want your clients to say, "I am so excited to be working with Susan, she really understands our business and is attuned to our safety and health needs." Or "Steve was the cheapest safety and health consultant we could find. His work reflects that."

... the question is how do you integrate client retention into your brand and reputation?

Recognize that just because you do great work doesn't guarantee they will fondly remember you. Solving today's crisis is only as memorable as the crisis is long. Once it's over, another crisis will take precedence. So the question is how do you integrate client retention into your brand and reputation? Some key areas to focus on include: identifying those personal values that will be ever-present for whatever client you work with (or decide not to work with), aligning your values with achieving the client results, and being clear in the various roles you assume while working with clients.

Personal and Business Values

The purpose of conducting a values exercise as a consultant is to clarify what's important as you embark on your work. A values exercise also enables you to discover your core beliefs, which will ultimately undergird fundamental decisions about the work you engage in with clients. The outcome of this values exercise will:

- keep you focused;
- help you determine when to make adjustments in your client relationships;
- enable you to feel more confident when dealing with a difficult client problem or situation;
- form the basis of how you want to grow and develop your business.

Below is a values exercise that I offer to clients who wish to take their consultancy to the next level. Complete this exercise with a small group of like-minded consultants. It is a terrific networking tool, and is much more fun and self-enlightening when others provide input. Group sharing in the exercise enables an exchange of various perspectives, and will help you to articulate intangible concepts. Feedback from people within the group will make your language crisper and more concrete. This values exercise can also be completed individually.

Values Exercise

Step One: In the back of this chapter is a sample listing of different values. Print the pages and cut the values into individual cards. Pull out those values that make no sense, or you wouldn't consider. Add any that you think might need to be captured.

Step Two: Sort through the deck, placing the cards into three piles: most important, important, and least important.

Step Three: Now you want to focus ONLY on the stack you identified as the most important. You are going to cull this stack down to only five cards. This can be quite challenging, so allow some reflection time. You might want to take an initial pass, and take a break for a day or so. As you go through the activity, ask yourself: How do I want my clients and anyone associated with my business to think of me? Do these values accurately reflect that?

Step Four: For verification purposes and in consideration of your selected top five values, ask yourself the following questions:

- Do these adequately represent me and my business?
- Is there anything missing?
- How do I feel with these top five?
- What might cause these to change in the future?

If you are not doing this exercise with a group of other consultants, now might be the opportunity to talk with a trusted advisor, family, or close friends. The ability to articulate your top five will help verify their validity for you.

Now that you know your top five values, think about how you are going to reflect these values when you are working with your client. Determine what actions and behaviors you will put in place, and verbalize them so that clients, employees, subcontractors, and service providers begin to associate these values with you and your business.

> *... if I don't have solid partnering relationships ... then I will lose passion and energy for the work I do, and the people with whom I interact.*

As an example, one of my values is partnering and team work. Whenever I take on work with clients or am speaking with prospective clients, I will ask them how they define partnering and team work. I will then ask, based on their definition, what they believe this will mean for our working relationship during the course of the project. I want to discover how they view this concept and what it means to them. I then share my perspective, using their frame of reference.

When I meet and interview associates or subcontractors with whom I want to work, I will pose questions to reveal how they interpret partnering and team work. I want to know that, when they represent my company to clients, their actions will support the values of partnering and teamwork my company embodies.

Most of the service providers I work closely with know that eventually I will talk about our relationship together, and how to best partner and support each other to be successful. As a boutique business owner, if I don't have solid partnering relationships with those with whom I spend an inordinate amount of time and energy, then I will lose passion and energy for the work I do, and the people with whom I interact. This value is so ingrained in my psyche that making decisions as to what to do when this comes into question becomes crystal clear.

Now take a few minutes to list each of the five values and identify the corresponding actions and behaviors you will undertake that embodies each of them. These actions and behaviors will now serve to guide you and your business.

Value #1: _____

Actions/Behaviors: _____

Value #2: _____

Actions/Behaviors: _____

Value #3: _____

Actions/Behaviors: _____

Value #4: _____

Actions/Behaviors: _____

Value #5: _____

Actions/Behaviors: _____

> *. . . I only take on clients with whom I want to work, regardless of their needs or financial offerings.*

As part of your marketing effort, you should identify your target market, and the types of clients with whom you want to engage. It's just as important to identify if there are specific entities or people with whom you do not want to work. As a new consultant you will often feel like you need to take on any work to pay the bills. The reality, however, is that you do have choices. So consider what's important to you, and be intentional about your approach.

I have a colleague who will not work with companies unless she knows up front that they have some type of corporate social responsibility interwoven into their business. This is not only a value for her, but it is a key characteristic of those clients that she wants to work with. She shared that early in her consulting business, she worked with clients who didn't have these values, and the relationships always seemed to go sour before the engagement was completed. She wrestled with this, and realized that life would be so much easier if she just didn't take on these clients. According to her, her business took off because she became clear about who she would and would not work with.

As for me, I only take on clients with whom I want to work, regardless of their needs or financial offerings. Part of it goes back to the value of partnership and team work, and part comes from when I was an employee and worked in bureaucratic corporate settings. There were many times when my boss would assign me to work on safety and health issues with leaders who did not view what we were doing as a priority or part of their responsibility.

I often felt like I was hitting my head against a brick wall, getting bruised and battered for nothing. Because of the circumstances, I was forced to work with someone who didn't want the relationship in the first place. When I started my company, I was very clear I *only* wanted to work with clients who wanted to work with me. If they didn't, I walked away from the work.

In my first few years of business, I walked away from several projects at a time when my business coffers were exceedingly low, and I have always been grateful for having the vision and determination to make those tough decisions.

Aligning Your Values with Client Results and Their View of Your Business Value

Once you are clear on your personal values, part of client retention involves aligning your work and personal values with the clients' expectations for results and business value that they see in your work. Rod James (2007, 35) defines this business value as "when the customer perceives that balance is right," and the customers are willing to make an exchange between the service you offer, and the cost they are willing to pay for it. If you can be clear on how to align these up front, then a strong foundation for both a successful partnership and accomplishment of the work expected is established.

Client results are the "what" you achieve when engaged in doing the work for them. These are the agreed-upon outcomes of what is to be accomplished once your work is completed. Obtaining agreement between yourself and your clients on these results is imperative. Too often, these desired outcomes are left too vague, which results, at the end of the assignment, in your thinking you have done a terrific job, while the client perception is that you only half-finished the job.

One of the easiest ways to clarify the results the client expects is to ask the client directly during your initial conversations and throughout the scoping of work phase. You can also bring up these questions periodically during the project to ensure nothing has changed. These few opening questions trigger this important conversation, and have worked well for me:

- When we are finished with this work, what results are you anticipating we will have accomplished?
- At the end of this project, what does success look like for you?

- What are you expecting will be done differently by people within your organization?
- Based on the work we are talking about, who within your organization will be directly and indirectly affected?
- What will people within your organization who are both directly and indirectly affected be saying about this work once it's done?

The gap between what is being asked by your client and the results they want to accomplish can create missed communication opportunities. . . .

You are attempting to learn from the client's perspective what results they want to achieve based on the work you will be doing. Once you know what their expectations are, you can be clear if the results your client expects align with what you think and know from experience is possible. It is much easier during preliminary discussions with the client, prior to signing a formal contract, to shape the expectations and clarify the expected outcomes than it is to try to accomplish this mid-way through a project.

Here is an example from a colleague: He was asked to conduct a safety inspection of the maintenance shop. My colleague initially expected that, at the end of the assignment, the mechanics would know their equipment was within code, and met regulatory requirements. As he and his co-workers talked with the client at the start of the project, they began to understand that the client expectations were very different. The client believed that once the inspection was completed, injuries would be reduced, and the mechanics would work safer. He told me later that it was at this point alarm bells began going off in his head.

He walked in thinking this was just an assignment to conduct an inspection, and to let the maintenance group know what safety violations they had. In reality, the company wanted him to engage and involve the mechanics in a better understanding of how to work more safely, what actions they could take to be more engaged in their work environment, and how they could improve their equipment so that it would meet regulatory requirements. He told me that knowing this information helped him to completely shift his line of questioning and develop a proposal that was much more in keeping with the client expectations.

The gap between what is being asked by your client and the results they want to accomplish can create missed communication opportunities and eventual lack of agreement on results occurring further into the project scope. The wider the gap, the lower the probability is that you will be successful in retaining this client in the future. The effort and work you spend in closing this gap early on during client discussions, especially in achieving alignment with the client expectations and in your ability to deliver those results, increases your chances of success.

The other part of this equation is clarifying the business value that the client places on the engagement. This value, once identified, can be used to determine why the expected results are important to the client. Knowing this information can also help you to determine how to price the project if you are using value-based pricing. Refer to the chapter on finances to learn more.

Value, in this case, is defined as the financial and personal worth that your work will achieve towards improving the client's condition. You will want to work with your clients to clarify both tangible and monetary worth and intangible worth, such as reduced stress and recognition, to define the value for them. Most of my clients have difficulty thinking through this concept, partly because they don't readily discuss it within the corporate environment. Most people just have a project that needs to be accomplished, and they reach out to a consultant to solve that need.

> *One client revealed to me that the reason I was selected for a project was based on the time I took to clarify the expected results and the business value with them.*

This discussion about business values, regardless of whether you incorporate it as part of your pricing structure or not, allows you to identify the client motivators for moving forward with the work. By discussing these up front, you can ascertain how valid and significant they are to the overall operating of the client's business. If mid-way through the project, parameters shift or other competing projects surface, revisiting these business values may help to appropriately prioritize the project.

Clarifying the business value of the project to the client means asking questions that will help put concepts into words. Realize that some clients may have not thought about this, so don't be too worried if this is new for them. Think of it as a benefit you offer them, even before you have actually formally started the work. Several questions that have helped me to move this conversation forward are:

- Why is this project important to you now?
- What are the downsides or consequences if you don't move forward with this work? Could there be compounding negative results?
- How much will the work we are going to do save your company? If there are no direct dollar savings, how will it reduce your liability exposure or associated fines?
- How important is this work to the greater organization, or how will the results of this work affect the greater organization?
- When we complete the work, will it improve the efficiency of the organization/department or group of people? And if yes, by approximately how much?

Once you can get the client to articulate for themselves the business value of the work you offer to them, their perception of what you have to offer may change for the better. One client revealed to me that the reason I was selected for a project was based on the time I took to clarify the expected results and the business value with them. They indicated that my assistance in helping them to achieve clarity on the values for this work provided the needed data and talking points to convince senior leadership of the project's importance, and to push for more resources, specifically budget dollars, to hire the best talent.

After working with your client to clarify what they expect in the way of results, and to ensure you both understand the business value of the project, you are now ready to have a discussion about the personal values of how you will work together, and what is important to you. When clients come to you, they are primarily interested in whether you can solve their problem or need. They don't immediately think about the long-term consequences of working together, or how to build the relationship between themselves and you as the consultant. This focus and responsibility is up to you.

How do they (the client) define partnership and working in collaboration on this project?

The groundwork you do before moving forward with the work will set you up for success in the future. However, until the client is assured that you have the skills, knowledge, and capability to meet their needs, they typically won't engage in any meaningful conversation to discuss your personal values, and how you as a consultant want to work. I have found, in most cases, they just don't have the time for this discussion.

Once you understand what is important to your client, it is relatively easy to open up the discussion. In my colleague's previous example, he could have a discussion about the values his company espouses only after he was clear about his prospective client's true expectations for the scope of work.

My colleague might ask: If I were to take this work on, how might I be able to interface with the mechanics and their supervisors to ensure the project would be successful? He would also want to know how they feel about working in partnership with a consultant. Another question might be: How do they (the client) define partnership and working in collaboration on this project? Realize that all these questions are helping to ensure an alignment between the results the client wants, and the values you have as a consultant. Yet, you can't get to this stage of questioning until you know what the work entails, what the client expects, and why the work is important to them.

If you have worked with these clients in the past, then your line of questioning will likely adopt a different approach. You can gently remind them of the results achieved in the last project, and iterate how the values of your work helped them to achieve those results. While discussing the new scope of work, determining expectation alignment and business values with your client, you can also reinforce your personal values for working with them, and what's important for both of you to be successful.

This discussion of aligning your personal values with your client's results and their perceived business value for your work becomes an ongoing dialog that you are continuously championing to keep the awareness level high—front and center for any conversation. By establishing this discussion at the onset of any client work, it becomes second nature as to how all parties will work together.

When challenges arise as part of the project, which will inevitably happen, you can loop back to this discussion about your values as a consultant, client expectations for the project, and the intended value of the project. You both are grounded in fundamentals of how you want to work together, and what is to be achieved. Having this common language then lets you determine what led the project or work astray, and how can it be brought back on track for successful results.

Consultant Roles in Client Relationships

Regardless of what niche you possess as an OS&H consultant, it is important to be clear on how you want to interface and work with your client. One of the best graphics I have come across was developed by Alan Weiss (2003, 18), and entitled "Consulting Interventions" (see Figure 1). In the lower left corner, the consultant serves only as an analyst, low in actually resolving the issue or transferring their skills to the client. They move from this lower left corner to the upper left corner when they bring expert technical skills, as most of you will, based on your expertise in OS&H. The question is how do you move from just being an independent expert for your client to a collaborator, high in both resolving their issues, and transferring skills to them? It is the classic case of whether you "do the fishing" of problem resolution for the client versus "teach the client to fish," so they have the skills to continue the work of problem resolution once you leave.

I have found they typically retain you . . . because of your ability to transfer that knowledge and those skills to their organization.

As a consultant, you bring a variety of skills, knowledge, and experience to the client situations you will encounter. The client may initially hire you because of the expertise you have. I have found they typically retain you and keep bringing you back not because of your expertise, but because of your ability to transfer that knowledge and those skills to their organization.

Unless you have a skill set or knowledge that is unique, which most of us just don't have, you are constantly competing against other qualified consultants and, in some cases, employees within the company. For this reason, what sets you apart from others will be your ability to elegantly transfer your knowledge so that it can be applied by the client. Your ability to successfully transfer this knowledge will have you standing head and shoulders above most consultants, and will be the secret sauce for why your clients come back again and again for your services.

Referring to Figure 1, part of your brand and reputation is dependent on how you want to be viewed as a consultant by your clients. You have the ability to build your brand and reputation by being specific about who you are as a person and business, what you offer that makes you unique, and your ability to develop sustainable client-consultant relationships. Those relationships need to focus on shared values and trust, role clarification (are you just an expert or are you actually transferring knowledge to the client), agreement on results, and ultimately, financial value for the business.

When you and your client can step back from any individual engagement, and clearly recognize how you worked together to bring financial value to their business, then you are a consultant they will want to retain and re-engage to access your skills and services. You will know when you are truly successful in forging successful client relationships when your client brings a problem to

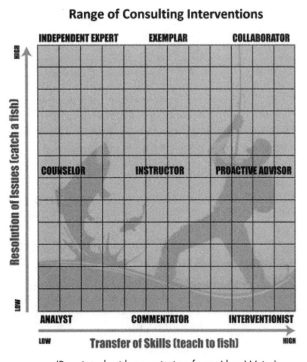

Figure 1
Expert Position vs. Skills Transfer

(Reprinted with permission from Alan Weiss)

you and claims they know it's not your specialty, but asks if you would take it on regardless. Why? Because they know that, by working together, at the end of the day they will be successful in whatever endeavor is attempted.

DESIGNING FOR CLIENT-CONSULTANT SUCCESS

I was meeting with a non-profit steering committee to discuss a special project initiative that would be rolled out to its members. As a new member, I was tactfully asking questions to determine how the initiative had come into being, especially since there were so many varied interpretations of what the initiative was to accomplish. Finally, one of the non-profit staff members remarked, "The reality is that we didn't have a plan in place. The initiative grew organically, just sort of coming together. I guess now the problem is that, since we didn't know what we intended in the first place, we have to figure it out at the back end."

Consultants are intent on landing work to support their businesses' growth and development. And most consultants are focused on doing exceptional work for their clients, especially if consulting is their primary source of livelihood. The more you can deliberately plan and design for your business and your clients' success, the more successful you will be.

Unlike the non-profit example, you cannot just let your success grow organically, and figure it out at the back end. By that time, it may be too late. A lost client damages your reputation and, as famously used in World War II propaganda, "loose lips sink ships." Though you may not lose your practice, a dissatisfied client who believes you over-promised and under-delivered can wreak significant havoc. As part of your first interaction with a potential client, you have to design for client-consultant success.

One of the best books on consulting, particularly related to the intricacies of how to design for a consultant's success at the front end of a client engagement, is Peter Block's *Flawless Consulting*. Many of the concepts and ideas presented here build on his precepts. In addition to identifying and staying true to their values, as discussed above, successful consultants are grounded in how they will approach their work. Their foundation is built upon four key goals, which I have adapted from Block (1981) as:

- Build collaborative client relationships.
- Solve the client's problem in a sustainable manner.
- Address the technical or business issues, along with the people dynamics.
- Obtain and maintain client ownership and agreement for action.

Build Collaborative Client Relationships

Right from the start, your goal should be to build and co-create a collaborative client relationship. There are many reasons for this, not the least of which is that having a relationship of mutual collaboration and support makes the interface between a client and consultant so much more enjoyable. Developing a collaborative relationship sets the boundaries for how you will work together, what's important to each of you, what are personal and business time constraints, how you will communicate, and how decisions will be made between the two of you. It may seem like a simple request, but learning up front what mode of communication (i.e., e-mail, text or phone) your client prefers makes a huge difference.

... as a consultant, you should be serving as a role model for your clients.

As an example, a client and I were working through these details. She mentioned that she liked receiving project updates via e-mail to review prior to our bi-weekly check-ins. She told me that she would rather have me contact her by phone when I really needed to talk with her, since her e-mail inbox was typically overloaded. These types of details, and working knowledge of each other, made working together much easier and helped in achieving a work-life balance.

A collaborative client relationship builds goodwill and serves as ballast in stormy seas. Let's face it, if you have been working on building a collaborative open relationship with your client, it is much easier for them and you to be open with each other when mistakes (either on your side or theirs) are made or shifts to the project need to be made. Being upfront about how to approach each other with unpleasant information makes for a healthy collaboration.

Additionally, as a consultant, you should be serving as a role model for your clients. Discussing with them what makes a collaborative relationship will encourage them to have those same discussions with their own bosses or direct reports. Modeling how you want to be treated, as well as demonstrating this for your client, makes a huge impression.

During a meeting with one client, the client described a performance problem she had been having with another employee, and how she had approached the employee with the problem. While the conversation was difficult, the client was pleased with the final outcome, since the employee understood the specific behavior changes expected. When I congratulated my client on her actions, she shared that her ability to approach that conversation with openness, positive intent, and the ability to name specific behavior changes had been due to our past working relationship. She commented, "I approached the meeting thinking how you would handle the situation, and it carried me through." I was floored by her comment, and had no idea that our collaborative relationship, built over time, had positively affected her ability to more effectively handle employee performance issues.

Solve the Client's Problem in a Sustainable Manner

Our job as consultants is not just to determine what needs to be done to solve the client's need, but to dig deeper and determine the root cause or real need that is leading to the problems being experienced. We know intuitively that helping them to develop a program for locking out equipment will not correlate to an increase in equipment being locked out, unless the barrier and challenges for locking out equipment are identified and corrected. The policy only sets the clearly defined expectations. The real questions are, among others: How will the expectations be presented? Will the employees locking out the equipment be involved in creating the solutions? Is there support from the various layers of leadership?

There is an old adage that a consultant is someone who borrows the client's watch to tell them what time it is. Yet the truth is that as a consultant you are dealing with the client's environment and their problems. Like a doctor, you have to diagnose what is going on in that environment, and what is causing the problems they are experiencing. You then need to be able to apply your skills, knowledge, and best judgment to work collaboratively with the client to resolve the problems identified. You are not there to create more problems. Similar to a physician, your motto should always be, "Do No Harm."

When you finish the engagement, you should have clearly and succinctly identified the real reasons for the problem, so that the solution is sustainable, and doesn't fall apart just as you walk out the door. I often tell my client: "When we finish, I want to know in my gut that when I walk away, you will be better off than when I arrived. And if I haven't accomplished that to the best of my ability, you shouldn't be paying me." The next section will address the need to ensure that the client fully understands and owns the problem, which I believe goes hand in hand with ensuring that the solution to the problem is sustainable.

While you should approach your work with the belief that your solution will be sustainable for your client, be forewarned that unforeseen circumstances can happen. Companies are bought and sold, new people are brought on board or let go, extenuating circumstances occur, and the environment you left with a sustainable solution is no longer applicable. This is the life of working in any type of dynamic, human-centered system: Change happens.

Thus when I talk about solution sustainability, it is within the given and known parameters of the immediate situation. Based on information provided by the client, you can extrapolate for possible eventualities and plan contingencies. In the final analysis, your recommendations for improvement and subsequent implementation have to be based on what is currently known, measured and observed.

Address the Technical or Business Issues, Along with the People Dynamics

For most any engagement, there will be both a technical or business issue, and a people dynamic component. Clients tend to hide behind the technical issue, believing that if you are a competent consultant, and can solve the technical issue, the people dynamics will be less relevant. The opposite is more correct; figuring out how to solve or more aptly engage the people will result in the technical issue being more easily addressed. As a consultant, you have to be willing to call out the people dynamics, not in a negative or unflattering light, but rather in an objective and descriptive way.

You, as the outside third party, have the advantage of not being constrained by politics, reporting relationships or pre-determined biases. During one engagement, the lead for the administrative section confided that she was so enthused by having me work there. When I asked why, she shared that now all the issues that she had explained to her boss could be resolved without any lasting incriminations. She was one of the first people I talked with as part of my fact finding and assessment.

One of the worse things to do is try to gloss over the people dynamics. Many a change project or work initiative has been stopped midstream due to significant people resistance that could have been much more adroitly handled if addressed early on. During one consulting project, I was paired up with the internal operational excellence coordinator in a school district. According to her, we just needed to get the processes developed, and then everything would be okay.

The bottom line is that you must address the people dynamics. . . .

I tried to persuade her that the dynamics of the organization were such that the people needed to be involved in developing the new processes. If not, there would be significant resistance when it came time for implementation. While the initial involvement would make the start-up for the project a bit longer, the results gained would be tremendous. Unfortunately, we hadn't been working together for that long and, more importantly, she was almost ready to launch the process rollout when I was brought on-board to support the change.

The new process was presented, and the presentation was met with stony faces, an assault of questions, and universal concurrence from the leadership on down to the staff that the processes were not implementable. We then spent the next month following up with damage control. I interviewed individual team members, and then brought them together for several process improvement sessions to map out a new process.

Was the resulting process any better than the one previously recommended? No, in fact it was pretty much the same process, with minor tweaks and adjustments. The difference is that the people themselves had developed the process, and took ownership for its success or failure. Organizations are comprised of complex, interconnected dynamics of human beings. The bottom line is that you must address the people dynamics, regardless of how good or fabulous your solution for the business or technical issue.

Obtain and Maintain Client Ownership and Agreement for Action

Similar to addressing the people dynamics, you need to obtain and maintain client ownership and agreement for action during each step of the consulting process. While you may bring the best solution to your client's challenge, it may not be implemented if you haven't brought them on-board relative to the work that needs to be accomplished. As someone once told me, you have to be both able to help your client visualize the future, as well as be clear about what it's going to take to achieve that future. Each step of the journey needs to be a recommitment to that future goal.

If at any time, you reach a point where the client says, directly or indirectly, "I just don't see how this is going to work," you need to pause and reconnect. It is never a good time to say, "Just trust me because I am the consultant, and know what's good for you." While you probably have a very cogent idea of what needs to happen next, a key part of your job is to circle back to ensure there is commitment and agreement for the next step before moving forward. There is a back-and-forth type of motion required of consultants to ensure clients are clear about what they have to do, where they are going, and what has been accomplished.

Client agreement can be a slippery slope when multiple stakeholders are involved in the project. You may be brought in by one person to conduct the work, interface with another person for the day-to-day project support, report to a cross-functional project team, and present before a senior leadership team. All of these people are your clients, and with each interface, you may be the only common bond among all of them.

It is incumbent upon you to determine where each person is within the structure of the project, identify what it will take to bring them along, and then be open to the insights and different perspectives they share. Even when you have a central point of contact, which is typically not the standard, you still have the responsibility to ensure that they have the information, resources and tools necessary for obtaining internal agreement. It seems like a lot of moving parts, and in some cases it is, but all this makes for a wild and adventurous ride in the ever-present road to client agreement and commitment.

Additional Insights for Client-Consultant Success

In addition to the above four goals recommended for designing for client-consultant success, keep these additional words of wisdom in mind. These have either been shared by others or personally gleaned from my own practice:

- Approach the engagement with the belief that the client is healthy. Similar to the interpretation of law that everyone is innocent until proven guilty, always approach working with your client from the standpoint that they want the best for the project, your success, and their success. Be open to listening to their concerns and issues. This does not mean you should ignore any danger or warning signs that would preclude this belief, but approach them with an open mind and interest in what they have to say. Most times, they will be wonderfully supportive and welcoming of a healthy client-consultant relationship.
- Start the work where the client is, and not where you want them to be. As a consultant, you enter the client's environment where they are. This doesn't mean you won't be shocked or surprised at what occurs within the client's culture, but you have to start where they are. You have the opportunity to bring them along, raise their level of capability and capacity for improvement, and affect change throughout the organization. When you meet them where they are, warts and all, you infuse them with hope for a future that elevates the safety and health of all working in the environment.
- Clearly define and sketch a picture of success, then work steadily toward it. As a consultant, you bring two very powerful forces. The first is the ability to envision a future different than where your client is. You have this ability because of the other clients you have worked with, and maybe from your own personal experience of working in an environment that achieved this success. The second is your process and structure, along with associated tools and resources, to partner with the client to navigate the journey, and achieve the vision. Be mindful and prepared that the vision may need to be altered to meet the dynamics of the changing business needs.

- Propose the Cadillac, but be ready with the Volkswagen. Be very clear about meeting the client in their current situation. Based on where they currently are, suggest recommendations that will immediately resolve their situation, along with those solutions that are more comprehensive. While clients may initially say they want the fancier approach, there may be logical and cogent business reasons for modifying and retrenching. And as the consultant, you have to be flexible to those approaches, and constantly be ready to shift course to meet the prevailing winds of the business.
- Assume positive intent. Similar to assuming your client is healthy and undamaged, approach your interactions with everyone assuming positive intent. I do not believe people get up in the morning and think, how can I make my consultant's life miserable? What happens is that they have good days and bad days just like the rest of us, and often they make decisions, take action or say things that, if reflective time were provided, they probably wouldn't have. Assume your client has positive intent for what they do, and give them the benefit of the doubt.

CLIENT-CONSULTANT SOCIAL CONTRACTING

Developing a social contract with your client is the way to establish and achieve the items we have already talked about: your values, client results and business values for the work, and the design of the client-consultant successful relationship. Think of this as a road map you can work through during your first and subsequent meetings with the client to achieve clear understanding and engagement, and to set the stage for a successful working relationship.

You can use this information to help establish your formal and legally binding contract with the client, but that is not the intention of this section. It is, instead, focused on the interpersonal relationship setting and engagement between the two of you (or more, if there are multiple stakeholders on the client side). The information provided in Table 1 is not the only way to approach the work, but it is one that has worked for me over the years. Modify those areas that do not align with your business. Ensure, though, that the sections you decide to eliminate are covered in other areas, such as client agreement.

Part of your job as a consultant is to help the organization bridge some of the gaps in communication and dissemination of the work. . . .

In working through the social contract with the client, know that this does not stop once the written and legal contract is agreed to and signed. Con-

Table 1: Creating a Client-Consultant Contract

Create the work agreement	• Understand the client's needs and business value • Scope boundaries and roles of the project • Decide to work with the client on this project
Define the problem and work	• Identify the key issues • Identify who will be involved in the project • Select the method for the work and how results will be measured
Gain commitment for recommendations	• Data collecting, analyzing, and summarizing • Discuss options, insights and recommendations • Gain agreement on next steps
Implement and follow up	• Align organizational, operational and individual issues • Ensure readiness, tools for rollout and reinforcement • Follow up, track results, and pivot as needed

tracting, re-contracting, and getting feedback on your agreements is a dance that you and the client will engage in during every interaction (regardless of the mode of communication) and with all the stakeholders, regardless of the size of the organization. Never assume that each person you talk to, and achieve agreement with, has the same level of understanding as the previous person you talked to.

Part of your job as a consultant is to help the organization bridge some of the gaps in communication and dissemination of the work, unless you discover the person assigned as your liaison is superb at doing this. And if so, then your job is to point that out to their boss and have them be recognized for the excellent work they are doing. I have discovered the more I praise those I enjoy working with, the more they will come back to work with me, regardless of whether the project is within my immediate area of expertise. As one project manager shared with me, "When I work with you, you take the time to help my boss recognize and realize my value and worth to the organization."

Create the Work Agreement

Up to this point, we have talked quite a lot about understanding the client's needs, expectations, and business results. Now let's take some time to talk about scoping boundaries and roles of the project. Scoping boundaries and role clarification is a little about the work and lot about the interpersonal interactions. Use the work you are considering as the context for this discussion, but the heart of the matter is how you want to be perceived by the client, what you will do, what the client will do, and how you both will navigate working together.

During the first few meetings, you should be asking yourself and discovering what is important to the client about this project. Is your client driven by ego and recognition for the success of this project? Do they have a vested interest in the final outcomes and results of the work? Are they being coerced to do this work by others in the organization, or is it something they see as relevant to them, the department, or the company?

The other opportunity is to define and explore how you will support the client during the length of the project. Referring back to Figure 1, how can you best work with your client to satisfy their needs? Will a part of your work involve the transfer of skills and knowledge to the client or other staff? What does the client expect from you as the consultant? To initiate this discussion, explore the client's historical experience with consultants. Some questions to ask are:

- Have you worked with other consultants before?
- What has your experience been like?
- What did you like best and what frustrated you?

Once you obtain the client's perspective on historical consultant interactions, you can use this information as context to discuss how your work with them will be different (or similar) to that of other consultants with whom they have worked. You and the client can also explore more deeply how your relationship will support meeting their objectives for the work.

This is also the opportunity for you, as a consultant, to begin setting your own boundaries. For example, I will let clients know that I use all manner of communication media to stay in touch, from phone, which also rolls to my cell phone, e-mail, and text. I gain agreement from them that we will not play Ping-Pong regarding e-mail. If there are lots of questions, or responding to an e-mail is taking too many paragraphs or leaving too many unanswered questions, we pledge to schedule a phone call to shorten the back-and-forth responses, and increase our communication effectiveness.

A consulting colleague shared another boundary-setting mechanism. She was challenged by a client who would frequently schedule last-minute meetings. Instead of re-juggling all her other clients and priorities, she established some boundaries up front with them. She let the client know that if contacted at the last minute, she would attempt to accommodate by participating via teleconference or having an associate (if one was working with her on the project) present. If those options were not available, she would not be able to attend. She said that once the client was aware of her boundaries, that habit of scheduling last-minute meetings was reduced.

If you take on work with a client with whom you don't want to work, . . . you will be miserable.

So now you're thinking, what if I don't know this about my client until a third of the way into the project? Let me reiterate, contracting does not finish after the first few meetings. You will continually need to revisit and negotiate boundaries that work for you and your client. The more you can establish that this is a 50-50 client-consultant partnership, the better off for both of you. What are some boundary-setting parameters that you might want to consider for your business?

The final analysis of the work agreement phase involves you making a conscious choice about whether you want to work with this client, can actually solve their problem, and whether it is in your best interests to take on the work. If you take on work with a client with whom you don't want to work, if you can't solve their problem or if you realize it's not in your best interest, then you will be miserable. You will spend an inordinate amount of time (particularly if it is not your specialty) working with people you don't like and don't care about. Being clear about what work you are willing to walk away from and then doing just that—walking away from it—is very liberating.

The upside is that when you say no, other exciting projects will open up for you. When you are clear on the projects for which you are well qualified, and the types of clients for whom you want to work, you will ultimately have more work than you know what to do with. Stacy Hall and Jan Brogniez wrote a book entitled *Attracting Perfect Customers: The Power of Strategic Synchronicity* that deals much more in depth with this concept. They truly believe that when you get crystal clear on the right client and the right kind of work for you, everything you do, from marketing, networking, and sales, attracts those individuals to you.

Define the Problem and the Work

As you know from being an expert in the field of OS&H, you are often brought in to address symptoms: established programs not complying with regulatory requirements, employees concerned about their health and safety, and supervisors not fully vested in holding individuals accountable for safety. It may take some considerable digging, based on the symptoms exhibited, to uncover the root cause, and define the problem. A quote cited on the Internet as being attributed to Albert Einstein, though not verified, states: "If I had an hour to solve a problem I'd spend 55 minutes thinking about the problem, and 5 minutes thinking about solutions." Even if you are not clear on the full extent of the problem initially, as a consultant, you can work with your client to put some boundaries around the scope of the problem.

Determine if you are the only consultant working on a particular project, or if others are involved. During one client assignment, I was brought in to conduct a strategic team retreat. The client let me know I had a half-day to work onsite with a cross-functional international team. As I asked more questions, I learned that they were actually meeting for three days. I asked if they were working with any other consultants on the retreat, and they indicated that there were four other people leading different sections. Thank goodness for that question.

I recommended that all of the consultants get together to decide which portions of the retreat we were covering, and to work together to make the client's overall retreat a success. I guess I was the last one brought on board, because I learned none of the other consultants had suggested or recommended this. Once we met, the client realized how vastly different our approaches were, and that all of us would need to do some upfront work to ensure our efforts were seamless during the retreat. As it happened, because of my questions, my client asked me to take the lead in pulling the whole retreat together to ensure its success. You never know where your questioning is going to lead you.

Does the information need to be shared up the chain to senior leadership . . . ?

Be clear, when first defining the problem, that you also know which stakeholders from the client's side will be involved with the project. Sometimes, this may be not be immediately apparent, but obtain as good an idea as you can. Determine who will be involved in any type of assessment or data gathering. How will they be informed and communicated with?

I have had several projects where I have offered to provide both a communication plan, and resulting communication tools to support the client in adequately conveying the project messages at different stages of work. This added work brought in additional money from the project, but more importantly, it helped me and my client to ensure the project was that much more successful.

Another key identifier for involvement is asking who will review your final results and analysis of the work completed. Does the information need to be shared up the chain to senior leadership, is it only for a middle manager's review, such as the Director of OS&H, or are there other stakeholders within the business who will be involved? Knowing this will help you determine how to work with your contact to prepare all of these people for the final project results.

Find out how comfortable your contact is in presenting to various levels of leadership. One of my client contacts used to cringe every time she had to make a presentation to her boss. She complained that he didn't like her and wanted her projects to fail. By asking questions, I learned that the person I was working with was very thin skinned, and her boss actually thought she did excellent work. However, he was not the type to share such feelings. Whenever she presented something to him, he would pick and find flaws. His focus was to make the presentation more appealing to the senior leader audience. Once she was presented with this perspective, it shifted the working dynamic between these two people. They were never best friends, but at least my contact knew her boss was in fact looking out for her best interests.

Select the most appropriate method to approach the client's problem. I believe that the reason a client is hiring you is for your expertise in how to solve their problem. Be careful that the client does not dictate the terms or conditions for how the work will be solved nor the appropriate methodology. We've all been faced with a client who thinks they know what the problem is, and in most cases hasn't a clue, but then tries to dictate how to solve the wrong problem. For that client, you have your work cut out for you. My recommendation is to immediately bring out a piece of paper (or use the nearest whiteboard) to draw out where they think they are, where you think they are, and the gap that exists. This may be a timeline, work-flow diagram, or some other visual aid that enables a meeting of the minds to occur.

Gain Commitment for Recommendations

There are often times when you need to collect some type of data, analyze it, and summarize it to make an accurate recommendation for your client. There are other times when the "what" of the consulting assignment is as plain as the nose on your face. Either way, once you are clear about how to address the client's problem, you need to engage the client, and gain their commitment for the recommendation you propose.

While you are drawing your conclusion as to the recommendations, your client is forming their own opinions as well. Perhaps you have been involving them along the way, so that when you are ready to present your recommendation, they are prepared for the message. While this is helpful, sometimes it's not possible.

Another approach is to involve your client in some aspect of the final analysis. Call it a beta test of information learned, asking for their input and thoughts based on their cultural understanding. During this beta test, you can hear from your client what concerns have surfaced and then incorporate those into the final recommendation. You are trying to prepare the client for the information and to open their perspective on a possibility that hasn't occurred to them. It may take some time for them to get comfortable with the information, especially if there are significant organizational and department ramifications.

A final approach is providing several options for consideration. . . . This is probably the best way for gaining full-on, client buy-in. . . .

A final approach is providing several options for consideration. Similar to the discussion in the previous section, attempt to present a Cadillac, a Volkswagen, and even an intermediate version for discussion and input. This is probably the best way for gaining full-on, client buy-in, since it is the client who approves the final improvement action. As the consultant, your job is to actively listen to the client, discern his or her concerns, find out what the client likes and what the client doesn't like, and determine what could both resolve the problem and achieve the objectives you both agreed upon at the start of the engagement.

Perhaps the most difficult job as a consultant is to not be too wedded to your recommendation for improvement. While there are certain black and white areas (compliant vs. non-compliant) with regards to OS&H regulatory requirements, how clients will achieve compliance may be vastly different. From a successful client-consultant relationship, you need to be that sounding board to talk through the various options and considerations.

If you are too committed to only one right way to approach the solution, then it will be difficult to step back and look at the opportunities with fresh eyes, and from the client's perspective. There is a significant difference between consultants who enter the relationship as only the expert, rather than as a thought partner and collaborative advisor (refer back to Figure 1). While your clients absolutely look to you for the specific skills, knowledge, and experience you bring, your ability to help shape and guide them to come up with the right answers and actions for moving forward will do more for your relationship than almost anything.

Once agreement for resolution is co-determined, the next step is recommitting to the next steps and actions for moving forward. While this is a new social contracting opportunity, this may or may not be a new legal contract between the two of you. For some jobs, particularly if you are clear on the final outcomes or what the client may need to do, you can contract only for the assessment piece, which may include surveys, focus groups, onsite observation, and other types of behavioral observation.

The follow-up contract, once both the client and you agree as to what needs to occur, will be a new legal contract for the implementation work. Other times, the legal contract may be comprehensive enough to cover the assessment, recommendations or findings, and implementation. When this is the case, you can identify key milestones for achievement and celebration. These milestones for recommendation and client commitment may include not just laying out the next steps, but a celebratory lunch or some type of team activity to congratulate the team on achieving this stage of agreement.

BEWARE THE ELEPHANT IN THE ROOM: CLIENT RESISTANCE

There is a phrase often used by facilitators and consultants for recognizing and addressing the "elephant in the room." This idiomatic expression refers to a truth, action or behavior that is so obvious everyone is aware of it, but no one wants to address, name, or even discuss it. This may be because of political reasons, friendships, or concern with the resulting consequences on the part of other people. As a consultant, you have to know how to address obvious issues as part of the normal course of conducting work with clients. When these "elephants" are left unaddressed, they simply get bigger, and if left too long, will form a wedge in the client-consultant relationship. When this happens, the results can be disastrous for the current work, as well as for any future work with a client.

A fellow consultant told me that she had lost a key client, worth over 45 percent of her business because, according to her, she had directly observed, but refrained from bringing to the client's attention, behavioral actions that did not support the project's success. At the time, she assumed they understood the ramifications of what they were doing. You may ask: Why is a client's inappropriate action my problem? If my client contact wants to commit political suicide, then isn't that his or her problem, as opposed to mine?

The difficulty for this consultant was that when the project began to stall, she brought what she had observed to her client's attention. Unfortunately, by then it was too late; the damage was done, and the project was re-assigned to another manager. My friend was replaced, and lost a significant piece of work. In that company, no one wanted to work with her again for the simple reason that they believed she would not look out for their best interests, readily share her insights, or help them to be successful. One of our jobs as consultants is to support our client in being successful, even if that means putting a mirror in front of them, and confronting them on behaviors that will not serve them well. For this reason, it is important to know how to address those behaviors and to be willing to have open conversations with your client about what you are observing.

Why is a client's inappropriate action my problem?

Identifying Client Resistance

Client resistance can take many different forms; you need to be on the lookout for it to surface. Most typically, resistance will arise as you get closer to defining the real or underlying problems, as opposed to addressing the symptoms raised by the client. However, resistance can also surface at other times during

Table 2: Client Resistance Types, Definitions, and Examples

Types of Resistance	Definition and Example
Asking for more detail	Asking for increasing levels of detail that moves beyond reasonable knowledge needed to actually resolve the problem. *Example:* "We appreciate your aggregate data. And while you broke it down by shift, could you please provide us more data by gender, length of time, and position level."
Deluge of information	Providing an overabundance of information, in such exquisite detail, that the true facts get glossed over. *Example:* "To understand this problem, you need to be familiar not just with our last few years, but when it when it really started, which was 20 years ago, when our company first started requiring that the mechanics be responsible for conducting safety checks on their equipment. Let me explain."
Time	Being too busy to put the effort into the project, and meet with you, constant interruptions during the project, or putting off the start of the project with continued delays. *Example:* "You just don't understand how busy I am with this work. We may need to delay for another two weeks. There just really isn't any good time to get our people together for this training."
"Real world" or uniqueness syndrome	Shifting responsibility or blame to the consultant or characterizing the problem as unique to the company or industry. *Example:* "If you really understood us, you'd realize this is really a unique problem or situation."
This was expected	Upon receiving data, to report that the information was known all the while. *Example:* "This is very helpful information, though, of course, we actually expected this when you were brought on board. We're not really surprised."
Attack the consultant	Shift the focus or blame to the consultant and his or her knowledge, expertise, or credibility. *Example:* "We were not sure you were the best person for this job. There has been some questioning of your methods for obtaining the data."
Client confusion	Initial confusion or uncertainty is legitimate. Confusion that lasts beyond the second or third explanation is suspect. *Example:* "I realize we have talked about this on several occasions, but could you please reiterate why we need to present this to the senior leadership."
Client silence or acquiescence	The client has absolutely nothing to add, no objections are raised, or everything you say or do must be right because you are the expert. *Example:* "You're the expert; whatever you say is fine with us."
Better than others	Downplaying a problem by elevating your circumstances compared to other shifts, departments, business, or industry. *Example:* "Well, in comparison with the swing shift, we are not so bad."
Solution-oriented	Focus on just wanting to know how to handle the problem, without getting clear on what the real problem is. *Example:* "Let's cut through this right now. Just tell us what we need to do to solve this problem and move on."

(Adapted from Block 1981)

the course of the project. Table 2 identifies the most common types of client resistance, along with supporting definitions and examples. This table will help you to better understand resistance when you see or hear it from your client.

Addressing Client Resistance

When, as a consultant, you believe that resistance is occurring, or an inappropriate client behavior is surfacing, there is a five-step approach you can take to handle the situation. Each of these steps provides concrete actions you can take. Understand that addressing client resistance is not always easy, even for seasoned consultants. The downside, as we've discussed, is that the client-consultant relationship may be damaged or, worse, the client project may be cancelled. In some instances, this may be okay, as there are some clients you just need to be willing to let go of, or in some intolerable situations, fire. However, the upside is that addressing these can improve the client-consultant relationship, and significantly raise your client's satisfaction of your services and value to the organization.

Most typically, resistance will arise as you get closer to defining the real or underlying problems. . . .

Step One: Identify and be clear in your own mind the type of resistance or aberrant behavior you are noticing from your client. Have a few examples you can reference and use for illustration purposes. This is also an opportunity to examine your own personal biases, and determine if they may be clouding the situation.

> *Example:* I have begun to realize my client contact uses her involvement in other work activities and extracurricular interests as a screen for not getting too deeply involved in this project. While we are just getting started, my concern is that, if this continues over time, she will not be present, able to function in a fully collaborative relationship, or execute required activities. The result: We will eventually miss critical deadlines. Assessing my personal bias, I have a tendency to get overcommitted myself on work projects. While I am aware of my own failing, I need to realize that my client and I have to support each other from the very start of this project.

Step Two: Name the behavior. Share with your client, in a neutral voice and nonjudgmental manner, what behaviors you have observed. Provide clearly described examples that enable them to also see the behaviors. Obtain a series of "Yes" answers to questions that help them recognize their own behavior.

> *Example:* (1). "Jane, I need to talk with you about our working relationship, and the success of our project. I want to ensure we are both fully

committed to its success. Are you open to having this discussion?" Jane responds, "Yes."

(2). "Are you in agreement that as this project escalates, we are both going to need to invest more time, be more accessible to each other, and give more time than we currently are to its success?" Jane responds, "Yes."

(3). "The last three meetings we have scheduled have either been cancelled, pushed off, or you have been late and arrived halfway through the meeting. I am concerned that this pattern of delayed, missed or partial meeting misses could inhibit our ability to make this project successful, as well as damage our collaborative working relationship."

... addressing client resistance is not always easy, even for seasoned consultants.

Step Three: Maintain a pregnant pause, and do not fill the silence. Pregnant pauses are those moments of silence that are filled with the possibility for reflection and insights. It is tough, because the inclination of most people is to remain talking, explaining away the behavior, or to keep pushing the point home. Pausing gives people time to reflect on their behavior and, most importantly, make it their own.

Example. After sharing the behavior with Jane, I remained silent. Jane responds after a time, "Yes, you are right. I have been concerned about this as well. My boss has loaded up my plate with projects, along with several extra work activities I have taken on. I guess I'll just have to try to be better for the future."

Step Four (optional): If the client does not suggest specific behavior changes, you may have to support them in identifying them. Focus on the end results for the project, and why they are necessary. Obtain buy-in from them, and ensure they own the outcomes and identify their own behavior changes.

Example: (1). "Jane, I certainly know what it is like being over-involved in too many activities. My concern is that if changes are not made early on, our project will not be as successful as it could be. Do you agree?" Jane responds, "Yes."

(2). "What do you see as options to ensure you have time to be fully vested and available for this project going forward?"

Step Five: Identify and agree to clearly defined behavior changes. These behavior changes need to be actionable, and with a realistic date prescribed to accomplish. Once the agreement is made, identify accountability measures to ensure follow-through is accomplished.

Example: (1). Jane responds, "I suppose I could talk with my boss about the workload on my plate, though I am not sure he will remove anything. My other option is to withdraw myself from one of the extra work activities I am involved with."

(2). "Jane, what would be a doable first step for you?" Jane responds, "I can withdraw from the extra work activity by the end of next week. Though I am still worried that my boss doesn't understand the work load this project is going to require."

(3). "So, by Monday, in two weeks, you will have withdrawn from the extra work activity?" Jane responds, "Yes."

(4). "As for your boss, would it help if together we laid out a more thorough project plan, so you could share with him some of the more heavy-lifting activities needed for this project?" Jane responds, "Yes, that would be very helpful. It would also be helpful if you and I could present this information together, since you have done this with other clients before."

(5). "Jane, this is not a problem. I'll pull together a draft plan in the next day or so that we can review at the end of this week. In the meantime, you schedule a meeting with your boss, and withdraw from the work activity. We'll check in on Monday to prepare for the meeting with your boss, and see what happened with your withdrawal from the extra work activity. Does that work for you?" Jane responds, "Yes."

The step-by-step approach provided above does work, though realize that some of the steps take longer to achieve than others. If resistance is strong, it may take several meetings and quite a few back-and-forth conversations to move fully from Step Three into Step Five. As a consultant, you may have to maintain a "tough love" approach to help your client take responsibility for behavior changes, and resulting actions that will address the resistance. There is also a delicate balance between support and co-dependence that you will need to monitor within yourself.

Don't let your propensity to help or your propensity to ignore get in the way of resolving and moving beyond the resistance. Often, the client will not want to acknowledge ingrained behaviors, and may use this to turn around and blame you as the consultant. This is a very human response, as is yours, to get defensive, angry or silent. Acknowledge your feelings, but do not buy into the emotional blackmail. Keep your responses as neutral as possible, and focus on easy-to-achieve behavior changes. Small steps are what will lead to your success.

BEWARE THE OTHER ELEPHANT: CONSULTANT RESISTANCE

Just as your client may be resistant or have barriers that do not support the project, the same is true for you as a consultant. There may be actions you are doing or behaviors that are not supportive to the client's success. Depending on how self-aware you are of your actions, you may easily discern what these are, and be able to make changes relatively seamlessly. The difficulty is when you don't notice or acknowledge your own resistance, but everyone around you is aware of it. There are a couple of ways to tackle this.

First and foremost, rely on your close family and friends to help keep you on the straight and narrow. They can often spot behavior aberrations, and bring them to your attention. As an example, my husband is usually the first one to recognize when I am tired and overstressed. His remark, "Let's schedule a long weekend getaway" is shorthand for you are overstressed, and you need to take a break from work. Use these family and friend clues to modify your behaviors, and make necessary changes to bring your life back into balance. I also recommend reading the last chapter of this book for some insights into how other consultants are tackling and achieving overall work-life balance.

Realize there may be actions or behaviors that only your client sees. Unlike the shorthand you have learned over time with a spouse, partner or close friend, you and your client have not yet developed that relationship. In these cases, you have to demonstrate for your client how to have these discussions in a way that lets the both of you grow and develop. The process outlined below is similar to the one above on client resistance. The difference is that, as a consultant, you have to help your client with language and information that will enable you to clearly see your own resistance, and enable you to take resulting action.

> *There may be actions you are doing or behaviors that are not supportive to the client's success.*

To ensure these discussions are handled in a constructive manner, as opposed to outbursts of frustration, you will need to build in time for you and your client to provide each other feedback. This may be initially done as part of the social contracting, but you will then need to follow up at the end of meetings, especially early on to establish their importance, and a pattern of asking for client feedback. Ask how the relationship is working for them, and if there is anything that you can do to improve it. Refrain from asking this because you have something you want to share with them about their behavior. This should be done long before that happens. More importantly, it muddies the water, and gets too many emotions intertwined. So, follow a similar process to the one presented in the section above.

Step One: Ask your client for feedback. Prepare yourself ahead of time, so that you are open to whatever they have to share. Set the context for the discussion by letting the client know the feedback they provide will help ensure the end results of the project are achieved.

> *Example:* "Jane, we have been working for the last few weeks on this project together. It is my custom to check in with my clients, and learn how I am doing in building our relationship. I find this is helpful to ensure a healthy working relationship. Is there any feedback you could provide me that would help ensure the success of this project?"

Step Two: Be open to listening what they have to say. Acknowledge the feedback. Refrain from arguing or justifying your behavior. Ask for specific examples to help you understand the behaviors they are seeing, and how they are interpreting those behaviors. While understanding your client's point of view, do not immediately suggest behavior actions you can change.

> *Example:* (1) "Susan, I appreciate your taking the time to bring up any issues. To be honest, and this is difficult to share because I really like you, but I have found it difficult working with you over the last few weeks."
> (2). "Jane, thank you for sharing your perspective. Can you offer me some examples of what's not been working for you?"
> (3). "Yes, my schedule is very busy. Often, you will call me a few days prior to our needing to meet. I then have to re-arrange my schedule to try to fit the meeting among already scheduled meetings. This project is important, and I want you to know I am committed, but this lack of notice is frustrating to me and my team."

Step Three: Acknowledge the feedback and, if you agree with it, recommend possible behavior changes you can make. If you don't agree, you may have to ask for additional information to determine how the behavior is manifesting and to clarify what you can control to improve.

> *Example:* (1) "Jane, thank you for helping me to understand your concerns. How much lead time do you typically need for appointment scheduling?" Jane responds, "Two weeks is best case."
> (2). "Would it help to have a weekly (or bi-weekly) scheduled check-in time that could be a standing meeting between the two of us for the remainder of this project?" Jane responds, "Yes, that would be helpful."

(3). "Not a problem. My one concern is what do we do if emergency decisions need to be made, or we need to connect right away? What would be the best way to coordinate that with your schedule needs?" Jane responds, "Send me a text that we need to connect, and I'll do the same for you. I will then either call you back by the end of day, or have my support team schedule time.

Step Four: With any behavior changes identified, recommend dates to complete and follow up to ensure accountability is ensured.

Example: "Jane, let's check in at the end of two weeks hence and ensure the changes we have made are working out for both of us." Jane responds, "That works for me. Thank you for being open to improving our working relationship."

Owning and taking actions to adjust our own human failings is not as easy as presented in the process above. Just as our clients' behaviors are ingrained, so are our own as consultants. Allow yourself some emotional support to make mistakes and learn from them. Use the check back with clients to gauge your success, and celebrate milestones achieved either on your part or that of your clients.

Be honest with yourself and your client if there are behaviors you know will take longer to change, or that you know you don't want to change. Acknowledge this with respect to your client's situation as well. In some cases, this may mean having another person on your team step in or bringing in a subcontractor to coordinate the work with your client because of extreme differences. Most often, it will not come to this type of dilemma, but be prepared to go there if needed.

CLIENT RETENTION AFTER THE ENGAGEMENT

> . . . about a third of the way through the consulting assignment, ask your client for a written testimonial. . . .

Once the engagement or project is completed, this should not end your relationship with the client. Unlike the old Western movies where the cowboy rides off into the sunset after saving the town, you need to stay in contact with your client. This is not just because you have built up a healthy relationship (and perhaps a friendship) over the length of the project, but also for future work opportunities, and ways to elevate each other's success.

When you are about a third of the way through the consulting assignment, ask your client for a written testimonial, as well as for referrals to other clients. This was always difficult for me until I learned from a client how much they appreciated my effort and follow-up. Look for other ways you can involve them in your work, and get them some publicity as well. Perhaps there might be an opportunity to co-write a paper on the results of a project or co-present at a future professional association conference. What about writing up the results to be featured in an internal house newsletter? All of these activities will help the two of you stay connected once the project has been completed.

Other ways to stay in touch include adding your client as a recipient to your company's newsletter or whatever periodic publication you provide. Share with them special articles you have read or papers you have written that might be especially helpful to the work you know they are doing in their company, or that is occurring within the industry. Invite them to networking events or presentations where you will be speaking, if you believe the topics will be of interest to them.

Another activity that several consultants have suggested to me is to hold an Executive Breakfast for several of your client contacts. Bring them together, share information you have been researching on a topic relevant to them, and then create the opportunity for them to discuss the latest issues they have been dealing with in their business. As part of your marketing strategy, you might want to invite a few individuals who are not currently clients, as a way to acquaint them with the work you do and the successful results that other clients have achieved.

GROWING AND DEVELOPING AS A CONSULTANT

While this entire chapter has been about client retention and building successful client-consultant relationships both during and after the engagement, you also need to be growing and developing yourself as a consultant and business owner. This means not just retaining clients, but also, according to Alan Weiss (1992), having a plan for relinquishing the bottom 15 percent of your market. At some point, maybe not your first or second year into business, but eventually, you will realize that projects you did when you first started are not as profitable or fulfilling to you as a consultant. Having built up a reputation for client retention and successful client-consultant relationships, how do you plan for this inevitability? There are a couple of options.

The first is to determine if you want to bring on associates (often termed subcontractors) or employees to handle this type of work. If so, what types of individuals would best represent you, your business values, and your level of excellence in working with clients? Certainly, you are looking to bring on subcontractors or employees who have the skills, knowledge, and expertise to do the work. Even more important is how they will fit within the culture and environment you have established for your business. Realize that if you choose this route, you are really not getting rid of the business, merely shifting it to others, while it is still under your purview. And that may be fine. Just recognize that the client will still associate you with this type of work.

The other option is to determine, based on how you want your business to expand, that you will not accept certain follow-up engagements. If there are certain ongoing client projects or work that you do which just don't fit your business model any longer, you might want to bring in someone on a subcontractor relationship on a one-year basis. Get that person and the client acquainted, and use this as the opportunity to transition the work. Then, turn over that portion of the business to the subcontractor for the future. Have him or her bring you back in when there is some juicy project that would fit your expanded business model.

Most importantly, have the conversation early on with your client about your decision to divest your company of certain types of business. Let them know you will find a replacement to fill the void or better yet, work with them to determine how the work can be handled internally. Perhaps there is an add-on portion of the project that enables you to train certain individuals within the client organization to take on work that you have normally done as a consultant. The client will appreciate your looking out for their best interests, as well as your willingness to educate those within the organization on what you do and how to transfer those skills and knowledge.

CONCLUSION

As you've probably figured out, client retention takes time, energy, and investment in the client-consultant relationship. As shared in the beginning, the payoffs are tremendous for both establishing, and then growing and developing your business. More importantly, successful client-consultant relationships turn out to be the honey that sweetens each and every day of consulting. As you move forward in developing these relationships, ask yourself the following:

- How do I continue to incorporate client retention concepts and beliefs into my business values and brand, especially as they evolve over time?
- Based on lessons learned from past client engagements, what do I need to further incorporate into my client discussions to ensure successful client-consultant relationships?

- How am I assessing client resistance and discussing in a way that supports both me and my client's development?
- What practices have I incorporated to ask my clients for feedback throughout the course of the consulting engagement, as well as afterwards?
- What actions am I taking to continue my learning and growth, both as both a consultant and business owner?

This chapter has discussed how to develop successful client-consultant relationships. And while it has touched on making decisions and choices as a consultant that are aligned with your values, part of that means also being clear about the ethical practices and policies you will follow with respect to your business, and the work you do with clients. The next chapter shares specific guidance and direction for you in those areas.

BIBLIOGRAPHY

Block, Peter. 1981. *Flawless Consulting: A Guide to Getting Your Expertise Used*. San Diego: Pfeiffer & Company.

Hall, Stacy and Jan Brogniez. 2001. *Attracting Perfect Customers: The Power of Strategic Synchonicity*. Oakland, CA: Berrett-Koehler Publishing.

LaGrossa, Virginia and Suzanne Saxe. 1998. *The Consultative Approach: Partnering for Results*. San Francisco: Jossey-Bass/Pfeiffer.

Jones, Rod. 2007. "Interview with Rod Jones" in Levinson, Jay Conrad, et al., *Marketing Strategies That Really Work!* Sevierville, TN: Insight Publishing.

Small Business Administration, Office of Advocacy. 2014. "Frequently Asked Questions" (retrieved December 8, 2014). www.sba.gov/sites/default/files/advocacy/ FAQ_March2014_0.pdf

Weiss, Alan. 2002. *How to Establish a Unique Brand in the Consulting Profession: Powerful Techniques for the Successful Practitioner* (The Ultimate Consultant Series). San Francisco: Jossey-Bass/Pfeiffer.

Weiss, Alan. 1992. *Million Dollar Consulting: The Professional's Guide to Growing a Practice*. New York: McGraw-Hill, Inc.

Weiss, Alan. 2003. *Organizational Consulting: How to Be an Effective Internal Change Agent*. New Jersey: John Wiley & Sons, Inc.

Weiss, Alan. 2001. *The Ultimate Consultant: Powerful Techniques for the Successful Practitioner*. San Francisco: Jossey-Bass/Pfeiffer.

APPENDIX

Value Cards

Note: Use the words that speak to you as an individual or as an organization. Add words if you do not see them there. Take out ones that do not make sense. In other words, tailor the deck to your needs.

Adventure	**Service**	**Be imaginative**
Collaboration	**Stewardship**	**Build**
Influence	**Inspire**	**Contribute**
Serve	**Improve**	**Learn**
Detect	**Facilitate**	**Foster**
Catalyze	**Have Impact**	**Design**
Teach	**Be part of family**	**Be expert**

Questions to ask:

Do I know the code of professional conduct for the safety profession? Is it voluntary or mandatory?

What standard of ethical behavior is required in the safety profession?

What are the consequences if I act in an unethical or unprofessional manner?

CHAPTER 9

Ethics and Other Professional Issues

BY DANIEL J. SNYDER, M.Ed, CSP, CET, CHMM, OHST, CHST, STS

Daniel Snyder holds a B.A. in Science and Biology and an M.Ed in Adult Education and Human Resource Development. He is a past-president of the Arkansas Chapter of the ASSE and serves on several ASSE/ANSI standards committees. Dan has 20 years of global consulting experience helping clients develop strategies for improving safety performance through gap analysis, coaching top management, developing supervisors and facilitating a safe work culture. He is a recognized professional demonstrating expertise in the technical subject matter of certification exam blueprints, psychometrics, human performance technology, and instructional systems design. An accomplished facilitator of applied adult learning principles, Dan is dedicated to advancing professional development. Based in Nixa MO, Dan owns the Performance Based Safety LLC consulting firm and SPAN International Training LLC specializing in certification examination preparation and mentoring. He is currently a doctoral candidate at the University Arkansas for Adult and Lifelong Learning.

T<small>HE QUESTIONS THAT</small> opened this chapter are only a few of the questions that any reputable consultant must think through and answer. The consultant, perhaps more than other safety professional, must develop an internal moral compass, his or her own guiding principles. No company or supervisor will be on hand to provide this guidance or to hold you accountable. You need to generate your own sense of self-respect and responsibility.

Before you considered a career in safety consulting, you had many influences working upon you (this is what socialization is all about): teachers, mentors, employers, and more. The questions we will raise here will provide you the opportunity to think for yourself, to break free of group-think, and to think through potential dilemmas before they arise. As a consultant, you have the opportunity to question a prior employer's ethics, and to act for yourself. A consultant is only as good as his or her independence of judgment, as his or her ability to make timely but surefooted decisions. With more latitude for action, you will discover quickly that there is no substitute for sound judgment, reasoned reflection, a robust sense of justice and fair play.

Ethical reflection creates an immediate benefit for the individual who, through reflection, can discover other possibilities of being and behaving. But it is also invaluable for another reason. You are in a position of genuine responsibility. In fact, you are assuming an extensive range of responsibilities. The welfare of other people depends directly on the choices you, as a consultant, make.

The top five things I've learned about ethics are:

1. It is important to understand ethics and to know the professional codes of conduct before being faced with an ethical dilemma.
2. Published codes of professional conduct can serve as guidance.
3. Being objective helps to keep a steady moral compass. "Objectivity" in professional ethics means that there are principles and values outside of oneself that the members of the community share and can discuss, and that individuals will be measured against.
4. It helps to seek the advice of colleagues. Ask what a reasonable peer would do in the same situation. Solving ethical problems is more clear-cut when one is informed, well-intentioned, objective, rational, detached but empathetic, unbiased, sane, and sober.
5. Every consultant will need to make decisions that challenge personal ethics.

DEFINING ETHICS

Ethics is a rational reflection upon good and evil (without weighing in on the question of heaven or hell, angels and demons). The word *ethics* refers to our identification of the "good" in any given situation as well as the rationale for the identification. Consider an example:

> A friend has come to your door seeking a place to hide. He says that he is being pursued by a maniac and that his life is in danger. The good, in this context, might be identified as friendship or as loyalty. If so, it is likely you will take the desperate man into your home. Let's say that this is what you do.
>
> Sure enough, Crazy Dave (the maniac) appears at your door. He demands that you produce your friend so that he can shoot him. As you can see, everything depends at this moment on what gets identified as the good. We know what the good is for the friend (staying alive and unharmed) and for Crazy Dave (shooting your friend). But what will it be for you? Let's say you call to mind the old adage

that honesty is always the best policy, so you confess that the friend is hiding in a closet just down the hallway. Because you don't see any advantage in physically grappling with Crazy Dave, the maniac pushes right past you, and shoots and kills your friend.

> *You must not only behave ethically; you must strive to encourage ethical behavior in others.*

At every step there has been a reflection, however brief, upon the desired outcome (the good). But it is not at all clear that the rationale at each point, the justification for choosing one good over another, is sensible. Ethics engages each of us at the level of the thought, the reasoning process that goes into every decision we make, whether for our own happiness or that of another. Sound ethical judgment arises when proper habits of thought have given way to confidence in the right conduct and in doing it.

As safety consultants (and mature adults), there is no flight from precisely this kind of deliberation. We have to make choices that are responsible, defensible, and appropriate. Decide upon the highest good and order all of the others, the lesser goods, in a hierarchy. This could be applied to a risk assessment or matrix.

There are rigorous professional guidelines and regulations regarding ethics for a safety consultant. Below is a list of some of them:

- American Society of Safety Engineers' Code of Professional Conduct (see Appendix A)
- Board of Certified Safety Professionals Code of Ethics and Professional Conduct (see Appendix B)
- American Industrial Hygiene Association and American Conference of Governmental Industrial Hygienists Joint Ethical Principles
- American Board of Industrial Hygiene Code of Ethics (see Appendix C)
- International Code of Ethics for Occupational Health Professionals
- Federal Contractor Code of Business Ethics and Conduct (48 CFR 3.10)
- American Society of Civil Engineers Code of Ethics
- National Society of Professional Engineers Code of Ethics
- Institute of Hazardous Materials Management Code of Ethics

As a consultant, you must be familiar with the codes of conduct pertinent to your work. However, in and of themselves, they are insufficient. You must also develop a robust code of personal ethics. The avoidance of wrong is not the same as doing right. The disinclination to behave improperly is not the same as a lifelong commitment to human dignity and ennobling goals. Consultants must honor a high ethical standard, one that encompasses not just yourself but your clients, your colleagues, and your community. You must not only behave ethically; you must strive to encourage ethical behavior in others.

Examples of unethical behavior in the realm of occupational safety and health (OS&H) consulting could be found in any of the countless aspects of the job, just a few of which we will discuss in this chapter. However, one especially sensitive responsibility is for the training of others. Consider the following:

A training consultant documents the full number of OSHA-required hours while having, in fact, only provided some fraction of them. In this case, problems arise not simply because the consultant made a decision concerning his relationship to extant law, the decision that he or she needn't honor it. There are more far-reaching consequences: The trainee now is ill-equipped to achieve legal compliance, possibly without his knowledge. And in this case, the compliance at issue concerns the safety of the workplace, and hence adverse consequences for an incalculable number of people. In the single gesture of falsifying documents, the consultant providing training has potentially discredited the safety profession and the moral understanding upon which it rests (e.g., the right to be reasonably free from harm in the workplace, the right to be properly informed by an employer of potential hazards, and the tacit compact between well-intentioned people of the barest minimum of vigilance concerning each other and the general welfare).

Now consider some concrete instances of ethically informed choices, choices that may or may not have been in the immediate best interests of the consultant. (This too is something that will have to be thought through.) Imagine a situation in which you, as a consultant, despite extraordinary pressures, go on record with a client about a reporting error that would entirely undermine the company's claim of a million man-hours without an accident, resulting in lost time. You may be encouraged to keep quiet about the reporting error—and this encouragement can take any number of forms—and while you might be intimidated or tempted and envision some such short-term self-interest in honoring the client's wishes, the long-term consequences for you are disastrous. It isn't only a matter of losing credibility, and by no means limited to the single client (who may be motivated to retaliate against you in any number of ways), but the choice made suggests poor judgment and, at the barest minimum, a failure to take into account all pertinent variables. A consultant with poor judgment is not long for the profession. Illicit deals made in private seldom stay private.

There will also be quite public choices to be made, ones that will broadcast immediately the state of the consultant's judgment. Imagine you are working with a small construction firm. You visit a site that involves trench work. The foreman is pushing to complete the job quickly; however, you believe the trench is in peril of immediate collapse. You draw upon your own authority to evacuate workers from the trench over the demonstrative objections of the foreman. In such a case, your ability to reach a sound decision that reflects widespread standards of human decency will be available for all to see and evaluate. In fact, in this moment, both you and the client occupy a uniquely public position. You can as directly retain the good standing of the client (by vetoing the foreman's wishes) as condemn the company to public disgrace. In the absence of prophetic foresight, the best course is to take the best course, to choose what is best, to take a rationally grounded ethical stand.

ETHICS FOR OS&H CONSULTANTS

Consider the philosophy on professional ethics in Supreme Court Justice Sandra Day O'Conner's dissenting opinion on the case of *Shapero v. Kentucky Bar Association*, a lawyer advertising ruling:

> One distinguishing feature of any profession is that membership in that profession entails an ethical obligation to temper one's selfish pursuit of economic success by adhering to standards of conduct that could not be enforced either by legal fiat or through the discipline of the market. Both the special privileges incident to membership in the profession, and the advantages those privileges give in the necessary task of earning a living, are the means to a goal that transcends the accumulation of wealth. That goal is public service. (Lewis 1995)

It is true that all manner of professional codes and criteria exist for OS&H consultants, and for good reason. There are the Codes of Ethics and Professional Conduct as set forth by the Board of Certified Safety Professionals (BCSP), the standards of the American Society of Safety Engineers (ASSE), those of the National Society of Professional Engineers (NSPE), and of the American Board of Industrial Hygienists (ABIH). These myriad protocols and regulations, norms, and expectations are grounded in the obligation to further the human welfare generally. That this is the central preoccupation is hardly surprising. Ethics, the mere existence of ethical questions, implies the shared assumption that human beings—of necessity generally conceived—have value, and no ethical discussion is possible in the absence of this assumption. That is, if I argue that smoking cigarettes is bad, I don't have to further stipulate "bad for human beings." The assumption of the scope of the assertion (as one concerning the welfare of human beings) goes without saying. If I make this assertion about cigarettes, and my opponent makes the counterclaim that human life is without value, there can be no discussion. We cannot reason the difference through together. We cannot collaborate in ethical discourse.

So the scope of our concern has widened without losing any of its focus. The overlap between your professional and your personal well-being is complete. Forget about any hard and fast application of the adage about the firewall between personal and professional life ("Don't take your private business to work," "Don't drag your work home with you," and so on). The all-important judgment you exercise at work has been formed in every aspect of your life, and this same judgment or executive reason will forever be called upon in affairs professional and private—and, quite literally, constantly. Every choice, monumental and trivial, refers to the identification and belief in (the placing of credence upon the assumption of strong reasons) some "good." Ultimately, each of us must be responsible for our choices, whether we are group-thinkers or not. We will each be responsible, at least, in the sense that our lot, for better or worse, will be determined by them. However, as already intimated, the consulting profession has treated the distinction between right and wrong, justifiable and unjustifiable behavior with supreme seriousness, and you will have to find your place within the guidelines that have already been established. Your place will be unique, your own, the result of the ethical contemplation you undertake, but at the same time within the established framework.

> *You are a professional, and as such your work cannot be "all about you."*

One key feature of this framework can be expressed in the word *service*. In this word, no connotation of degrading subordination is intended. It is crucial that you come to understand your profession as always "in service to. . . ." Your work is only about you to the extent that it is in service to some wider objective. You are a professional, and as such your work cannot be "all about you."

Potential Ethical Dilemmas for Consultants

Ethical choices are not simply "in the eye of the beholder." "How well you sleep at night" is not of ethical significance. If such commonplace assumptions were even remotely accurate, there would be so little basis for law and social order that it would all seem transparently arbitrary and pointless. But it doesn't. Individuals and corporations face indictments, lawsuits, fines, and jail sentences every day, and we distinguish between Enron and Costco, Bernard Madoff and Albert Schweitzer. We do not think the difference merely imaginary.

Since the Sarbanes-Oxley Act (2002)[1] and the bundled-mortgage catastrophe of 2008, momentum has been building in the general public for a higher standard of ethics in the business community. In 2013, JP Morgan faced fines

---

[1] The Act mandated a number of reforms to enhance corporate responsibility, enhance financial disclosures, combat corporate and accounting fraud, creating the Public Company Accounting Oversight Board, to oversee the activities of the auditing profession. The full text of the Act is available at www.sec.gov/about/laws/soa2002.pdf.

in the billions of dollars to settle the mortgage-backed securities fraud case with the Justice Department (DOJ OPA 2013b). In 2013, Johnson and Johnson agreed to pay more than $2.2 billion to resolve criminal allegations that include off-label marketing and kickbacks to doctors and pharmacists. In October of 2013, a federal judge sentenced the former president of Port Arthur Chemical and Environmental Services LLC (Texas) to one year in prison, ordering him to pay fines in the amount of $5,000 for violations of the OSH Act and for making a false statement about transportation documents to conceal wastewater shipments with high concentrations of hydrogen sulfide (DOJ OPA 2013a).

From the garment industry, with its disastrous outsourcing to Bangladesh and other less-developed countries, to the multinational banks that fixed overnight bank rates, every sector of the economy has reason to be more ethically introspective than ever before. As a consultant, you may find that many large companies you work with have invested in ethics training for management as a response to these recent high-profile cases. You would do well to become familiar with your clients' ethical guidelines.

In many cases when unethical or unprofessional behavior is identified, the individual company determines the disciplinary action, up to and including discharge of the safety professional or safety consultant. Where you do not have a corporate entity determining your code of ethics, as a consultant you would be wise to develop one yourself. Professional organizations such as ASSE, ABIH, and BCSP all have professional codes of conduct that can be adopted.

The Safety Consultants' Code of Conduct

The adoption of the properly ethical attitude is dependent on giving time over to introspection. Let's look at several possible ethical situations that you may face as a safety consultant.

Case Studies in "Throat-Cutting"

Imagine you are working under contract for another consultant (X). Consultant X's client approaches you and inquires whether he can hire you directly, thereby cutting out Consultant X. The client insists that he is not motivated by the potential cost savings, but that he prefers your work to that of Consultant X and is looking for a new consultant. In this situation, you could:

- Reject the offer.
- Go to work for the client, making Consultant X's client your client.
- Explain that you are working for Consultant X and must remain in that capacity with respect to the scope of the contract.

- Inform Consultant X that you have been approached by the client to work directly for him.
- Suggest the client take his issues directly to Consultant X.
- Recommend that the client, Consultant X, and you schedule a meeting to determine the issues and how to best proceed.

Let's look at additional questions for each option:

- If you reject the offer, would you then continue to work for Consultant X?
- If you accept the offer, converting Consultant X's clients to yours, what would you then do about your relationship with Consultant X? Have you violated any contractual obligations? What happens to your relationship with Consultant X? What happens to future referrals? Could this impact your reputation in terms of referrals from other consultants?
- If you reject the offer, keeping the relationship with Consultant X, do you lose a potential new client? Is your professional reputation at stake? If so, in what way?
- If you let Consultant X know that the client approached you, are you clear on what you hope the outcome will be? Why let Consultant X know? Does this option provide the opportunity to determine a mutually agreeable outcome?
- If you suggest the client talk directly to Consultant X, are you putting the client in an awkward position? Does that matter? What are the advantages and disadvantages to this approach? Can a mutually agreeable outcome be determined?
- Under which scenarios would you want to review the language of your contractual obligations with Consultant X?
- If you schedule a meeting with all parties, could Consultant X feel as though you and the client are "ganging up?" Are there steps you can take before the meeting to facilitate a mutually beneficial outcome?

In this case, a couple of the bullets may be appropriate depending on the circumstances, but perhaps the best ethical solution is described in the last option, whereby all parties are involved with a win-win solution.

Case Studies in "Padding the Hours"

You are working with a client who discovers the amount budgeted for a project is significantly more than anticipated. A contact with the client company suggests that you "pad" your expenses, as the client was prepared to pay more for the project anyway. You could:

- Pad expenses to use up the client's budget.
- Reject the suggestion to pad the expenses and add billable hours to the invoice.
- Reject padding the hours and/or expenses as unethical and counter with an offer to explore other projects where you can add value.
- Reject padding as unethical and report the incident to the contact's supervisor.

This type of scenario is fairly common in the consulting world, and you will likely face it. The best option is to reject the idea of padding hours or expenses and explore other projects.

The BCSP Code of Ethics and Professional Conduct states that safety professionals must "be honest, fair and impartial; act with responsibility and integrity." In addition, they must, "[c]onduct their professional relations by the highest standards of integrity and avoid compromise of their professional judgment by conflicts of interest" (BCSP 2012). Padding hours could be construed as not acting with integrity.

Padding hours would violate the American Board of Industrial Hygienists' Code of Ethics, which states: "Provide truthful and accurate representations to the public in advertising, public statements or representations, and in the preparation of estimates concerning costs, services and expected results."

Case Study on Fees and Expert Witness Work

You have been approached by an attorney to serve as an expert witness. The attorney offers you 5% of the award when the case is won. What are your choices?

- Accept the percentage offered.
- Reject the offer and suggest a flat hourly fee.
- Accept the offer but only after you have examined the case thoroughly to ensure that it is winnable.
- Reject the offer after reviewing the case.

What other options come to mind?

It is always best to counter with a flat hourly rate. Consider how you would answer the question of compensation when you are on the witness stand. You can indeed serve as an expert witness, but not as an interested party (one who receives a share of any monetary award). Your testimony ought to be impartial and determined only by the merits of the case.

Case Studies in "The F-Word"

Falsification is the F-word in OS&H profession; it epitomizes unethical behavior. The following are several case studies highlighting the pertinent ethical principle of candor and transparency.

As an external safety consultant for a high-profile international company, you discover that a site safety professional has intentionally falsified the OSHA 300 log. You also discover that management receives significant bonuses based partially on the OSHA log numbers. Here are a few options:

- Let the discrepancy go, and assume there is other oversight.
- Say nothing, as this is an internal company issue.
- Verify your numbers, and notify your handler/point of contact of the discrepancy.
- Identify the discrepancy in the next management meeting.
- Request a meeting with the CEO to express concerns about the recordkeeping.
- Contact the regional OSHA administrator, and report the falsification.
- Call a press conference, claim whistleblower protection, and bask in your five minutes of fame.

Can you think of other options?

This scenario is based on a 2013 Justice Department case (DOJ ED Tenn 2013) against a company where management received over $2 million in bonuses due to the falsified data. Once discovered, the company paid over $5 million in fines and the safety professional was indicted, convicted, and is currently facing jail time.

The issue of honest reporting comes into play constantly, applying to more than just OSHA 300 logs. Consider another situation: After being hired as the new interim OS&H consultant, you discover that the previous environmental consultant appears to have falsified pollution discharge permits. You cannot replicate sample results, even though company testing procedures have not changed. How would you handle this?

- Assume that your predecessor's results are correct and modify your results to match the historical results.
- Stop monitoring and wait until the new full-time OS&H professional is hired.
- Investigate any process changes that may account for the increased levels as compared to previous results.
- Contact your predecessor to determine methods or other information that may support his data and explain the discrepancy.

- Contact EPA and the state Department of Environmental Quality/ Natural Resources and ask for an inspector to visit and verify results.
- Submit your results in the next report to the state.
- Contact the regulatory authority and schedule a meeting to modify the parameters of the discharge permit.
- Notify your contact at the company about the discrepancies, your concerns, any due diligence, and propose a plan to move forward.

Are there other options that you think of?

A combination of some of these choices may be ethical, but the best solution is to notify your client in the capacity of an unbiased agent. You would thereby be in compliance with the ASSE code of professional conduct that obligates you to "serve the public, employees, employers, clients, society, and the profession with fidelity, honesty, and impartiality" (ASSE 2012).

In a case quite similar to the hypothetical one above, a contracted consultant in the state of Mississippi provided false laboratory reports for effluent readings. The environmental consultant was found guilty in an eight-day trial and is facing sentencing of up to 20 years' incarceration and a $250,000 fine (DOJ OPA 2013c).

Case Studies in "Making the Client Happy"

A manufacturing firm hired me to evaluate their programs and facility for hazards and OSHA compliance gaps. The facility was very subpar, and the culture was that of compliance avoidance. During the audits, it was determined that the previous consulting firm sent unqualified consultants into the facility monthly for a 15-minute walk around and safety meeting. The previous consultants did not evaluate site hazards or make recommendations to management. After the third visit without the client implementing any recommendations for hazard control or improving OSHA compliance, I requested a meeting with the plant manager, my liaison. He informed me that during their site visits, the previous consulting group recommended that if OSHA showed up, the company should just call the consultants to get out of the OSHA fine. Based on that, he believed he didn't need to fix the issues. If you were faced with this situation, what are some possible options?

A consultant will invariably at some point come upon a client who is compliance-avoidant.

- Continue with scheduled site visits and focus only on issues not previously reported.
- Continue reporting on all OSHA compliance gaps discovered during the site audits, make recommendations for hazard abatement, and encourage management to address the issues as per the scope of your contract.

- Contact the union and help organizing efforts.
- File an OSHA complaint.
- Refuse to continue to work with that client.

Are there other options that you can think of?

A consultant will invariably at some point come upon a client who is compliance-avoidant. Such a client can be abetted by consulting firms that serve to conceal violations and otherwise make detection difficult. If the client's attitude towards compliance cannot be changed, as a consultant you must decide if you want to continue working for this type of company. Along with reviewing your insurance liability, consider related OS&H professional codes of conduct:

- "Make informed decisions in the performance of professional duties that adhere to all relevant laws, regulations, and recognized standards of practice" and "inform all appropriate parties when professional judgment indicates that there is an unacceptable level of risk of injury, illness, property damage, or environmental harm" (ASSE 2012).
- "Be honest, fair, and impartial; act with responsibility and integrity. Adhere to high standards of ethical conduct with balanced care for the interests of the public, employers, clients, employees, colleagues and the profession. Avoid all conduct or practice that is likely to discredit the profession or deceive the public" (BSCP 2012).
- "Deliver competent services with objective and independent professional judgment in decision-making (ABIH 2007).
- At the beginning, follow appropriate health and safety procedures, in the course of performing professional duties, to protect clients, employers, employees and the public from conditions where injury and damage are reasonably foreseeable" (ABIH 2007).

Case Studies in "Authority"

A serious violation of OSHA regulations has been brought to your attention by a facility employee during a walk-around inspection. After a brief discussion, the employee tells you that he has notified his supervisor, and nothing is ever corrected. Should you:

- Direct the employee to correct the hazard himself.
- Advise the employee to contact OSHA.
- Get the employee's name and contact OSHA on behalf of the employee.
- Submit a work order.
- Verify that the concern is a legitimate OSHA compliance issue and document it on your report to the client.

- Recommend that the employee notify his supervisor again and discuss the issue with the client, without identifying the employee.

What other options can you think of?

Again, more than one option could be ethical, depending on your level of authority with the client. The key here is to know, without a doubt, what your role is as a consultant and what authority, if any, you have to initiate corrective action. At a minimum, you should immediately notify the client of the OSHA violation and register concern about employees having reported the hazard without abatement. This could be an opportunity to work with the client on hazard identification, proper reporting and abatement, and efficient processing of employee complaints. Be certain to address any activities in the scope of work and specific contractual language that will provide guidance for all parties.

> *I have found that the best clients are forgiving. In other words, they trust your guidance and value your advice as a consultant.*

The ethical course will always be to:

- maintain and respect the confidentiality of sensitive information obtained in the course of professional activities unless: the information is reasonably understood to pertain to unlawful activity; a court or governmental agency lawfully directs the release of the information; the client or the employer expressly authorizes the release of specific information; or, the failure to release such information would likely result in death or serious physical harm to employees and/or the public (ABIH 2007).

There are caveats to any scenarios, such as: Is this a current client with whom you have a strong relationship, or a new client? Does that make a difference?

I have found that the best clients are forgiving. In other words, they trust your guidance and value your advice as a consultant. This rapport is built over time, so if it is a current, long-standing client, you may be in a better position to work though issues with more latitude, since you understand the business of the client and their goals. New clients pose a different issue, since it takes a fair amount of time to get up to speed with the client's culture, goals, and business environment. You must assess the environment, commitment to safety, budgeting for projects, and so on. Different clients call for different solutions.

Case Studies in "Professional Competency"

Suppose that you are a consultant, a CSP with a degree in adult education, and you have been asked to approve plans for a fall protection system design on a work platform. You do not have any experience with designing fall protection systems, and you are not a registered professional engineer. How should you handle this scenario?

Consider these options:

- Reject the offer and recommend the company hire a professional engineer with fall protection design experience.
- Reject the offer and recommend another consultant who has expertise in the design of fall protection systems.
- Accept the offer and then find a subject matter expert as a subcontractor to review the plans and advise you if you should approve the system design.
- Accept the offer with a stipulation to bring in a professional engineer to review the structural drawings before the system is built.
- Accept the offer and read up on fall protection design systems to acquire the requisite knowledge.

Are there other options that you think of?

When evaluating whether or not to accept work outside of the scope of your core competencies, consider whether you can bring yourself up to a level of competency needed for this work in a timely manner that best serves the client.

The solution is not a one size fits all. Your relationship with the client (new, long-standing, casual, on-site weekly) may influence your decision. It may also depend on exactly what the client is asking of you. Professional competency and credibility is the bread and better of consulting. You must determine if what the client is asking for is within your scope of expertise. If not, can you realistically bring yourself up to speed to serve the client needs, or would it be best to subcontract or refer the company to a more competent consultant in that specialty area?

Anyone who claims to specialize in all areas is likely to be working outside of his or her areas of competence.

There are several reasons to consider referring to a qualified professional. When possible, as noted in the ABIH Code of Ethics, you should "make a reasonable effort to provide appropriate professional referrals when unable to provide competent professional assistance" (ABIH 2007). This course of action is not only ethically appropriate, it avoids possible liability, and it is consistent with self-interest. It is an opportunity to build a consultant referral network and win the goodwill of a number of parties.

It is my experience that knowing when to refer, as well as the professional to whom you are referring, is critically important. Referrals and subcontracting can bolster your credibility, serve the client, and broaden your network of professionals that, in turn, will pay dividends. The client will also know that you are honest about your abilities and will more likely trust and implement your advice.

As a consultant, you will undoubtedly face the limits of your knowledge, skills, and abilities as you work with clients to meet their needs. OS&H professional ethics provides guidance for these situations, including:

- "Continually improve professional knowledge, skills, competencies, and awareness of relevant new developments through training, education, networking, and work experiences.
- "Consider qualifications before undertaking any professional activity and perform only those services that may be handled competently.
- "Accurately represent professional qualifications including education, credentials, designations, affiliations, titles, and work experience.
- "Undertake assignments only when qualified by education or experience in the specific technical fields involved.
- "Accept responsibility for their continued professional development by acquiring and maintaining competence through continuing education, experience, professional training, and keeping current on relevant legal issues" (ASSE 2012).
- "Recognize the limitations of one's professional ability and provide services only when qualified. The certificant/candidate is responsible for determining the limits of his/her own professional abilities based on education, knowledge, skills, practice experience and other relevant considerations.
- "Make a reasonable effort to provide appropriate professional referrals when unable to provide competent professional assistance" (ABIH 2007).

You may find, as a safety consultant, that clients look to you for management consulting as well, especially if the company is looking to hire an in-house OS&H position. You may be asked to assist in identifying and defining the competencies required for a specific task, such as when a Request for Proposal (RFP) is issued for other consulting work or for in-house jobs.

While serving as an interim contracted safety officer for a large regional medical center, I was tasked with assisting the management team with interviewing candidates for the full-time safety position. The favored candidate presented an ideal resume for the position and had successfully made it through two rounds of interviews that were focused on the medical center environment. During the final interview, I began to ask specific safety professional questions that any Certified Safety Professional (CSP) with the background displayed on her resumé should have been able to easily answer and discuss. The responses were surprisingly deficient, to the point that, during the break, I checked the BCSP website and determined that this person was not a CSP. The candidate did not return for the final phase of the interview. This situation can apply to hiring consultants as well.

Misrepresentation of your qualifications and certifications can result in being disqualified from achieving professional certifications in the future. The ASSE Code of Professional Conduct states that you should "accurately represent professional qualifications including education, credentials, designations, affiliations, titles, and work experience" (ASSE 2012). In addition, the Code stipulates that you should achieve and maintain competency in the practice of the profession and perform professional services only in areas of competence.

The OS&H profession is very broad, with numerous areas of specialization. Anyone who claims to specialize in all areas is likely to be working outside of his or her areas of competence. Instead, successful consultants focus on those areas in which they are the most competent. Those areas could be anything: system and process safety, fire protection, industrial hygiene, ergonomics, training, hazardous material management, construction safety, and so on.

The mere possession of a given credential does not in itself constitute proof of competency. Competency must be evaluated in terms of education and training, both formal and informal, and practical experience. Most areas of specialization also offer additional certifications. Putting in the effort to achieve the specialized certification extends one's expertise beyond the basics and can open the way to opportunities in business or professional growth.

OS&H consultants can be called upon to work in an enormous variety of settings: manufacturing, insurance, risk management, government, education, consulting, construction, healthcare, engineering and design, waste management, petroleum, facilities management, retail, transportation, and utilities. Whatever the context, consultants must tailor their capabilities to fit the mission, operations, and culture of their clients. As such, the consultant should consider the knowledge, skills, and abilities needed to provide ethical, competent service to those clients.

Simply attaining a certification is not sufficient. OS&H consultants must be committed lifelong learners, willing to acquire and maintain the knowledge and skills to perform their functions effectively. Continuing education and training will allow one to remain current with emerging technologies, laws and regulations, and changes in the workforce, workplace and world business, political, and social climate.

By acquiring the requisite knowledge and skills, the attitude and wisdom to act responsibly in the employment context; by keeping up with changes in all aspects of your field, the OS&H consultant is able to perform to the highest standards with confidence, competence, and authority.

CONCLUSION

Making ethical decisions is not easy, especially when the situation involves multiple points of view, conflicting objectives, competing priorities, incomplete knowledge or ambiguity. A valued OS&H consultant must learn to recognize ethical issues and think through the consequences of alternative solutions to make sound moral judgments.

The keys to an ethical OS&H consulting practice are to demonstrate fairness, honesty, and impartiality in all situations. Consider the following basic questions as they apply to your consulting practice.

When advising clients:

1. Am I competent? I consider the scope of work and required qualifications before undertaking professional services.
2. Is it legal? I deliver informed advice about relevant laws, regulations, and standards of best practice.
3. Is it fair? I serve as a competent, unbiased, faithful agent providing truthful statements.
4. Is it right? I demonstrate uncompromising professional conduct, avoid conflicts of interest, and serve with fidelity, honesty, and impartiality.

A moral dilemma occurs when two moral explanations lead to conflicting moral decisions. The following are three solutions to a moral dilemma:

1. Develop a creative third alternative that satisfies both moral outcomes.
2. When possible, act sequentially on each to satisfy both sides of the dilemma.
3. Evaluation over time will show which is the strongest moral explanation and decision.

Strong moral reasons are those that are relevant to the decision, are concerned with the person most affected by the decision, and are focused on values of central importance. Moral perspectives help us to resolve conflicts between rules and conflicts between values. Published codes of ethics and professional conduct serve as a physical representation of attitude and commitment to the safety profession. They may serve as touchstones to your performance as a safety consultant, and guide you in all the practices and procedures of your business.

This chapter is intended to introduce OS&H consultants to ethics as applied to the profession. I hope the questions, scenarios, and appendices serve as guidance throughout your career, aid you in incorporating professional codes of conduct into your practice, and contribute to the success of your business.

And now that you've considered ethical dilemmas that could arise, along with having developed your business plan, learning about finances, legal issues and insurance for a business owner, developing a marketing plan, and considering how you will retain your clients, it is time to look forward. The next chapter introduces you to considerations as your business matures, along with reviewing some of what you've already learned (but will use over and over in the years ahead).

BIBLIOGRAPHY

Academy of Industrial Hygienists, American Conference of Governmental Industrial Hygienists (ACGIH), American Industrial Hygiene Association (AIHA). 2007. *Joint Industrial Hygiene Association Member Ethical Principles* (retrieved May 23, 2014). www.aiha.org/get-involved/Academy/Documents/MemberEthicalPrinciples52107.pdf

American Board of Industrial Hygiene (ABIH). 2007. *American Board of Industrial Hygiene Code of Ethics* (retrieved July 11, 2013). www.abih.org/sites/default/files/downloads/ABIHCodeofEthics.pdf

American Society of Civil Engineers (ASCE). 2006. *ASCE Code of Ethics* (retrieved July 11, 2013). www.asce.org/code-of-ethics/

American Society of Safety Engineers (ASSE). 2012. *Code of Professional Conduct* (retrieved July 11, 2013). www.asse.org/about/code-of-professional-conduct/

Board of Certified Safety Professionals (BCSP). 2012. *Code of Ethics* (retrieved July 11, 2013). www.bcsp.org/Portals/0/Assets/DocumentLibrary/BCSPcodeofethics.pdf

Eckenfelder, D.J. 1996. *Values-Driven Safety: Reengineering Loss Prevention Using Value Inspired Resource Optimization*. Rockville, MD: Government Institutes.

English, W. "The Moral Component of Our Professional Challenge." *Professional Safety*, July 2006.

Institute of Hazardous Materials Management (IHMM). 2010. *CHMM® Code of Ethics* (retrieved October 10, 2014.) www.ihmm.org/about-ihmm/code-of-ethics

International Commission on Occupational Health (ICOH). 2012. *International Code of Ethics for Occupational Health Professionals* (retrieved July 11, 2013). www.ocohweb.org/site_new/multimedia/core_documents/pdf/code_ethics_eng_2012.pdf

Kapp, A. "Ethical Climate & Safety Performance: Design better programs, improve compliance and foster participation." *Professional Safety*, July 2008.

Leemann, J.E. "Delivering business value by linking behavioral EHS competencies to corporate core competencies." *International Journal for Sustainable Business* 12(1), 3–16. (2005).

Lewis, L.G. "The Cultivation of Professional Ethics." *Engineering Ethics Update*, September 1995 (retrieved December 1, 2013). www.niee.org/sept_95.htm#Cultivation

Manuele, F.A. 2003. *On the Practice of Safety*. 3rd Ed. Hoboken, NJ: John Wiley & Sons, Inc.

National Society of Professional Engineers (NSPE). *Code of ethics examination*. (retrieved July 17, 2013). www.nspe.prg/resources/ethics/code-ethics

Nick Nichols, George V. Nichols Jr. and Patsy A. Nichols. "Professional Ethics: The importance of teaching ethics to future professionals." *Professional Safety*, July 2007.

Newton, L.H. 1989. *Ethics in America Study Guide*. Englewood Cliffs, New Jersey: Prentice Hall.

Patankar, M.S. 2005. *Safety Ethics, Cases from Aviation, Healthcare and Occupational and Environmental Health*. Burlington, VT: Ashgate Publishing Company.

Petersen, D. 2003. *Techniques of Safety Management: A Systems Approach*. 4th Ed. Des Plaines IL: ASSE.

Robbins, S.P. 1994. *Essentials of Organizational Behavior*. 4th Edition. Englewood Cliffs, New Jersey: Prentice Hall.

Schneid, T.D. 2008. *Corporate Safety Compliance OSHA, Ethics and the Law*. Boca Raton, FL: CRC Press.

United States Department of Justice, Office of Public Affairs (DOJ OPA). 2013a. "Former President of Port Arthur, Texas, Chemical Company Sentenced for Federal Crimes Related to Employee Deaths." www.justice.gov/opa/pr/2013/October/13-enrd-1145.html

_____. 2013b. "Justice Department, Federal and State Partners Secure Record $13 Billion Global Settlement with JPMorgan for Misleading Investors About Securities Containing Toxic Mortgages." www.justice.gov/opa/pr/2013/November/13-ag-1237.html

_____. 2013c. "Mississippi Laboratory Operator Found Guilty of Falsifying Records on Industrial Wastewater" (retrieved January 2, 2013). www.justice.gov/opa/pr/2013/May/13-enrd-596.html

Department of Justice (DOJ), United States Attorney William C Killean, Eastern District of Tennessee (ED Tenn). 2013. "Former Shaw Group Safety Manager at TVA Nuclear Sites Sentenced to 78 Months In Prison For Major Fraud Case Against The United States." www.justice.gov/usao/tne/news/2013/April/041213%20Cardin%20Sentencing%20Fraud.html

U.S. National Archives and Records Administration. 2011. *Code of Federal Regulations*. Title 48 Section 3.10. Contractor Code of Business Ethics and Conduct.

Wachter, J. "Ethics: The Absurd Yet Preferred Approach to Safety Management." *Professional Safety*, June 2011.

APPENDIX A

American Society of Safety Engineers Code of Professional Conduct (2012)

Membership in the American Society of Safety Engineers (ASSE) commits one to serve and protect people, property and the environment. Members are accountable for following the Code of Professional Conduct:

- Serve the public, employees, employers, clients, the Society, and the profession with fidelity, honesty, and impartiality.
- In all professional relationships, treat others with respect, civility, and without discrimination.
- Abstain from behavior that will unjustly cause harm to the reputation of the Society, its members, and the profession.
- Continually improve professional knowledge, skills, competencies, and awareness of relevant new developments through training, education, networking, and work experiences.
- Consider qualifications before undertaking any professional activity and perform only those services that may be handled competently.
- Make informed decisions in the performance of professional duties that adhere to all relevant laws, regulations, and recognized standards of practice.
- Inform all appropriate parties when professional judgment indicates that there is an unacceptable level of risk of injury, illness, property damage, or environmental harm.
- Maintain the confidentiality of information acquired through professional practice that is designated or generally recognized as non-public, confidential, or privileged.
- Accurately represent professional qualifications including education, credentials, designations, affiliations, titles, and work experience.
- Avoid situations that create actual, potential or perceived conflicts between personal and professional interests, and if a potential conflict of interest arises disclose all applicable facts to potentially affected parties.

And now that you've considered ethical dilemmas that could arise, along with having developed your business plan, learning about finances, legal issues and insurance for a business owner, developing a marketing plan and considering how you will retain your clients, it is time to look forward. The next chapter introduces you to considerations as your business matures, along with reviewing some of what you've already learned (but will use over and over in the years ahead).

APPENDIX B

BCSP Code of Ethics (2012)

Below is the code of ethics and professional standards to be observed by holders of documents of certification conferred by the Board of Certified Safety Professionals (BCSP). (Reprinted with permission from BCSP. Please check the BCSP website to verify the current version of the BCSP Code of Ethics.)

"Certificants shall, in their professional activities, sustain and advance the integrity, honor, and prestige of the profession by adherence to these standards.

1. HOLD paramount the safety and health of people, the protection of the environment and protection of property in the performance of professional duties and exercise their obligation to advise employers, clients, employees, the public, and appropriate authorities of danger and unacceptable risks to people, the environment, or property.
2. BE honest, fair, and impartial; act with responsibility and integrity. Adhere to high standards of ethical conduct with balanced care for the interests of the public, employers, clients, employees, colleagues and the profession. Avoid all conduct or practice that is likely to discredit the profession or deceive the public.
3. ISSUE public statements only in an objective and truthful manner and only when founded upon knowledge of the facts and competence in the subject matter.
4. UNDERTAKE assignments only when qualified by education or experience in the specific technical fields involved. Accept responsibility for their continued professional development by acquiring and maintaining competence through continuing education, experience, professional training and keeping current on relevant legal issues.
5. AVOID deceptive acts that falsify or misrepresent their academic or professional qualifications. Not misrepresent or exaggerate their degree of responsibility in or for the subject matter of prior assignments. Presentations incident to the solicitation of employment shall not misrepresent pertinent facts concerning employers, employees, associates, or past accomplishments with the intent and purpose of enhancing their qualifications and their work.
6. CONDUCT their professional relations by the highest standards of integrity and avoid compromise of their professional judgment by conflicts of interest. When becoming aware of professional misconduct by a BCSP certificant, take steps to bring that misconduct to the attention of the Board of Certified Safety Professionals.

7. ACT in a manner free of bias with regard to religion, ethnicity, gender, age, national origin, sexual orientation, or disability.
8. SEEK opportunities to be of constructive service in civic affairs and work for the advancement of the safety, health and wellbeing of their community and their profession by sharing their knowledge and skills.

APPENDIX C

ABIH Code of Professional Conduct (2007)

As professionals in the field of industrial hygiene, ABIH certificants and candidates have the obligation to: maintain high standards of integrity and professional conduct; accept responsibility for their actions; continually seek to enhance their professional capabilities; practice with fairness and honesty; and encourage others to act in a professional manner consistent with the certification standards and responsibilities set forth below (Reprinted with permission by ABIH).

ABIH Code of Ethics

I. Responsibilities to ABIH, the profession and the public.
   A. Certificant and candidate compliance with all organizational rules, policies and legal requirements.
      1. Comply with laws, regulations, policies and ethical standards governing professional practice of industrial hygiene and related activities.
      2. Provide accurate and truthful representations concerning all certification and recertification information.
      3. Maintain the security of ABIH examination information and materials, including the prevention of unauthorized disclosures of test information.
      4. Cooperate with ABIH concerning ethics matters and the collection of information related to an ethics matter.
      5. Report apparent violations of the ethics code by certificants and candidates upon a reasonable and clear factual basis.
      6. Refrain from public behavior that is clearly in violation of professional, ethical or legal standards.
II. Responsibilities to clients, employers, employees and the public.
   A. Education, experience, competency and performance of professional services.
      1. Deliver competent services with objective and independent professional judgment in decision-making.
      2. Recognize the limitations of one's professional ability and provide services only when qualified. The certificant/candidate is responsible for determining the limits of his/her own professional abilities based on education, knowledge, skills, practice experience and other relevant considerations.
      3. Make a reasonable effort to provide appropriate professional referrals when unable to provide competent professional assistance.
      4. Maintain and respect the confidentiality of sensitive information obtained in the course of professional activities unless: the information is reasonably understood to pertain to unlawful activity; a court or governmental agency

lawfully directs the release of the information; the client or the employer expressly authorizes the release of specific information; or, the failure to release such information would likely result in death or serious physical harm to employees and/or the public.
   5. Properly use professional credentials, and provide truthful and accurate representations concerning education, experience, competency and the performance of services.
   6. Provide truthful and accurate representations to the public in advertising, public statements or representations, and in the preparation of estimates concerning costs, services and expected results.
   7. Recognize and respect the intellectual property rights of others and act in an accurate, truthful and complete manner, including activities related to professional work and research.
   8. Affix or authorize the use of one's ABIH seal, stamp or signature only when the document is prepared by the certificant/candidate or someone under his/her direction and control.
B. Conflict of interest and appearance of impropriety.
   1. Disclose to clients or employers significant circumstances that could be construed as a conflict of interest or an appearance of impropriety.
   2. Avoid conduct that could cause a conflict of interest with a client, employer, employee or the public.
   3. Assure that a conflict of interest does not compromise legitimate interests of a client, employer, employee or the public and does not influence or interfere with professional judgments.
   4. Refrain from offering or accepting significant payments, gifts or other forms of compensation or benefits in order to secure work or that are intended to influence professional judgment.
C. Public health and safety.
   1. Follow appropriate health and safety procedures, in the course of performing professional duties, to protect clients, employers, employees and the public from conditions where injury and damage are reasonably foreseeable.

Questions to ask:

The doors are open, the financing is complete, the client list has been started, and marketing concept is complete. What can I expect now that I have conquered the first year?

What do I need as an owner to have staying power in the occupational health and safety (OS&H) consulting business arena?

How do I work with an ever-changing economy to keep my business healthy? How do I evaluate the adjustments needed to keep my business on target with my goals?

How do I determine if I need to grow my business or maintain it at the present level? What are my options? How do I determine which option works best for me?

What steps do I need to take to set long-term personal and professional goals?

Chapter 10

After the First Year

BY DONNA PEARSON, CSP

Donna S. Pearson is a Certified Safety Professional (CSP) who began her professional career with a mechanical contractor in Northwest Tennessee in 1987. Donna's college education focused on business management, which has aided in owning Pearson Safety Services, LLC (PSS) with offices and training centers in Memphis, Tennessee, and Murray, Kentucky. The corporate office is located in Jackson, Tennessee.

Donna became a CSP in 2003, earning trainer credentials in a variety of specialties, including the OSHA Outreach Program, CPR/first-aid, ergonomics, confined spaces, and the Drug-Free Workplace Program. PSS is a majority woman-owned business, specializing in all types of safety services. The S.O.S. program (Safety Orientation System), which Donna developed in 2005, has expanded to assist with multi-employer OSHA compliance for plants and achieve basic behavioral training for contractors.

Starting a safety consulting business can be both exciting and exhausting, as I discovered when I first opened my door to this wonderful opportunity. Many safety consultants will tell you that they did not actually decide to start their own safety consulting firm; it just happened. Career changes, plant closures, and unexpected opportunities are all examples of how a safety professional is suddenly also a business owner. That is what happened to me. I did not actually plan a career in safety; it evolved from filling out a first report of injury for my previous employer to owning my own professional safety company. Whether you planned to be a safety professional business owner or it seemingly just happened, after the first year, a time of reflection will be needed to move forward in a productive manner for your company.

The most interesting thing I learned about business ownership was that I was not really very good at it. Even though I took business management and accounting classes in college, I soon discovered I just did not like the business side of owning a business. My passion lies in actual safety services; that was a real shock to me, given my educational background, and the time I spent in office work prior to this career. I discovered that there were ways to overcome my less-than-enthusiastic accounting duties by using others to make sure this aspect of my business was handled professionally.

A hard lesson to learn was how to say "NO," something I find difficult even today. I value every client, so telling someone that I cannot do whatever the task is whenever they want it has been my most difficult obstacle, even to the point of hurting my personal life in a most painful lesson. We will discuss this later in the chapter, so that you can learn from my mistakes. After the first year, you will need to establish what works with your business and what does not. We will list several ways to accomplish this and how to use this workbook to prevent obvious, and some not-so-obvious, mistakes.

> *Give the client a quality service with a sincere desire to make a difference.*

Having good time management (a tool I still struggle with) will also be a major asset as you go forward past the first year and into the ensuing years of your business. Since billable hours are a safety consultant's method of salary, proper time management skills are a must in this industry. Without those, you may find you are better off working for others.

Knowing how to grow your business while maintaining your sense of balance will be a key factor in its success. Marketing tools may include advertising, utilizing online media venues, or joining professional organizations. We will discuss ways to determine how to maximize the non-billable time you put into marketing yourself and your company.

Learning how to be consistent in what services you provide, the hours you work, and the quality of your service will be the trademarks that will set you apart from your competition. When asked how I managed to maintain a career in this industry for almost 30 years, the answer is simple: Give the client a quality service with a sincere desire to make a difference.

WHAT HAVE YOU LEARNED?

While it may seem that the first year is a blur of activity, from seemingly simple to do's such as naming the company, to serious heart-searching decisions such as how much to finance, the first year many times can be the easiest. The previous chapters have outlined assistance in making all of these difficult decisions. They'll prove valuable to you as you work through all of these items. Oh, that I could have had such a tool when I started my safety business years ago. The rush of ownership will move you through the decision-making process the first year, and you will need it. Excitement and enthusiasm for your business is the strongest selling point of success. You MUST believe in what you are selling. F. John Reh wrote, "When you are passionate about what you do for a living you enjoy it more. You also do it better. You are more committed to the success of the operation if you believe in it passionately" (Reh n.d.). The trick is to structure your business so that it continues to spark that passion long after the first year is over.

However, a company does not survive on adrenalin rush alone. It takes work, strong skill sets, ethics and professional pride in what you bring to the table to succeed in an occupational safety and health and environmental (OS&H) business. You'll need to call on skills you were taught long before you entered this profession. Strong ethics, self-motivation, and passion for your fellow men are requirements that you won't get from any publication. You'll need to use the safety knowledge you've gained from your work so far, along with your personal experiences, to continue forward in business after the first year.

Making Adjustments

Once the first whirlwind year is complete, it may be time to consider the services you provide, using the first year as an evaluation process to decide where to go from here. Don't be discouraged if, after the first year, you are not where you thought you would be. Establishing a business, securing repeat customers, and a steady clientele, can take a few years. It is rare that all the kinks of a new business will be ironed out by the end of the first year. In fact, building repeat business and your reputation is an ongoing process, not a first year project only.

It is crucial after the first year to make some adjustments to your business. Many times, when first getting started, consultants take on any and all work just to build the business and their reputations. Once you've started to be established, which may be after the first year or may take longer, look back over all of your business planning. You will find you need to make a few changes, or you may even need to completely overhaul your plan.

First, back to your passion for your business. What did you like best about the first year of your business? How have you set your business up? Is it a sole proprietorship or did you decide to add personnel during that first year? I have worked as both, alone and with employees, and found both to have their own challenges. Are you happy with where you are?

Beyond a Solo Practice

If you are happy as a sole proprietor, then what is it you like about being a one-person show? For many, the best part of being a sole proprietor is that you know every aspect of the business, and you can guarantee the work will be to your liking. In other words, you are the BEST employee you have. You can control quality, time, expectations, and so on, of every aspect of the business. Your reputation, which is so very important in this business, is closely held.

There are other factors to consider with a solo practice. Is working solo allowing you to meet your profit expectations and your time expectations? Is the whole business ownership idea working for you? Since it is a solo business, every decision on what you do and how you do it generally impacts only your immediate family. Looking back over your experiences in the last year, determine if you are still happy with the services you are providing, the income you are receiving, and if the time and effort you have put into this business in the past year has reaped the rewards you anticipated. If not, then look at what changes you feel you must make to get to those anticipated rewards.

Define Your Strengths

Ask yourself if you are where you thought you would be when you started your consulting practice. Are you doing the type of work you anticipated when you decided to start the business? If training was your primary passion, what percentage of training do you actually do? Do you love being outside, on the jobsites where the actual hazards are, identifying those hazards and assisting others on a more one-on-one basis? How much time did you spend in the office away from what you love to do? As a business owner, you will always have to tend to the business. Was the amount of time spent on the business reasonable?

What do you feel is your best product or service? How much of that service did you actually get to do? We can easily get sidetracked in our need to pay the bills, taking on work we really don't want or like to do. Sometimes this is just essential. Sometimes you may have an essential client, important to your success, who needs you to do something outside of your primary focus. In the larger picture of owning your own business, you should try to secure work that includes your favorite part of safety, e.g. training, site audits, ergonomics, and so on. After all, that is generally why owners of consulting firms decide to own their own businesses in the first place.

Clientele

Sometime after the first year, review the clientele you have acquired. With your current book of clients, are you still able to do what you like to do best? The types of services expected by your clients may change your focus periodically as you provide both the services they need, such as site audits, and those you love the most, such as training. The customers' requests and your favorite aspect of safety may vary as the customers' needs change. However, you will be able to control some of the amount of each service by your own marketing techniques and decisions on how to run your business going forward.

When I started in safety, I loved being outdoors, on the construction sites, in the thick of things, working one on one with individuals and seeing their personal commitment to safety. I provided training on a daily basis, literally "in the trenches." Construction safety was my specialty, and I loved it. Now, years later, I don't climb ladders like I used to do because age, time, and the needs of my clients have required me to look at doing more training in house. Group training has become more the norm for me, which means working with larger facilities instead of small, individual construction sites. While change is sometimes hard, it is inevitable; adapting your business to your own personal challenges will keep your company strong and viable. While I do miss the outdoors, I still do what I love the most: training; I just do it in a different setting now. It is not necessary to give up the part you like the most. But it is important to be open to changing your clientele, your market, or your venue to be able to keep doing what you love in this business.

Business Size

As your business matures, you have other important decisions to make. You will need to make some decisions on the overall structure of your business. You may need to think about the size of the business. Are you happy working as a sole proprietor or do you wish to expand, either now or in the future? What are the pros and cons of expanding your business? Does this mean bringing in business partners or only employees? Are you better off subcontracting? Do you have the network to subcontract? Going from a sole proprietor to multi-personnel business is a large step, and should not be without a lot of well thought-out plans on managing it.

Managing Workload

Sometimes the workload (as in my case) may make this decision for you. Be careful not to let the current demand overrun your original business plan and your financial capabilities. Also, be careful not to step out of your management comfort zone. One of my original mistakes was letting the company run me instead of me running the company. My business started in a spare bedroom, and grew very quickly the first year. Soon, the decisions being made were based on meeting the demands of the business, not my own personal or professional goals.

The growth of your business should be a steady process, which requires discipline and devotion to your clients, as well as to your own time management.

When the scope of work exceeds the hours you had originally planned to put in your business, stop and evaluate your personal wishes for your company (and your family) before adding personnel, expanding your business loans, and increasing your clientele. Do you want to spend every day just trying to get it all done? Believe me, this can happen before you know it. Then you have lost control of your business and, more important, your personal life. The business should be what you DO, not who you ARE.

Controlling Growth

The growth of your business should be a steady process, which requires discipline and devotion to your clients, as well as to your own time management. It is easy to overbook yourself and make promises for services that you simply cannot fulfill. This is not to say that you don't need to expand your business, just that controlling your growth and allowing yourself a little time to evaluate what you personally want is time well spent. Taking the time to evaluate allows you to really think about what you wish to focus your skill sets on; the time you want to put into your business; whether you wish to expand to bring in more employees; and what level of professional qualifications and capital are needed to achieve all this. Whether you realize it or not, as you delve into these decisions, you will be setting up the future of your business. By looking back at what worked, what didn't work, what parts were the most exciting for you to accomplish, and what work caused the most stress, you will actually be setting the tone for many years to come. Taking the time to evaluate and reflect on the first year will provide a clearer vision for what you really want to achieve out of your business, so that the business does not run you.

Make a list of what you feel worked well since you started, and what you wish to continue doing going forward. Also, look at what did not work that needs to be changed.

First, list the things you feel you did right:

THINGS I DID FOR MY COMPANY THAT I WOULD DO AGAIN AND WHY?

1. _____
2. _____
3. _____
4. _____

It is important that this is your list. To get your mind rolling, here are some examples from my list:

1. Picking the right bank. This bank works with me, assist me with loans, credit card set-up, etc.
2. Picking the right IT support group was a valuable win.
3. Getting a website in place has created several new leads.

We can learn as much from things that did not go as planned. Look at what did not work and what lessons were learned:

THINGS I DID FOR MY COMPANY I WOULD NOT DO AGAIN AND WHY

1. _____
2. _____
3. _____
4. _____

Items that might need to be looked at could include:

1. Will not pay for weekly advertising in local paper. It was expensive and did not generate any leads.
2. Rented too large a space, which is cutting into my profit margin.
3. Tried to grow too large too fast and could not meet demands of clients, which hurt our reputation.

Also, personally, what did you like about the way you set up the business in the first year? Do you like working alone, or do you wish you had help? Did you hire staff, and now you are spending too much time trying to keep them busy? The same rules of making a list will work here too.

HOW HAS THE PERSONAL SETUP OF THE BUSINESS WORK FOR ME SO FAR?

1. _____
2. _____
3. _____

Examples of these may include:

1. I like running the business as a sole proprietorship and the freedom that allows.
2. I realized I like working out of my home and the low overhead that gives my business.
3. I love being able to train and that is 80% of my business, so I want to stay on course with that.

Just as important is asking yourself what you don't like about the way you have set up your personal part of the business.

WHAT DO I NOT LIKE ABOUT MY PERSONAL SETUP OF THE BUSINESS SO FAR?

1. _____
2. _____
3. _____

Examples could include:

1. I don't like working out of my home. It is too distracting, and I don't feel like a professional owner of a business.
2. Being by myself is making it too hard to have any time off.
3. My favorite part of the business is ergonomic assessment and somehow, all I do is train.

Again, these are just suggestions. Think about what lessons you have learned that are both good and bad, for both your business and for yourself. Being able to identify what worked and what didn't is a valuable learning tool. It could also save you a lot of money and hard lessons, as you discard what does not work and enhance what does. This is NOT the time to beat yourself up. You will do that on and off again, as any business owner will tell you.

Your mistakes, or lessons, may be costly. The key is to learn from mistakes. Realize that as a business owner, minor mistakes may always be a part of your company. If you can learn from these mistakes, they can become the building blocks of your future.

SELF-EVALUATE (YES, AGAIN!)

An honest self-evaluation will assist with keeping you on track with your business plans, setting goals, and going forward as your business matures. As you list the items you feel good about and the ones that you would do differently if you could go back, evaluate what starting up your business taught you about yourself and being in business. Use that information to move forward. Before you move forward, you must look at what you have established. Ask yourself the following questions:

1. Are you following the business plan you developed at the beginning of your decision to start your own business?

2. Are you on target to offer the services you planned to offer when you started?
3. How far apart are you from the financial goals that you envisioned?
4. Are you still as excited about what you are doing as when you started? If not, what obstacles have altered this? How can you overcome them?

Ask yourself if you are fully committed to owning your own business. By now, you have learned that it is not as easy as it appears. The obligations of business ownership are many (as are the rewards). To be successful, be very honest with yourself about your own personality, abilities, and commitment. It takes a very committed individual, who is willing to do tasks that you may not enjoy, to be the owner of a consulting firm, regardless of whether you decide to do this as an individual or whether you are working with others.

It is time to ask yourself some very personal questions. Cheating on the answers will not work here!

Effect on Family

First, look at your family structure. When you go into business, it is a family affair; there is more than just you to consider. You will need the support of your immediate family. Do you share your life with someone? If so, how does he or she feel about the time, money and energy you have been putting into your business so far to make it successful? This should be discussed together. Not discussing this with the people with whom you share your life could lead to serious issues as your business grows and consumes more of your time. How much time is your business taking out of your day-to-day life? Is this acceptable to you and those around you, especially your family?

Not everyone in the family may have signed up for the long hours, the stress, and even possibly the travel involved in your business that self-ownership can bring, especially in the beginning. If your business is successful, what impact will that have? We all list success as our primary goal, if not directly then in an "assumed" way.

My business was successful and that altered our family finances. For some, that is wonderful, and everyone is happy. For others, it can be intimidating or make the other person in your relationship feel inadequate, as though he or she is not contributing to the household income at the same level. I have known cases where, all of a sudden, it is your money, not our money. This can affect the overall health of your relationship, and needs to be discussed. If you are in a relationship, money can be a real stumbling block. This is true whether you have it or don't have it.

The same holds true if your business is slow to start or slows down. Fluctuating income is a part of small business ownership. How will that affect your current relationship? How critical is your income to the overall success of your home? During a money crunch with my business, I had to go several weeks without a salary, making sure everyone else and the bills were paid before I was. I had savings to fall back on, since I had walked this road before.

It is important for the small business owner to realize that a savings account is not just a want but a need. Having a savings account is critical to cover bills and mortgages if money isn't flowing in regularly. Income may not be consistent, as it is when working as an employee for a company. Payments from clients may be delayed, projects take time to finish before they can be billed, and so forth. The small business owner must have resources, such as a personal nest egg, for these times. Early on, learn to discipline yourself, not just with time management, but with money management as well.

Consider reviewing your notes on the Chapter 3, "Financial," regarding money management, adding ideas that are now coming to mind. The notes you take now will be pulled out years from now for review. They are worth a second look now that you have gained some experience in this portion of your business.

Setting Priorities—Learning to Say No

Second, look at the setup of your business. Do you still own it, or does it now own you? As mentioned before, this is one of my greatest challenges. Like many in this profession, I had a huge problem with saying "no" to any request for assistance. It has been my experience that owning your own business, whether as an individual or in a group setting, can take away free time, and lead you to make personal decisions about your priorities as you work to juggle personal and professional time. So the next challenge of your evaluation is how are you with time management?

President Dwight D. Eisenhower has been attributed with saying, "What is important is seldom urgent and what is urgent is seldom important" (Eisenhower 1954). Many times, we create our own chaos through overbooking and trying to "do it all." One of the advantages of owning your own consulting business is the ability to schedule your own time; it can also be the greatest disadvantage. Being able to schedule appointments allows you the opportunity to do things with your children, for example, that others with more structured working hours can't do. I have been able to help with field days, go to a movie in the afternoon with my children, or be a room mother when others could not, because their jobs did not provide flexibility. For consultants, flexibility is a big advantage for your family. However, it is also one of the disadvantages, if you do not stay focused and on track with your time.

Time Management and Scheduling

Using a calendar is imperative if you wish to keep all your appointments, making time for your personal schedule, and your family's schedule as well. Full-time consulting is that: full time. So when you take time away during the day and work week, it generally means making up the time elsewhere, working late nights or weekends. Some services that you provide, such as accident investigations and immediate training needs (such as for the client to be able to work on a particular project), will also dictate the "free" time you have in your business. You may find companies calling with last-minute safety needs when their own staff is overwhelmed, if they lack an in-house safety person, or when they have an immediate need for training. Be prepared for some long days, as those will be necessary to take care of clients' needs. Employees, if you expand to that level, and general accounting tasks will always be part of the demands of any business.

Incorporate balancing work and life outside work into your business plan and goals from the very beginning. . . .

Once, a longtime client called me, stating they had been told they could not start their construction project until they completed a jobsite hazard analysis (JHA) for every tasks assigned to the project, both for them (the general contractor) and every one of their subcontractors. They also had to have a full-time safety professional on the project for the duration of the project. They needed help, and they needed it now. My team and I worked long hours, making many phone calls. We were able to provide the client with the much-needed paperwork to prevent a work stoppage. It was not easy to meet this client's needs, and required lots of overtime for me and my staff, but it was worth it because the client was able to stay on site and provide jobs for a lot of people. Knowing that we are a part of that is a wonderful feeling that goes beyond the monetary rewards of this business.

Clients may contact you at the eleventh hour. Your ability to make their world work will set you apart, establishing your reputation, as well as opportunities for repeat business, as nothing else can. To this day, getting that heartfelt thank you is still such a great feeling for me and my staff. Knowing you accomplished what others would say cannot be done; knowing that the hazards for a specific project have been identified and safety measures are in place prior to work starting on that project; knowing that safety just gained another higher niche in the big scheme of things is what keeps many safety professionals going long after the monetary rewards are met. This wonderful experience is not without its downside. Thus the greatest asset in owning your own business is sadly one I have never quite achieved: time management. It is crucial to your business, but much more so to your balance of career and life outside of your career.

Ownership of any business requires finding a balance between providing the service and enjoying a life outside of work. "Our career is an extension of who we are and why we are here on this planet. It should be an enjoyable outlet that utilizes our skills and talents in a productive way" (Perry 2006). Finding a balance between enjoying your work and enjoying your family without feeling guilty may be a delicate balancing act for you, as it has been for me.

Incorporate balancing work and life outside work into your business plan and goals from the very beginning, and as you review and refine it. As a business owner and consultant, where time and knowledge are the primary services you provide, evaluate how you organize your time and activities to maximize both the time spent at work and time away from work.

Time Management Assistance

There are many ways to manage your time and many avenues to utilize to learn how to do this. The National Association of Professional Organizers (NAPO) even offers certification of time management and professionals to assist you if you wish to resource this out. There are books on the subject and articles too numerous to mention at your fingertips through the internet. Many people use web-based calendars, purchase specialized computer software, and install smart phone applications to help manage their appointments. All of these are handy and very helpful, but as I have found out, they are only as good as what we take the time to input. That's when human factor (aka mistake factor) that creeps in, causing double booking, forgotten appointments, and so forth. How do you minimize your chance for error? In her article, "How to Improve Organizational Skills", Cheryl Hinneburg (2013) advises, "Good organizational skills are crucial to maximizing your productivity and helping you achieve a well-balanced lifestyle."

Minimizing the chances for error includes becoming super-organized. Now, if you are like me and that is not a natural trait, you must look outside of yourself to achieve this much-needed skill. Many options are available. You can utilize computer-based systems, such as Microsoft Outlook Calendar or i-Planner from APPLE. You could also use online scheduling calendars, including Big Contacts or Doodle, which also hold client information for a small fee each month. You can even use the old-fashioned daily calendar/scheduler, which allows for instant reference without the use of any electronic device. If you use a daily calendar/scheduler, purchase one that also allows you to hold business cards, brochures, and so forth, in order that you may portray confidence when you go to meetings and sell to the potential client the persona of being an organized person. We all want this so badly that we stand a little in awe of the person who seems to achieve this.

A great first impression to instill in your clients is the confidence that you can deliver the product or service you are marketing to them on time. Not being organized in a first impression meeting could cost you that account. I found that including a writing pad to take notes, a pencil (you will learn not to write your appointments in ink), an ink pen, and a $20.00 bill for unexpected tolls/car lots that take cash only can come in very handy sometimes.

Being disorganized can lead to double booking, which is stressful, and embarrassing because you cannot be two place at one time (even with teleconferencing) effectively. It is important to know where you are supposed to be, scheduling correctly to make sure you meet the needs of the client. It is important not to forget to put your personal appointments in as well. Sometimes, we may schedule while talking on the cell phone, in a restaurant, or at a doctor's office. It is easy to forget to place that appointment, whether personal or professional, in our calendars. When I first started my business, I prided myself on my memory, and my ability to keep up with my schedule. After canceling several dentist, eye, and hair appointments because I forgot and booked over them, I realized that scheduling in a consulting business is a key component of de-stressing your life. It is also critical if you wish to keep the same hair dresser and dentist!

All the tools of the trade: time management, organization, and yes, even your family structure, as well as your own individual personality and self-motivation, must be evaluated after the first year. You need to determine if this is still what you want and where you want to be. Look at the effect of your business on your family structure to see if the business is still what you want to pursue going forward. Once all of these questions have been answered and all systems are still go, then it is time to look at where you want your business to grow.

GROWING FORWARD

After the first year, it is time to see if you are on track for where you need to be with the overall aspect of the business. It is a time to look back and look forward at the same time. What are the lessons learned that can be taken and used to increase your profitability, ease your stress, expand your client base, and secure the future of your business? According to statistics published by the Small Business Administration (SBA), 50 percent of new employer establishments survive at least two years and 51% survive at least five years (SBA 2012). "This is a far cry from the previous long-held belief that 50 percent of businesses fail in the first year and 95 percent fail within five years" (Schaefer 2011).

With this ratio of small businesses being successful, the worry is not so much failing but being able to handle the success. It is important to work on steadily growing the business, and assisting your clients for customer satisfaction. I have always said, "It is a whole lot harder to get new clients than to work on keeping the ones you have." Both require work but long-term relationships will increase your profits by reducing the need to invest in marketing. Additionally, the consulting business is based on relationships. Year after year of providing services to your clients will develop friendships that last a lifetime. A lesson learned when I first started my business was that customers become friends who refer you to others, making business never just business.

With a consulting business, every day you are selling a part of you, so it does become personal. Your reputation is on the line every day. How you respond to clients, issues, and your own staff will determine, in a large part, the future success of your company. While you will never be able to please everyone, you can develop a reputation for good service at a fair price in a timely manner. This will carry you through when that project just does not work out, or that training was not to up that particular client's expectation. Being able to learn from those lessons, to grow from setbacks, poor choices, and bad decisions will determine the strength of your backbone and belief in yourself. People watch business owners to see how they react under fire. Whether you realize it or not, your reaction to your worst moments will be when you can shine the most.

Getting Input from Clients

How do you apply lessons you have learned from the first year? How do you take these lessons and intertwine them into your business going forward? Get input from your clients. After my company had been in business for a couple of years, we decided to send out a survey to our clients asking for feedback. We made it very quick and easy, with checkmarks for specific questions, and a small box for feedback on how we could improve our service. While we sent out over 100 surveys, we only received about a dozen back. While that may sound disappointingly small, it is the 10% average you can expect in a survey. Those twelve clients gave us some valuable feedback on how they felt we were doing, along with useful recommendations for going forward. With e-mail and online surveys so accessible these days, the percentages of responses should actually increase.

I also offer a seminar on OSHA recordkeeping each year, free for my retainer accounts. This seminar actually gets the in-house safety personnel to my facility so I can meet them face to face, and they get valuable information on OSHA logs, recordkeeping, and OSHA compliance. I have found clients are wonderful resources for providing feedback on services, and how my company is viewed by their management.

You may want to consider a client review board, drawing from both clients that have been with you the longest, as well as more recently acquired clients. Engage these clients by asking them to a breakfast or lunch meeting, asking for specific comments on services and customer satisfaction. Most people will give you a few minutes of their time, especially if you feed them. Also, company owners are generally interested in helping other business owners (you), especially in startup stages. Conducting client feedback meetings or compiling a client review board will help you get valuable feedback and strengthen your client relationships, as when you adopt their personal recommendations they become part of your success. Another advantage of soliciting, and modifying services, based on direct feedback from clients, is that they may be more willing to be a reference for you.

The Buck Stops Here: Your Reputation and Client Retention

Another way to gather feedback is a brief (no more than 15 minutes) visit to the client to inquire about their recommendations for improvement. For years now, I make a habit of visiting one client a month, either at their site or by taking them to lunch just to see if they are happy with our services. Staying in tune with clients' needs and your ability to deliver to those needs is what keeps your business growing. Again, feedback is always a good idea. In your survey or personal meeting about customer satisfaction, ask a couple of questions about the overall quality of the service you are providing. Waiting until they call to cancel their account with you is too late. If you have invested the time in building a good relationship with your clients, then they will discuss their concerns with you prior to just calling and canceling your services with them. Clients appreciate that you are interested in their feedback; it builds long-term relationships that can see you through the occasionally booking mix-up or weak training class. I believe the in-person visit is imperative if you own a business with multiple consultants working for you. While consultants know they represent themselves as well as the company, sometimes their failure to perform can cost you an account if you have not previously developed your own relationship with the clients.

"It is a whole lot harder to get new clients than to work on keeping the ones you have."

One of the hardest lessons learned was that I needed to meet with new accounts myself. As we grew, I was allowing the new accounts to be assigned to consultants without me meeting them. When the consultant left or there was a conflict, I came to realize that the client did not know to call me to let me try to make it right. This cost me a client or two; the same may happen to you. It's a hard lesson to learned but one you will never forget. Remember, it is your business and your reputation at stake. Guard it wisely.

Adding Employees: Changing the Dynamic

Speaking of safety professionals who may work for you, it is a big step to decide to add personnel. I don't think anything changes the dynamics of a business by adding employees more than the consulting profession. When you are a sole proprietor, you are selling you and only you. You know the work is good because you did it. The old saying, "If you want something done right, do it yourself" is never truer than with consulting services. Once you decide to add an employee, that person is also selling you and your business. The reputation you spent so much time building is now on the line with the people you add to your firm. If you are hiring staff, that means you have reached the point that you no longer can be everywhere, anytime, any way for your clients. You now have to trust others to provide the same or better level of service than you have been providing. That is hard to get comfortable with, believe me. Your business is your baby when you start from the ground up. Giving it over to someone else to hold and help raise can cause a multitude of issues, all of which need to be addressed prior to making the decision to expand.

However, the other side of the coin is that if you start growing and cannot meet the demands of the increased work load, you can hurt your own reputation, the one you worked so hard to build. Being overworked can be as detrimental as not having enough work. Also, how you approach your business and your attitude toward it will be reflected in how others see your company. As you think about the time since you started your business, you should be able to recognize that you are your greatest asset or your worst one. After the first year, is the time to evaluate which one you are. Think about it. Ask yourself these questions.

My investment in assistance for that one day a week proved invaluable to my ability to get the work completed.

1. Do I show up for work eager and ready to go, or do I let the fact that I am my own boss put off my starting time?
2. How many hours am I devoting to my business?
3. Am I treating it like a full-time job or a (just whenever I get around to it) hobby?

Over the years, I have worked with many consultants who have trouble establishing their own work hours. Remember, this job requires a lot of time and commitment, and it is rarely viewed as a "hobby." Too much preparation work goes into knowing what you need to know to be a safety consultant, so it would be hard to see how it could be viewed as a hobby. Self-discipline is needed in the role of safety consulting; this is even more the truth when you own the company. A good self-evaluation at this point is to really look at how you have treated your business in the last year, including such questions as:

- What are your hours of operation? Do you have hours of operation? How available are you to those who would use your services?
- How many days and hours do you average for actually coming in and going to work?
- How many billable hours do you average?

You need to start having a handle on how your work days fall in line with billable hours and non-billable, or administrative overhead, time. While starting a business can consume many hours of planning and meeting with bankers, lawyers, accountants, and so on, as you move forward, this non-billable time should be minimized as much as possible to allow you to spend your time on billable activities. Not knowing this by the end of your first year could result in a painful and expensive realization very quickly. Not only must you stay healthy and excited, but your bank account needs to as well. Be prepared to be the hardest worker in your business for years to come. You will set the attitude and pace of others. Thus, the decision to work alone or as the head of a team is one that requires deep thought and assessment of both the pros and the cons.

When I first started my business, I worked solo. This was when having a cell phone involved taking out a major loan just to use it (long before unlimited minutes). I felt I could not afford any help. This meant booking my own appointments, driving to them, and conducting my consulting work. Then I returned to the office, typed the reports, called on a landline for the next day's appointments, and had to find time to market for the next client. Many times my next potential client would call back when I was out of the office and could not take the call. The following day put me in the office trying to contact the clients I missed the day before. I found out quickly that I was averaging about three days a week of billable time; the rest of the time was spent doing clerical tasks. One of my best decisions right after the first year was to hire clerical help. At first, I could only afford it for one day a week, but having someone come in that one day a week, take calls, schedule appointments, type reports, and file was a great asset to my business. In no time, she started generating new business. My investment in assistance for that one day a week proved invaluable to my ability to get the work completed. Sometimes, we have to learn how to work smart. This was a prime example of my business growing because I invested in having someone there to make sure I could work five days a week and log in billable hours every day.

Adding clerical help can allow for growth, since you are then able to do additional marketing, which can lead to adding safety professionals to your staff as well. Adding personnel can add to your reputation in a positive way, allowing you to increase your business productivity. However, many successful safety professionals make a manageable customer base for themselves with maybe one part-time or full-time clerical employee. The key is to know what size works for you to maintain your professional goals.

Remember also that adding personnel will take away from your ability to be in the field doing what you love to do. When our company grew to include other branches, it was a difficult period for me personally. My love was to be out there working with the clients, their employees, and other safety professionals. Suddenly, I found myself the president of the company, and my role changed. I made the mistake of thinking I could let others do the in-house activities, take care of personnel, and so on, while I still spent most of my time doing what I enjoyed the most. This resulted in lack of direction for my employees, in-house chaos, and a very overworked, overstressed owner. Client satisfaction suffered, personnel left, internal issues abounded, and yes, my personal life imploded through complete neglect.

> *Step out of any pre-conceived ideas of what you think you "have to do" to have a successful business. . . .*

Realize that no one person is an island. If you are going to have multiple branches and multiple personnel, you as the Owner must be that, the Owner. You will not be able to be the consultant who travels to that one- or two-week project; you cannot be out of the office days on end working (or playing). You have commitments to clients, personnel, and your own personal life. I found out I am not Superwoman, and you will find that out as well. Don't even try.

Through the years, I have heard many stories like mine. You start your business out of your home, it starts growing, you start reacting and, before you know it, you have staff, clients, multiple rents for offices, and you are getting up earlier and earlier just to meet the needs. If this is starting to happen in your first year, take a time out! Seek assistance from someone who has been where you are going, your financial advisor, or a mentor you trust. Step out of any pre-conceived ideas of what you think you "have to do" to have a successful business, and look at the bigger picture. Don't emulate others or their businesses. The beauty of owning your own consulting firm is that it is just that, yours. Find the comfort level of business that works for you personally, and incorporates your and your family's goals.

Stepping Back

I found that I did not want to be as big as our company grew. It was too much for me and my comfort zone. I downsized, bought out my partners, closed a branch, and worked on reaching a level that I could manage and be proud of. Bigger is not always better, which I found out the hard way. I implore you to let your business work for you, not for others' ideas and dreams. At the end of the day, it will be your name, your reputation, and your accomplishments that need to be met. Your staff piggybacks off those deciding factors. This is why you need to be happy with your comfort level in order to provide leadership to your group.

The last step in evaluating the lessons learned from the first year would be the service. Look at the bottom line. Are you making a profit yet? Most companies do not anticipate a profit the first year, as there are too many startup expenses to repay. However, consulting businesses can sometimes see a profit in the first year if they keep their overhead low. This is a good time to see what is working, what needs to be revised, and what needs to be retired. Review the services you offered when you opened your business. Do you have one service, such as ergonomic assessments, that you focus on, and that is all you offer? Are you an industrial hygienist, and your focus is solely on that specialty? If so, is that working for you? Are you as busy as you want to be, or are you finding you could have more opportunities if you expanded the services you provide?

There is nothing wrong with having a specific safety expertise that you offer and focusing on just that one service. It is important though, if that is the case, to make sure the market need exists to support your focus. It is also important to be very good at that particular service. When I set up my business plan, I wanted to be a one-stop shop. I hired a staff of professionals with varied expertise. This way, I could give the clients everything they needed, so they would not have to look elsewhere. This was, in theory, a great idea, but one area of service just did not generate enough requests to make it feasible to offer in-house. It also involved an area of expertise that we actually did not have among our current staff. After losing several dollars on this idea, it was decided to not offer this to our clients, referring it to someone who was a well-known professional in the industry. This enhanced our reputation, as we still provided the clients what they needed; we just contracted it out. The professional we referred to added to our reputation of quality service. Being honest with a client about what you can and cannot do is healthy, and builds much stronger relationship than trying to do something in which you do not have sufficient expertise. In fact, it hurts the services that you do excel in and your reputation for those quality services.

UNDERSTANDING THE MARKET GOING FORWARD

While you might have some business fall in your lap, most consultants find that, sooner than later, they have to really understand the market in which they are performing their services. Since you don't have a nine-to-five work environment, you will find out very quickly that the hours you devote to your company after the first year (and many years after that) will be a difficult balance of performing billable work and taking time to market. There is no "catch up" or "slow down." A healthy consulting business is always adding, deleting, and maintaining clients.

Each client is your most important client because that is how they feel. They are investing money into your services, and they are not concerned about your other clientele, only about their need for your services. Be careful about putting off one client to satisfy another. Consulting work means that, many times, your scope of work is actually controlled by others. Being able to manage this will become one of your greatest assets or liabilities. This is where Chapter 6, "Marketing and Sales," and Chapter 8, "Client Retention," become very important and should be read and reread to make sure you catch the tips offered (taking notes at the end of the chapters). My advice to you is to learn quickly how to assess what constitutes an emergency on the part of your client and their needs. If you do not, you will find yourself working later hours, weekends, holidays, and so forth. After years of doing this, I finally realized that a good OS&H owner never really gets caught up. If you do, then you are back to marketing to get more work. So, you will market to get the work, work, market to get more work, and so on.

...I finally realized that a good OS&H owner never really gets caught up.

A key element of successful marketing is knowing the area in which you are trying to market, and the services you are trying to bring to that market. This includes knowing the safety needs of the states, cities, or towns to which you have decided to provide services. If the geographic market where you intend to work has already established plants and general industry work, the safety services most in demand may be services that appeal to the general industry market. Likewise, if the area is in growth mode, then consulting services that include construction training and site audits may be the immediate need. It will be beneficial to your consulting business to evaluate the area in which you are trying to grow, identifying the market's safety services' needs. Marketing your ability to provide services to these areas should be well thought out as to how and when to spend money on marketing ideas to bring your services to these clients. Knowing the types of clients to which you wish to focus your marketing resources should net a better return of your marketing dollars.

Annual Review of Goals

My first business plan and the goals we set for that year are still in my drawer. We take them out each year to review where we thought the market was then, and what actually happened when all the factors were put into play. I am always amazed at how different my goals, and the actual finish of that year turned out to be. I was so far off. I set a goal for the first year, which we exceeded by 70%. It was a good thing, too, since if we had reached just our goal, we would not have made payroll. You can't just pick a number based on current anticipated work. I just jumped in, thinking I had a business plan and goals, and knew the market.

In developing my first business plan, I used my experience from my previous employer, my clients' needs from the time working with that firm, and a long discussion about my plan with my insurance agent, who was very knowledgeable about construction market trends. I also discussed market trends with contractors who had been in the business for a long time. I watched for association meetings that addressed market trends and speakers that would educate me on what to expect and why. I read articles in national safety magazines, including *Professional Safety* (the American Society of Safety Engineers) and *Safety and Health* (National Safety Council) to review what they believed was going on in the industry at the time. Many of these magazines are part of association dues, and some are even free to safety professionals just by signing up for a membership. To this date, I still receive several magazines through my professional associations. I always take a minute when they arrive each month to check out the table of contents, highlighting in yellow any articles I feel will assist me in keeping abreast of current trends, both in my chosen market and the safety industry as a whole.

When I first began, I thought I researched my market carefully. I realize now that I did not do the research that I recommend that you do. Watch the trends of the market as a whole; what is going on around you in other businesses will directly affect you and your business. There is an ebb and flow to our economy, consistent with time. If you stay involved with what is going on around you, and continually review what the experts will tell you through various media, you will be able to more accurately judge your business plan each year, and adjust your plan accordingly.

Geographic Location

Another factor that will affect the success of your business is where you want to work: your geographic location, and your industry focus. When you decide to market, it is generally for growth of your services, or to let potential clients know who you are and what you offer. It is important to have a concept of what you wish to achieve with the time, effort, and money involved in marketing.

Your marketing success and failures can help you decide if you need to change your venue or the scope of services you provide. The results of your marketing will help you define what potential clients, if any, out there are interested in your services. After years in this business, I attribute a part of our company's success in knowing the trends of the market for which we are working, and the needs of the areas in which we choose to work. One of my hardest decisions was to close an office branch. The geographic area appeared to be a wonderful place to grow our business, and we already had clients in the area. However, after a few years of trying to get the branch started, including a few changes in management, it became obvious that the market had too much competition to be viable. Sometimes, you can throw good money after bad trying to recoup what is already lost. We finally admitted it was not going to happen, and chose to close the branch.

Meanwhile, in looking in another direction, north instead of east, we saw an untapped market. We redirected our resources to that area, which resulted in a positive response. While it is sometimes a little harder to start in an area where there is no previous activity for safety, it is also a wonderful challenge and opportunity to bring a safety consulting group into an area where they did not have your help before. Remember, you are bringing a much needed service into a new area. Many small companies and several large ones may not have the internal expertise that they need, and your consulting company can offer, in order to achieve their safety goals.

Marketing

As you established your company, you need to keep on remembering to market. Chapters 6–8 on marketing, networking, and client retention are worth reviewing now that you've been in business for a while. Are your marketing strategies effective? Do you need to look at new ways to market? Are you bringing in the clients you want?

An inexpensive marketing campaign through e-mails, ads, marketing booths at safety related functions, and so on, can assist you in finding out how much your services are needed. Having a booth at a safety function can net many contacts. It can be extremely helpful when going into an area in which you are not established and evaluating the need. Having a booth at a safety function will bring potential customers to you instead of you having to seek them out, which is very time consuming and hard to do. It also puts you in contact with potential clients, and can open that door to an appointment you may not have otherwise gotten.

One of my greatest marketing assets has been being a member of the American Society of Safety Engineers (ASSE).

The goal is to balance the backlog of work with the current log of work, to learn to anticipate the need for additional help, and to accept when your plate is full, and be happy with that level of workload. Remember that balancing all of that does not mean you don't have to continue to market. Companies will come and go, clients will come and go, and sometimes contacts within our client facilities will move, causing us to have to resell our services and reestablish the relationship. If you are not steadily increasing your clientele at least a little bit, then you are slowing dying as a business. It is imperative that you continue to have a marketing and growth plan, even if you have reached your comfort level of clients, staff, and workload.

Make sure you belong to at least one association that aids you in your endeavor to be an OS&H firm. One of my greatest marketing assets has been being a member of the American Society of Safety Engineers (ASSE). I have been a member for well over 20 years now, and this has been a lifeline that I have found extremely helpful in my career. It provides a network of people who understand your frustrations with starting and maintaining your business, relating to clients, employees, and regulatory situations. Association membership can provide lifelong friendships, open doors to potential customers, and offer moral support in the down times of business ownership.

It is imperative as you go forward past your first year to continue to sell the value of your services. This is not necessarily done by word of mouth but by results of service. It is important for the client to understand the value gained by bringing safety services to their company and your company's part of it. It is so much easier to get repeat business than to constantly have to market for new business and more profitable as well.

Marketing is an essential tool if you decide to change gears sometime throughout our career. While my background in safety was from the construction industry, I developed an interest in general industry through my CSP studies. This actually caused me to decide to market an idea that combined the two industries. I wanted to market this training venue to see if it would assist contractors working in general industry. My business now has a program that promotes this idea. Marketing this concept involved both meeting with one contact and sometimes a safety group, to identify and access the right people in order to sell it. I now provide services that have expanded past the construction industry. When I started my business, I focused on just construction but, for several years now, I have expanded our marketing efforts to include potential clients in both the construction and general industries.

Marketing efforts need to have achievable goals.

Associations and Relationships

You can use your relationships with associations to assist in getting your name and the services you provide out there in the general public arena. Belonging to associations such as the American Society of Safety Engineers (ASSE) both locally and nationally enables you to make many contacts that will assist you in promoting your business. Marketing does not have to be about full-page ads and billboards. As emphasized in the networking and client retention chapters, in consulting, it is more about building relationship and referrals, which will net the long-term results that you are looking for in building your client base.

Along with building relationships, make sure people know who you are by getting your name recognized. Our company has T-shirts embroidered with our company logo. We have given out hats, coolers, shirts, hard-hat stickers, and other items with our company name and logo as a way to promote our company. We also participate in local charities. Small items like these will help promote your business.

Customer Satisfaction and Referrals

Having your name and logo on shirts may get your name out there, but the major marketing tools for any safety consultant are customer satisfaction, and with that, referrals. Customer satisfaction will sell your company faster than any T-shirt ever can. Understanding the needs of the client and making them love the services you provide will be your best marketing tool.

Marketing efforts need to have achievable goals. You need to know where to place your marketing focus, before you continue to spend the time and money on marketing or before you think about branching into offering a new service. Look at the past year and the business plan for growth first. Consider the following questions:

1. In what area did I start my business? (Consider construction or general industry, manufacturing, oil and gas, insurance, and so on. What geographic area?)

   _____

2. How is the economy for my specific area? How does it relate to the services I provide?

   _____

3. What is the current economy? If it is going well, and the economy is unusually strong right now, have I developed a false sense of security? Is my staff, lease, overhead, and so on, appropriate?

   _____
   _____

4. How is my team working together? Evaluate my time management and my team's time management

   _____
   _____

5. If I decide to grow into another area, what are the costs both in money *and* time? How will that affect my current list of clients? What marketing demands on my time and resources will I need? How will that affect my current business plan and service where I am already established?

   _____
   _____

While we have touched on these a little from my own experience, each of these questions will need to be evaluated for your individual area and efforts. What other considerations can you think of? List them as well.

CONSISTENCY EQUALS LONGEVITY IN THE CONSULTING WORLD: FINDING YOUR OWN PERSONAL NICHE

One critical avenue to address if you choose to enter into ownership of an OS&H business is your own personal professional credentials. I am often asked how I got into the safety business. When I entered the safety profession, it was not as well-known as it is now. At the time I started, I did not even know there was a safety engineering degree; I was going to school to be an accountant. In 1986, when I attended the Tennessee Right To Know seminar held by Tennessee OSHA, I listened to the compliance officer discuss the Right To Know law. I was fascinated by everything he had to say, and realized that safety was more than just a bunch of written programs. Safety education, when introduced correctly into a working environment, could impact lives, jobs, and the community as a whole. I was hooked. From that point forward, I wanted to learn more, so I attended any training on safety I could talk my employer into letting me attend. However, it was not until I was actually 40 years old that I convinced myself that I wasn't too old to go back to school and learn what I needed to pass the Associate Safety Professional (ASP) and the CSP certifications. I was then able to obtain my Certified Safety Professional certification (CSP).

Safety needs to be sold positively.... Respectful retraining works wonders.

My late husband, my former employer, and my children all encouraged me to go back to school to get the certification I so desired. I wanted to be recognized as the professional I had spent years becoming. I had been in safety for well over ten years. While I was known for my hard work and knowledge regarding safety, I knew the importance of obtaining this certification and what it would mean to my career going forward. My previous employer, a CSP, encouraged me to sit for my exam. My late husband also felt it would be beneficial going forward. While my husband did not live to see me reach this goal, he was my inspiration to finish it. Going back to school, working full time and trying to restart my brain for college at 40 years old was a challenge, but studying for the ASP and then the CSP, and passing both tests was so rewarding. The knowledge I gained through these studies will continue to be used throughout my career. Another benefit is that becoming a Certified Safety Professional has opened doors to clients that would never have been opened without it.

As you plan your career, plan to also further your education or certifications in this field. You need credibility if you are to be considered a professional consultant. One of the greatest things about this business is that you are always learning, growing, and expanding in knowledge. This business is a learning experience that insists we stay at the top of our game. Regulatory mandates constantly change, and vary from state to state. It is imperative that you enjoy reading, learning, and staying up on the most current rules and regulations in this business. Allow time for updates on education, interaction with others in your field, and staying current on regulatory items. This is an ongoing part of your having a successful business with a great reputation.

Safety needs to be sold positively. I have made it my lifelong mission to sell safety in a positive manner. Respectful retraining works wonders. Safety should not be a "have to" for your client's employees, it should be a "want to." You can be a part of instilling this in the workplaces where you teach if you sell this mindset to others through your training.

Defining Your Area of Expertise

Now is the time also to look at your business for the long haul. Safety consulting has many areas of service that can be provided to the client. It is time to fully develop your area of service and the areas of expertise that you intend to market to your clientele. What is the direction you enjoy the most, construction safety, general industry, ergonomics, industrial hygiene, healthcare? Ask yourself the following questions to help you define the areas of expertise you wish to pursue:

- Do you wish to include training, site audits, ergonomic assessments or specialized fields, such as industrial hygiene?
- What skill sets do you have currently?

- What skill sets have you discovered that you need to work on, or that you need to obtain?
- Have you achieved the credentials to be recognized as a professional in that field?
- What is the next step in getting what you need to be able to go in the direction you wish to go?
- What obstacles must be overcome to achieve the services that you wish for your company?
- And, most important, are you focusing on the available market in your area?

Sometimes we must be open to change. Through the years of owning my own consulting business, the economy has ebbed and flowed. Keeping abreast of the changes in the economy and adapting to those changes is the reason my own consulting business has stayed alive through both the busy years and the lean years of economic changes. While my strength was originally new construction safety, several times over the years the economy forced me to look at general industry safety, and I would then shift my focus to that market as well. I enjoy teaching confined space training as much as I do excavation and trenching. There are the same issues in many cases, but different setups in the workplace. I enjoy having a seasoned worker say "I never knew that" in response to something he learned in my class. Your goal in every training class is to teach them something they did not already know about the subject you are teaching.

If someone in my classroom asked me a question I could not answer, I always admitted I did not know. . . .

Make sure if you do switch gears and go into a different area of service that you are an "expert" in that field. It is better to know everything about one field, stick to that field, and be known as the best in that field, than to be mediocre in several areas. Sometimes, the economy or the client may request you go into an area of safety you are just not comfortable with. At that point, you will need to either say no to that request, or go back to and learn that area, making sure you do know what you are trying to teach.

Remember, your classrooms are full of students who know more than you do. You need to be prepared, since students will often challenge you. I discovered this early on. If someone in my classroom asked me a question I could not answer, I always admitted I did not know, telling them I would get right back to them with an answer. I utilized my resources and professional network to get the answers, staying away from subjects that I did not feel comfortable teaching. It is sometimes hard to say you don't provide a certain service, but poor service in one area will hurt the great service you provide in another area. Stick to what you know, or do the homework to learn the subject *before* you say you will provide the service. Reestablishing your credibility is hard to do. You will be better served to say no to services you are not comfortable providing.

Keeping up to Date

Another matter to consider as you plan out the longevity of your business is internal structure. Subjects to keep up to date on so your company can grow include:

1. As an owner, you must keep abreast of the current local, national, and worldwide economy. Plan ahead as well as be prepared. Don't hesitate to make difficult decisions, including employee reduction, personal pay cuts, or moving your business space. I have done all of these, and while they are decisions not to be made lightly, there may be times when they need to be made. Hesitating can cost you your business. Utilize your history as you get through the first years. Learn to plan your next year based on more than just what you did last year, as that is not always the best source. Outside factors will affect your next year's goals and profits. Your business needs to be as fluid as the circumstances around it.
2. Know what is needed in the way of certifications and credentials to be taken seriously. Many plants expect their third-party safety professionals to be accredited, as a CSP or Certified Industrial Hygienist (CIH), for example. You may lose potential business by not having achieved these credentials. Also, it may be that you can qualify for a nationally recognized certification that will help your client. I have been a woman-owned business for several years, but it was not until a client asked me to obtain my National Women's Business Enterprise Certification (WBENC) that I took the time to check out what that was, and what it would mean to our company. I did it for the client who asked, but now it has opened doors for our company that I never expected. I am always happy to consider any certification that would help my client.
3. Picking out the size of your company. This decision can really be tricky, so it will need to be discussed and reviewed more than once throughout the longevity of your business. With my first business, I started solo. I wanted it to stay small as my husband travelled for work, and we had four children at home, so I wanted to minimize the time

I gave to my business to focus on family. However, my clients told their friends who told their friends. Add that to my inability to say no, and I found myself in real need of a little help. Your business, along with your geographic area and industry specialization, may dictate some of the size of growth. I lived in a large metropolitan area, so growth potential was large. I grew so fast that I finally decided to merge my first business with a larger company so I could be part of a larger organization and have other consultants to assist with the workload. I also did not want the business responsibilities and obligations that went with expanding the company at that time in my life.

You will need to consider all the factors in your life as you decide on your business. The old saying, "timing is everything," is out there for a reason. Years later, after my husband had died, and my children were grown, the opportunity to start my own business presented itself again. This time, I decided to go for it. As I suspected, it consumed a large part of my time and energy, as well as presenting a whole new set of challenges, as we have discussed throughout this chapter. The size of you consultancy should be based on your own personal wants and needs, not by the demands of the market. Sometimes however, the current economy will strongly influence this. The main recommendation here is to have an idea of what you would like to see your business grow to become. When I started the first time, I had no goals, no idea of what size I wanted my business to be. I simply did not have a good business plan to follow. When my business did take off, I was not prepared for the growth nor did I manage it successfully. Luckily for me, I was able to merge it with another reputable firm. Your future business plan should not be based on luck. Evaluate both sides.

4. Know the key ingredients for consistency and longevity in the safety consulting world. They are relatively simple. Quality work is first and foremost. Without quality work, customer satisfaction will not happen and, without customer satisfaction, repeat business will not happen and without that, you will be spending way too much time chasing new work, and non-billable time will put you out of business. Quality work includes knowing the clients' needs, knowing the services you provide, and working hard to provide those services on time and at a good price.

Proper staffing is also crucial if you decide to expand your business to include others. They are an extension of your products and services, so you will be held accountable for everyone's quality of work. Remember, you are only as good as the last good service you provided to your clients. Don't make the mistake of thinking you can tell a client that you had no idea the person you hired was not as ethical or good as he said he was. As an owner of a consulting business, you are responsible for every good or bad decision that each of your employees makes. I pride myself on our name, and what that means in the safety community. We live and grow by referrals. There is no greater compliment.

> *It will be your personal responsibility to appease the client when you or your employees make an error.*

I received a phone call one day that a client was exercising their right to drop us as their safety consulting firm. I was so dismayed. I asked the owner if I could come personally and sit down with him. I drove two hours to meet with him. When I sat down to discuss his decision, he stated he had told the safety director of his company that either we went or he did. Businesswise, to this date that was one of the most devastating conversations I have ever had with another person. The consultant assigned to him had not returned his calls, had not sent in reports from site audits in a timely manner, and generally had provided poor service in every way. The owner was not mad at the consultant, he was mad at me—and we had never met! It was one of my first hard lessons when I started my business. I was clueless that this client was so unhappy until it was too late. The consultant admitted he had not serviced the client as he should, but the damage was done. I found out very quickly that, as far as the client was concerned, it was my fault.

As the owner of the company, you are ultimately responsible for any and all hiccups and mishaps and, yes, even employees oversleeping and being late to a training appointment. It will be your personal responsibility to appease the client when you or your employees make an error. I called that client, and told him I did not expect to get his business back, but that I wanted to get my reputation back. I gave him six months of free service. I did not get his business back, but he did tell me I had restored his faith in our company, and that he respected my efforts to make it right. Mistakes will be made. You and your employees are only human. So it is crucial you do two things: minimize the chances for error and, when you make an error, work to make it right.

5. Be the best at what you do. Whenever someone asks why they should use our company, I always reply, "Because we are the best

at what we do." That statement does not take away from any other safety consulting firm, as they are the best at what they do. You should be the best at what you do. If you don't believe in your own business and services, then others will not either. How many clients will you get by saying, "Well, I am okay at what I do?" Finding your niche in this market is what will determine your success rate.

A *niche* is defined by the Merriam Webster Dictionary as, "the situation in which a business's products or services can succeed by being sold to a particular kind or group of people" (Merriam Webster 2014). Once you start providing services, it will not take very long for you to realize what you excel at, and what you enjoy the most about the services you offer. Most of the time, you've determined that prior to starting your own business. In fact, most people start a business based on what they enjoy doing the most.

People who love to bake open cupcake shops, those who love to fix hair open salons, and safety consultants generally gravitate towards what they enjoy in the safety industry. This can include training, working on jobsites, building safety programs, and so forth. The list is quite diverse when you start providing safety services. For some, the variety of providing service in several areas is what attracts them the most. For others, the focus is on a particular field in which they feel the most knowledgeable. Either way, finding your niche will assist you in achieving your goals. Most people will work harder if they are doing something they love to do.

Know the key ingredients for consistency and longevity in the safety consulting world.

Your reputation for being very good at a particular safety service will follow you, leading to referrals and repeat business. When you become the go-to person for a particular service or services, your marketing time goes down, and billable time goes up. I can remember when the phone finally starting ringing with clients contacting us instead of us having to call or market them. That is a great day indeed, one that doesn't just happen. It is a well thought-out part of your business plan and the goals you set for yourself and your company.

SETTING AND ACHIEVING PERSONAL AND PROFESSIONAL GOALS

Now let's talk about goal setting. Everyone thinks they know what they want to do with their safety business. I can tell you from experience, many times the market will reestablish the very goals you set. While I am a firm believer in goals, they should be realistic and achievable. To set unrealistic goals is to sign up for disappointment and failure. You want to learn from all the decisions you made, both good and bad, using that information going forward. If you set goals before you started a year ago, now is the time to pull them out, and see how close you are to meeting them. When you look over your last year, what have you done right? List these. Pat yourself on the back. Many times, I would be so focused on what else I had to do, I forgot to take a minute and just be grateful and pleased that I made it this far. That is an accomplishment in itself. You made it through the first year. Your passion for what you are doing is intact.

I did not set goals. I did not have a plan of action. I literally just reacted to the calls and requests for safety services. I should have known better. I had had goals for my other business but they were mostly set by the parent company, and I would work to achieve them. This time, I had to set the goals myself. Frankly, I did not know how. I learned two ways to set goals that you may find helpful.

Salary Goals

First, set what you want your salary to be. It has to be realistic to the time and resources you have to invest in making this happen. Breaking down your salary goal, how do you achieve this? Does it involve bringing in others? If so, where are you going to get these "others," and how are you going to pay for them? Do you want to manage others? As we discussed earlier, when you bring in personnel, it changes the dynamics of your business. While it can prove to become more profitable to you, doing so must be researched and thought out prior to expanding your business in that direction.

Sometimes bigger does not mean more money and sometimes, your goals are not completely motivated by money.

If you decide to work solo, you will be limiting your income to the number of hours you devote to and achieve billable time. For some, this is no problem. I have a former employee who knew from the beginning, when he went off on his own, that he did not want to grow too big. He had already determined the salary he wanted, broken it down to weekly accomplishments, and identified the area of safety in which he was going to specialize. He ended up going a totally different route than what we do, but it worked for him. He did add a couple of safety professionals, but has maintained the level of growth he wanted, and has been happy with that level of business. I, on the other hand, have opened as many as three branches at one time, and employed over 25 professionals during good economic growth times. In the end, our salaries were not really that far apart. You have to ask yourself what your goals are, how they will play out in salary, and what you hope to achieve. Sometimes bigger does not mean more money and sometimes, your goals are not completely motivated by money.

Work Model

The other option is to set goals based on your model of work. How many hours a week do you want to work? Are there certain times of day you want to work? Do you want to travel? This can limit your ability to grow, and will call for realistic expectations of what you can achieve with the limitations you set on your business. The hours you are willing to devote to your business, and the distance you are willing to travel will determine your clients and your services. Remember, you are selling your knowledge, your expertise, and your professionalism. You will need clientele whose needs fit into your model of work.

> *My biggest mistake in starting my own business was in not setting goals that meant something to me.*

One thing most consultants will share with you is that without goal setting, you will not run your business, it will run you. In Arina Nikitina's article, "7 Little Known Goal Setting Tips," she lists as the second of the seven tips, "Ask yourself, why do I want to achieve this goal?" (Nikitina 2008). Many times, you set goals because that is what everyone tells you to do. But really, what are the goals for your business? Is it to make lots of money? Is it pride of ownership? Is it to be your own boss? Do you want to make a difference in your area for safety services? The list is as endless as goals may be. It is imperative that you know why you are doing what you are doing.

My biggest mistake in starting my own business was in not setting goals that meant something to me. I set goals based on immediate need: pay off the business loan, secure accounts that would meet payroll, build my company's reputation, and so forth. While these are important items, they are actually simply necessary parts of any business, not true goals. Goals should challenge you, but should also support your ideas about your company, and what made you start it in the first place. They should be used to define your company and motivate you and any personnel you have.

To this day, goal setting is still a challenge for me. I tend to let the company run me, and then I run the company based on clients' needs and expectations, not necessarily my own needs. This is an easy trap to fall into, especially when you first start a business focusing on customer satisfaction. It is not, however, the element that should determine the size, scope, or success of your business. You have to do that, and it takes a some soul searching and goal setting to get there.

When you set goals, they must be specific. Setting a goal to make lots of money or to be the best safety consulting firm in the area is too vague and hard to define. True goal setting is not a simple statement; it is an outline that starts with the end result.

You will find that the challenges to meet the payroll, pay vendors, draw a salary, and so on, will almost set your goals for you. In fact, if you are not careful, the constant running of the business (taxes, payroll, bills, financials, and so on) may be overwhelming; it still is for me, even after all these years. One of the ways to combat this is to take the part of the job that you dislike the most, and subcontract it out. I personally do not like payroll, payroll taxes, and so on; because of that, I have an accounting firm that does all that. When I looked at the cost of outsourcing versus keeping payroll in-house, I was surprised to find it was less expensive to outsource our payroll. Now I know this is being taken care of, and I don't have to worry about it. I can spend my time on other areas, like marketing or client satisfaction.

Remember, anything you add to your plate will have an impact on your greatest resource, your time.

If a time comes that you feel you are losing your passion for safety in the midst of all the bills, financial decisions, personnel issues, and client complaints, then pause and look back before you grow forward, or decide not to continue as an independent consultant. It is important to find the level of ownership that allows you to believe in your business and still love what you do. Don't be afraid to scale back or outsource tasks if you need to.

Setting Goals for the Future

As you set your goals for the future, you will need to learn a few tools of the safety consulting trade. As we discussed, it is important to introduce yourself to scheduling and self-discipline, as well as reasonable expectations. Get some system that requires you to be accountable for your time during the normal work week, and start filling up that calendar. Then make sure the work you are filling up is actual billable time. If you don't have enough billable time scheduled, fill up the time with marketing, prospect contacts, or continuing your education. What works well with your day? I realized I had to diversify my business so that I could conduct site audits and client visits on some days, and write safety programs and training on others. I always keep work at hand. I have never had a goal to get caught up. A safety professional does not want to get so far behind that he or she can't deliver to the client, but getting caught up is putting yourself out of business. Also, it is so easy to work day after day and never really get anything done. I still struggle with that, even after all this time. You will need to find something that keeps you focused on the goal.

Set professional and personal goals; sometimes, they may even be a little of a blend of both. But don't forget that it is important to have a life outside of your business. Again, balance is the key. Many times when you own your own time, you are looked at as being able to volunteer for many outside activities. Either people do not see consulting as a "real job," or they believe you "can't be fired." Well, not showing up for your own business will get you "fired" just as quickly as if a boss lets you go for not showing up to work. You just basically fire yourself. Learning to say *no* was and still is one of the traits that I consider a weakness. I have gotten better over the years, but I had my fair share of years of trying to be Superwoman. It was not that I wanted to do everything, be everything, and please everyone; it was that I just could not say "no" to requests to help others. If you are this type of person, believe me, it will be discovered quickly, and you will be taken advantage of in the workplace, as well as in your community.

Some professional goals may include becoming more active in professional associations. I have been a member of American Society of Safety Engineers (ASSE) for many years, active in various projects, but had not been in a leadership role. When I first started my second safety consulting business, I relocated to another town and joined the local ASSE for networking opportunities. I recommend it to anyone wanting to have their own safety consulting business. In fact, networking at the chapter level will assist you in making the right decisions of where to spend your time in the positive, non-billable aspects of your business. I was very happy to see that we had a strong ASSE chapter in my new town. However, very soon after joining the local ASSE chapter, as I was establishing my new consulting business, one of the other members volunteered me as the membership chair for the local chapter. I, of course, could not say no, and so there I was with one of the most time-consuming positions in the chapter. While I enjoyed my role, the timing was not the best for me.

Two years later, I was asked to be the Chapter President. At that time, my business was more established, so I could commit to the obligation without it having a negative impact on my business. In fact, it was a very positive experience. I developed long-term friendships from this experience that continue to this day. Make sure that when you commit to your outside activities, the timing is right to actually commit to the project. Remember, anything you add to your plate will have an impact on your greatest resource, your time. It is imperative that you judge what benefits (and they don't have to be monetary) you will get from volunteering for outside activities.

Get some system that requires you to be accountable for your time during the normal work week. . . .

Set Timelines for Goals

Goals should have deadlines and timelines. Ask yourself what goals mean the most to you. How close were you to achieving those goals? Then add a three- to five-year plan to the numbers. Break it down into billable hours. Do you need additional staff to accomplish the goals? This helps your decision-making process for achieving what you want with your business. Some questions to ponder include:

1. What were the goals you set a year ago?
   _____
   _____

2. Did you achieve them?
   _____
   _____

3. What factors affected your ability to achieve these goals?
   _____
   _____

Take the time to list things you feel very good about accomplishing in the first year of business. Revisit your business plan and original goals, looking at how you accomplished them. Whether you reached a goal of a certain number of clients, a monetary sales goal, or paying off a bank loan, knowing you accomplished some of your initial goals will increase your confidence as a business owner. You can use that knowledge going forward.

Money is rarely the only goal for a business.

Just as important as listing the goals you met is listing the goals you did not meet, maybe even more so. Now is the time to reset your business plan, if your goals are not being met. While it may be a little painful to admit to some mistakes, it will also be very constructive to be honest about the mistakes you made in the first year, and to adjust accordingly. Find out now why those goals were not obtained. This critical evaluation is beneficial going forward.

Whether or not you accomplished the first year's goal, now is the time to set some new ones or to revamp the old ones. Every year when I am setting my goals, I pull out that first year's goals, and use them to think about where we were then and where we are now. I also look back at the year before. In fact, my profit and loss statements are set up to show both last year and this year, so I can do a quick comparison of where we are today as opposed to a year ago. By setting the P&L up this way, I can do a quick comparison of sales every month. It gives me a bar to use for comparison, allowing me to monitor my monetary goals easily.

What goals do you wish to achieve going forward?

Money is rarely the only goal for a business. In fact, if that is the only reason for starting a safety consulting business, you may be disappointed at the end of the first year. Pride of ownership and knowing you can bring a much-needed service to the world of safety may be a motivator that exceeds the weekly paycheck. Again, goal setting and reviewing those goals many times provides us with an insight on why we are trying to achieve the goal in the first place.

1. What personal goals have you set?
   _____
   _____

2. Did you meet them?
   _____
   _____

3. What are your next goals?
   _____
   _____

4. What long-range goals have you set?
   _____
   _____

5. Have you included goals for your personal life, such as time away?
   _____
   _____

6. Do your goals include your family?
   _____
   _____

Without goals, you will find yourself in reactive mode instead of proactive mode, wasting a consultant's most important commodity, time. Setting goals with realistic and specific deadlines will prevent the derailing of you, your business and the success that is waiting for you.

HOME RUN: WHEW, WE ARE DONE

Well, by now you should know the above will never be true. A safety consulting business is a moving target. Safety is always growing, always changing. With the daily introduction of knowledge, as well as the growing need for experienced safety professionals, the field itself keeps evolving. The tools we have today astound me sometimes. When I first started, we did not have computers, PowerPoint, Excel spreadsheets, and the Internet at our fingertips. Instead, we had overhead projectors (look it up if you don't know what I'm talking about), handouts, and fax sheets. There were not a lot of resources to draw on to assist in teaching and research.

The wealth of knowledge we have today is a valuable tool. To be able to conduct an ergonomic study and go to the Internet for backup resources is so much easier than going back to our books for formulas on range of motion (ROM), as in the "old" days. We did not have cellphones when I started. You had an appointment, and you went and hoped they were there. Or you called ahead, planning every detail to maximize your time, because drive time was down time. Anytime you were away from the landline telephone was a business interruption. Now, with scanners, cellphones, the Internet, and online scheduling techniques, being in touch with your business has become so much easier. This also allows your income to increase but then, so has your stress level! It is easy to find yourself on the clock 24/7. This is very true for me, and something I have to watch. Now, when I go on vacation, I only check my emails and make a call to the office once a day; then I shut it all off. Life is short, and time with family and friends shorter.

Having a safety consulting business can be one of the most rewarding parts of your life. It will not be for everyone, but it may be for you. This workbook is all about discovering if you are that person or not.

To this day, I still go back over the notes of pros and cons that I put down on paper when I decided to start my own consulting business. I still have days when I will ask myself if I did the right thing. I have fired myself more than once, only to rehire myself immediately. You will have days when you will question whether you did the right thing or not. You will also have days of great accomplishment. In the end, no one can make this decision but you. Use this workbook as the tool it was intended to be, letting it assist you in making the right choices for you. Whatever you decide, if you utilize the information you have gained in this workbook, you will be able to be know that you are making an educated decision on what you choose to do and be comfortable in that decision.

For me, it has been a journey, one that is not over, and one that has been rewarding and fulfilling in the discovery of my passion for this business, and the ability to teach others to save their own lives. There is nothing I would rather do than what I am doing in my career. At the end of the day, when you evaluate where you are and where you want to be, add the plus column and the minus column, and see where you are. I encourage you to do this every year, so your goals and your commitment to safety will always be in the plus column, whether you own your own consulting business or pursue other avenues. It is ultimately your choice, and isn't that in itself exciting?

Lessons Learned

These are some of the lessons I learned about being a consultant:

I have fired myself more than once, only to rehire myself immediately.

1. Know what you are good at and passionate about, and what you need others to do.
2. Recognize your limitations.
3. Learn to say **No**.
4. Time management is critical.
5. Review your goals and state of your business every year.

CONCLUSION

Now let's bring this information together to pinpoint your strengths and areas that are now in place, as well as those which need improvement. Let's use a list to organize our thoughts:

1. Are you comfortable with your business structure? This could include the bank you have chosen, your accounting firm, even your clerical help (if applicable). List the items that you believe are working for you in your financial setup. After you list the items you feel good about, list those that you would change.

    Good:

    _____
    _____
    _____

    Changes I would like to make:

    _____
    _____
    _____
    _____

2. Now look at the client-service relationship you are providing, and see if the services correlate with the clientele you are trying to attract. Again, list what works and what does not. Include the reasons you think each works or does not work.

    Client-service relationship that is working and why?

    _____
    _____
    _____

Client-service relationship that is not working and why?

_____
_____
_____

3. Finally, is your business moving towards providing the rewards you had originally anticipated? These could be monetary, personal satisfaction, peer professional acknowledgement, and so forth. Again, include your reasons, particularly if you think they will help you understand your answers when you look back at them later.

Rewards are what I expected (List what and why):

_____
_____
_____

Rewards are not being met (List what and why):

_____
_____
_____

I encourage you to review the chapters as you need to, complete any and all questionnaires, and challenge yourself to complete the review process of this workbook. Then take the information, study it, and let it help you decide if safety consulting is right (or is still right) for you. Include all factors such as family, your own personality, how much time you wish to devote to this endeavor, and the overall feasibility of making this work. There is no pass or fail on this test. The information provided here is to assist you in making the right choice for you. Only you can do that. Either choice, providing safety services whether through your own consulting firm or working for others, is still a worthy career.

You've processed a lot of information, from marketing to client relationships, evaluating what has or has not worked, and, hopefully, considered your needs and the needs of your family. We've discussed living and working through your passions, saying "no" when you need to, and taking lessons learned forward as your business matures. The next chapter has short essays from safety consultants on how they've made all this work—what brought them into consulting and how they balance (or attempt to balance) work and life.

BIBLIOGRAPHY

Eisenhower, D. D. 1954. *Public Papers of the Presidents Dwight D. Eisenhower.* (Retrieved DATE) http//coursesa.matrix.msu.edu/~hst306/documents/domino.html

Hinneburg, C. 2013. How to improve organizational skills (retrieved November 14, 2014). www.ehow.com/how_6180952_improve-organizational-skills.html

Merriam Webster Dictionary. 2014. "Niche" (retrieved November 14, 2014). www.merriam-webster.com/dictionary/niche

Nikitina, A. 2008. 7 Little Known Tips That Will Turn your Vague Dreams Into Tangible Reality (retrieved November 14, 2014). www.achieve-goal-setting-success.com/support-files/7tipsreport.pdf

Perry, Y. 2006. *Job satisfaction—finding balance between work and play.* (Retrieved November 14, 2014). http://ezinearticles.com/?Job-Satisfaction—Finding-Balance-Between-Work-and-Play&id=356079

Reh, J. F. 2013. *Passion pays* (retrieved November 14, 2014). http://management.about.com/cs/yourself/a/PassionPays.htm

Schaefer, P. 2011. *The seven pitfalls of business failure.* (retrieved November 14, 2014). www.businessknowhow.com/startup/business-failure.htm

Small Business Administration, Office of Advocacy. 2012. *Frequently Asked Questions about Small Business* (retrieved February 3, 2014). www.sba.gov/advocacy/7495/29581

A lot of work went into developing the technical content of this book. The Editors worked very hard to identify the most important information that was essential to OS&H consultants who were just getting started and for existing consultants who wanted to check their progress and look for ways to improve their business.

As we were soliciting proposals from potential authors, Kathy Hart suggested that we not forget to talk about the "soft" side of consulting—how to "make it work". She suggested that we explore the variety of ways in which consultants were already successfully making it work by asking them to write a short essay about their journey. We thought we could write that chapter on our own, but decided that listening to the voices of consultants who have been at it for a while was the best way to provide readers with a multitude of perspectives for consideration.

We put out a call for essays and what follows are the best that we received. We hope they will provide you with a variety of perspectives on success so that you can decide for yourself what success will mean. The technical chapters are critical to successful consulting, but Chapter 11 will help you know when you have arrived.

Carol Keyes
J. A. Rodriguez, Jr.
Pam Walaski

CHAPTER 11

Making It Work on Your Own

Editor's Comments

Introduction

The day comes when Robert N. Andres discovers and realizes that his skill set can do more, can be more than his position demands, and how he can capitalize on this discovery. Robert shares the primary reasons why consultants are in business and the responsibilities bestowed upon us to deliver value at every opportunity. He expounds on several crucial lessons learned from his decades of experience.

Rules of the Road to a Successful Consultancy
ROBERT N. ANDRES, CSP, CPE, CMFGE, DABFE, INCE

Like many, I segued into the safety profession. My particular route was from manufacturing and plant engineering in the aerospace industry, followed by production management in automotive aftermarket manufacturing. Along the way, including a three-year stint in the Army, I picked up the skills that would help develop my career.

I became a consultant in safety and noise control as an offshoot from an existing job as a reasonably competent technical salesman in the same fields. It became evident that I knew enough about machine and facility safety, and noise control, to offer more than other salesmen, and that there were instances where a solution may not require the purchase of any equipment or materials. Fortunately, capitalization was not an issue, as I shared office space and equipment with my other company.

Over the years, I have learned that to be a good consultant, you must be keenly aware that you are hired by a client:

- Because someone feels that you have a particular talent they need, and they have no one readily available with your mix of expertise.
- Because someone feels that you are a cost-effective investment, and that you can solve (or help solve) a problem or add something to their operations/organization.

If you can't do that (no matter how much money you're making), you are wasting your time and talent, and the client's money!

You are in a service industry. This means providing a service that will help better your client's outcome. It's not about your ego. It's not about the money or whatever else you may want. It's all about the client's needs.

Here are a few valuable lessons I learned as a consultant over the past 34 years:

1. *Never compromise your integrity.* You aren't hired to win a popularity contest. With few exceptions, your client is looking for candid advice and critical evaluation. You need to be ready to tell them your expert, unvarnished opinion.

    If you are a testifying expert, you will often be asked by attorneys to mold your opinions to suit their needs. Even though they are paying you, you must make it clear that you are a professional, and will not compromise the truth, as you see it, when testifying. If you twist the truth in a deposition or on the witness stand, it will come back to destroy your credibility. These days, everything you say can be discovered, whether or not you want it to be.

2. *Network.* A good consultant, in my opinion, specializes. He/she also knows other consultants who may specialize in other fields and will not hesitate to pass on clients needing that expertise. Take every opportunity to meet and talk with other safety and health professionals and learn what they do best.

    I would say that about 90 percent of the consulting business I get is from "word-of-mouth" communication, with well over half being referrals from my esteemed colleagues in the profession. I still keep in regular touch with a safety director I worked with over 40 years ago.

3. ***Stay on Top.*** Attend monthly ASSE meetings and, when possible, professional development conferences, shows, and seminars to stay current on advances within the field of safety and health. Also, take advantage of specialized offerings for consultants and small businesses. All of this helps you build your "network" as well.

    Work on your communications skills. Technical people are notorious for having poor communication skills. Knowing the answers is only half of the equation; communicating your findings and opinions is the other half and what will really set you apart.

    Always carry a supply of well-designed and professional-looking business cards. Business cards are the least costly form of advertising.

    If you look at the schedule for Safety 2015, the ASSE Professional Development Conference & Exposition being held in Dallas, you will see a selection of nearly 260 presentations over three days, covering virtually every aspect of safety and health. There's a lot there to absorb.

    In the alternative, if you look at the schedule for any ASSE Professional Development Conference & Exposition, you will see a varied and selection of presentations.

4. ***Charge a fair price.*** Do an objective analysis of the market in the territory you wish to cover, and see how your particular talents fit. Find out what others are charging, and adjust accordingly.

    Keep in mind that, if you charge too much, you will generally get less work; if you charge too little, you will not be seen as having value, and will also get less work. (This is one of the valuable pieces of information I got from attending a SEAK Seminar for Experts a few years ago.)

    I lost a job up in northern Michigan last year because I was trying to control costs for the prospective client (a governmental agency) by scheduling the site visit along job nearby. I knew from experience that the observations would take little time, but they questioned why I priced it so low and, ultimately, hired an engineering firm for twice the price. Perhaps they were using that old formula that tells the purchasing people to reject the highest and lowest bid.

5. ***Be Confident.*** If you want to be seen as an expert in your chosen field of safety and health, you need to keep "on top" and exude confidence, but exercise care to never be arrogant or condescending.

This is particularly important if you are a testifying expert, as the jury's perception is sometimes even more important than the substance of your testimony. Know your topic, and know your data, but do not think or act like you have all the answers.

When in court, present yourself as humble, but extremely knowledgeable on your subject. Talk in everyday terms that the judge and jury can easily understand. I have found this to be a winning formula. On a drowning case many years ago, I used an analogy to explain the defendant's actions. In the subsequent appeal (which was denied), the NYC attorney said that I had "inflamed" the jury. I received congratulatory calls from attorneys all over the country. (Apparently, expert witnesses are better known for putting juries to sleep than creating any emotion.)

6. *Be Available.* Again, you are in the service business. This means being available when you are needed. This alone can set you apart from the competition.

7. *Take Advantage of New Forms of Communication.* If you are trying to get established as a consultant, find a professional to design and establish a Web site, get on LinkedIn, Facebook, and other social media sites, and utilize Internet communications to enhance your network. A qualified consultant can help you select key words and get you great placement on online directories that are being routinely used by prospective clients.

I recently received a call at 4PM on a Monday, requesting me to take sound level readings at 6AM the following morning. I drove 120 miles, took the readings and photos, drove back to the office, downloaded the data, wrote and e-mailed the report with recommendations by 2PM, in time for their 5PM meeting.

Editor's Commentary

Many of Robert's lessons are segues to the chapters in this book. Say what you do, do what you say, be a super connector of people, add value, demonstrate confidence, be there, and keep up with the times are the price of admission to the consulting stage. We often tackle the big things well. It is focusing on the little things that offer your clients a glimpse of your potential and uncompromising competitive advantage.

Editor's Comments

Introduction

Jeffery C. Camplin takes us on a familiar journey; one of finding your calling, and determining what is important in your life. This is easier said than done, and is often the cause of sleepless nights and long workdays. He unveils the path that has helped him shift from a struggling consultant to a highly successful one. Jeffery also offers a glimpse into his discovery of wealth and what it really means to him.

The Foundation of a Successful Consulting Business
JEFFERY C. CAMPLIN, MS, CSP, CPEA

My goal when I started my consulting firm in January 1991, at the ripe old age of 27, was simple: become rich by age 35. Along the way to this goal, I learned quite a bit about being a consultant, while also clarifying what being "rich" actually meant to me. In the end, I learned more about myself and how to live a truly meaningful life. What follows is some brief insight into how I found my life's calling and how my consulting practice continues to help facilitate that end. My story is conveyed in four points that I hope will benefit you in becoming a successful consultant on your way to building your own legacy.

1. *Have a Life Strategy; Then Align Your Business Goals.* When I first started my consulting practice, I had a vision for growth. I beat the bushes for business, and started hiring people. Within two years, I had 15 people on staff. Money was coming in, and going out just as fast. Managing employees, jobs, cash flow, and new work consumed my time. I was busy; actually, more liked swamped. But I wasn't happy or satisfied. I now found that I dreaded going to work. My company was running me, instead of the other way around.

    An epiphany occurred one day as I was driving to a client, listening to a cassette tape on goal setting (back in those old days we didn't have iPods, which I do now). The presenter stated that, "in order to be successful, you have to pay the price." In this case, the price he was referring to was sacrificing your relationships with family and friends as you climbed to the top. I decided right then I wasn't going to pay that price.

Then the second epiphany occurred. I was listening to another presentation on goal setting. This presenter stated that to really have meaningful goals you have to begin with the end in mind. "Imagine your funeral . . . what do you want people to say about you? How do you want to be remembered? What is your legacy?" After pondering and really thinking through these questions, I ended up with a hierarchy of my life priorities: my marriage, my kids, volunteerism, my profession, and my business. It became clear to me that the path I was on was leading me away from those things that were most important to me in my life. This is why I was unsatisfied and unhappy.

My advice: Know what is really important to you, and make that your priority. Your business goals should get aligned and support your life strategy. You must run your business; don't let it run you.

2. *Learn Sales and Negotiating Skills; These are Required 24/7.* As stated above, I listen to books/presentations while traveling. I read a lot, too. The top skills I believe any consultant must develop and enhance are in salesmanship and negotiation. These two skills go hand-in-hand. Knowing how to present your value, overcome objections, find the decision makers, and negotiate and close a deal are the keys to your success. There are many steps and variations to making a sale.

Salesmanship to me simply means understanding what the other person wants/needs and finding a way your services can satisfy them. Salesmanship also means selling yourself and developing a personal relationship. Have several elevator speeches ready on all of the services you provide. Imagine having a ten-second "elevator ride" with a decision maker. How would you gain their interest and educate them on your value in two or three sentences? Salesmanship teaches you how to do this.

The second skill is negotiation. We negotiate and are being negotiated by others all of the time. A good consultant must know all of the negotiation styles and, particularly, the countermoves to those styles. When negotiating a price for your services, do you know the countermove when someone says, "Let's split the difference?" Do you know if you split the difference, they will usually try to split the difference again?

An equally important point in both negotiation and salesmanship is to have confidence in your value. Too often, we lose confidence in our value and undersell the monetary worth of our services. Don't sell yourself short. Believe in your value; if you don't, then why would anyone else? Once you know your value, use salesmanship to negotiate for its full potential, while also seeking a win-win by satisfying the client's wants and/or needs.

Salesmanship and negotiations are also important for cash flow. Getting and doing the work is only half of the battle. You must be ready to use salesmanship and negotiation skills to get your invoice pushed through the system and paid in a timely manner. You will need that money to grow, pay bills, and pay yourself.

3. ***Build up Your Credentials; Demonstrate Your Competencies.*** As stated above, I listen to books/presentations while traveling. I read a lot, too. The top skills I believe any consultant must develop and enhance are in salesmanship and negotiation. These two skills go hand-in-hand. Knowing how to present your value, overcome objections, find the decision makers, and negotiate and close a deal are the keys to your success. There are many steps and variations to making a sale.

It is important to work on your image and how others perceive you. In fact, in order to get interest in your consulting services, you have to gain their attention first. Building relationships with clients as a consultant requires their confidence and trust in you and your abilities. This takes character, but it also requires competency and results in what author Steven Covey calls trustworthiness: having both character *and* competency. Without trust, a consultant is worthless to a client. Therefore, being able to demonstrate your competency is important.

Competency can be demonstrated with credentials: certifications, degrees, and accreditations. Never use lack of time as a reason for not pursuing credentials that validate your competency. We can always use the excuse that we don't have time. My advice: Make time!

4. ***Volunteer: The Return on Your Time Investment Is Huge.*** The perception from others of your experience, knowledge, and competency can be further enhanced through public speaking, professional writing, and volunteering/contributing to professional organizations. As consultants, we often find our subject matter expertise and clientele to be very narrow in focus. Volunteerism offers an avenue to expand your knowledge, experience, networks, and audiences, while also giving back to your profession.

Volunteerism provides an opportunity to try new things, develop new skills, and find new opportunities with very little downside for failure. As an unpaid volunteer, I learned how to write professionally, after failing numerous times. As an unpaid volunteer, I enhanced my knowledge and speaking skills by presenting at various venues. After years of working on these skills, I now get paid to write and speak on my areas of expertise. Had I not honed these skills as an unpaid volunteer, I may not have been proficient enough or be able to demonstrate my competency enough when these paid opportunities came my way.

Finally, volunteer activities give you the opportunity to get in front of large audiences of potential clients. An easy start can be within your own community. Look for clubs, trade groups or professional associations that have local chapter meetings in your areas, as they are always looking for luncheon speakers or authors for their newsletters. I have generated a lot of leads and many sales from articles I wrote, presentations I made, or from credentials/experience I acquired from volunteerism.

My final advice is: When in doubt about any aspect of improving your consulting practice, just rely on the old NIKE slogan and "Just Do It." Good luck!

Editor's Commentary

In the end, consulting is about adding tremendous value in the eyes of your client. Understanding your life strategy and utilizing that springboard to align your business goals is a great place to start. Building up your sales and negotiating skills along with your credentials will offer the gift of presence, the X factor of the most successful consultants. Focusing on giving back pays forward in many ways, often in ways that cannot be measured.

Editor's Comments

Introduction

Work-life balance is a term that implies simplicity and equality. This is often better said than done. Paul Gant discusses how he and others achieves work-life balance, despite the demands and challenges as a working consultant. He notes how his work adds meaning to everything he does, and how everything he does adds meaning to his work.

Balancing a Life of Safety
PAUL GANTT, M.ENG, CSP, CET

The issues associated with assessing one's work-life balance are clearly something that should be addressed, given the potential for negative consequences to arise. For most occupations, it is important to leave your work behind when you leave the office and come home. Failing to do this can result in a number of problems, including those related to physical and relational consequences. But in the field of occupational safety and health, there is a bit of a dilemma given that what we do, the application of safety, impacts all aspects of our life. So how does one deal with this, and gain a real balance?

My situation is somewhat unique in that I work in a family business that provides occupational safety and health services. Other members of my family work with me, and share a passion for what we do. Safety is not just a job; it is the way we live our lives. We talk safety, we practice safety, and we look for ways to apply what we do to all aspects of our personal and professional lives. As one might expect, this situation does present a number of opportunities that can be both positive as well as negative. After all, can one ever be too safe, or can the obsession to be safe ever become too much?

As with many other areas of our lives, too much of a good thing can result in problems. And even though we are passionate about what we do, we need to also fold in other activities to allow our minds and bodies to remain in a healthy state. Some of those that work for most people are obvious, and include maintaining the proper physical and mental health. This can and should include proper diet, regular exercise, and taking time out to relax. That time does not need to be excessive, but getting a mind vacation is important. Many experts also suggest having hobbies that allow you to change gears and focus on other aspects of the world outside of your primary work. However, everyone is different and requires a different formula to achieve the correct balance. In some cases, longer periods of time are required to achieve balance. For others, shorter mini-breaks are all that are required.

For many seeking to get that needed break, reading fiction or some type of unassociated literature is helpful. In my case, I don't have a lot of free reading time and instead, use the time that I do have to catch up on safety periodicals and books that are related to what I do. As Steven Covey identifies in his book, *The 7 Habits of Highly Effective People*, this is the one related to sharpening the sword. I find that I am more effective and less stressed in my primary work as a safety professional when I am up to date on my reading. So I prefer to not read much that is significantly unrelated to what I do in my work life.

However, there are other ways to clear one's head and essentially "drop off the planet" that do not involve reading. The use of a hobby, as we identified previously, is one way. For some, that can incorporate physical aspects that allow both mind and body to get away and get strengthened in the process. Bicycle riding, hiking, swimming, and even golf are good examples of those that work for many. But hobbies do not necessarily need to be standard ones that others use. While there are many definitions of the term hobby, most agree that it is an activity that is done outside of one's primary occupation for the purpose of finding relaxation or pleasure. I have a number of associates who go to movies on a regular basis, and see almost every new one that comes out, who work on cars or motorcycles, who play or act in community groups, or who travel. Any of these types of activities can provide the necessary mind and body rest that is needed to remain both healthy and productive.

When I advise others in our industry about my approach to this, I generally point out that they have chosen a profession that is not like many others. It is not one that you simply can walk away from at the end of the day, and expect that when you return, everything will be fine. The world of professional occupational safety and health is one that requires more than the standard "it's only a job" mentality. Our choice of vocations is one that requires us to continually stay abreast of changes that are continuing to occur. To not do so would cause one to fall behind, given all of the changes that we are starting to see unfold. So we need to work outside of work in order to keep up. Also, our vocation is one that requires us to pay attention to all aspects of our lives, and apply our trade continually, both on and off the job. It is one that requires us to think safety pretty much all of the time. We cannot and should not let our guards down just because we are off duty. Others who see us talking one way when we are working, and living another way outside of work, will soon realize the hypocrisy of what is happening.

As part of my advice to those in our profession, I also remind them that we are not all the same. Those may require far less time off than others might. I actually prefer to work more than others might, as I have a passion for what I do. What I do with my life is what I have chosen to do, and so my balance is not defined as either work or play. For me, working is fun, and it is part of my play. For others, this alignment may not work, and they should look to find the proper balance in their lives, balance that will keep them healthy and productive.

Editor's Commentary

How is work-life balance defined or achieved? The likelihood is high that if ten people were asked this question, you will record ten different answers. It is this very personal definition that quarantines the perceptions of being overworked or of feeling underutilized or of achieving the elusive state of work-life balance. The key to your definition of success is to find your norm and commit to living by it whether at work or at play.

Editor's Comments

Introduction

Terry Grisim (as many of us know him) first established his consulting business during a recession in the 1980s. I've known Terry for several years and highly respect his experience and perspective. While a work lay-off pushed him to start his own business initially, it took a few additional employers and training before the self-employment stuck. Terry shares some great nuggets of advice about company name, considerations when heading out on your own, debt, and determining your niche.

Good Advice Taken and Mistakes Made
J. TERRENCE GRISIM, CSP, CDS, CPSM, ARM

Much of what I have learned about business, and just about all I learned about work/life balance, I learned from my dad. One of my earliest memories of advice from my dad, who owned his own business, was his frequent admonition to my younger brother, Jeff, and I, "You'll never make any money working for someone else." It would be many years later, just before his untimely death, that the advice soaked in. Sadly for me, he never saw the fruits of his sage guidance. I spent countless hours at my dad's auto and truck repair and body shop from a very tender age. My dad used to reminisce about my brother Jeff standing on a milk crate, running the electric shop door up and down for minutes at a time when he was about five years old. When we were older, he actually paid us some money for things like cleaning his office, and sweeping the floor, which was also a gift, because both of us freely raided his Coke machine all day. He never tired of teaching us all he knew, and sending us to the General Motors Training Center to teach us the more complex things about automobiles. When I was a teenager we, mostly he, were building hot rods for Jeff and me. I don't think I ever remember him losing his patience with us. When I was about 19, I came to the conclusion this is not what I wanted to do. Jeff reached the same one as well. Dad told us, "You two better get an education, because neither one of you wants to get your hands dirty."

Like so many consultants, I started my company in 1982, upon being fired from a job. I was working for a national insurance brokerage firm, and was on contract to a major client of that firm as a full-time employee, performing as the safety director of their manufacturing operations. One day when I was on the road in Detroit, I received a call from the office manager of my employer, telling me I had 30 days, and I was on the street. I knew the client was having major financial problems, but did not see this coming. To this day, I remember that the five-hour drive back to Chicago to tell my wife what had happened was one of the longest of my life.

At this time my wife, Mary Ellen, was a stay-at-home mom, and our two sons, Kevin and Mike, were four and five years old. For those of you that weren't around at the time, 1982 was in the midst of a very serious recession, and marked the beginning of some very large changes in the insurance industry, including the first of many massive layoffs of safety people whose positions would never return.

After some long soul searching with my wife, we decided that my going into business for myself was the best option. She went back to work, so we had insurance, and I went to see our family accountant for advice. In addition, I attended some startup classes at the local junior college. Of course, there were some adjustments to be made with her going back to work that I didn't anticipate, like trips to doctors and schools.

To this day, Mary Ellen and I refer to these as my "Mr. Mom" years. It was a real adjustment, but we got through it.

Some of the best advice I received was from our accountant, who gave me some sage guidance, which included warning me that the biggest cause of start-up failures was spending too much, and getting in too much debt. A second was the name of my company. As many do, I was going to call the company Grisim Associates. He told me that was a lousy idea, because it didn't tell anyone what we did, so I settled on Safety Management Consultants, Inc. He also got my business incorporated as a subchapter S corporation.

If there is one mantra I have never forsaken, it is my disdain for any debt, no doubt because of my parent's Depression-era stories. I believe it is at the core of where I am now. When I got fired, my then employer sold me my four-year-old company car. Just a few months prior, my employer had paid to build an office in my basement for me to work, as their Chicago division office, where I had been headquartered, had closed. As a result, I started out with a virtually overhead-free place to work. All these years later, I'm still there, but I came out of the basement and built an addition to our house in 1992 with a more spacious office.

This initial adventure only lasted about four months, when I realized I wasn't cutting it in business. This was especially true because I had no real business plan, except waiting for the phone to ring. Believe it or not, it did, a few times, just not enough. Following this initial foray into business, I went on to have three further employers, the last of which gave me some valuable sales and marketing training before they decided they did not want to be in the safety business anymore. I had a few months to get my house in order, and they gave us the business they had, so we had some regular income to start.

By this time, our boys were 11 and 12 years old. Between my working from home and our moms helping out, we made it work. It was during this time I decided to explore expert witness work. I had always wanted to do it, but none of my employers would let me. After a couple of years, it became obvious that I was not going to make it in the accident prevention business, but the expert witness business was looking promising. By about 1997, it was virtually all I did and continue to do. It was the best decision I ever made in terms of the business. The second most important thing I did was to invest in training in the field. I have attended a two-day expert witness seminar every year since I have been in business. I credit that ongoing training, more than anything else, for keeping my skills on top of my field. I cannot overemphasize the importance of ongoing skills development.

As far as potholes, I've learned some valuable lessons. The first one is being self-employed is not for everyone. My brother Jeff did it for years, got increasingly unhappy with it, and went back to work for someone. I could never work for someone else again after 24 years on my own. Anyone contemplating this decision to be self-employed owes themselves a lot of soul searching before striking out on their own.

Another lesson learned is by working alone at home, I do not have a partner to whom I can sell the business when I decide to retire. So as of this moment, succession planning is an area where I have fallen short.

Editor's Commentary

As Terry exemplifies, just because you start a business once and return to working for someone else, does not mean failure. It is an opportunity to learn from the experience, and gain additional knowledge you may need to be successful. A concern that all consultants, whether working on their own or in a small group, must face once their business is established, is succession planning: what to do for retirement.

Editor's Comments

Introduction

Similar to Terry, Steve High had family who set the example for owning your own business. He also he had small children at home who played into business decisions. As so many other essay authors noted, the flexibility of consulting may help you meet the obligations of family, but you have to balance that with the demands of business. Your business is essentially another child, one that is always demanding. Learning to say no, to set boundaries, and have a support network (professional and family/personal) are some of the reminders that Steve offers.

Consulting as a Way of Life—A Work-Life Balance . . . or Not
STEVEN HIGH, MS, ARM, CSP, CHST

There are others, I am sure, who have mastered the work-life balance much better than I have. In fact, by most measures, I would presume that many would say that I've failed miserably in this aspect. So perhaps this is a lesson in what not to do as much as what to do. I was born in 1964, just making into the "baby boomers" generation. The motto of the boomers is "live to work," and I've done this well.[1]

I had the luxury of starting my business within the context of a larger family company, which could support the start-up costs and cover negative cash-flows of a new business venture. I have great respect for colleagues who have risked financial peril in establishing their businesses without the safety net that I had. Our family business was started by my conservative grandfather in 1931 as a small welding company in the middle of the depression. He was known as a hard worker, and his perseverance is fabled in family lore. This work ethic carried over to my father, who is more successful in his work-life balance, but clearly, he has intensity for the business, and his efforts grew our companies significantly. Often, he jokes that my grandfather told him that working in the family business only requires half-days. Family members could choose any 12 of the 24 hours in the day to work.

Today our businesses include structural steel bridge manufacturing, precast concrete, steel service center processing, construction, various forms of real estate holdings, and a number of other companies (www.high.net). I served in the safety

---

[1] Gursoy, D., T. Maier, and C. Chi. 2008. "Generational Differences: An Examination of Work Values and Generational Gaps in the Hospitality Workforce." *International Journal of Hospitality Management* 27(3): 448–58.

department, and we had successes in safety performance, including being an early adopter of the VPP STAR. In 1997, I decided I wanted to start consulting instead of managing our own companies' safety programs.

My kids were ages six, three and one. I had secured my CSP, and completed the Associate Risk Management (ARM), but decided that my undergraduate degree in business should be supplemented by a Master's degree in Safety Sciences. This necessitated giving up my weekend security job at Tyson Foods, as well as my role as an EMT volunteer with the local ambulance service.

When I started, every project was "new." Training programs took hours to develop and, as workloads increased, we had to meet our obligations. I remember preparing a site-specific training program. The finishing touches were finally in place at 4 am for my 7 am session. Bedtime was immediately following the session. The peaks and valleys of consulting are part of the business. The peaks have to be managed, and the air can be rather thin at the top of some of them.

I tried to be involved with my kids while starting a new business and going to school. I changed my share of diapers. I attended the dance recitals, went on family vacations, and spent time in Cub Scouts. There is always more you can do in the business, and there is always more you can do with your kids. It is important to balance these. In retrospect, I could have done more with my kids. A business associate told me that kids spell love as T-I-M-E.

A business is a lot like another child. You care about it intensely, and it needs your attention to remain healthy. It needs the most attention when it is just born, but always needs your support. If the business is the primary source of family income, it is important for the financial health of its real-world siblings as well.

I am passionate about health and safety. This passion has evolved over the years, starting with care of sudden illness and injury as an EMT, progressing to injury and illness prevention in organizational structures. Now I am interested in community environmental health considerations, as I complete a Masters in Public Health (MPH) at Johns Hopkins with the intent to continue to a terminal degree. This is it: It is what I love to do. Many individuals don't align their passion with their work. They go home at the end of the day, and do woodworking, play sports, watch movies, or attend community-related activities. For me, what I do for work is my hobby, my sport (although I do run), and my entertainment. This is how I justify that my work weeks are rarely less than fifty hours: They are fifty hours of pure fun!

Consulting can provide flexibility that can benefit your family. You may choose to work at home when a child is sick. Often, you can schedule around family obligations when they are known in advance. At the same time, some commitments are nearly unbreakable, with death being the only good excuse for not showing.

So with a look in the rearview mirror, here are a few suggestions:

- Develop a network of associates who have similar skill sets and who could cover for you. If you have a personal crisis, this could be very helpful. Developing an agreement in advance could define a mutually beneficial relationship.
- It will work well if you have the support of your spouse; it will work best if both of you view the business as something you are raising together.
- If you have a bolus of work, celebrate after you complete it by taking the day off, and spending downtime with your family. Put messages on your voicemail and e-mail that you are unavailable.
- Be willing to say no. Clients will ask you to do more at the same price. They will ask you to give up your Saturdays. They will ask you to postpone your vacation, or miss your daughter's school play to train the third shift. You will need to draw lines. Sometimes, it will be a difficult decision about what to do. Be creative about solutions.
- When determining project proposal costs, be liberal with time estimates. Schedule projects so that you have plenty of breathing room to complete the work. Most projects take longer than you think. Underestimated project hours are a double-edged sword; they will require you to work more hours, and result in less income potential.
- Today, we are always connected. I respond to e-mails, phone calls, and texts at all hours of the day. Consider the consultant who left a birthday party to address an urgent customer need. When the client found out that consultant had left the party to address their request, the client asked, "Whose birthday is it?" The consultant responded, "mine," which was probably a much better answer than "my wife's" or "my son's."

Being a business owner requires a significant commitment of time. Your business plan must incorporate any assumptions of personal time away from the business. Clients will respect the lines you draw, but if they are too taut, some may decide you are too difficult. If you drew them in the sand, they may be washed away and never seen again.

It is up to each individual to determine where the lines are between their personal life and the business. Consider how your lines could be different from how other family members perceive these lines. The lines may bend or blur. Consider creating a work-life-balance manifesto that defines how you will preserve your personal life. Sharing this with others in your life may give you more perspective about where to draw the lines.

Editor's Commentary

How is work-life balance defined or achieved? The likelihood is high that if ten people were asked this question, you will record ten different answers. It is this very personal definition that quarantines the perceptions of being overworked or of feeling underutilized or of achieving the elusive state of work-life balance. The key to your definition of success is to find your norm and commit to living by it whether at work or at play.

Editor's Comments

Introduction

John Leseganich tells a compelling story; what worked in your prior job may not work as a consultant. Having knowledge and expertise is critical, but when you work as a consultant, you need much more than that. Your clients may respond differently to you as their consultant than if you were an employee in the company, or a loss control representative, or an OSHA inspector, or whatever your job was/is before consulting. Client motivations may need to be uncovered, you may get frustrated at lack of progress, or you may take offense because a client doesn't see safety as important as you do. Your role will change and the expectations of your clients may need to be defined.

So You Want to Be a Consultant
JOHN P. LESEGANICH, CPEA

Several years ago, I wrote an article about becoming a consultant. While some of that material still holds true, here are a few new things I have learned since that article.

I am sure many of you professional occupational safety and health individuals out there are entertaining the possibility of becoming a private OS&H consultant, once you retire from your current OS&H position, or possibly even now due to cutbacks, closings, or just for a change. If you are like me, you enjoy what you do, you believe in what you do, and you have invested the time to learn your trade. Why wouldn't you want to share all of that knowledge, life experience, and training with others and, make a few bucks doing it? Just being a consultant has a charismatic sound to it, doesn't it?

After spending more than 30 years working with the Occupational Safety and Health Administration, both in compliance and then later in the On Site Consultation sector, I retired and entered the private consulting arena. I presumed my years of experience working with the agency, which so many employers fear (and truly seek compliance based on that fear) would make it a slam-dunk job opportunity. My years of field experience, my years of standards application and interpretation, my hundreds upon hundreds of investigations, my years of rubbing elbows with the agencies' shakers and movers in all of those long sessions on standard development, application, interpretation, program development, new direction, and required action training had to be worth something. Even if I hadn't paid attention, by accident I had to learn a thing or two.

So I retired and began Independent Consultation Services, LLC (known as ICS:), my consulting service. Why the "Independent" title? I wanted to suggest my services were not associated with any other agency or any company that provides any other type of product. Strictly independent between my client and me. The ICS: was sort of a play on the many police investigation shows you've see on TV lately, plus I just couldn't leave behind all of the acronyms I have learned. You know them: OSHA, EPA, NFPA, SST, LEP. I can go on, but I'm sure those of you in the field can add a dozen or so. Allow me to point out that when choosing a name for your consulting firm, do a little marketing research: What would identify you, how would potential clients remember you, what are you all about; thus the ICS: as explained. Easy to remember, fits in with the regulatory acronyms, suggest a one-on-one relationship.

I did everything that had to be done. I incorporated, obtained the necessary insurance, had business cards and the fliers printed, set up the office area at home. I was ready, willing, and able. The first year, right out of the chute, business was good, I must admit. Word got out I had retired, and many of my clients were individuals, employers, or employer representatives whom I had met during my time with the agency. I thought, *Maybe I should have done this years ago*. Being own boss, with none of that time-consuming paper work to complete: time sheets, where you were, what you did, and so on. I was enjoying my decision, and felt good about who I was and what I had accomplished.

A Difficult Time Getting Results

You perhaps are thinking at this point that it sounds pretty good. I may be leading you into making that move sooner than you thought. You have the experience, the training, the education and, so far, you haven't read anything negative as to my decision. Well, allow me to explain what I have found, and what you may experience if and when you become a private OS&H consultant.

I knew and know my trade. I honestly believe that I provide the correct and adequate response when it comes to questions of standard (OSHA) application, interpretation, means of abatement, and hazard recognition, and can assist in litigation in the event of an issued citation. Again, I've done it for over 30 years. I also have seen my services work when I was with the agency. Areas of concern I identified during my many inspections were abated, hazards removed; or, at a minimum, risk factors were reduced. It was very rewarding. That's why we are in the business, right? Why would it or should it be any different as a private consultant? You identify the concern, you explain what needs to be done so as to eliminate or reduce the risk of injury, and it's done, you would hope.

One of my first clients contacted me to assist in an informal complaint received from OSHA, a letter questioning a number of alleged safety hazards existing at the client's facility. They contacted me and asked how to respond. I went out to the location, reviewed the letter, and looked at the areas of concern. There was some validity to the complaint, but the problems were easily and quickly remedied. We took photos, and explained what was done, and how the previous areas of concern would be monitored to ensure recurrence would not take place. We responded with the photos and a letter written in the acronyms only the agency would understand, a very important means of response guaranteeing acceptance. Shortly after, we received a letter from the local OSHA office accepting our findings and the action taken, and informing us the case was closed. It was obvious to my client that my years of experience, and understanding the agency paid off, they were pleased.

It was a win, a slam dunk. I had proven my services worked, and were well received. Life couldn't get any easier. So I continued advertising my services. Through talks to local organizations and client and acquaintance referrals, requests began to flow in. Then something happened. I landed a fairly nice consultant contract with a company looking for a full-time OS&H director. I contacted them, informed them that I wasn't looking for a full-time, position but suggested they have a comprehensive survey performed (third party) so as to identify and prioritize areas of concern. That way, when they hired the full-time director they were seeking, they would know what they needed to have done, and what to look for in that individual. They agreed, and the contract was signed. During this service, I explained I was going to perform a comprehensive survey, looking at every operational procedure and support service their employees performed.

My findings were somewhat extensive. I was somewhat surprised by the hazards, risk factors, and regulatory violations I found, because they'd had an OS&H director for years who recently had left. How could all of these faults exist? I finalized my report and submitted it.

During the meeting, or what may be called the closing conference, we went over my findings. I was asked by the ranking management official whether I would be willing to stay on under a contract provision and assist in abating the noted concerns. I thought about it, drew up a nice contract, and agreed to assist in bringing them into full compliance. I was looking forward to the challenge, and achieving my and their goals.

I began full steam ahead, bringing all of my past experience, knowledge on standard requirements, and acceptable abatement procedures to the table. I was excited. As I continued and held meetings, talking to maintenance personnel and supervisors and showing them what needed to be done, I found not much was being accomplished or completed. I put together all of the required programs, held introductory training sessions, explained responsibilities, and delegated authorities. Everything was in place, but I really wasn't seeing any change.

I couldn't understand what was happening. I mean, when I was with OSHA, I had always seen action taken, and had never had much problem getting my findings taken care of; why not here?

I can recall on one of the accident investigation forms I was reviewing under this client contract, the supervisor had written *"stupid mistake by operator"* as the reason for the accident, with no mention of the unguarded component I had previously identified. I know that I had conducted an accident investigation training class for all supervision; I know that I shared my findings with all supervision, and I get this type of response. I needed to change this quickly.

After bringing this concern and all the other findings up at every production meeting, and seeing no action taken, I finally requested a meeting with the top dog, and informed him that previously noted concerns not only could and would result in injuries, but also could bring some large penalties in the event of an OSHA inspection. I informed him that nothing is being done about these areas of concern. His response was, *"That is why we have you here, to keep them (OSHA) out."*

I then realized that, although I had seen results when I was with the agency, as a private consultant, I really had no power. I had lost the "hammer" I once had. I also quickly realized clients of a private consultant can decide what they want to do when it comes to my suggestions; I have no direct authority with any of my clients. As a consultant, you simply identify, explain, and educate; you have no managerial, direct order powers.

That lack of power or lack of management authority to mandate changes is part of being a consultant. That powerless position, when you know things need to be done, is somewhat disturbing and frustrating. I remember driving home asking myself, how I could get this organization to respond? *What am I doing wrong? What can I do?*

The truth of the matter is, so many establishments, so many companies, hire consultants and end up wasting both their and the consultant's time, either because of their management set-up or the fact that they really do not know how to use the consultant. This is costly to the client, and a waste of time for the consultant.

Advice for Both Consultants and Clients

Now, please don't accept this as the norm. I have many clients who have truly understood what a consultant provides, and how to use their (consultant) services. Many of my clients have changed their safety and health culture completely, based on my findings and recommendations. They knew what they wanted, how to use the guidance they paid for, and what questions to ask.

If you are considering becoming a private consultant, be prepared. Accomplishments that you may have had in a previous position may not be as easy to achieve as a private consultant. Be prepared to provide a service or guidance, just to have it placed on a shelf. Don't take it personally, as I did in the beginning.

As a future client, or if you as an employer are considering using an outside consultant, know what you want to achieve, what you want that service to accomplish. Be realistic. Remember, consultants are just that, consultants. They are not administrators; they are not part of, and should not be part of, your management structure. You need to take their guidance, their knowledge, and their recommendations, and implement those into your system. If not, you are wasting each other's time, and your company's money.

If you don't understand the consultant/client relationship, you may end up disappointed. It's sort of like buying that piece of exercise equipment, putting it in the corner, never using it, and then saying, "It didn't work."

Editor's Commentary

John points out an interesting aspect of consulting that goes beyond the business requirements: your relationship with clients will be different than when you were an employee, regardless of your position. As a long-time OSHA employee, John had a lot of knowledge. But as a consultant, the way that knowledge is received by the client changed. Learning to not take things personally and to be aware of your clients' motivations will help you become successful.

Editor's Comments

Introduction

In his essay, Chris Ross reflects on the last-minute angst he felt just as he was about to embark on his journey as a consultant. He expresses a feeling just about every consultant I have ever talked to shares; the "what if" questions. And interestingly enough, he later reflects that the worries and concerns were unfounded; his business started strong, and he has never looked back. These sentiments are again what I have heard over and over again.

I have known Chris for many years, and one of the things about him that I find most interesting is that he is always reading about new ideas and theories. In the following essay, he introduces us to some new thinking on noted business author Fred Reichheld.

How to Sleep Well at Night
CHRIS ROSS, CSP, OHST

I vividly remember the six months before I started my business. There were so many, very short nights of sleep, as I would awaken and wonder, "Is this the right decision," "What if the clients don't materialize," "What if I can't generate enough revenue to meet expenses," and myriad other questions along those lines.

I also remember being so preoccupied about my start-up while driving down a secondary road, coming up to a main highway. I stopped at the stop sign, and while so deep in thought that I sat there for several minutes, waiting for the stop sign to change.

While that may be a funny story, I know that most everyone who embarks on their newfound journey of being in business for themselves has had similar experiences.

But the day I started my business, I had dozens of clients lined up, and six months of work. And I have never looked back. And I have never really done any real advertising. Sure, I have done some marketing, I have a Web site, and I speak at a lot of conferences, but I really don't sell much. The selling has already been done.

When I think about running a successful business and having a good work/life balance, it is all about being secure, about feeling somewhat in control of my schedule, and about having enough work booked to be relatively stress free.

For me, that comes from building long-lasting relationships with my clients. I believe that trust is everything; I will do whatever it takes to build that deep level of trust and help to build a sustainable and mutually beneficial partnership with them.

That is the reason I sleep well at night, and it is the reason why I have more work than I can hope to accomplish, why my schedule is penciled in months in advance. Ninety-nine percent of my work comes from either repeat business from existing clients or referrals from those clients. They are the ones selling my services and my value, based on their experiences and results.

Several years ago, I had the opportunity to listen to Fred Reichheld, founder of Bain & Company's Loyalty Practice, and author of several notable business books, including *The Loyalty Effect* (1996), *Loyalty Rules!* (2001), *The Ultimate Question: Driving Good Profits and True Growth* (2006), and *The Ultimate Question 2.0: How Net Promoter Companies Thrive in a Customer Driven World* (2011). His message keys in on the distinctions between good profits and bad profits. He describes bad profits being made in ways that damage the customer relationship and can strangle growth. I think of bad profits as taking a job that you may not be fully qualified for, or don't have adequate time or enthusiasm to complete in a professional way.

He describes good profits are earned with customers' enthusiastic cooperation. They create promoters who, in turn, fuel an organization's growth. These are the types of projects that create a real win/win situation for both the consultant and the client. The client gets excellent results, core issues are addressed and solved, the consultant is well-rewarded, trust is built, and there is a focus on the ongoing relationship, not just a quick win.

According to Reichheld, only one question correlates to an organization's profitable growth: "How likely are you to recommend this product or service to a friend or colleague?"

Promoters (9 or 10) are loyal enthusiasts who keep buying from a company and urge their friends to do the same. Passives (7 or 8) are satisfied but unenthusiastic customers who can be easily wooed by the competition; and Detractors (6 or lower) are unhappy customers trapped in a bad relationship.

Then the follow-up question is, "Why did you rate us the way you did?" After you truly listen to the answer, you can ask other questions such as: What job do you want us to do? What are we not doing that you'd like us to do? What part of the experience could we improve?

I always begin every engagement with a very robust dialogue and assessment. I never presume to know what the solution is until being very diligent in gathering information. There is a direct correlation between the ability to gather information and developing trust. If we measure trust by the free flow and examination of information, we can actually gauge the probability of both our delivering real value, and the client's willingness to act on it with us. This trust/meaningful information measurement, combined with our competence, credibility, and reliability, can create the pathway that clears the way to achieve success.

To become true value creators or trusted advisors, we must find a way to fuse our IQ, EQ, and XQ together. IQ defines our intellectual horsepower; our business acumen, industry knowledge, and expertise. This is our competence and credibility. Our XQ is our ability and reliability to execute and make things happen. The best programs and strategies in the world, if not properly executed, are worthless. And finally, our EQ is our ability to communicate, to empathize, to share, to frame effective dialogue and inquiry. EQ, in a way, will measure our ability to listen and decipher complex messages.

We must become skilled at dialogue, inquiry, and diagnosis. There is a famous proverb, "Prescription without diagnosis is malpractice," which rings as true for safety professionals (consultants) as it does for physicians.

We must have a thorough understanding of the needs, the desired outcomes, and the success measures of our clients before proposing solutions.

My objective with every project is not only to complete the project in a satisfactory manner, but to create an intensely loyal customer; not by giving anything away, but having open, sometimes brutally honest dialogue; naming whatever elephants may be in the room; and always looking for ways to expand the pie, thus creating opportunities for both of us.

By following this framework of trust, advocacy, inquiry, dialogue and communication, I create intensely loyal customers, who become my promoters, who keep me very busy. This allows me to take time away from work to pursue my other interests; but most of all, it allows me a very sound sleep every night, knowing that I have created value for a client, and the phone will soon ring

Editor's Commentary

I think I speak for all of the editors and authors of this book in saying that we would all universally recommend trying your hand at consulting if it is something you think you want to do. We are not advocating jumping in without thinking through many of the aspects that are discussed in previous chapters, but we would also suggest that sometimes, you just simply have to take a leap of faith and do what you feel called to do. If you have laid the ground work that we have advocated in the previous pages, we believe you will do well.

Editor's Comments

Introduction

I have known Debby Shewitz for many, many years. She was one of the first members of the Consultants Practice Specialty Advisory Committee I met way back in 2005. Since then, we have remained colleagues and friends, and in her essay she reminds us of the power of networking. For many consultants who remain in either a solo practice or with a very small group, this marketing strategy is powerful, and it works. I had the same experience when I first started in consulting and for many years afterwards.

Making it Work
DEBBY SHEWITZ, CSP

My initial foray into becoming a consultant came about in a fairly typical way. The company I worked for was bought out by a larger corporation, and there was no job for me with the new owners. When I parted ways with them, I did some traditional job hunting, while at the same time investigating what it would take to go into consulting. By the time the job hunting had convinced me that I really didn't want to get back into the corporate rat race, I had collected a lot of good information from colleagues who had already been consultants for a number of years (several of whom have written chapters for this book), and attended one of ASSE's courses on how to be a successful OS&H consultant. And so, I decided to take the leap.

I started out with a very simple business plan (if it even deserves to be called that). I knew myself well enough to realize that I would not be any good at selling my services, and even more than that, I would hate having to do so. Since the point of going into consulting was to improve my quality of life over what the corporate world had to offer, I decided that my basic criterion of whether I was successful as a consultant or not would simply be whether I could get enough work, primarily through basic networking activities, and with no selling. I also made the conscious decision (one I know that not everyone can afford to make) that I would gladly trade off money for quality of life, which I loosely defined as working fewer hours, and having more flexibility and control over when I worked those hours.

One approach that fit well with this strategy was that some of the time that was no longer being taken up with the endless budgeting processes, goal-setting and performance reviews that are part of working for a corporation, could be spent getting more involved with professional organizations. I joined the advisory board of ASSE's Consultants Practice Specialty, and later the executive committee of my local ASSE Chapter. Eventually, I also got involved with the Auditing Roundtable, an organization of OS&H professionals who focus on auditing functions (both regulatory and management systems). I'll say very honestly that a big part of my initial motivation for some of this participation was that it earned points towards maintaining my CSP certification (and of course, consultants have to string some letters after their names). But I found quickly that the involvement with these organizations was helpful to me in multiple ways. I got to know and work with some really bright, energetic and well-respected professionals in the OS&H field who I wouldn't have met otherwise. Some have been people who gave me work, some have been people who affiliated with me so that I could accept work I couldn't have done on my own (or to whom I could refer clients knowing that my reputation would be protected or even enhanced), and some have become friends outside of work. At times when work was slow, or when it consisted of sitting in my home tied to the computer, the local chapter activities forced me to get out, put on real clothes, and keep up my professional image.

I also reached the conclusion over time that an important way to build a business network is to not focus on the business network per se, but to just stay in touch with people in whatever way feels most natural and comfortable. For me, at least, it was a whole lot easier to add, "Oh, by the way, I'm consulting now and would appreciate it if you'd keep me in mind if you or anyone you know needs my type of services" to a relatively routine e-mail or other communication with someone than to send them something that said, "I know we haven't been in touch for years, and now my first communication in all that time is to ask for favors, but I'm consulting now and...." Again, this fit my business plan of networking versus selling, and it has brought me a nice amount of business over the years for minimal time investment beyond what I enjoy doing anyway in terms of keeping in touch with people.

As for the quality of life piece of my definition of successful consulting, I know that everyone will have a different idea as to the appropriate work/life balance. That's true no matter what type of work someone does. Financial needs will obviously drive a large part of the equation—and I've been fortunate in that I had affordable medical benefits through my husband, and didn't need to worry too much about cash flow as long as I generated enough income over the long term to support a comfortable retirement. But if nothing else, I appreciated right from the start having the flexibility to make my own decisions about what conferences/training courses I wanted to attend without having to go through the third budget reforecast, to decide there was work I didn't want to take, or travel I didn't want to do. The phrase, "I'm sorry, but I have commitments at that time that can't be changed," became my best friend.

Another huge driver of anyone's decision about the proper work/life balance is obviously the circumstances that arise in the life portion. My plans for how much time I expected to put into my business got thrown completely out the window when a serious illness came up in my family. As hard as those times were, being a consultant at that point was a definite godsend. I had to pull back from work a lot, and really fell back on my network of affiliates more heavily than ever to keep servicing existing clients. The importance of having a group of colleagues upon whom I could rely both to provide quality services and to deal ethically with me and my clients was never greater than it was during that period. At the same time, it really saved my sanity to be able to keep doing some amount of work. Here again, the flexibility of having total control over how much, and what type of work I felt I could take, on was critical to me.

These days, I don't need to take advantage of the flexibility to nearly as large an extent, but I still find it quite valuable, since I have aging parents with whom I want to spend time. The ability to go with them to doctors' appointments, shopping, and so on, during the daytime, and do a lot of my work at night or on weekends is a huge benefit for all of us.

If I had to pick the single best advice I could give to anyone thinking of getting into consulting, it would network, network, network. Ideally, you should be doing this before you even start a consulting business, so that your relationships are well established, and so that you've had practice at it, if it's not something that comes naturally. Make sure that your network includes fellow consultants, not just potential clients. I know some consultants who look at colleagues in the business strictly as competition. But in my experience, there's plenty of work out there for all of us, and fellow consultants are a source of support, resources who can help fill in gaps (technical and geographic) that I can't cover, and great sounding boards when I hit an issue I'm not sure how to handle. Everyone will hit different combinations of quirks in the course of their consulting lives, but somebody out there has already dealt with each of the individual situations, or something very like it. In spite of all the jokes about consultants, they're a great community to be part of.

Editor's Commentary

It has often been said that it is not what you know, but who you know. For many of us in consulting, our networking efforts are a primary reason why we realize our initial successes, and it is often how we stay in business. Linda Tapp gives you some excellent ideas in her chapter on marketing, but we would all be remiss if we didn't strongly encourage you to harness the power of who you know. This is a tried and true (and relatively free) method that you would be wise to use to your best advantage.

Editor's Comments

Introduction

Dave Smith shares some practical advice with you in his essay, and he also addresses the topic of balance from a unique and simple perspective. He reminds you to schedule your vacation just like any other appointment. How many times have you heard people complain that they never have time for a vacation and, when they do, they end up attached to their phone or laptop and spend another two days digging out from under their email when they return? He extols you to remember that work/life balance also means things like eating right, exercising regularly, and managing stress, which are just as important as reviewing your financial statements and business plan.

Balancing Professional Success with the Rest of Your Life
DAVE K. SMITH, CSP

Balancing the demands of running a business that helps people and organizations with your life can be a challenge. I am not sure I am particularly qualified to give advice on this topic as I too struggle with work/life balance. My wife thinks it is a losing battle.

There is an old adage that states, "Why work 40 hours a week for someone else when you can work 80 hours a week for yourself?" This definitely applies in running a professional safety consulting business. It is just critical to make time in your life for things other than work. Make sure to make time for the important people in your life.

When starting any new venture, key questions to ask are: What do you want to do? How will you do it? These apply to the rest of your life as well. The only thing you can really do is make a conscious effort to achieve work-life balance.

Planning

When being a professional, making and sticking to a calendar is a prerequisite. So, for vacations or personal time, why not do the same? As professionals, we promote Plan-Check-Do-Act models, and there is no reason why this cannot be applied to our non-work lives.

Friends and colleagues think we are a little crazy, but my wife and I calendar our vacation time six to twelve months in advance. Days are blocked on the calendar to avoid booking service work then. If you don't protect your days off, they will get filled up with appointments, and you'll have a hard time planning a vacation. Consider taking shorter duration vacations or long weekends, which may be easier to schedule

Trade Offs

Others may tell you to just get a regular job (most likely for less money) to achieve balance. However, the reality of the 21st century workplace is that it never ends, and there are no boundaries. "Regular" jobs are time-consuming too, especially with higher level responsibilities (and compensation). If you don't come in Sunday, don't come in Monday.

Actually, I think you have greater freedom running your own show. If you want (and can afford) to take a day off, schedule it, and do it. If you want to spend two weeks in Europe or the Caribbean, save up the money, calendar the time, and do it. There are no vacation request forms, and no last-minute administrative "emergencies," like redesigning the vacation request forms, and no irritating supervisor dropping inconsequential items on your desktop the afternoon before you leave on vacation.

Coverage

When you take vacations, make sure to arrange coverage. Many times, the phone does not ring unless there is a crisis for which people need help in responding. If you are not there, make sure someone else is. This is a value of networking with other consulting firms.

Fear

There is always fear: fear of failure, fear of going broke, or fear of error. Conquering fear of failure must be foremost on the list. As President Franklin Roosevelt said in his first inaugural address at the height of the great Depression:

> "Let me assert my firm belief that the only thing we have to fear is fear itself—nameless, unreasoning, unjustified terror which paralyzes needed efforts to convert retreat into advance." (http://avalon.law.yale.edu/20th_century/froos1.asp)

There is always the fear that all clients will leave, and I will never work again. I will be a homeless vagrant, mumbling to myself pushing shopping cart in the rain, starving and alone.

Yes, clients may leave if you go on vacation, but that has never happened to any consultant I know. And even if it did, do you want those unreasonable clients anyway? They were probably unreasonable about other issues too, like paying their bills.

In most organizations, there is a type of vendor inertia. It is hard to change vendors (like safety consultants), unless something really bad happens. Put yourself in the client representative's role. To replace any vendor may involve a search, interview, and internal approval process, and the process is more cumbersome as the size of the organization increases. This is why even marginal vendors in just about any field can stay in business; it is too much work for the internal person to replace them. Once you are approved, you are approved, so stop worrying.

Exercise

We have all heard, it but maintaining physical fitness is really important. The experts say exercise one hour every day, which includes walking around customer locations. It is hard to schedule, but we all really need to make a priority of getting sufficient exercise. If I miss workouts, I pay for it!

Diet

You already know this, but maintaining a proper diet is important to healthy living as well. While it is hard to eat properly, especially while travelling, you simply have to make the effort.

Stress Management

Everyone needs to figure out what works for them to help manage the stress of modern living, plus running your own business. For me, exercise, especially outdoors, is the most important thing I can do to manage stress.

Another stressor in OS&H consulting is the rather uninformed pushback on what we see as very obvious hazard exposures. In part, this is a form of denial on the part of people, and we have all heard it. Such statements as, "It hasn't happened yet," or "I've been doing this for x years, and nothing has happened" illustrate that the risk perception hasn't adjusted to reality. The truth is that nothing has happened, until it does. As safety professionals, we just have to accept this as part of the territory, and work on changing that risk perception at all levels, from senior management to the lowest person on the organization chart. Do *not* take this personally; many younger safety people burn out from this sometimes constant pushback, and you just can't take it personally.

Try to avoid frantic work periods, which is easier said than done. We have to allow sufficient time to complete tasks, with no all-nighters or other stressors. If we always strive for smooth work operations, this will provide more resilience for those crunch times that inevitably occur.

Right Livelihood

In his famous Stanford University commencement address, Steve Jobs said:

> "... for the past 33 years, I have looked in the mirror every morning and asked myself: "If today were the last day of my life, would I want to do what I am about to do today?" And whenever the answer has been "No" for too many days in a row, I know I need to change something." (http://news.stanford.edu/news/2005/june15/jobs-061505.html)

Steve Jobs' entire speech is quite inspirational, and I encourage you to read the entire work.

A great benefit of working in the OS&H field is that we are actually doing something useful and helpful to people, society, and the planet. Enjoy that, and remember why we choose to do this work in the first place. There must be easier ways to make a living, but few provide the satisfaction of being a safety professional. This is a job and career that you can love to do; I do, and that in itself makes it all worthwhile.

Editor's Commentary

And so we end this chapter on essays. As we noted at the beginning, we wanted to make sure we left you with an understanding of the softer side of consulting by letting some of your fellow OS&H professional share their stories of success by defining how the concept of work/life balance works for them.

As you have undoubtedly realized, there is no one way to balance work and life. This is true for all of us, not just consultants. We believe that once you take the first step into consulting, you will need to create your own balance in the way that works best for you, and you alone.

We believe that reading this book and following the guidance of successful OS&H consultants who have authored the previous chapters will help lay the foundation that will greatly increase the chances that your foray into OS&H consulting will also be successful. We have not attempted to provide a rigid prescription that must be followed; each chapter was designed to provide ideas, resources, and things for you to consider and, as the saying goes, "Take what you need and leave the rest." We also believe the book will provide a reference for you to come back to as you work your way through the first weeks, months, and years of your consulting career.

We all wish you the best of luck.
The Editors and Authors

ABOUT THE CONTRIBUTORS

ROBERT N. ANDRES, CSP, CPE, CMfgE, DABFE, INCE, is the principal of Environmental and Safety Associates, LLC, specializing in community, industrial, and building noise measurement and control; machine and facility safety; and incident forensics. Now based in Naples, Florida, his consultancy was launched as an offshoot of Oshex Associates, Inc., Baldwinsville, NY, in 1981. Bob has a BS in Engineering and Management from Clarkson University, and has served as Administrator of the Engineering Practice Specialty, Chapter President, and Chairman of the landmark ANSI B11.TR2 subcommittee. He currently serves as Director of Government and Public Affairs for the Florida Suncoast Chapter of ASSE, and is a recent recipient of the first Lifetime Achievement Award from the Central New York Chapter.

JEFFERY C. CAMPLIN, MS, CSP, CPEA, is president of Camplin Environmental Services, Inc., a safety and environmental consulting firm he founded in the Chicago area in 1991. Jeff has a BS in safety from Northern Illinois University (NIU), remaining involved on their Board of Directors of the College of Engineering Alumni Society. In 2008, he received the College's outstanding alumni award. Jeff also has a MS in Safety and Emergency Management from Eastern Kentucky University. He is currently a member of the American Society of Safety Engineers' Board of Directors, while also serving in the role of their Vice President of Practices & Standards.

PAUL GANTT is the President of Safety Compliance Management (SCM), a firm which delivers occupational safety and health services. Prior to founding SCM in 1991, Paul spent 15 years in the Fire Service, working through the ranks to Chief Officer.

In addition to providing services to SCM's clients in both the private and public sectors, Paul also provides testimony as an expert witness in several areas. Paul holds certification as a Certified Safety Professional, Certified Environmental, Safety and Health Trainer, and Construction Health and Safety Technologist. He has a Master's Degree in Advanced Safety Engineering and Management. Additionally, Paul is a prolific author of textbooks and articles published in numerous safety journals.

TERRY GRISIM is President of Safety Management Consultants, Inc. He has two homes and two business locations. He lived in west suburban Chicago since before he started in business in 1982, and in Englewood, Florida, for the last ten years. He's been in safety since 1968, and started his own business in 1982. For the last approximately twenty years, Terry has specialized in litigation consulting.

His focus areas are:
- Premises Safety and Liability (mainly retail stores)
- Transportation, Warehousing and Distribution (fleet operations and warehouse safety)
- Product Safety
- Automotive Service
- Workplace Safety and Health

STEVEN HIGH is the President of High Environmental Health and Safety Consulting Ltd., based in Lancaster, Pennsylvania. The group provides a wide range of occupational and environmental health and safety services, and can be located on the internet at www.highehs.com. Steve has been in the safety/health field since 1986, and started his consulting practice in 1999. He has specific interests in applying bio-statistical and epidemiological methods to occupational safety and health problems; evaluating slip-resistance on walking surfaces; implementing safety management systems; and delivering engaging and competent education for his clients.

JOHN P. LESEGANICH is OS&H Consultant and President of Independent Consultation Services LLC. He is also a professional member of ASSE, a Certified Professional Environmental Auditor–S&H (BEAC-CPEA), and a Commissioned Deputy Sheriff in Mahoning County, Ohio. John has over 40 years working in the field of occupational safety and health. He began his career with OSHA working as a Compliance Officer, retired with the OSHA On Site Consultation Program as Public Relations Coordinator with the agency, and continued his career, after retirement in 2005, as an industry OS&H consultant and founder of Independent Consultation Services, LLC.

CHRIS ROSS has been a performance consultant, trainer, lecturer, and presenter for over 30 years. He owns The Engagement Effect, a multi-discipline training and consulting firm in Anchorage, Alaska, with clients throughout North America. The Engagement Effect provides leadership and supervisory development, employee selection, strategic planning, business performance improvement, risk management, regulatory compliance, and emergency response planning. Ross has earned professional certification in Workplace Learning and Performance (CPLP) through the American Society of Training and Development, and is additionally recognized by the Board of Certified Safety Professionals as a CSP and OHST. Chris has presented over a thousand training classes, workshops, seminars, keynote speeches, and presentations. He is also a frequent contributor and columnist for *Alaska Contractor*, *Council Prospector*, and many other publications.

DEBBY SCHEWITZ has over 30 years of experience as an OS&H generalist. As the principal of Shewitz Consulting for about 15 years, she has focused on Process Safety Management, OS&H Management Systems, compliance auditing, and implementing new OS&H programs for clients in a variety of industries. Debby is the lead technical author for four regulatory compliance guides for Specialty Technical Publishers. She is a professional member of ASSE, and is on the boards of the Consultants Practice Specialty and the Northern Ohio Chapter. Debby has received the CPS SPY award for 2004-2005, 2007-2008 and 2012-2103.

DAVE K. SMITH is a safety professional with experience in construction, manufacturing and service industries and is Managing Consultant of Dave Smith & Co Inc. He has been an independent consultant for over 17 years. Dave is a published author, and has been invited to speak before groups from the World of Concrete to the National Safety Management Society. Dave is a Certified Safety Professional, an Associate in Risk Management and a Certified Safety and Health Manager. He is a graduate of Cogswell Polytechnical College (Safety Management) and Ohio University (Government/Communication).

SUGGESTED READINGS

Please refer to the Bibliographies at the end of each chapter for additional reading.

Allen, David. 2001. *Getting Things Done: The Art of Stress-Free Productivity*. New York: Penguin Books.

Barr, Chad, Linda Henman, and Aviv Shahar. 2013. "Alan Weiss on Consulting." East Greenwich, CT: Summit Consulting Group, Inc.

Bellman, Geoffrey M. 2002. *The Consultant's Calling: Being Who You Are to What You Do*. San Francisco: Jossey-Bass Publishers.

Cialdini, Robert B. 2007. *Influence: The Psychology of Persuasion*. Rev. ed. New York: Collins Business.

Conklin, Todd. 2012. *Pre-Accident Investigations: An Introduction to Organizational Safety*. Burlington, Vermont: Ashgate Publishing Company.

Dekker, Sidney. 2006. *The Field Guide to Understanding Human Error*. Burlington, Vermont: Ashgate Publishing Company.

Friedman, Thomas L. 2005. *The World is Flat: A Brief History of the 21st Century*. New York: Farrar, Straus, Giroux.

Gerber, Michael E. 2004. *The E Myth Revisited*. New York: HarperCollins Books.

Hollnagel, Eric. 2009. *The ETTO Principle: Efficiency-Thoroughness Trade-Off*. Burlington, Vermont: Ashgate Publishing Company.

Kaner, Sam, Lenny Lind, Catherine Toldi, Sarah Fisk, and Duane Berger. 2007. *Facilitator's Guide to Participatory Decision-Making*. 2nd ed. San Francisco: John Wiley & Sons, Inc.

Konrath, Jill. 2006. *Selling to Big Companies*. Chicago: Dearborn Trade Publishing.

The Safety Differently blog at http://www.safetydifferently.com

Schein, Edgar. 1992. *Organizational Culture and Leadership*. 2nd ed. San Francisco: Jossey-Bass Publishers.

Weiss, Alan. 2008. *Value-Based Fees: How to Charge—and Get—What You're Worth*. 2nd ed. San Francisco: Pfeiffer.

Weiss, Alan. 2002. *Process Consulting: How Launch, Implement, and Conclude Successful Consulting Projects*. San Francisco: Jossey-Bass/Pfeiffer.

Wickman, Gino. 2011. *Traction: Get a Grip on Your Business.* Dallas, TX: BenBella Books, Inc.

Williams, Oscar, ed. 1957. *Immortal Poems of the English Language.* New York: Pocket Books.

INDEX

A

Accounting, 102–116
    balance sheet, 106–108
    collections, 111–114
    credit, 115
    financial statements, 102–108
    invoicing, 109–111
    non-routine collection, 114–115
    profit and loss (P&L) statement, sample, 104
    taxes and, 109
    write-offs, 114–115
Affordable Care Act, 133, 146–147
Age Discrimination in Employment Act of 1967 (ADEA), 169–170
A. M. Best, 137–138
American Board of Industrial Hygiene (ABIH), Code of Professional Conduct, 323, 330–332, 342–343
American Industrial Hygiene Association (AIHA), 211
American Society of Safety Engineers (ASSE)
    networking at, 367–368
    seminars for consultants, 29, 32, 411
    social media and, 209–210
    volunteering at, 412
American Society of Safety Engineers (ASSE) Professional Development Conference, (PDC)
    networking at, 221, 246, 265, 389
    speaking at, 211
Americans with Disabilities Act of 1990 (ADA), 168–169
Assessment tools, 29–32, 408
Attributes of OS&H consultants, 3, 8, 12–13, 408
    business knowledge, 27–29
    challenge seekers, 9
    "life changers" or "transitioners," 9–10
    personal characteristics, 14–25
    practical skills, 25–26
    recent graduates, 10–11
    seasoned experts, 8–9
Auditing Roundtable, 409–410
Auto insurance, 126

B

Bellman, Geoffrey M., 215
Block, Peter, 292
Blogs, as marketing tool, 203–204
Board of Certified Safety Professionals (BCSP) Code of Ethics, 323, 327, 330, 340–341
Board of Directors (BOD), 51–52
Branding, 193–194
    appearance and dress, 195–196
    client retention and reputation, 282–292
    business address, 195
    Web site, 194–195
Branson, Richard, 14–15
Bring Forward System, 25
Brogniez, Jim, 301
Bureau of Labor Statistics (BLS), and failure rate of consulting businesses, 5
Business(es), 53–55, 68, 147–150. *See also:* Networking
    address, 195
    adjustments after first year, 347–349
    C corporation, 54, 68, 148–150
    card sorter, 259–260
    cards, 260–261
    compliance with OS&H laws and regulations, 172–173
    downsizing, 362–363, 409
    expense deductions, 152
    failure, 5, 32–33, 40, 57, 281
    federal employment laws, compliance with, 164–172
    funding, 60–61
    knowledge, 27–29
    incentives for economically distressed areas, 153
    insurance, determining amount, 142–143
    limited liability company (LLC), 54, 68, 148, 150
    partnership, 54, 148, 150–151
    property and general liability insurance, 122–126

Business(es) *(cont.)*
    regulatory compliance, 172–173
    S corporation, 54, 148–150
    sole proprietorship, 54–55, 148, 151–152
    taxes on, 68–69
    Web sites, 202–203, 390
    workload, managing, 349–352
Business cards, 260–261, 389
    sorter, 259–260
Business failure, reasons for, 281
Business funding, initial, 100–102
Business plan, 33, 398, 409. *See also:* Executive summary of business plan
    appendices, 64
    branding, 193–194
    cash flow, 49–50
    confidentiality clause in, 63
    distribution record of, 63
    elements, 44–55
    financial outlook projections, 61–63
    financial planning and advisement, 69
    funding, 60–61
    government certifications, 71–72
    information, control, 63
    insurance and, 138
    marketing and sales, 57–60
    mission statement, 46
    need for, 41–42
    networking. *See:* Networking
    organization and management, 51–55
    ownership, 53–55
    personal tax planning, 70
    products and services described in, 55–56
    purpose, 42–44
    reasons for, 40–41
    regulatory issues, 63
    research and development activities, 56–57
    retirement planning and, 69
    revisions, 64
    start-up, 43, 46, 65–70
    subcontracting, 65–68
    succession planning, 70–73
    taxes, 68–69
    technology advances and workload, 382

C

C corporation, 53–55, 68, 147–150
Canadian Society of Safety Engineering (CSSE)
    Consulting Skills Course, 29, 30–32
Case studies, ethics
    authority, 330–331
    falsification, 328
    fees and expert witness work, 327
    making the client happy, 329
    padding hours, 326–327
    professional competency, 331–332
    "throat cutting," 325–326
Cash value life insurance, 132
Certificate of insurance (COI), 136–137
    sample form, 142–143
Certifications, government-based, 71–73
Certified Health and Safety Consultant (CHSC), 30–32
Challenge seekers, 9
Chamber of Commerce, networking and the, 265–266
Civil Rights Act, Title VII, 167
Client
    input, 358–360
    needs, 48–49, 405–408
    satisfaction and referrals, 368–369, 408
    saying no to, 401
Client resistance
    addressing, 307–309
    identifying, 305–307
    types, definitions, and examples, 306
Client retention, 281–315, 359–360
    addressing business and technical issues and people dynamics, 295–296
    aligning consultant's values with client work expectations, 286–290
    brand and reputation, 282–292
    business and personal values, 283–286
    collaborative relationships, 293–294
    consultant resistance, 310–312
    consultant role, 290–292
    contract, creating, 299
    defining problem and work, 301–303
    designing for, 292–298
    and maintaining client ownership and agreement for action, 296–297
    post-project, 312–313
    problem-solving in sustainable manner, 294–295
    recommendations, commitment, 303–304
    resistance, 305–309
    review after first year, 348–349
    satisfaction, 368–369
    social contract with, 298–304
    work agreement, creating, 299–301

Close corporations. *See:* S Corporations
COBRA benefits, 147
Collections, 111–114
    non-routine, 114–115
Communication skills, 388, 408
Competitive rates, 84–86
Conferences, attendance at, 210–212, 220–221, 389
    follow-up 221–223
Consultancies. *See also:* Business(es); Business plan
    adjustments after first year, 347–349
    business size, 349
    client retention. *See:* Client retention
    competitor's recommendations, 216
    compliance with OS&H laws and regulations, 172–173
    confidence, 389
    downsizing, 362–363
    employees, hiring, 313–314, 360–362
    federal employment laws, compliance with, 164–172
    financial outlook projections, 61–63
    flexibility of, 400
    funding, 60–61
    geographic location, 365–366
    goals, annual review, 364–36, 391
    government-based certification of, 71–73
    growing business, 346, 350–352, 357–363
    legal and regulatory requirements for, 145–188
    legal privilege and, 174–176
    lessons learned, 346–347, 383
    longevity in, 369–370
    management, 52–53, 70
    multiplier, rate determination by, 82–84
    networking, 221. *See also:* Networking
    priorities, setting 354–355
    pros and cons of, 382–383
    reasons for starting, 345–346
    relationship with other consultants, 400
    reputation management, 218–219, 359–360
    regulatory compliance, 172–173
    retirement planning, 69
    saying no to business, 346
    set-up, review after first year, 350–352
    start-up business plan, 43, 46, 65–70
    subcontracting, 65–68
    subcontractors, hiring, 313–314
    taxes, 68–70
    technology advances, workload and, 382
    understanding market going forward, 363–369
    workload, managing, 349–352
Consultant(s). *See also:* Attributes of OS&H consultants
    areas of expertise, defining, 370–372
    client retention. *See:* Client retention
    credentials, build up, 392
    competencies, 392
    debt, getting into, 397–98
    defining strengths 348
    ethics for, 323–335
    growth and development, 314–315
    integrity, 388
    keeping up to date, 372–375
    knowing what it takes to be a, 11–27
    planning for success, 292
    personal and professional goals, 375–381
    personal niche, finding, 369–375
    professional code of conduct, 325–335
    professional reputation, 359–360
    reasons for becoming, 402–403
    reasons for hiring, 5–8
    resistance, in relationship with client, 310–312
    self-evaluation, 352–357
    setting and achieving personal and professional goals, 375–381
    social contract with client, 298–304
    subcontractors, divesting work to, 314
    time management and scheduling, 355–357
    work/life balance. *See:* Work/life balance
    working with subcontractors, 11
Contact database, 259
Contingency pricing method, 95
Contracts, 153–159, 176
    adhesion, 153
    clients, 155
    client-consultant, social, 298–304
    common terms, 180–181
    office space and facilities, 154
    other consultants, 155–159
    professional liability exposure and insurance, 156–157
    regulatory compliance and contractor prequalification, 157–159
    subcontractor liability and risk management, 155–56
    work agreement, creating, 299–301
Copyrights and patents, 56
Costs of running business, 60, 401
Credit, 115, 146
Critical and creative and thinking skills, 21–25. *See also:* Practical skills of consultants

Customer value propositions (CVPs), 229

D
DBEs (Disadvantaged Business Enterprises), 71–73
Department of Homeland Security (DHS),
    employee immigration issues and, 166–167
Diet, work/life balance and, 414
Disability insurance, 122, 134
Downsizing, becoming consultant after, 362–363, 409
Dun & Bradstreet ratings, 146

E
E-mail, and targeted marketing, 198–200, 221
Elevator pitch, 256–257
Employee Misclassification Initiative, 161–162
Employees, 313–314
    benefits, 146
        discrimination, laws against, 168–170
        immigration issues of, 166–167, 177
        sample rate schedule for firms with, 87
Employment at will, 160
Employment discrimination, 167–168
Employment Eligibility Verification (USCIS Form I-9), 166
Employment law
    basics of, 164–172
    contracts, 159–172
    discrimination, 168–170
Entrepreneurship, 1–37
Environmental Protection Agency (EPA),
    regulatory compliance under, 172–173
Equal Pay Act of 2009, 168
Errors and omissions (E&O) insurance, 128–130
Ethics, 319–336
    ABIH Code of Professional Conduct, 323, 330–332, 342–343
    ASSE Code of Professional Conduct, 323, 330, 339
    BCSP Code of Ethics, 323, 327, 330, 340–341
    case studies, 325–332
    defining, 320–323
    OSHA, case studies, 329–331
    National Society of Professional Engineers (NSPE), 323
    potential dilemmas for consultants, 324–325
    professional guidelines and regulations, 321
Executive summary of business plan, 45–51
    company description, 45–47
    financial information, 46
    future objectives, 46
    historical performance, 46
    market analysis, 45, 47–51
    mission statement, 45–46
    products and services, 45, 55–56
    start-up companies, 46
Exercise, work/life balance and, 413–414
Expert witness, 389, 398
    case study, 327
External business funding, 60–61

F
Facebook, as marketing tool, 208–209, 219, 390
Failure, fear of, 413
Failure rate, business, 5, 32–33, 40, 57, 397
Fair Labor Standards Act of 1938 (FLSA), 165–166
Family, effect of consultancy on, 32–33
    business plan for family, 33
Family and Medical Leave Act of 1993 (FMLA), 170–171
Federal employment laws, coverage and scope, 182–183, 162–172
Fee schedules. *See:* Schedules *and* Multiplier
Financial planning
    advisement, 69
    and business plans, 69
    outlook projections, 61–63
    retirement and, 69
    wealth building, 71
Funding of business, 60–61

G
Garr, Douglas, 254
Gattis, Chris, 224–225
Geographic location of consultancy, 365–366
Gitomer, Jeff, 207–208
Goals, 375
    annual review, 364–365
    future, 378–379
    salary, 376–377
    timeline, 379–381
    work model, based on, 377–378
Godin, Seth, 214
GoForth Institute, 29
    Self-Assessment Guide for Entrepreneurs, 29
Google
    Ads, 59
    Alerts, 219

H

Hall, Stacy, 301
Hashtags, use of by Twitter and Instagram, 201
HUB Zone certification, 72
Hrycenko, Ed, 18

I

Incorporation, 146
    articles of, for C corporations, 148
    choice of state, 152
    organization, for LLCs, 150
Immigration Reform and Control Act of 1986 (IRCA), 166–167
Independent contractor, IRS rules determining, 162–164
Individual retirement accounts (IRAs), 131
Instagram, as marketing tool, 201, 209–210
Insurance
    agencies, 137–138
    auto insurance, 126
    business owner's policy, 122–126
    Certificate of Liability Insurance form, 141
    certificate of insurance (COI), 136–137
    disability, 122, 134
    errors and omissions (E&O), 128–130, 139
    finding coverage, 137–138
    determining what kind and how much, 120–122, 142–143, 139
    life, 131–133
    medical, 133–134
    personal loss exposures and risk financing, 131
    professional liability, 128–130, 139, 146
    professional malpractice, 146
    subcontractors, coverage for, 134–137
    property and general liability, 122–126
    state regulation, 139
    umbrella, 126–127
    Workers' Compensation, 127–128
Insurance Services Office, 122
Intellectual property issues, 56
Internal Revenue Service (IRS)
    common law rules for classification of workers, 162–164
    S corporations, 149
Invoicing, 109–111

J

Jantsch, John, 215–217

K

Kotter, John, 23

L

Legal privilege for consultants, 174–176
Life changers, 9–10
Life cycle of product or services, 55–56
Limited liability companies (LLCs), 54, 148, 150
Limited liability partnerships (LLPs), 151
LinkedIn
    as marketing tool, 207–208, 390
    networking and, 268–269

M

Management of consulting business, 52–53, 70
Management-Based Safety Process (MBS), 56
Market analysis, in business plan, 47–51
    cash flow, 49–50
    client needs, 48–49
Marketing, 57–58, 60, 191–215, 366–369
    advertising and, 192–193
    branding, 193–194
    business address, 195
    and business growth, 58
    campaigns, 59–60
    changes in 192–193
    communications, 58
    definition, 191–192
    distribution of products and services, 58
    e-mail as marketing tool, 198–200, 221
    follow-up, 221–223
    groups and associations, participation in, 197–198
    networking, 221
    penetration, 58
    plans and research, 223–225
    press, use of 201–202
    proposals, 229–230, 234, 240–243
    public relations, 200–202
    publishing, 196–197
    and sales, 57–60, 191–237
    sales and marketing funnel, 220–221
    services, 192–193
    social media and, 202–210
    speaking and writing, 210–215
    strategy, 57–59
    targeting specific groups, 198–200
    Web site, professional, 194–195
Marketing Action Plan, Sample, 226
Marketing plans and research, 221–223

Marketing proposals, 229–236
    additional components, 232
    alternative options, 231
    approach to project, 232–233
    cancellation clauses, 233
    outcomes, 232
    proposal template, 234–236, 240–243
MBS. *See*: Management-Based Safety Process
Medical insurance, 133–134
    COBRA coverage, 147
Menzel, R., 25
Meshel, Jeffrey, 254
Military
    employment after service, 171–172
    leave and military caregiver leave added to FMLA, 171
Mine Safety and Health Administration (MSHA), 149
    regulatory compliance under, 172–173
Mission statement, 46–47
Moody's, 138
Multiplier, rate determination by, 82–84

N

National Association of Women Business Owners, 266
National Council on Compensation Insurance, 128
National Speakers Association (NSA), 211
National Trade and Professional Associations of the United States, 265
Negotiation skills, 391–392
Networking, 221, 245–277, 388, 410–411
    after event, 274–275
    before event 269–271
    business card sorter, 259
    business cards, 260–260
    Chamber of Commerce, joining, 265–266
    company information, 258–259
    complementary process partners, 250
    contact database, 259
    coverage for vacations, 413
    during event, 271–274
    elevator pitch, 256–257
    external business development, 247–248, 252
    event, guidelines for maximizing, 274–275
    follow-up, 221–223, 274
    foundational guidelines, 275–277
    internal business development, 249, 252
    opportunities, 261–269
    personal development, 251–253
    philosophy, 253–256
    professional and trade associations, 265–268
    professional electronic connections, 268–269
    provocative questions, 257–258
    reasons for, 247–253
    spheres of influence, 262–265
    strategic alliances, 249–251
    technology partners, 250–251
    tools, 256–261
Non-disclosure and non-compete agreements, 56

O

Occupational Safety and Health Administration (OSHA)
    ethics, case studies, 329–331, 403–405
    legal privilege and, 174–175
    regulatory compliance under, 172–173
    10-hour courses for general industry and construction, 85
O'Connor, Sandra Day, 323
Online networking, 221
    follow-up, 221–223
Organization and management of consulting business, 51–55. *See also*: Business(es)
Organization Development Network, 246
Overhead rate pricing, 90–91
    sample, 91

P

Partnerships, 54, 148, 150–151
    damages, jointly and severably liable for, 151
Pascale, Blaise, 16–17
Payroll tax deductions, 146
Personal characteristics of consultants, 14–21
    communication skills, 18–19
    entrepreneurial spirit, 14
    ethics, 20–21
    interpersonal skills, 17
    investment, 16–17
    leadership, 17–18
    optimism, 15–16
    passion, 14–15
    personal relationships, 19–20
    positivity, 15–16
    resilience, 16
    risk tolerance, 16
    self-knowledge, 16–17
    vision, 14

Personal tax planning strategies and business plans, 70
Petersen, Dan, 23
Pinterest, as marketing tool, 209–210
Plan-Do-Check-Act, 412
Potential ethical dilemmas for consultants, 324–325
Practical skills of consultants, 25–26
    decision making, 26
    organization, 25
    planning, 25–26
    self-discipline, 25
    time management, 25
Press, marketing, use of, 201–202
Pricing for services, 80, 389, 401
    contingency method, 95
    fixed price method, 91–92
    multiplier, rate determination by, 82–84
    overhead rate method, 90–91
    process or method, developing, 87–95
    retainer method, 92–93
    subcontractor's fees, 97–98
    time and materials method, 88
    travel expenses, 98–99
    value-based method, 93–95
Price fixing, 86
Priorities, setting, 354–355
Products and services, 55–56
    intellectual property, 56
    life-cycle implications, 55
Professional liability insurance, 128–130
Professional trade associations, 265–268
Public relations, and marketing, 200–202
Public speaking and writing, as marketing tools, 210–214
Publications, as marketing tools, 213–214

Q
Qualified retirement plans, 131

R
Rates for services, 80–87
    billable time and revenue mix, 99–100
    competitive, 84–86
    options, 82–84
    schedules, 86–87
    travel expenses, 98–99
Recent graduates, 10–11
Record retention and destruction, 175–76
Referrals, 215–218, 273, 313, 332–333, 368–369
Regulatory issues, business plan, 63

Reichheld, 407–408
Reputation management, 218–219
Research, marketing plans and, 223–225
Research and Development (R&D), 56–57
Resistance
    client, 305–309
    consultant, 310–312
Retirement planning, 69, 131
    life insurance and, 132–133
Revisions to business plan, 64
Risk management
    and business plans, 70
    insurance, 131
RoAne, Susan, 270
Rogers, Everett, 268
Roy, Deb, 32

S
S corporations, 54–55, 149–150
    legal requirements for forming, 150
Safety consultants' code of conduct, 325–335
Sales, 391–392
    back-of-the-room, 214
    cold calling, 215
    referrals, 215–218
    strategy, 59–60
Sales and marketing funnel, 220–221
Sales taxes, state, 153
Sarbanes-Oxley Act, 149
SBA. *See:* Small Business Administration (SBA), U.S.
SBDCs, 72
Scott, David Meerman, 203
Search engine optimization (SEO), 202–203
Seasoned experts, 8–9
Securities and Exchange Commission (SEC), 149
Self-Assessment Guide for Entrepreneurs, 29
Seminars, as marketing tools, 213–214
Services
    marketing, 192–193
    state taxes on 153Simplified employee pension (SEP) plan, 131
Small Business Administration (SBA), U.S., 42, 72
    8(a) certifications, 72
Small Business Development Centers. *See:* SBDCs
Small business failure, causes, 5, 32–33, 40, 57
Small Business Readiness Assessment, 29
SMART (Specific, Measurable, Achievable, and Time Limited), 26, 225

SMARTER (Specific, Measurable, Achievable, Time Limited, Evaluate, and Reevaluate), 26
Social media in marketing
    blogs, 203–204
    Facebook, 208–209, 225, 390
    Instagram, 209–210
    LinkedIn, 207–208, 390
    Pinterest, 209–210
    Tumblr, 203–204
    Twitter, 204–207
    YouTube, 209
    Web sites, 202–203, 390
Social Security, 122
Sole proprietorship, 54, 148, 151–152, 347–348
    sample rate schedule for, 87
Sparks, Felica, 224, 225
Spheres of influence, 262–265
Standard and Poor's, 138
State labor and employment offices, 184–188
State taxes, on consulting services, 153
Stress management, work/life balance and, 414
Subcontracting
    and business plans, 65–68
    referrals for competent professional, 332
Subcontractors, 146
    divesting work to, 214
    insurance coverage for, 134–137
    starting as, 11, 65–68
    working with consultants, 11, 313–314
Succession planning, 70–73, 398
    using government certifications, 71–73
    wealth building, 71
SWOT (Strengths, Weaknesses, Opportunities, and Threats) analysis, 26

T

Taxes, 68–69, 109, 152–153, 177
    advantages of S corporation, 149
    corporate tax return, filing, 152
    state, on services, 153
Term life insurance, 122, 132
Testimonials
    client, 313
    in proposal, 236
Time and materials, rate method, 88–90
Time management, 25, 355–357, 401
    assistance, 356–357

Trade-offs, 412
Transitioners, 9–10
Travel expenses, 98–99
Tumblr, 203–204
Twitter, as marketing tool, 201, 204–207

U

Umbrella insurance, 126–127, 151
Unemployment insurance, 146
Uniformed Services Employment and Reemployment Rights Act of 1994 (USERRA), 171–172
Universal life insurance, 122
U. S. Citizenship and Immigration Services (USCIS), 166
U.S. Employment Eligibility Verification (Form I-9), 166
U. S. Immigration and Customs Enforcement (ICE), 166
U. S. Small Business Administration (SBA), small business failure statistics, 281

V

Value-based pricing method, 93–95
Vaynerchuk, Gary, 193, 199, 205, 209–210
Volunteering, 393

W

Wealth building, succession planning, 71
Web sites, as marketing tool, 202–203, 390
Weiss, Alan, 231–233, 253, 282
Whole life insurance, 122
Work/life balance, 32–33, 346, 353–354, 391, 394–396, 399–401, 410–415
Work model, goals and 377–378
Worker misclassification issues, 161–162
Workers' compensation insurance, 127–128, 146, 173
Write-offs, 114–115

Y

YouTube, as marketing tool, 209

Z

Zarella, Dan, 202–203, 207
Zuckerberg, 207